CAMBRIDGE STUDIES IN EIGHTEENTH-CENTURY
ENGLISH LITERATURE AND THOUGHT   20

Swift's politics

CAMBRIDGE STUDIES IN EIGHTEENTH-CENTURY
ENGLISH LITERATURE AND THOUGHT

General editors Dr HOWARD ERSKINE-HILL, Litt.D., FBA *Pembroke College,
Cambridge* and
Professor JOHN RICHETTI, *University of Pennsylvania*

Editorial board Morris Brownell, *University of Nevada*
Leopold Damrosch, *Harvard University*
J. Paul Hunter, *University of Chicago*
Isobel Grundy, *University of Alberta*
Lawrence Lipking, *Northwestern University*
Harold Love, *Monash University*
Claude Rawson, *Yale University*
Pat Rogers, *University of South Florida*
James Sambrook, *University of Southampton*

Some recent titles
Eighteenth-Century Sensibility and the Novel
The Senses in Social Context
by Ann Jessie Van Sant
Family and the Law in Eighteenth-Century Fiction
The Public Conscience in the Private Sphere
by John P. Zomchick
Crime and Defoe: A New Kind of Writing
by Lincoln B. Faller
Literary Transmission and Authority
Dryden and other writers
Edited by Earl Miner and Jennifer Brady
Plots and Counterplots
Sexual Politics and the Body Politic in English Literature, 1600–1730
by Richard Braverman
The Eighteenth-Century Hymn in England
by Donald Davie
Swift's Politics: A Study in Disaffection
by Ian Higgins

A complete list of books in this series is given at the end of the volume

Swift's politics
A study in disaffection

IAN HIGGINS

Lecturer in English,
The Australian National University, Canberra

CAMBRIDGE UNIVERSITY PRESS
Cambridge, New York, Melbourne, Madrid, Cape Town, Singapore, São Paulo

Cambridge University Press
The Edinburgh Building, Cambridge CB2 2RU, UK

Published in the United States of America by Cambridge University Press, New York

www.cambridge.org
Information on this title: www.cambridge.org/9780521418140

© Cambridge University Press 1994

This publication is in copyright. Subject to statutory exception
and to the provisions of relevant collective licensing agreements,
no reproduction of any part may take place without
the written permission of Cambridge University Press.

First published 1994
Reprinted 1995
This digitally printed first paperback version 2006

A catalogue record for this publication is available from the British Library

Library of Congress Cataloguing in Publication data

Higgins, Ian.
Swift's politics: a study in disaffection / Ian Higgins.
p.   cm. – (Cambridge studies in eighteenth-century
English literature and thought; 20)
Includes bibliographical references and index.
ISBN 0 521 41814 3 (hardback)
1. Swift, Jonathan, 1667–1745 – Political and social views.
2. Politics and literature – Great Britain – History – 18th century.
3. Satire, English – History and criticism. 4. Tories, English, in
literature. 5. Jacobites in literature. I. Title. II. Series.
PR 3728.P6H54   1994
828′.509–dc20   93–8593   CIP

ISBN-13 978-0-521-41814-0 hardback
ISBN-10 0-521-41814-3 hardback

ISBN-13 978-0-521-02568-3 paperback
ISBN-10 0-521-02568-0 paperback

Contents

Preface

This contextualist study is concerned with the contested critical question of Jonathan Swift's political character. Attending to topical polemical circumstances the historical criticism in this book attempts to recover the partisan meanings of Swift's texts and their original political impact. This study offers a reassessment of Swift's political writing and recorded opinion. While contesting current conceptions of Swift as a Whig, it offers a partial revision of that scholarship which describes Swift as a non-Jacobite Tory. Swift's first readers claimed he was a disaffected High Churchman. Swift did not subscribe to traditional royalist Tory principles of absolute, divine-right monarchy and indefeasible hereditary succession, yet his Whig adversaries came to regard him as 'a great Jacobite'.[1] The question of Swift's 'Jacobitism' has been often canvassed in modern Swift studies and it is the scholarly orthodoxy that Swift was not a Jacobite.[2] In constructing the author of *A Tale of a Tub* and *Gulliver's Travels* as a Whig or as a loyal Tory, modern scholarship has occluded a militant polemical strain in his great satires, poems and pamphleteering on affairs of state. Whether or not Swift was a Jacobite cannot be determined. He claimed in private and in print to be a Whig. Rather than dismiss the judgement of Swift's contemporaries, however, this study asks whether there is anything about Swift's political writing in polemical context that could have led

---

[1] *The Life and Errors of John Dunton*, edited by John Nichols, 2 vols. (1818; rpt. New York, 1969), 'Appeal to George I', p. 740.

[2] Ellen Douglass Leyburn, 'Swift's View of the Dutch', *PMLA*, 66 (1951), 734–45 (p. 735). Assessing the evidence of Swift's statements on the succession issue, both F. P. Lock and J. A. Downie have concluded that although Swift was often accused of Jacobitism his professions of innocence can be accepted: see F. P. Lock, *Swift's Tory Politics* (London, 1983), esp. pp. 119–20, 133; J. A. Downie, *Jonathan Swift: Political Writer* (London, 1984), Appendix II, 'Swift's Alleged Jacobitism', pp. 344–5. See also John Irwin Fischer, Review of *Jonathan Swift: Political Writer*, *Scriblerian*, 17 (1985), 170–3: Swift 'was no Jacobite' (p. 172). An historian of Jacobitism, however, finds Swift 'ambivalent' on Jacobites and their doctrines; see Frank McLynn, *The Jacobites* (London, 1985), p. 148.

contemporaries to construe Jacobite Tory meanings. The consonance of
Swift's political rhetoric with Tory and Jacobite polemic is registered
here. Echoes of the proscribed Jacobite voice in the political polyphony
of Swift's culture can be found in his work. What can be shown is that
Swift's writings in the 1690s, during the last four years of Queen Anne's
reign, and after the Hanoverian succession, contained Jacobitical political implication within the contemporary paper wars in which his texts
have their provenance. This study notes the complexity and ambivalence of some of the textual evidence of Swift's attitude to Jacobitism
and describes his discontent with the Revolution settlement.

The book is based on an analysis of Swift's prose, poetry and correspondence and contemporary (mainly printed) sources – books, pamphlets, poems on affairs of state and newspapers. It is centrally concerned
with the partisan political meanings of Swift's imaginative texts, particularly the great satires *A Tale of a Tub* and *Gulliver's Travels*. Some
new or neglected polemical contexts and analogues for Swift's works are
suggested. Chapter 1 considers some of the problems and contested
issues in interpretation of Swift's political biography and writing.
Chapter 2 witnesses Swift's combination of High Church attitudes with
a radical political critique of Whig Establishment. Swift is read in
juxtaposition with Jacobite Tory authors such as George Granville,
Lord Lansdowne. Chapter 3 relocates *A Tale of a Tub* in historical
context to reveal the satire's relation to High Church Tory polemical
languages. Chapter 4 discusses the disaffected Tory aspect of *Gulliver's
Travels*.

This book derives from my doctoral thesis (University of Warwick,
1989). An earlier version of chapter 1 with some commentary on the
Tory and ambiguously Jacobite aspect of *Gulliver's Travels* was
published as 'Swift's Politics: A Preface to *Gulliver's Travels*', in *Monash
Swift Papers*, Number One, edited by Clive T. Probyn and Bryan
Coleborne (Monash University, 1988), pp. 41–65. I would like to
record my gratitude to several people who have helped me in my
research and writing on Swift. I am particularly indebted to the
learning, generosity and encouragement of Professor F. P. Lock, with
whom I began my work on Swift, and Professor Claude Rawson, who
supervised my doctoral research. I am especially grateful to Jenny
Mezciems for generous support and for expert critical advice on earlier
versions of this work. At earlier stages of my research I benefited from
discussions with Dr Eveline Cruickshanks, Dr Daniel Eilon and Dr
Mark Goldie. I am indebted to the scholarship, encouragement and
patience of Dr Howard Erskine-Hill, the co-editor of this series. For

support during the later stages of preparation I would like to thank Jon Mee, Gillian Russell and Ben Penny. Andrée Poulter generously gave patient and painstaking critical attention to this manuscript. None of the above, of course, are responsible for the interpretations and short-comings of this book.

Periods of research in British libraries were made possible for me by a Commonwealth Scholarship under the Commonwealth Scholarship and Fellowship Plan and research travel grants from the School of Humanities, La Trobe University and the Faculty Research Fund, The Australian National University. I gratefully acknowledge this support.

Abbreviations

Editions of Swift's works

Complete Poems	*Jonathan Swift The Complete Poems*, ed. by Pat Rogers (Harmondsworth, 1983)
Corr	*The Correspondence of Jonathan Swift*, ed. by Harold Williams, 5 vols. (Oxford, 1963–5)
Discourse	*A Discourse of the Contests and Dissentions Between the Nobles and the Commons in Athens and Rome*, ed. by Frank H. Ellis (Oxford, 1967)
Exam	*Swift vs. Mainwaring: 'The Examiner' and 'The Medley'*, ed. by Frank H. Ellis (Oxford, 1985)
Poems	*The Poems of Jonathan Swift*, ed. by Harold Williams, 2nd edn, 3 vols. (Oxford, 1958)
PW	*The Prose Writings of Jonathan Swift*, ed. by Herbert Davis and others, 16 vols. (Oxford, 1939–74)
Tale	*A Tale of a Tub To which is added The Battle of the Books and the Mechanical Operation of the Spirit*, ed. by A. C. Guthkelch and D. Nichol Smith, 2nd edn (Oxford, 1958 [1973])

Other abbreviations

Epist. Corr.	Atterbury, Francis, *The Epistolary Correspondence, Visitation Charges, Speeches and Miscellanies of the Right Reverend Francis Atterbury, D. D., Lord Bishop of Rochester*, ed. by J. Nichols, 5 vols. (London, 1783–90)
LeFanu	LeFanu, William, *A Catalogue of Books belonging to Dr Jonathan Swift Dean of St Patrick's, Dublin Aug. 19. 1715: A facsimile of Swift's autograph with an introduction and alphabetic catalogue*, Cambridge Bibliographical Society Monograph no. 10 (Cambridge, 1988)

Parl. Hist.	Cobbett, William, ed., *The Parliamentary History of England*, 36 vols. (London, 1806–20)
POAS	*Poems on Affairs of State*, ed. by G. deF. Lord and others, 7 vols. (New Haven, 1963–75)
Proceedings	*Proceedings of The First Münster Symposium on Jonathan Swift*, ed. by Hermann J. Real and Heinz J. Vienken (Munich, 1985)
SC	Williams, Harold, *Dean Swift's Library. With a Facsimile of the Original Sale Catalogue and Some Account of Two Manuscript Lists of his Books* (Cambridge, 1932). Reference is by lot number in the catalogue.
Somers Tracts	*A Collection of Scarce and Valuable Tracts*, ed. by Walter Scott, 2nd edn, 13 vols. (London, 1809–15)
Swift	Ehrenpreis, Irvin, *Swift: The Man, his Works, and the Age*, 3 vols. (London, 1962–83)

Dates and quotations

In all dates the year is taken to begin on 1 January (rather than 25 March). Most contemporary works were published anonymously. Authors have been supplied where known. The original spelling, punctuation and italicization have generally been retained in quotations.

1

Swift's political character

... the modern Question is only, Whether he be a *Whig* or *Tory* ...
        The Sentiments of a Church-of-England Man (1708; published 1711)

If possible, to learn his Story,
And whether he were *Whig* or *Tory?* ...
In State-Opinions *a-la Mode*,
He hated *Wh——n* like a Toad;
Had giv'n the *Faction* many a Wound,
And Libell'd all the *Junta* round ...
        Part of the Seventh Epistle of the First Book of Horace Imitated (1713)

But, I confess, that after I had been a little too copious in talking of my own
beloved Country; of our Trade, and Wars by Sea and Land, of our Schisms in
Religion, and Parties in the State; the Prejudices of his Education prevailed so
far, that he could not forbear taking me up in his right Hand, and stroaking me
gently with the other; after an hearty Fit of laughing, asked me whether I were
a *Whig* or a *Tory*.
        Gulliver's Travels, II, iii (1726)

Swift's politics is a large, complex and controversial subject upon which
there is a considerable corpus of commentary. This chapter considers
briefly some of the contested issues in interpretation of Swift's political
biography and writing.

The exegesis of Swift's political principles and party-political allegiance is a matter of continuing disagreement in modern Swift studies.
A complexity in the case is that Swift was reputed to be a Whig at the
beginning of Queen Anne's reign but a Tory by the end of it. An
apparent public change of parties in 1710 is reflected in his private
correspondence. Tory names start to replace Whig names in the list of
Swift's English correspondents after 1710.[1] However, modern scholars

[1] *Corr*, I, xxi–lxx; W. A. Speck, 'From Principles to Practice: Swift and Party Politics', in *The
World of Jonathan Swift: Essays for the Tercentenary*, edited by Brian Vickers (Oxford, 1968),
pp. 69–86 (p. 69).

find an integrity and coherence in Swift's mature political convictions. What is contested is the precise nature of his ideological identity, which remained essentially unchanged during his adult life, and the topical meaning of his political principles and language.

Essentially there are three basic and contradictory accounts of Swift's politics in the critical commentary. One position is that Swift is a post-Revolution Tory who was temporarily associated by circumstance with the Whigs. The case for Swift as a Tory in politics and ecclesiology has been advanced in detail in the work of F. P. Lock.[2] Swift's break with the Whigs and public 'conversion' to a Tory party-political position in 1710 is seen as an ideological homecoming rather than an apostasy in the 'Tory' reading of Swift's politics. A second position in Swift studies tends to see Swift as a paradoxical, idiosyncratic political figure whose political attitudes include elements from Tory and Whig extremes of contemporary political argument; that there are reactionary and libertarian strands in his political ideology. This second position argues that it is probably a futile exercise to try to site Swift in the terrain of post-Revolution party politics or that both 'Whig' and 'Tory' descriptions of Swift are appropriate. Swift is represented as a political nonconformist in the Age of Party.[3] A third view is that Swift is essentially a Whig in state politics and remained so despite his 'conversion' to the predominantly Tory administration of 1710–14. This view, which can be found stated or expounded in the work of many Swiftians, is a modern scholarly orthodoxy.[4] The Whig case for Swift

---

[2] F. P. Lock, *Swift's Tory Politics* (London, 1983).

[3] Daniel Eilon, *Factions' Fictions: Ideological Closure in Swift's Satire* (Newark, London, Toronto, 1991), esp. pp. 15–20, 94–122, 160–4. Eilon's analysis of the Whig and Tory cases for Swift accepts a final verdict of 'Tory by temperament and a Whig by principle' (p. 114); David Nokes, 'The Radical Conservatism of Swift's Irish Pamphlets', *British Journal for Eighteenth-Century Studies*, 7 (1984), 169–76.

[4] For some modern studies that, despite other differences, identify Swift's fundamental Whig politics: Arthur E. Case, *Four Essays on Gulliver's Travels* (Princeton, 1945; rpt. Gloucester, Mass., 1958), pp. 107–9; Ricardo Quintana, *Swift: An Introduction* (London, 1955; rpt. Oxford Paperbacks, 1962), pp. 7–8; J. C. Beckett, 'Swift as an Ecclesiastical Statesman', in *Essays in British and Irish History in Honour of James Eadie Todd*, edited by H. A. Cronne, T. W. Moody and D. B. Quinn (London, 1949), rpt. in *Fair Liberty Was All His Cry: A Tercentenary Tribute to Jonathan Swift 1667–1745*, edited by A. Norman Jeffares (London, 1967), pp. 146–65 (pp. 150, 152, 159); Kathleen Williams, *Jonathan Swift and the Age of Compromise* (Lawrence, Kansas, 1958), pp. 100–3; James A. Preu, *The Dean and the Anarchist* (Tallahassee, 1959), esp. pp. 33, 99–102; Bertrand A. Goldgar, *The Curse of Party: Swift's Relations with Addison and Steele* (Lincoln, Nebraska, 1961), pp. 63–67, 83, 169; Basil Hall, '"An Inverted Hypocrite": Swift the Churchman', in *The World of Jonathan Swift*, pp. 38–68 (p. 60); W. A. Speck, 'From Principles to Practice: Swift and Party Politics', in *ibid.*, pp. 69–86 (pp. 80–1); Speck, *Society and Literature in England 1700–60* (Dublin, 1983), which sees *Gulliver's Travels* as reflecting 'Country more than Tory attitudes'. Political

squares with a literal reading of Swift's repeated profession that he was 'a Whig in politics' although a 'High-churchman' in religion; that he was 'of the old Whig principles, without the modern articles and refinements' (*PW*, VIII, 120; *Corr*, IV, 100). Swift's hostility to 'modern whiggery' and particularly to the Walpolean regime, it is argued, reflects his fundamental Whig principles rather than dis-affected Tory politics. Irvin Ehrenpreis's biography of Swift represents him as an 'Old Whig' in politics but Tory with regard to the Church. At one point Ehrenpreis implies that Swift's politics in the last four years of Anne's reign were an aberration from a Whig humanism. Swift 'defends a Lockean view of the limits of good government. When his friends stood on top, he forgot this view. One benign effect of defeat, for Swift, was that it recalled him to humanity.' It is observed during an expo-sition of the Drapier's third letter that 'Swift has in effect accepted his new rulers, the Hanoverian Whigs, and seems to urge them to judge their Irish conduct by their English ideals.'[5] The argument for Swift as a true Whig opposed to Tory ideology and Hanoverian Court Whig-gism has been put in detail by J. A. Downie. He sees a continuity in Swift's political writings from *A Discourse of the Contests and Dissentions Between the Nobles and the Commons in Athens and Rome* (1701), defending Whig lords, through his tracts of 1710–14, to his alliance with the Whig Archbishop King in Ireland during the affair of Wood's halfpence, *The Drapier's Letters* and *Gulliver's Travels*. Downie concludes that in *Gulli-ver's Travels* Swift

refers to the way in which old Whig ideals have been allowed to become corrupted since the Revolution by men like Walpole. Swift, in Gulliver's conversations with the King of Brobdingnag (and elsewhere), compares Modern Whig government with Old Whig political ideology ... In this, his

attitudes in the work are labelled 'Country Whig' and 'Country Tory' (see pp. 27, 67, 82); Donald Greene, 'Swift: Some Caveats', in *Studies in the Eighteenth Century II: Papers Presented at the Second David Nichol Smith Memorial Seminar 1970*, edited by R. F. Brissenden (Canberra, 1973), pp. 341–58 (pp. 341–7). Like W. A. Speck, J. A. Downie (*Robert Harley and the Press: Propaganda and Public Opinion in the Age of Swift and Defoe* (Cambridge, 1979), pp. 127–9 and *Jonathan Swift: Political Writer* (London, 1984), esp. pp. 259–60) presents the argument that Swift straddled the contemporary party division between Whig and Tory. His anachronistic political ideology was Old Whig or Country. Swift is seen as essentially a Whig in political principle by Frank H. Ellis in his edition of *The Examiner* and *The Medley* (Oxford, 1985). J. G. A. Pocock ('*The Machiavellian Moment* Revisited: A Study in History and Ideology', *Journal of Modern History*, 53 (1981), 49–72) remarks 'the presence in opposition of Tories of the style of Swift, Bolingbroke, and Pope, whose ideology differed surprisingly little from that of the Old Whigs' (p. 63). Swift's 'Old Whig principles' have become a truism in Swift studies.

[5] *Swift*, II, 4, 46, 118, 252–4; III, 142, 243.

greatest statement on politics, Swift, through implication, outlines his ideal political system. And this turns out to be not Tory in inspiration, but Whig.[6]

It is a measure of the complex nature of the issues involved in historical criticism of Swift's political writings, and the effect on Swift criticism of current historiographical controversy about the nature of party politics and ideology after the Revolution, and especially in the early Hanoverian period, that there should be such opposed interpretations of Swift's political allegiance. Two authoritative scholars working on Swift's politics who appear to share a Hirschian critical methodology, who rehearse much the same evidence in their historical criticism of Swift's texts and who are in agreement about the 'Country' critique informing Swift's political satire in Gulliver's Travels, have arrived at spectacularly opposed verdicts on Swift's politics. For F. P. Lock, Swift is a natural Tory. For J. A. Downie, Swift is an unreconstructed Revolution Whig.

There is at least nominal inconsistency and contradiction in Swift's party-political alignment. In the early 1690s he wrote Pindaric odes to both King William III and the deprived Archbishop of Canterbury, William Sancroft. Swift's first political tract, A Discourse of the Contests and Dissentions ..., was published in a specific Court Whig political cause, although Swift's Tory answerers were able to demonstrate unwhiggish tenets in the work.[7] A Tale of a Tub (1704) is dedicated to the Junto Whig Lord Somers, but hostile contemporaries remarked that the ironic and parodic 'Bookseller's Dedication' to Somers was disrespectful.[8] The Dedication remained in the fifth edition of 1710. A Tale of a Tub was identified with the productions of heterodox radical Whigs, such as John Toland, and regarded as profane and irreligious by many.[9] Yet, as pointed out in chapter 3, Swift clearly thought that

---

[6] J. A. Downie, 'Swift's Politics', in Proceedings, pp. 47–58 (p. 58).

[7] See the excerpts from The Source of Our Present Fears Discover'd and from Charles Leslie, The New Association. Part II (London, 1703) and 'Supplement' reprinted as appendices in Discourse, pp. 228–51. Leslie, who assumed the work was by the eminent Whig polemicist Bishop Gilbert Burnet, triumphed at one point: 'Ah! Doctor, Doctor, Was this Always your Doctrine? Are you come to see it at last? And yet never Mend!' (p. 247). See the extended study of the pamphlet in F. P. Lock, Swift's Tory Politics, pp. 146–61, esp. pp. 160–1.

[8] William King, Some Remarks on The Tale of a Tub (1704) in The Original Works of William King, LL.D., 3 vols. (London, 1776), I, 215; William Wotton, Observations upon The Tale of a Tub (1705), reprinted in Tale, pp. 313–28 (p. 327).

[9] For a contemporary analysis of the Tale as the irreligious production of a libertine, see BL Add. MSS, 29, 612 fols. 15–25 (esp. fol. 25), the Letter-Book of Silvester Jenks 1703–1707. See also Brief Remarks On the late Representation of The Lower House of Convocation: As the same respects the Quakers only (London, 1711), pp. 13–14 where Swift duly appears in the company of those convicted of heterodoxy, heresy or irreligion. On the reception of the Tale as a profane, deistical and irreligious work, see William John Roscelli, 'A Tale of a Tub and the

authorship of the *Tale* made him welcome to the Church party, the book was admired by the High Church Tory, Francis Atterbury, and was regarded as the work of a 'violent Tory' by the Tory satirist William King. Swift's opposition to Whig ecclesiastical policy is well documented and well known, and in 1710 for principled and personal reasons Swift began to write for what he later described as 'the immortal Tory Ministry' (*PW*, V, 265) of the last four years of Queen Anne's reign. He emphatically wrote of the Whigs on 13 October 1710: 'I have done with them, and they have, I hope, done with this kingdom for our time' (*PW*, XV, 55). By the end of Anne's reign Swift was a famous Tory party publicist and a suspected Jacobite. In May 1715 the Tory printer, John Barber, wrote to Swift: 'We have 20 frightfull Accounts of your being sent for up, and your papers seized, for you are the reputed Author of every good thing that comes out on our side' (*Corr*, II, 168).

Swift's own statements about his political principles and party allegiance in the first Age of Party might seem to illustrate a Swiftian 'Thought': 'How inconsistent is Man with himself!' (*PW*, IV, 245).[10] Regularly charged in the Whig press after 1710 with venal political apostasy, and clearly sensitive to charges that he had deserted the Whigs for the Tories in 1710, Swift frequently claimed personal political consistency, representing himself as that idiosyncratic figure, a High Church Whig, and as a consistent if anachronistic 'old Whig'. Sometimes Swift averred that there was no real difference between the essential principles of Whig and Tory and that he was moderate and bipartisan.[11] It was only circumstantial and personal reasons, Swift claimed in *The Sentiments of a Church-of-England Man* (probably written in 1708 but published in 1711) that had associated him with one party (the Whigs) more than another:

I converse in full Freedom with many considerable Men of both Parties; and if not in equal Number, it is purely accidental and personal, as happening to be near the Court, and to have made Acquaintance there, more under one Ministry than another.

"Cavils of the Sour"', *Journal of English and Germanic Philology*, 64 (1965), 41–56, and Frank T. Boyle, 'Profane and Debauched Deist: Swift in the Contemporary Response to *A Tale of a Tub*', *Eighteenth-Century Ireland*, 3 (1988), 25–38.

[10] Swift also wrote: 'IF a Man would register all his Opinions upon Love, Politicks, Religion, Learning, and the like; beginning from his Youth, and so go on to old Age: What a Bundle of Inconsistencies and Contradictions would appear at last?' (*PW*, I, 244). There may not be a unified subject to reconstruct out of Swift's corpus. On Swift's inconsistency, see Patrick Reilly, *Jonathan Swift: The Brave Desponder* (Manchester, 1982), pp. 28, 120.

[11] See, for example, *Corr*, I, 212; *PW*, II, 13–14; VIII, 71–2; *Exam*, pp. 34–7 (*Examiner*, 16 November 1710); pp. 313–14 (*Examiner*, 22 March 1711); pp. 450–8 (*Examiner*, 31 May 1711).

He admits 'it seems every Man's Duty to chuse one of the two Sides', the course of 'the latter Cato', although 'before Things proceed to open Violence, the truest Service a private Man may hope to do his Country, is by unbiassing his Mind as much as possible, and then endeavouring to moderate between the Rival Powers' (*PW*, II, 2). The passages quoted here from the *Sentiments* may be Swift's oblique response to the 'Supplement' (dated 25 March 1703) of Charles Leslie's *The New Association. Part II*, an extremist High Church work in which Swift would have found his own nominally Whig *Discourse* of 1701 singled out for hostile attention. At the conclusion of the 'Supplement' Leslie looked with some charity on those good men who find themselves listed among the Whigs: 'Allowances must be made for the *Prejudices* of *Education*, of *Acquaintance* and *Friendship* contracted, which have *Byass'd* many *Well-meaning* and *Good Disposed* Men on the side of this, as of other *Wicked Parties*.' But the time has come for those good men to '*Examine* the *Truth*' to 'shew themselves *Men*, to Examine *Impartially*; And then Judge as they find'.[12] Swift accepts in the *Sentiments* that it is 'every Man's Duty' to unbias his mind but to choose sides. Swift aligned with the Tories.

In his *Memoirs, Relating to that Change which happened in the Queen's Ministry in the Year 1710* (written in 1714 although not printed until 1765) Swift states that in 1702 'I first began to trouble myself with the difference between the principles of Whig and Tory.' The formulation of his position is careful:

I talked often upon this subject with Lord Sommers; told him, that, having been long conversant with the Greek and Roman authors, and therefore a lover of liberty, I found myself much inclined to be what they called a Whig in politics; and that, besides, I thought it impossible, upon any other principle, to defend or submit to the Revolution: But, as to religion, I confessed myself to be an High-churchman, and that I did not conceive how any one, who wore the habit of a clergyman, could be otherwise.

(*PW*, VIII, 120)

Despite the strong inclination he expressed to Somers to be a Whig in politics, and thus to make his adherence to the Revolution settlement unquestionable, the High Churchman attempts to vindicate himself in the *Memoirs* from the charge 'by several of those poor pamphleteers, who have blotted so much paper to shew their malice against me, that I was a favourer of the low-party'. He instances several tracts written

---

[12] Charles Leslie, *The New Association. Part II*, 'Supplement', p. 22, N.B.

(although not all 'published' as Swift misleadingly claims) in opposition
to the Whigs 'during the highest dominion of that faction' – 'A Project
for the Reformation of Manners, in a letter to the Countess of Berkeley;
The Sentiments of a Church-of-England man; an Argument against
abolishing Christianity; and, lastly, a Letter to a Member of Parliament
against taking off the Test in Ireland' (*PW*, VIII, 122; see also *Corr*, I,
100). A Tory government propagandist between 1710 and 1714, Swift
had credit and acquaintance with a remarkable number of important
and prominent Jacobite Tories. His friends included men and women
who were either committed or sometime Jacobites, among others,
Francis Atterbury, John Barber, Lord Bathurst, Viscount Bolingbroke,
Charles and Mary Caesar, Sir John Hynde Cotton, Lord Lansdowne,
the Duke of Ormonde, the Earl of Orrery and the second Earl of
Oxford.[13] Swift wrote to Alexander Pope in 1723: 'I have often made
the same remark with you of my Infelicity in being so Strongly attached
to Traytors (as they call them) and Exiles, and State Criminalls' (*Corr*,
II, 464; a passage omitted in Pope's own texts of the correspondence).
During the Hanoverian period Swift was a bitter, public critic of Whig
political measures, especially of the government's Irish and ecclesiastical policies. Yet in his post-1710 correspondence he professed to
have always been a member of the Whig party in politics.[14] The inquest
into his party-political identity imagined in *The Life and Genuine Character of Doctor Swift* is in disagreement about him:

> He was an *honest man* I'll swear ---:
> Why Sir, I differ from you there,
> For, I have heard another Story,
> He was a most *confounded Tory* ---!
>
> (*Poems*, II, 547)

Historical criticism of Swift's writings seeks to disclose the meanings
of a particular text at the moment of its composition and reception, and
needs to register the full complexity of contemporary polemical and
ideological contexts within which Swift's texts and statements are to be
situated and their meanings determined. It is my contention that the
current received views of Swift as a Whig or at least an Old Whig (an

---

[13] See, for example, the list of persons in Swift's letter to Mrs Barber of 23 February 1731,
Corr, III, 439–40.

[14] For descriptions of himself as a Whig to Whig correspondents see: *Corr*, I, 359 (27 May 1713,
to Richard Steele); II, 236 (22 December 1716, to Archbishop King); III, 138 (7 July
1726, to Thomas Tickell); III, 484 (27 July 1731, to the Countess of Suffolk); IV, 100 (8
January 1733, to Lady Elizabeth Germain); IV, 230 (23 March 1734, to Francis Grant).
And see *Corr*, IV, 346 (8 June 1735, to Lady Elizabeth Germain).

identity Swift liked to project from time to time) and as a non-Jacobite
Tory are oversimplifications of a complex and extremist political
writer. Despite the Whig associations and influences of his period in
the household of Sir William Temple, and of his early political career
and intellectual inheritance, Swift may be recognized as, ontologically,
a 'naturalized' Tory of the Queen Anne and Hanoverian period. The
consonance of Swift's political and ecclesiastical attitudes with identifi-
able Tory party-political positions can be noted in his attack on
Dissent and occasional conformity in *A Tale of a Tub* (1704); in his hostility to the Union with Scotland expressed, for example, in his 'Verses
Said To Be Written on the Union' (1707); in his support for the Lower
House of Convocation; in his commitment to an exclusive Anglican
monopoly of public office and resistance to any extension of religious
toleration; in his hostility to Protestant immigration and the Naturalization Act; in his support for a non-interventionist foreign policy; and
revealingly, in his animus against the Dutch.

On the decisive question of political obligation, Swift's official ideological position is that the private subject owed allegiance and passive
obedience to the powers-that-be – the sovereign legislature of king in
possession with the consent of parliament. He propounds this conservative quietism in letters to friends suspected of Jacobitism, such as
Alexander Pope, Knightley Chetwode and Thomas Sheridan (*Corr*, II,
213; II, 384; III, 67). The *Sentiments* affirms that it is not lawful to
resist the legislative power which is 'absolute and unlimited' (*PW*, II,
16, 23). This view has impeccable High Church Tory polemical provenance.[15] Swift's doctrine of unlimited passive obedience to the legislature of king, lords and commons in settled possession of the government according to present law in force aligns him with the
contemporary view influentially expounded by the High Churchman
and former nonjuror William Higden against Jacobite indefeasible
divine hereditary right doctrine and Whig contractual resistance
theory.[16] As the paper war occasioned by Higden's *A View of the English*

---

[15] See, for example, Charles Leslie, *The Case of the Regale and of the Pontificat Stated* (n.p., 1700),
pp. 127–8: '*Civil Government*, which it is *Necessary* shou'd be *Absolute* and *Un-Controulable*; as
the *Supreme Power* is in all *Governments*, wherever it is Lodg'd, whether in *One*, or in *Many* . . .
The *Supreme Legislative Power* cannot Make it self not to be *Absolute*.'

[16] Swift possessed a copy of Higden's *A View of the English Constitution, with Respect to the Sovereign
Authority of the Prince, and the Allegiance of the Subject, &c. The Third Edition. With a Defence of the
View, by way of Reply to the several Answers that have been made to it* (London, 1710); see LeFanu,
p. 20; *SC*, no. 423. Higden's work went through several editions and prompted attacks and
defences. For witness of Higden's influence see: BL Add. MSS, 45,512, fols. 192–3 (Robert
Nelson collection); Charles Leslie, *A Battle Royal Between Three Cocks of the Game Mr. Higden*,

Constitution, with Respect to the Sovereign Authority of the Prince, and the Allegiance of the Subject (1709) and his *Defence* (1710) makes clear, this Swift–Higden view is ideologically neither Jacobite nor Revolution Whig. It regards post-Revolution government as a legal settlement and prescribes submission to the established legislature. Higden's case of allegiance, the Jacobite Tory Thomas Hearne remarked, 'resolves all into Possession, and makes all Usurpers have a title to Allegiance'.[17] While it provoked Jacobite legitimists, Higden's theory hardly satisfies Revolution Whigs, for it leaves a residual ambiguity about the constitutional legality of the Revolution itself and continues to insist on the Anglican Tory doctrine of non-resistance.

In the *Sentiments*, Swift contrives to suture adamant adherence to the Tory doctrine of absolute non-resistance with acquiescence in the cessation of James II's right at the Revolution in 1689. Swift's Tory politics are disclosed in his desire in the argument of the *Sentiments* to preserve intact the doctrine of absolute non-resistance, that under no '*Pretence whatsoever*' was it '*lawful to resist the supreme Magistrate*' (*PW*, II, 16). The Church-of-England Man argues that for most subjects the question of passive obedience is not concerned in the events of 1688–9. As for the '*Abdication* of King *James*' which nonjurors regard as 'forcible and unjust, and consequently void in it self', the Church-of-England Man thinks 'a Man may observe every Article of the *English* Church, without being in much Pain about it'. Whether James II's 'Removal were caused by his own *Fears*, or other Men's *Artifices*' (there is an innuendo against 'the Prince of *Orange*' in the passage), it was the supposition of 'the Throne to be vacant, which was the Foot the Nation went upon' at the Revolution (*PW*, II, 20). The Tory High Churchman, Henry Sacheverell, had made the same insistence in the notorious sermon, *The Perils of False Brethren both in Church and State* (1709) which had provoked a Whig government prosecution:

How often must they be told, that the *King Himself* solemnly *Disclaim'd* the Least Imputation of *Resistance* in his *Declaration*; and that the *Parliament* declar'd, That they set the *Crown* on his Head, upon no other *Title*, but that of the *Vacancy of the* Throne? And did they not Unanimously condemn to the Flames, (as it justly *Deserv'd*) that *Infamous Libel*, that would have *Pleaded* the

---

Hoadley, Hottentote. As to the State of Nature and of Government ... appended to *The Finishing Stroke* ... (London, 1711), pp. 125–239.

17 Thomas Hearne, *Remarks and Collections of Thomas Hearne*, edited by C. E. Doble, Oxford Historical Society, 11 vols. (Oxford, 1885–1921), II, 297 (2 November 1709). See also II, 284, 290, 293, 398; III, 93.

Title of *Conquest*, by which *Resistance* was suppos'd? So *Tender* were they of the *Regal* Rights, and so averse to infringe the least Tittle of Our *Constitution!*[18]

When in polemical combat with Whig ideologists, Jacobites as well as conforming Tories insisted that the Convention in 1689 went upon the supposition of vacancy in the throne and abdication, not the principle of resistance and deposition.[19] In the Church-of-England Man's casuistical account of James's '*Abdication*' or 'Departure', which preserves the Church party principle of passive obedience, Swift is officially subscribing to that contemporary conservative Anglican Tory interpretation of the events of 1688–9 which claimed that James had not been forcibly resisted by his subjects.[20] Tories who conformed to the Revolution settlement could be discomforted by the rigorous legalism of nonjurors, who argued that only the king, lords and commons in parliament could make and repeal law and that the Convention at the Revolution which transferred the crown did not constitute the supreme legislature. When directly confronting the problem of the legality of the deposition and alteration of the succession in the *Sentiments* (*PW*, II, 21–3) and in the *Examiner* (*Exam*, pp. 5, 317), Swift capitulates to a Grotian conservative natural rights position of resistance *in extremis* – that non-resistance is the rule but an exception can be allowed in an extreme case of necessity.

Despite Swift's compliance with the Revolution settlement and his recorded opposition to a popish successor to the crown of England, he can be legitimately understood in various places to be saying what some Jacobite political writers were saying. This does not make Swift a Jacobite, of course, but it does reveal him to be a more unsettling, less domesticated political animal than the conservative Old Whig repre-

[18] Henry Sacheverell, *The Perils of False Brethren both in Church and State: Set forth in a Sermon Preach'd before The Right Honourable, The Lord-Mayor, Aldermen, and Citizens of London, at the Cathedral-Church of St. Paul, On the 5th of November, 1709* (London, 1709; reprinted by The Rota at the University of Exeter, 1974), pp. 20–1.

[19] See, for example, Charles Leslie, *A View of the Times, Their Principles and Practices in The Rehearsals*, second edition, 6 vols. (London, 1750), I, 14–15; II, 94, 108, 126–7; V, 256–7, 262; Leslie, *The Best Answer ...* (London, 1709), pp. 1–2; Leslie, *Best of All ...* (London, 1709), pp. 12–13, 18; [Matthias Earbery], *The Universal Spy or, The Royal Oak Journal Reviv'd* no. 9 (2 September 1732), Public Record Office, State Papers Domestic (hereafter cited as PRO SP) 36/28, fols. 90–1.

[20] For Anglican Tory argument, see Mark Goldie, 'Edmund Bohun and *Jus Gentium* in the Revolution Debate, 1689–1693', *The Historical Journal*, 20 (1977), 569–86; Goldie, 'The Revolution of 1689 and the Structure of Political Argument: An Essay and an Annotated Bibliography of Pamphlets on the Allegiance Controversy', *Bulletin of Research in the Humanities*, 83 (1980), 473–564; Goldie, 'The Political Thought of the Anglican Revolution', in *The Revolutions of 1688*, edited by Robert Beddard (Oxford, 1991), pp. 102–36.

sented in much modern Swiftian biography and criticism. When read
in polemical context, the paradox often observed in Swift's political
writings of authoritarian and conservative Tory elements coexisting
with radical libertarian strands of argument may be evidence of a
Jacobite Tory political stance. It can be shown that conservative High
Church Tories adopted a radical, 'whiggish' idiom of revolution principles in their polemic against post-Revolution polity. Before he had
decided to enter the post-Revolution Church of England (and thus to
take the oaths to the Revolution monarchs) and in his disaffection from
the Hanoverian regime after 1714, Swift writes in the political language
of the dispossessed and proscribed – the language of a radical, ambiguously Jacobite, Toryism. Passive obedience and non-resistance but also
regicide and revolutionism engaged Swift the political writer.

Critical disagreement about Swift's political character derives in part
from disagreement about the nature of party politics and ideology when
Swift is writing. There has been historiographical controversy over
whether or not a Tory party retained an organizational, political and
ideological identity during the Hanoverian period and, if it did so,
whether or not the Tory party became a Jacobite one. There has been
debate over whether or not a Whig–Tory political polarity (with party
identity continuing beneath the bipartisan 'Country' attitudes of
Opposition Whigs and Tories on specific issues) was replaced by a
Court–Country configuration (with Tories and dissident Whigs
merging in a patriot, Country opposition to the Court).[21] W. A. Speck,
a prominent historian who believed that 'the Tory and Whig parties of
Anne's reign became less dominant under the first two Georges, while
court-country alignments became more prominent than they had previously been', is also a leading authority on Swift's politics and
exponent of the case for Swift as neither strictly Whig nor Tory but a

[21] See Geoffrey Holmes, *British Politics in the Age of Anne*, revised edition (London and
Ronceverte, 1987), 'Introduction to Revised Edition', pp. xii–xiii; J. V. Beckett, 'Introduction: Stability in Politics and Society, 1680–1750', in *Britain in the First Age of Party
1680–1750: Essays Presented to Geoffrey Holmes*, edited by Clyve Jones (London and Ronceverte, 1987), pp. 1–18. Essential studies of the Tory party after 1714 are: Eveline Cruickshanks, *Political Untouchables: The Tories and the '45* (London, 1979) and Linda Colley, *In
Defiance of Oligarchy: The Tory Party 1714–60* (Cambridge, 1982). Cruickshanks considers the
Tory party after the Hanoverian accession to have become a Jacobite one. Colley considers
the majority of the party to have been loyal 'Hanoverian' Tories. For a restatement of her
case for the Tory party as a Jacobite party, see Eveline Cruickshanks, 'The Political
Management of Sir Robert Walpole, 1720–42', in *Britain in the Age of Walpole*, edited by
Jeremy Black, Problems in Focus (London, 1984), pp. 23–43 (esp. pp. 28–33). See also Ian
R. Christie, 'The Tory Party, Jacobitism and the 'Forty-Five: A Note', *The Historical
Journal*, 30 (1987), 921–31.

State Whig and Church Tory, a 'Country' rather than 'Tory' writer. Speck, however, has now accepted

that the Tory party survived the trauma of the Hanoverian succession longer than I previously thought. But I have still to be convinced by the evidence that most Tories were Jacobite. If that could be documented more adequately than it has so far been, I would accept the case of those who claim that Jacobitism was a significant phenomenon.[22]

The nature of the case, however, precludes the kind of definitive documentary evidence of Tory Jacobitism scholars would like to see. Eveline Cruickshanks, the historian who has argued most forcefully for the view that the Tory party retained its political identity in the Hanoverian period but had become a Jacobite party, observes: 'One of the great and abiding problems of studying Jacobitism in Britain, especially in England, is the problem of identification, to discover who was a Jacobite. Because of the penal laws against Jacobites – these statutes should be prescribed reading for historians of Jacobitism – discretion had to be the better part of valour.' Very few could have had access to Jacobite ciphers and messenger services to the exiled Stuart court. 'And it would be even more naive, of course, for the historian to expect to find hard evidence of Jacobitism in a man's private papers: would someone whose personal effects were liable to be searched at any time be likely to leave proofs of treason? Jacobites did not, no more had the Whigs in the 1680s.' Cruickshanks comments that with 'an almost total lack of Tory papers for the post-1715 period, it is impossible to prove or disprove whether the party's rank and file were Jacobites. What one can prove is that *the leaders of the party were Jacobites and answered for the party*. Historians who declare the contrary are in fact seeking to know better than contemporaries: better than Oxford, Gower, Bathurst, Atterbury, Orrery, Cornbury, Cotton, Watkin Williams Wynn and Beaufort and better than Walpole.'[23]

    J. A. Downie argues that in the absence of definite evidence of Jacobitism in Swift's correspondence, printed and manuscript remains, which would contradict Swift's publicly stated support for the Hanoverian succession, 'we have no alternative but to accept his own protestations that, however much he found to criticize under the Hanoverians, he was a "true loyal Whig". Otherwise we must be

[22] W. A. Speck, 'Polemical Purposes', *The Times Higher Education Supplement*, 7 November 1986, p. 16.
[23] Eveline Cruickshanks, 'Introduction', *Ideology and Conspiracy: Aspects of Jacobitism 1689–1759*, edited by Eveline Cruickshanks (Edinburgh, 1982), pp. 3, 4, 7.

prepared to contradict Swift's statements on the succession, and allow conjecture to take their place.'[24] It is difficult to see how the Hanoverian Whig writer represented by Downie and many others could be regarded as 'extremist' or could have been under suspicion of Jacobitism by Whig governments or occasioned so much alarm in the Whig press and the accusation of Jacobitism. There is little attempt in 'Whig' readings of Swift to ask whether there is textual evidence of shifting or equivocal loyalties or any disturbance or qualification in statements professing allegiance to Revolution governments, or whether we should be sceptical of Swift's (and Pope's) public presentation of themselves as loyal Whigs. Some comments made by Christopher Hill on censorship and seventeenth-century English literature seem apposite and especially applicable to Swift. Hill has remarked:

Those who believe we should study only the words on the page, only texts, do not ask themselves whether there were certain words, or certain ideas, which could not be printed; and others which of conventional necessity had to be. The constraints shaping 'the text' might be social and economic (patronage, the market) or political (the censorship in all its forms . . .).

He also observes that 'it is always rash to be wiser than a contemporary' and that literary historians 'do not always bear sufficiently in mind the subterfuges which writers necessarily had to adopt in order not to expose themselves to danger'.[25] Swift was acknowledged to be 'at the Head of all the Pamphleteers in *Great Britain*'. The copy of the treason statutes in Swift's library would have been a cautionary reference book for a writer of seditious libels.[26] It can be assumed that Swift knew what it meant to imagine the death of his sovereign, call in question his sovereign's right to the throne, assist or correspond with the Pretender or any of his open or secret adherents. There is no expression of high treason in Swift's known corpus. He was not a Jacobite fugitive. But the partisan import of, for example, the daring monarchomach rhetoric in Swift's extremist satires has not been investigated fully.

The case for Swift as an Old Whig presented in modern scholarship gives a selective and over-simplified representation of the party-political and ideological contexts of Swift's political writing. For instance,

---

[24] Downie, *Jonathan Swift: Political Writer*, p. 345.
[25] Christopher Hill, *Collected Essays. Volume One: Writing and Revolution in 17th Century England* (Brighton, 1985), pp. 32, 160, 170.
[26] *A Letter to the Reverend Mr. Dean Swift, Occasion'd by a Satire Said to be written by Him, Entitled, A Dedication to a Great Man, concerning Dedications* . . . (London, 1719), p. 21. Swift possessed *A Collection of the Several Statutes, and Parts of Statutes, Now in Force, relating to High Treason, And Misprision of High Treason* (London, 1709), see LeFanu, p. 17; *SC*, no. 307.

the variegated character of Tory and Jacobite ideology is not sufficiently registered. It is quite possible for Swift to be understood as a
Tory even though he did not subscribe to a Tory ideology of indefeasible, divine hereditary right monarchism. The 'Whig' case for Swift
would appear to depend on premises and arguments that can be
empirically challenged – particularly the views that Whig–Tory party
differences lost ideological and political significance and were substantially replaced by a Court–Country dichotomy and that Swift's
political principles can be understood separately from his High Church
Anglicanism: that his religious views have little significance in deter-
mining his *political* identity. Downie, in his political biography, directs
readers to the scholarship on neo-Harringtonian, classical republican,
'Country' and radical Whig political languages, and sees Swift as
belonging to an independent Old Whig tradition, an adherent of True,
pre-Revolution and Revolutionary Whiggism. Swift is identified with
the 'Country' party of the 1690s and 1720s and 1730s and located in a
political world characterized by Court–Country rather than Whig–
Tory division after 1715. I believe this distorts Swift's actual political
character and the polemical significance of his writings.

As Swift described vividly in a letter to William Tisdall on the second
introduction of the Tory bill against Occasional Conformity in 1703
and later in his violent sermon 'On Brotherly Love' (preached in 1717),
'Party' division profoundly pervaded his society (*Corr*, I, 38–9; *PW*, IX,
176–7). Swift's correspondence in the reigns of Queen Anne and the
first two Georges attests to the continuing vitality of a Whig–Tory
party-political vocabulary and of the contemporary perception of Whig
and Tory as the primary polarity in parliamentary politics and in
political life generally. Writing to Pope on 20 September 1723, Swift
comments on Pope's posture of 'retirement' and philosophical disengagement from party:

Your happiness is greater than your Merit in chusing your Favorites so
Indifferently among either party, this you owe partly to your Education and
partly to your Genius, employing you in an Art where Faction has nothing to
do. For I suppose Virgil, and Horace are equally read by Whigs and Toryes
you have no more to do with the Constitution of Church and State than a
Christian at Constantinople, and you are so much the wiser, and the happier
because both partyes will approve your Poetry as long as you are known to be
of neither. But I who am sunk under the prejudices of another Education, and
am every day perswading my self that a Dagger is at my Throat, a halter about
my Neck, or Chains at my Feet, all prepared by those in Power, can never
arrive at the Security of Mind you possess.

                                                                    (*Corr*, II, 465)

Swift, from time to time, professed to be disengaged from party politics. His disavowals of party politics during the Hanoverian period are not evidence that Whig–Tory political division had ceased to be relevant or central to his own political experience after 1714 or that Swift was no longer engaged or committed in political disputes. Such professions of disinterest or disengagement are properly understood as the routine prudential epistolary and public manoeuvres of a politically suspect man during the rage of party. An instance is in 'A Letter From Dr. Swift to Mr. Pope' (10 January 1722)[27] where Swift, conscious of the accusation of Jacobite sedition, parades his ignorance of party politics and the ruling Hanoverian royal family after 1714, having lived 'in the greatest privacy, and utter ignorance of those events which are most commonly talked of in the world; I neither know the names nor number of the Family which now reigns, further than the Prayer-book informs me' (PW, IX, 25–6; Corr, II, 367). Remarkably, Swift shows his political 'disengagement' by specifically disowning 'a Treatise called a Dedication upon Dedications'. It is 'impossible for me to have been Author of a Treatise, wherein there are several pages containing a Panegyrick on King George, of whose character and person I am utterly ignorant, nor ever had once the curiosity to enquire into either'. A Dedication to a Great Man, Concerning Dedications (1718) is in fact now attributed to the loyal Old Whig Thomas Gordon (PW, IX, 28; Corr, II, 368–9). The banter about dedications in the pamphlet may have been thought reminiscent of A Tale of a Tub. But the pamphlet contains fulsome panegyrics of George I and the Hanoverian dynasty and such men as the Duke of Marlborough, William III and Benjamin Hoadly. Its radical Whig provenance is suggested in its hostility to ecclesiastical hegemony and to the Tory principle of non-resistance. One contemporary pamphleteer remarked that some 'have wonder'd how Doctor Swift, whose Affection to the Church was never doubted, tho' his Christianity was ever question'd' could have written the anticlerical, Hanoverian Whig tract. The pamphleteer 'defends' Swift's apostasy, 'in this Instance, you have put off Prejudice, and resum'd your Understanding'.[28] In disavowing authorship of the Whig work imputed to him, Swift manages to register his partisan position while affecting aloofness from the world of Hanoverian politics. In the 1720s and 1730s, when Tories and Opposition Whigs attempted to collaborate

---

27 Ehrenpreis dates the letter as begun on 10 January 1722 and completed during the year, see Swift, III, 136, 445.

28 [Thomas Gordon], A Dedication to a Great Man, Concerning Dedications. Discovering, Amongst other wonderful Secrets, what will be the present Posture of Affairs a thousand Years hence (London, 1718); A Letter to the Reverend Mr. Dean Swift . . ., p. 16.

against the Whig government on specific 'Country' platforms, Swift's
famous satiric ridicule of party distinction (through the King of Brobdingnag's speech in Part II of *Gulliver's Travels*, *PW*, XI, 106–7) is
appropriately understood as party-political polemical strategy. Though
an 'exile' in Ireland, Swift remained a combatant in the party-political
paper wars. As Swift put it in *An Epistle to a Lady, Who desired the Author to
make Verses on Her, in the Heroick Stile* (1733):

> If I laugh at Whig and Tory;
> I conclude a *Fortiori*,
> All your Eloquence will scarce
> Drive me from my fav'rite Farce.
>
> (lines 193–6; *Poems*, II, 636)

Swift's political writing, although it might affect to be disinterested,
nevertheless has a deeply occasional provenance and aspect. And
Swift's conclusions on contemporary political controversies can be
identified most often as 'for Tory'.

Contemporaries regarded Swift, after 1710, as a Tory High Churchman. Swift acknowledged the party of the High Church Tory Bishop of
Rochester, Francis Atterbury, as 'my party' in a letter to Atterbury of
1717 (*Corr*, II, 279). The Tory party leader and friend of Swift, Henry
St John, Viscount Bolingbroke, declared in a letter to Sir William
Wyndham that the Tory party, proscribed from the centre of power
under the Hanoverian Whig regime, became a Jacobite party: 'If
milder measures had been pursued, certain it is that the Tories had
never universally embraced Jacobitism. The violence of the Whigs
forced them into the arms of the Pretender.'[29] Atterbury was in the
service of the Pretender from 1716 and was involved in financing the
preparations for the projected Swedish-Jacobite expedition in 1716–
17.[30] Swift may or may not have suspected his friend Atterbury to have

[29] *The History of Parliament, The House of Commons 1715–1754*, edited by Romney Sedgwick, 2
vols. (London, 1970), I, 62; Cruickshanks, *Political Untouchables*, p. 6.

[30] G. V. Bennett (*The Tory Crisis in Church and State 1688–1730: The Career of Francis Atterbury
Bishop of Rochester* (Oxford, 1975)) observes of Atterbury's Jacobitism: 'He had no romantic
or theoretical attachment to the cause of Stuart legitimacy, and for the policies and persons
of Roman Catholics he continued to have a profound distaste. His loyalty was to the
Church of England and to a vision of its place in English life and society. He became
involved in Jacobitism only when he despaired that the Tory party would ever be able to
rise again in sufficient strength to restore the Church to its ancient status and authority. In
1716 it seemed that both Church and State had fallen into bondage to a Whig oligarchy
which rested on a standing army and a ruthless exploitation of political corruption'
(pp. 206–7). If Swift's private loyalties did shift from the settlement in the Protestant
House of Hanover and he entertained the Jacobite option, I believe his reasoning would
have been similar to Atterbury's as described here.

been a Jacobite, but it is indicative of his actual party-political sympathies that it is the High Church Tory Bishop of Rochester, the parliamentary leader of the Tory peers who were outvoted but defiant in their opposition to the passage of the Whig Septennial Bill in 1716, to whom Swift looks to preserve the nation from slavery in 1716. Swift wrote to Atterbury on 18 April: 'God Almighty preserve your Lordship ... it is a great deal your fault if you suffer us all to be undone; for God never gave such talents without expecting they should be used to preserve a nation' (*Corr*, II, 198–9). Independent or Old Whigs, such as Lord Molesworth and Walter Moyle, supported the establishment Whig Septennial Bill. At the end of George I's reign the sympathies of the author of *Gulliver's Travels* were perhaps Jacobitical. Swift made a private marginal annotation in 1727 against a passage in a copy of Joseph Addison's *Freeholder* that suggests his disaffection from the Hanoverian monarch and the ambiguity of his own allegiance at this time. The conservative Hanoverian Whig had written in *The Freeholder* of 9 January 1716:

And tho' I should be unwilling to pronounce the Man who is indolent, or indifferent in the Cause of his Prince, to be absolutely perjured; I may venture to affirm, that he falls very short of that Allegiance to which he is obliged by Oath.

Swift commented:

Suppose a King grows a Beast, or a Tyrant, after I have taken an Oath; a'prentice takes an Oath; but if his Master useth him barbarously, the lad may be excused if he wishes for a Better.

(*PW*, V, 252)

Swift's pro-Tory marginalia in Addison's *Freeholder* represent the Hanoverian Whig regime as a tyranny. The criticism is directed against the monarch as well as the ministry. It is not loyal criticism of the government (*PW*, V, 251–5).

Whether or not Bolingbroke's claim that the Tories were Jacobite is accurate is still debated among historians, but there is evidence that Swift believed that the Tory part of the political nation after 1715 had become Jacobite in sympathy (see *PW*, VIII, 165, 173) and that identification as a 'Tory' meant to be suspected of Jacobitism. The conditions under which Swift and his Tory friends wrote and corresponded should be constantly recalled by literary critics interpreting political meaning in Swift's writings. The Whigs 'call the Tories all Jacobites' Swift writes to Knightley Chetwode in August 1715, and notes that the 'suspending the Habeas Corpus Act has frightened our friends in England' (*Corr*, II, 183–4). Swift had been warned to hide his papers in early 1715 (*Corr*, II, 156). He wrote, 'When I was leaving England, upon the Queen's death, I burnt all the letters I could find, that I had received from ministers for several years before' (*Corr*, IV, 344). Letters to Swift from the Duke of Ormonde and John Barber had been intercepted by the government and Swift was understood by his English Tory friends and the Whig government to be saying that his friends should not endanger themselves and him by writing and remarking on affairs of state (*Corr*, II, 166–9; V, 230–3). On 2 September 1718 Swift is transparently telling the indiscreet Jacobite Tory Knightley Chetwode not to write or involve him in politics: 'I am the only man in this kingdom who is not a politician, and therefore I only keep such company as will suffer me to suspend their politics ... I am quite a stranger to all schemes and have almost forgot the difference between Whig and Tory' (*Corr*, II, 294). As Swift wrote to the second Earl of Oxford: 'Your Lordship judgeth rightly, that in some Cases it is a Happyness not to hear, and in this Country where Faction hath been so outrageous above anything in England, a wise or quiet man would gladly have his Ears stopt much longer than open' (*Corr*, III, 85). Swift understood himself to be in great danger as a suspected Jacobite Tory. Indeed, on 10 September 1718 Swift's Tory friend Peter Ludlow writes:

I send you the inclosed pamphlet by a private hand, not daring to venture it by the common post; for it is a melancholy circumstance we are now in, that friends are afraid to carry on even a bare correspondence, much more to write news, or send papers of consequence (as I take the inclosed to be) that way. But I suppose I need make no apology for not sending it by post, for you must know, and own too, that my fears are by no means groundless. For your friend, Mr. *Manley*, has been guilty of opening letters that were not directed to him.

(*Corr*, II, 294–5)

On 31 December 1724 Swift tells his Tory friend Charles Ford that Isaac Manley, the Postmaster-General in Ireland, 'opens all Pamphletable Letters' (*Corr*, III, 46).

Swift knew that his own correspondence and that of his friends suspected of disaffection were always subject to perlustration. John Gay tells Swift in 1730 that 'those dirty fellows of the Post Office do read my Letters ... If you will not write, come' (*Corr*, III, 403). In 1732 Gay writes: 'If I don't write intelligibly to you ['tis] because I wou'd not have the Clerkes of the Post Office know every thing I am doing' (*Corr*, IV, 63). The Jacobite Lord Bathurst remarks that a letter sent to Swift 'will certainly be open'd' (*Corr*, III, 401). There is a lacuna of more than seventeen years in the correspondence between Swift and his friend the printer John Barber, Lord Mayor of London in 1732–3 and a convinced Tory and acknowledged Jacobite. When their extant correspondence resumes in 1732 their friendship is as warm as ever and they express shared political sympathies and shared commitment to 'honest principles'.[31] Writing to Swift from London on 23 June 1737, Barber says 'I have many things to say, which in prudence I must defer' (*Corr*, V, 51). William King, the Jacobite Principal of St Mary Hall, Oxford, complained in a letter of 24 June 1737 of the interception of Swift's correspondence (*Corr*, V, 51–3). Swift tells Pope and Bolingbroke in 1738 that 'I have an ill name in the post-office of both kingdoms, which makes the letters addressed to me not seldom miscarry, or be opened and read, and then sealed in a bungling manner before they come to my hands' (*Corr*, V, 119). Pope and Bolingbroke attest to Post Office surveillance of their correspondence with Swift: 'no secret can cross your Irish Sea [but] every clerk in the post-office had known it' (*Corr*, IV, 253–5). Yet Jacobite sympathy can be detected in Swift's letters. He daringly praises (and hopes for the return of) the Duke of Ormonde and execrates Hanoverian tyranny in a letter to Barber in 1738: 'That glorious exil hath suffered more for his Virtues than ever the greatest Vilain did from the cruellest Tyrant' (*Corr*, V, 103). In a subsequent letter to Barber, Swift expresses his gladness at hearing (from Barber) that the Irish Jacobite plotter the Reverend George Kelly is Ormonde's chaplain – 'so valuable a companion' (*Corr*, V, 117, see V, 115).

Swift never seems to have called himself a Tory,[32] and modern scholarship refers to 'Swift's form of Irish Whiggery' and represents him as subscribing to Lockean Whig contract principles legitimizing the Williamite settlement in Ireland.[33] But it can be observed that Swift in

---

[31] For 'honest principles', see their correspondence on the defeat of the Excise Bill in 1733 (*Corr*, IV, 175, 188). For epistolary evidence of continued close friendship and shared political attitudes, see, for example, *Corr*, IV, 57, 62, 70–1, 175–6, 188–90; V, 18–20, 50–1, 85–6, 95–9, 114–16. Although no correspondence between Swift and his Jacobite friend survives for the period between 1715 and 1732 we know they corresponded and conveyed messages of goodwill: see *Corr*, II, 303, 308, 356, 360. Swift certainly knew of Barber's 'Tory Principles' (*Corr*, IV, 535). For documentation and an account of the Swift–Barber relationship, see Charles A. Rivington, '*TYRANT*': *The Story of John Barber 1675 to 1741 Jacobite Lord Mayor of London and Printer and Friend to Dr. Swift* (York, 1989).

[32] In Swift's marginalia there is the comment, 'He was a better Tory than I, if he spoke as he thought', on Gilbert Burnet's opinion that though James II's action against Magdalen College 'was indeed an act of despotical and arbitrary Power, yet I did not think it struck at the whole' (*PW*, V, 286).

[33] See Joseph McMinn, 'A Weary Patriot: Swift and the Formation of an Anglo-Irish Identity', *Eighteenth-Century Ireland*, 2 (1987), 103–13 (esp. p. 107).

his writings seemed unwilling to admit that Jacobites and Tories existed at all in Ireland (see, for example, *PW*, X, 132–3). An attack on occasional conformity (a *cause célèbre* of Tories and High Churchmen) in *A Letter From a Member of the House of Commons in Ireland To a Member of the House of Commons in England, Concerning the Sacramental Test* (1708) is put this way:

> the Parties among us are made up, on one side, of *moderate Whigs*, and, on the other, of *Presbyterians* and their *Abettors*; by which last I mean, such who can equally go to a *Church*, or a *Conventicle*; or such who are indifferent to all Religion in general, or, lastly, such who affect to bear a personal Rancor towards the Clergy.
>
> (*PW*, II, 118)

It was the difference in attitude on the question of the toleration of Protestant Dissent and treatment of Roman Catholics which principally divided Irish Protestants into Whigs and Tories. The party conflict was intense.[34] Archbishop King expressed surprise in a letter of 10 February 1709 that Swift could 'contrive to pass for a Whig' in England (*Corr*, I, 123). Swift's commentary on party issues and dynastic questions in England and descriptions of his politics are refracted through his Irish experience as an Anglican clergyman in a country overwhelmingly Roman Catholic, but with a militant Presbyterian minority. Swift saw himself on active combat duty: 'I look upon myself,

---

[34] *A New History of Ireland IV: Eighteenth-Century Ireland 1691–1800*, edited by T. W. Moody and W. E. Vaughan (Oxford, 1986), ch. 1, 'The Establishment of Protestant Ascendancy, 1691–1714' by J. G. Simms, pp. 3, 27–30; Simms, 'The Irish Parliament of 1713' in his *War and Politics in Ireland 1649–1730*, edited by D. W. Hayton and Gerard O'Brien (London and Ronceverte, 1986), pp. 277–87; David Hayton, 'The Beginnings of the "Undertaker System"', in *Penal Era and Golden Age: Essays in Irish History, 1690–1800*, edited by Thomas Bartlett and D. W. Hayton (Belfast, 1979), pp. 32–54 (esp. pp. 41–8, 52–3); Hayton, 'The Williamite Revolution in Ireland, 1688–91', in *The Anglo-Dutch Moment: Essays on the Glorious Revolution and Its World Impact*, edited by Jonathan I. Israel (Cambridge, 1991), pp. 185–213 (p. 212); Patrick Kelly, 'Ireland and the Glorious Revolution: From Kingdom to Colony', in *The Revolutions of 1688*, edited by Robert Beddard (Oxford, 1991), pp. 163–90 (p. 184). For studies on party politics in Ireland upon which I have drawn particularly see David Hayton, 'Walpole and Ireland', in *Britain in the Age of Walpole*, edited by Jeremy Black (London, 1984), pp. 95–119, and Daniel Szechi and David Hayton, 'John Bull's Other Kingdoms: The English Government of Scotland and Ireland', in *Britain in the First Age of Party 1680–1750*, pp. 241–80 (pp. 259–79). Swift's views that 'the highest Tories' in Ireland 'would make tolerable Whigs' in England (*PW*, II, 283) and that Whig and Tory were introduced to Ireland in 1702 (*Corr*, I, 55) are echoed in modern historical accounts: see Kelly, 'Ireland and the Glorious Revolution', p. 184 and note 97. J. C. D. Clark comments that the threat of insurrection in Ireland meant there were no Tories, only Jacobites and Whigs: see 'A General Theory of Party, Opposition and Government 1688–1832', *The Historical Journal*, 23 (1980), 295–325 (pp. 316–17).

in the capacity of a clergyman, to be one appointed by providence for defending a post assigned me, and for gaining over as many enemies as I can' (*PW*, IX, 262). The Anglican establishment to which he belonged ultimately owed its hegemony to the Williamite military victory in Ireland and depended on the security of English military support. The question of the succession and the potential ramifications of a Roman Catholic Stuart succession and the question of the place of Protestant Dissent in the state would have been intensely immediate to Swift. Swift's Irish experience must have contributed to the High Churchman's inclination to perceive politics in terms of Anglicanism versus popery and dissent. The Whig politician, the Earl of Wharton, Queen Anne's viceroy in Ireland in 1709–10, is significantly execrated by Swift in a libel of 1710 as 'a Presbyterian in Politics, and an Atheist in Religion; but he chuseth at present to whore with a Papist' (*PW*, III, 179). A favourite Swiftian nomenclature for Tory and Whig is the familiar Restoration one of 'church' and 'presbyterian' parties.

Swift was part of the strident High Church Lower House in the revived Irish convocation. He was elected as proctor to represent St Patrick's Cathedral and served for three months in 1707, during which time the Lower House agitated for action from the Upper House in securing remission from the Crown of the First Fruits and Twentieth Parts – financial imposts on the clergy – and engaged in factional controversy. Louis A. Landa remarks of Swift's part in the Convocational controversy of 1707: 'it reveals him early in two roles he assumed with frequency in later years: as a guardian of the rights of churchmen, sensitive to encroachments by laymen, and as a lower clergyman in set opposition to the higher clergy'.[35] Swift intensely opposed Whig projects between 1707 and 1709 to repeal the Sacramental Test imposed in Ireland in 1704. His experience as a representative of the Irish Church soliciting for the remission of the First Fruits and Twentieth Parts, an embassy thwarted by the Whigs but forwarded under the Tory ministry in England, undoubtedly has significance in Swift's political biography in confirming him in a Tory alignment and party 'conversion' in 1710. Swift clearly sided with the Tory party in Ireland, and remained a supporter of the Tory MP Samuel Dopping, the High Tory, crypto-Jacobite Sir Constantine Phipps, Lord Chancellor of Ireland between 1710 and 1714 and the Duke of Ormonde (see

---

[35] Louis A. Landa, *Swift and the Church of Ireland* (Oxford, 1954 (1965)), p. 51. See also Muriel McCarthy, 'Swift and the Foundation of the First Public Library in Ireland', *Swift Studies*, 4 (1989), 29–33.

Corr, I, 83; II, 7–8, 258, 375). Swift also had close connections with the staunchly Tory Rochfort family and the Leslies. The proscription of Tories from political and ecclesiastical patronage and the exile of Ormonde deprived the 'High Church and Ormonde' party in Ireland of effective leadership and direction in the Hanoverian period. The silencing of Convocation removed a recognizable High Church platform to challenge Whig domination.

Swift's Irish pamphleteering against the Hanoverian Whig English government, especially during the controversy over Wood's Halfpence in 1723–5, was in a bipartisan Irish cause. As he told the Earl of Oxford in 1725, 'Faction' in Ireland exceeded anything in England but 'a silly Accident of Brass Money hath more united them than it ever could have been imagined' (*Corr*, III, 85). He was the ally of prominent Irish Whigs in resisting English government measures. The political *rapprochement* between Swift and the Whig Archbishop William King has been taken to signify Swift's return to his supposedly natural Irish Whig allegiance. There is evidence, however, that Swift regarded the Irish Whigs as having changed their party-political colours. He describes the Archbishop of Dublin in a letter to Ford of 1719 as 'half a Tory' (*Corr*, II, 331). Disaffected Irish Whigs are 'perfect Jacobites' (*Corr*, II, 380). Although Swift's Irish patriot political discourse was careful to invoke pristine Whig principles of 1688 and canonical Whig authorities, and disavowed 'party', the Whig English government and its supporters claimed to see sedition in the radical natural rights case for Irish legislative independence put, for instance, in the fourth *Drapier's Letter*, which appropriates arguments advanced by William Molyneux in *The Case of Ireland's being bound by acts of parliament in England, stated* (1698).[36] Establishment Whig alarm is understandable. It was, after all, the Jacobite parliament of 1689 which had declared Ireland's judicial and legislative independence. Swift's approval of Molyneux's case was shared by Irish Jacobite High Churchmen such as Henry Dodwell and Charles Leslie.[37] In an electoral broadsheet of 1733, *Advice to the*

---

[36] *PW*, X, 51–68, esp. p. 62; BL Add. MSS, 6116, fol. 137, Bishop William Nicolson to Archbishop William Wake, 30 October 1724: 'if no Mark be set on this insolent Writer, little Safety will be expected'. For the Proclamation against the fourth *Drapier's Letter*, see *PW*, X, 205.

[37] Henry Dodwell to John Madden, 7 December 1700, in Historical Manuscripts Commission, *Appendix to Second Report* (1874), p. 241; Patrick Kelly, 'William Molyneux and the Spirit of Liberty in Eighteenth-Century Ireland', *Eighteenth-Century Ireland*, 3 (1988), 133–48 (p. 135, n. 9). On Leslie's wholehearted approval of Molyneux's case for Irish independence, but castigation of the Old Whig's acceptance of the English Act of 1691 imposing oaths to William and Mary, see [Charles Leslie], *Considerations of Importance to*

Free-Men of the City of Dublin in the Choice of a Member to Represent them in Parliament, Swift conducts his campaign on behalf of the mayor of Dublin, Humphrey French (a man approved by John Barber, *Corr*, IV, 190) by stating that Ireland consists 'of two Parties, I do not mean Popish and Protestant, High and Low Church, Episcopal and Sectarians, Whig and Tory; but of these *English* who happen to be born in this Kingdom, (whose Ancestors reduced the whole Nation under the Obedience of the *English* Crown,) and the Gentlemen sent from the other Side to possess most of the chief Employments here' (*PW*, XIII, 80). Despite its loyal patriot mode the paper sails close to the wind. Swift, for instance, has this anecdote:

I remember a Person of Distinction some Days ago affirmed in a good deal of mixt Company, and of both Parties. That the Gentry from *England* who now enjoy OUR highest Employments of all kinds, can never be possibly Losers of one Farthing by the greatest Calamities that can befal this Kingdom, except a Plague that would sweep away a Million of our *Hewers of Wood, and Drawers of Water*: Or an Invasion that would fright our Grandees out of the Kingdom.

(*PW*, XIII, 81)

The statement in a paper hostile to the Whig government, that (apart from the depopulation of the kingdom) only an Invasion (perhaps led by that glorious exile, the Duke of Ormonde?) could dislodge the oppressive English Whig establishment, is arresting. Swift prudently distances himself from the statement: it was made by 'a Person of Distinction', but, understandably, there 'were rumours that Swift's paper had been suppressed' (see *PW*, XIII, xxv). Swift's defence of the Church in his pamphleteering implicitly has a Tory party-political character, but Whig ecclesiastical policy largely prevented High Churchmen, like Swift, reviving a co-ordinated Tory 'Church in danger' campaign by depriving them of issues and political power and opportunities. While Anglo-Irish political opposition to the government was conducted in a loyal 'patriot' discourse rather than on Whig–Tory party lines or programmes, Swift's *political character* need not be presumed to have changed – he was for 'High Church and Ormonde' and not a true Whig.

There are cogent reasons why Swift did not call himself a Tory. 'Tory' in Ireland implied Jacobite. On 11 September 1725 Swift wrote

Ireland, In a Letter to a Member of Parliament there: upon Occasion of Mr. Molyneux's late Book: Intituled, The Case of Ireland's being Bound by Acts of Parliament in England, Stated (n.p., 1698); J. G. Simms, *William Molyneux of Dublin*, edited by P. H. Kelly (Blackrock, County Dublin, 1982), pp. 114–15.

to Thomas Sheridan (who had preached a sermon on the anniversary of
the accession of the House of Hanover from the text 'Sufficient unto the
day is the evil thereof') that:

> It is safer for a Man's Interest to blaspheme God, than to be of a Party out of
> Power, or even to be thought so ... I tell you there is hardly a Whig in *Ireland*
> who would allow a Potato and Butter-milk to a reputed Tory.
>
> (*Corr*, III, 93–4)

Swift counselled the Jacobite sympathizer to take the oaths to 'the
Powers that be' and not 'discover your Disloyalty in the Pulpit' (*Corr*,
III, 67, 94). Swift seems to have understood 'Whig' and 'Tory' generally in terms of acceptance or rejection of the Revolution (*Corr*, II,
236; *PW*, II, 118; X, 132). Swift says he thought that only on a 'Whig'
principle could one 'defend or submit to the Revolution' (*PW*, VIII,
120). Of course, High Church Tories and later Jacobites such as
Atterbury and the Duke of Ormonde (who supported the Revolution
and fought in William III's campaigns) and indeed any Tory who, to
use Swift's phrase, could 'defend or submit to the Revolution' would
presumably be listed as 'Whigs' in Swift's acceptation of the political
label. When Pope asks Swift in a letter sent through the post in 1730 to
help get subscriptions for a Commentary on Job by the Reverend
Samuel Wesley, a High Church Tory suspected of Jacobitism, he
cautiously puts his request for the 'honest man' in this way: 'Lord
Bolingbroke is a favourer of it, and allows you to do your best to serve
an old Tory, and a sufferer for the Church of England, tho' you are a
Whig, as I am' (*Corr*, III, 377–8). The Earl of Oxford recommends the
'worthy honest Man' and hopes Swift will take the 'Honest, Poor,
worthy Clergyman' under 'your Protection' (*Corr*, III, 378–9). In a
political atmosphere where 'Tory' signified Jacobite, Swift and Pope,
periodically accused of Jacobitism, called themselves Whigs, yet Swift
was expected to be sympathetic to a reputed Jacobite.[38] Swift stated
publicly in 1735 that he professed to be of the Whig party in politics.[39]
But to Lord Bathurst in 1737 Swift remains 'a disaffected person, such
y^u will be reputed as long as y^u live, after y^r death perhaps y^u may stand
Rectus in Curia' (*Corr*, V, 79).

To call Swift a Whig in politics at least after 1710 is otiose. Indeed, it

---

[38] On Samuel Wesley's politics, see Linda Colley, *In Defiance of Oligarchy*, p. 113 and J. C. D.
Clark, *English Society 1688–1832: Ideology, Social Structure and Political Practice during the Ancien
Regime* (Cambridge, 1985), pp. 51n, 237.

[39] 'Swift's Advertisement to *Poems*, 1735', in *Swift: Poetical Works*, edited by Herbert Davis
(London, 1967), pp. xxix–xxx (p. xxix); Downie, 'Swift's Politics', p. 48.

obfuscates the actual political character of the man and his writings in political and religious context. It has been argued that Swift is 'uncompromisingly Whig' in politics because he 'believed in the Whig principles current at the time of the Revolution', opposed 'Corruption' and 'the threat posed by an encroaching executive', insisted on the separation of the executive and the legislature, agreed with the Declaration of Rights of 1689, opposed Septennial bills, approved annual parliaments and detested standing armies.[40] But historical criticism of Swift also needs to note contemporary Tory polemical languages. A few examples must suffice. The Tory MP Archibald Hutcheson, for instance, in his speech against the Septennial Bill in 1716 approves annual parliaments (confirmed in the ancient constitution) and the Triennial Act, sees the liberties of a people threatened by the executive and 'corruption', detests Henry VIII's tyrannical invasion of 'the liberties of his people' and traces the encroachments of the Crown's prerogative to his reign. Hutcheson also argues that the Act of Habeas Corpus is 'essential to the being of a free people', reminds the parliament 'of the prerogatives claimed and exercised by king James the 2d, to dispense with the laws ... recited by the Claim of Rights' from which the Revolution rescued the nation, reflects on 'how wanting we were to ourselves upon that turn, in not retrieving and securing for ever, by the Claim of Rights, our ancient constitution of frequent new parliaments', and so on.[41] The Jacobite Tory, William Shippen, in the same debate said:

I think you ought not to repeal the Triennial Act, except in the last extremity, and in the most imminent danger of the State. This law was one of the fruits of the Revolution: This law restored the freedom and frequency of parliaments, so far as was consistent with the circumstances of that reign, which was involved in a war, and had occasion for constant and heavy taxes.[42]

Bolingbroke's *Craftsman* extols '*that Act*, which is call'd the *Declaration of Rights*; by which, we hope, an End is put to the dangerous Claims and Practices of some *former Reigns*; such as That of a Power in the Crown to *dispense with the Execution of the Laws*; as also That of keeping up a *standing Army in Time of Peace, without Consent of Parliament*; and some

[40] Downie, 'Swift's Politics', *passim*.

[41] *Parl. Hist.*, VII, cols. 339–67. On Hutcheson, see the entry by Eveline Cruickshanks in *The House of Commons 1715–54*, ed. Sedgwick, II, 163–4; Linda Colley, *In Defiance of Oligarchy*, see pp. 28–9, 98–9; Jeremy Black, 'Archibald Hutcheson as Author', *Notes and Queries*, n.s., 32 (1985), 207–8.

[42] *Parl. Hist.*, VII, cols. 317–18.

other Particulars, which are contained in *that Act*'.[43] The Jacobite *Fog's Weekly Journal* supports annual parliaments, the separation of the legislative and executive parts of the government, and contractual resistance, for example.[44] And Robert Walpole stated:

> No man of common prudence will profess himself openly a jacobite ... Your right Jacobite, Sir, disguises his true sentiments; he roars out for revolution principles; he pretends to be a great friend to liberty, and a great admirer of our antient constitution; and under this pretence there are numbers who every day endeavour to sow discontents among the people, by persuading them that the constitution is in danger, and that they are unnecessarily loaded with many and heavy taxes.[45]

It now seems too undisturbed a reading to state that 'Pope and Swift are still occasionally accused of Jacobitism, despite the fact that, in reality, they are predominantly influenced by "Country" or "Old Whig" principles, though one was a Roman Catholic and the other vehemently High Church'.[46] The Country opposition, and the 'Country' political critique of excessive power in the executive, corruption, placemen and pensioners, high taxation and standing armies, became increasingly Tory after the early 1690s.[47] 'Country' principles are a significant strand in Jacobite ideology and polemical argument.[48] Attention to the possible polemical provenance and resonance of some of Swift's political statements allows us to understand how a contemporary might have construed Swift's political discourse as the speech act of a disaffected Tory. It is a hermeneutic injunction, but both the conceptual meaning of words on the page *and* their functional meaning in a polemical moment need to be recognized in interpretation of Swift's

---

[43] *Lord Bolingbroke. Contributions to The 'Craftsman'*, edited by Simon Varey (Oxford, 1982), p. 153 (no. 375, 8 September 1733).

[44] *Select Letters taken from Fog's Weekly Journal*, 2 vols. (London, 1732), II, 26, 158–9, 172–3.

[45] *Parl. Hist.*, X, cols. 400–1. See Eveline Cruickshanks, *Political Untouchables*, pp. 14–16.

[46] T. N. Corns, W. A. Speck and J. A. Downie, 'Archetypal Mystification: Polemic and Reality in English Political Literature, 1640–1750', *Eighteenth-Century Life*, 7 (1982), 1–27 (p. 24).

[47] David Hayton, 'The "Country" Interest and the Party System, 1689–c. 1720', in *Party and Management in Parliament, 1640–1784*, edited by Clyve Jones (Leicester, 1984), pp. 37–85.

[48] See especially Howard Erskine-Hill, 'Literature and the Jacobite Cause: Was There a Rhetoric of Jacobitism?' in *Ideology and Conspiracy: Aspects of Jacobitism, 1689–1759*, edited by Eveline Cruickshanks (Edinburgh, 1982), pp. 49–69; Paul Chapman, 'Jacobite Political Argument in England 1714–1766' (unpublished Ph.D. thesis, University of Cambridge, 1983); Paul Monod, 'Jacobitism and Country Principles in the Reign of William III', *The Historical Journal*, 30 (1987), 289–310 and his *Jacobitism and the English People 1688–1788* (Cambridge, 1989), see esp. pp. 17, 23, 27, 28, 32–3, 38, 42, 102, 243, 336. For scholarship on Jacobitism after 1714, see J. C. D. Clark, *Revolution and Rebellion: State and Society in England in the Seventeenth and Eighteenth Centuries* (Cambridge, 1986), Appendix B, pp. 174–7.

political texts. Certainly this was a reading procedure of politically
literate contemporaries. Daniel Defoe, for example, in his *Review* in
1705 considered the 'Reception to my Exhortation to *Peace*' in one of his
previous papers and found that 'it seem'd absolutely necessary for me
to Enquire, What is meant by *this Peace?* And not only what Peace it
self means, but what every particular sort of People *mean by it*, and why
they all pretend to it, and yet so few pursue it.'[49]

In 'A Letter from Dr. Swift to Mr. Pope' (1722) Swift declared:

> I ever abominated that scheme of politicks, (now about thirty years old) of
> setting up a monied Interest in opposition to the landed. For, I conceived,
> there could not be a truer maxim in our government than this, That the
> possessors of the soil are the best judges of what is for the advantage of the
> kingdom: If others had thought the same way, Funds of Credit and South-sea
> Projects would neither have been felt nor heard of.
>
> $\qquad\qquad\qquad\qquad\qquad\qquad\qquad\qquad$ (*PW*, IX, 32)

The 'neo-Harringtonian', 'Country' opposition to the City 'monied
Interest' expressed here, and presented as a criticism of the Revolution
settlement by the parenthetical observation, also had party-political
significance, as Swift was well aware. In a private letter to the Tory
leader Bolingbroke in September 1714 Swift had written:

> if I see the old Whig-measures taken in the next elections, and that the court,
> the bank, East-India, and South-sea, act strenuously, and procure a majority, I
> shall lie down and beg of Jupiter to heave the cart out of the dirt.
>
> $\qquad\qquad\qquad\qquad\qquad\qquad\qquad\qquad$ (*Corr*, II, 129)

The Tory political character of Swift's support for a 'Country' measure
such as a Triennial bill is revealed in the following comment on William
III's veto of the Triennial Bill in 1693 in his autobiographical fragment
'Family of Swift': 'The Consequence of this wrong Step in His Majesty
was very unhappy; For it put that Prince under a necessity of introducing those People called Whigs into power and Employments, in order to
pacify them' (*PW*, V, 194). Swift wrote to Lady Elizabeth Germain in
1733: 'I know you have been always a zealous Whig, and so am I to this
day ... I am of the old Whig principles, without the modern articles
and refinements', and he drew Francis Grant's attention in the election
year of 1734 to 'Standing armies in times of peace; projects of excise,
and bribing elections ... not forgetting septennial Parliaments, directly

---

[49] *Review*, 28 April 1705; *Defoe's Review*, Reproduced from the Original Editions, with an
  Introduction and Bibliographical Notes by Arthur W. Secord. Facsimile Book 4. February
  27, 1705, To August 23, 1705. Of Volume II (New York, 1937), p. 93.

against the old Whig principles, which always have been mine' (*Corr*, IV, 100, 230). But in October 1733 the *Craftsman* noted: 'the *Body* of the *present Tories* have adopted the Spirit of the *old Whigs*'.[50] A contemporary Whig commented that Bolingbroke's *Craftsman* undertakes 'his old Trade of libelling, under the Pretext of propagating *Whig Principles and Tenets*'.[51] Swift knew well enough that to advance 'certain old whiggish principles' was to pass 'for a disaffected person' (*PW*, IX, 33).

In a letter to Charles Ford of 15 April 1721, in which Swift says he is at work on *Gulliver's Travels*, he refers to 'The letter of Brutus to Cicero', one of the classic Old Whig *Cato's Letters* (1 April 1721) which Swift feels 'should have been better translated'. He remarks that the English 'Ministry seems to me to want Credit in suffering so many Libells published against them; and here there is a worse Matter; for many of the violent Whigs profess themselves perfect Jacobites, and plead for it the Miseryes and Contempt they suffer by the Treatment of England' (*Corr*, II, 380). In fact, however, the defence of Brutus in Trenchard and Gordon's *Cato's Letters* was carefully dissociated by Thomas Gordon from Jacobite Tory polemic, which also celebrated Brutus and approved assassination.[52] *Cato's Letters* are strongly pro-Hanoverian and critical of establishment Whig governments for not proscribing and punishing the crypto-Jacobite High Church Tories for their crimes against the Revolution state. Queen Anne's Tory ministers (and presumably their propagandist, Swift) are capital criminals in the eyes of true Old Whigs:

Lenity to great crimes is an invitation to greater; whereas despair of pardon, for the most part, makes pardon useless. If no mercy were shewn to the enemies of the state, no state would be overturned; and if small or no punishment be inflicted upon them, no state can be safe. Happy, happy had it been for this unhappy people, if these important and essential maxims of government had been duly regarded by our legislators at the *revolution*; (and I wish too, that the sincere and hearty endeavours of our present legislators to punish the betrayers of the late unfortunate queen had met the desired success:) for I

---

[50] Quoted in Paul Langford, *The Excise Crisis: Society and Politics in the Age of Walpole* (Oxford, 1975), p. 13.

[51] *The Grand Accuser The Greatest of all Criminals*, Part I (London, 1735), p. 77.

[52] John Trenchard and Thomas Gordon, *Cato's Letters: Or, Essays on Liberty, Civil and Religious, And other important Subjects*, 4 vols. (n.p., 1754), I, Preface. And see Trenchard and Gordon, *The Independent Whig: or, A Defence of Primitive Christianity, And of our Ecclesiastical Establishment, Against the Exorbitant Claims and Encroachments of Fanatical and Disaffected Clergymen*, 3 vols., sixth edition (London, 1735), I, no. II, p. 14, on the High Church clergy who preach up their 'Votaries to Rebellions and Assassinations'.

doubt that all our misfortunes have flowed from these sources, and are owing to these disappointments.[53]

'"What was the end of our killing the tyrant, but to be free from tyranny?"', translates 'Cato' in the *'letter from* Brutus *to* Cicero' referred to by Swift in his letter to Ford.[54] The Old Whig publication castigates corrupt modern Whig government, but it also condemns High Church prelatical tyranny, the imposition of Anglican uniformity through persecutory statutes, and Tory Jacobitism. King George I in speeches to the parliament in 1716 and 1717 (after the Jacobite Rising of 1715) referred to 'the numerous instances of mercy which I have shown' and his 'clemency' in the treatment of Jacobite rebels.[55] Old Whigs such as Trenchard and Gordon regretted such 'Lenity'. Establishment Whigs such as Joseph Addison commended George I's mercy and grace. But Swift regarded George I's treatment of the rebels as savage, and he wrote sardonic comments on the Hanoverian King's 'clemency' (*PW*, V, 254–5). George I is one monarch whose face appears in Swift's satiric 'Glass' in the account of the Emperor of Lilliput's euphemistic 'Mercy' and *'Lenity'* in Part One, Chapter VII of *Gulliver's Travels*.

As Swift indicates in his letter to Ford, some radical Whigs did embrace Jacobitism in the 1720s. Philip, Duke of Wharton, son of the Junto Whig, was one and Swift was acquainted with him and approved his performance in defending Atterbury in the House of Lords (see, for example, *Corr*, II, 285; III, 10). Swift forged political links with radical Whigs in the 1720s as did Tory MPs such as Archibald Hutcheson and Sir Thomas Hanmer.[56] In parliamentary debates on the Mutiny Bill in 1718 Tory MPs could highly commend Lord Molesworth's original Whig anti-army writing.[57] Swift said of his fellow nationalist Lord Molesworth in 1723, 'excepting in what relates to the Church, there are few Persons with whose Opinions I am better pleased to agree', though Swift is antagonized by the Old Whig's political attack on clerical *'Liberty* and *Property'* (*PW*, IX, 58–60). The 'Drapier' dedicated a Letter to Molesworth and voiced the language of Old Whig radicalism in attacking the English Whig government. Readers of Swift need to realize the Tory and Jacobite appropriation of Old Whig principles and rhetoric from the 1690s when reading the political signs in his work.

Swift's *Examiner* is 'not sensible of any material Difference ...

[53] *Cato's Letters*, I, 116–17 (no. 20, 11 March 172[1]).
[54] *Cato's Letters*, I, 146 (no. 23, 1 April 1721).
[55] *Parl. Hist.*, VII, cols. 386, 448.   [56] See Colley, *In Defiance of Oligarchy*, pp. 98–9.
[57] See *Parl. Hist.*, VII, col. 536; Colley, *In Defiance of Oligarchy*, p. 92.

between those who call themselves the *Old Whigs*, and a great majority of the present *Tories*' (*Exam*, p. 314). But despite the contingency and nominalism of political argument in contemporary pamphlets and periodical literature some real differences between 'Old Whig' and 'Tory' political positions can be registered. Considering some of the differences, it is evident that Swift's politics are 'Tory'. Historians and literary critics who deny the existence of a 'Tory party' political position in the Hanoverian period and believe the basic alignment to be between a Court Administration and a Country Opposition[58] obscure crucial differences in the political attitudes of 'Opposition' figures, which has enabled a misleading conflation of Swift's political attitudes with pro-Hanoverian Old Whig writers committed to a rapport with Dissent.

An essential element of Old Whig or Country Whig ideology is its religious heterodoxy and anticlericalism – its opposition to 'priest-craft'.[59] A principal object of Old Whig animus is Anglican clericalist hegemony in the civil, religious and educational establishment. A continuity in radical Whiggism is its commitment to liberty of conscience, toleration, and the ultimate removal of statutes imposing Anglican uniformity in public life. True Whigs, such as the third Earl of Shaftesbury, Andrew Fletcher, Robert Molesworth, John Trenchard, Thomas Gordon, Anthony Collins, John Toland, Matthew Tindal and others, opposed a Tory party hostile to religious dissent and toleration even though the Tories became the party synonymous with Country (traditionally exclusionist Whig) political ideology. Swift, however, a High Church Anglican in religion, had no trouble identifying with the modern 'Church party'. Conformity to the established religion is a positive in *Gulliver's Travels* (*PW*, XI, 50, 60, 131). Old Whigs were committed to the succession in the Protestant House of Hanover (as they were to William III) because these Protestant monarchs would preserve the nation from prelatical tyranny whether papist or High Church Anglican. Old Whig criticism of corruption and illiberal measures in post-Revolution government is characteristically *loyal* criticism. Old Whigs criticized Williamite government for losing the radical opportunity the Revolution afforded and for the mistake of employing

---

[58] For a restatement of such views, see Peter D. G. Thomas, 'Party Politics in Eighteenth-Century Britain: Some Myths and a Touch of Reality', *British Journal for Eighteenth-Century Studies*, 10 (1987), 201–10.

[59] See especially Mark Goldie, 'John Locke and Anglican Royalism', *Political Studies*, 31 (1983), 61–85, and his 'The Roots of True Whiggism 1688–94', *History of Political Thought*, 1 (1980), 195–236.

Tories. Swift, however, blamed William III for introducing Whigs into the government and for discarding Tories. For Swift, the Revolution had activated a radical Protestant revolutionism countenanced by Whig politicians. As historian, Swift wrote of the Junto Whig John Somers, 'reputed the Head and Oracle of that Party':

> the old Republican Spirit, which the Revolution had restored, began to teach other Lessons: That, since we had accepted a new King from a Calvinistical Commonwealth, we must likewise admitt new Maxims in Religion and Government: But, since the Nobility and Gentry would probably adhere to the Established Church, and to the Rights of Monarchy as delivered down from their Ancestors; it was the Practice of these Politicians to introduce such Men, as were perfectly indifferent to any or no Religion; and, who were not likely to inherit much Loyalty from those to whom they owed their Birth. Of this Number was the Person I am now describing.
>
> (*PW*, VII, 5)

The author of *A Discourse Concerning the Mechanical Operation of the Spirit. In a Letter to a Friend. A Fragment* remarked:

> I do not remember any other Temper of Body, or Quality of Mind, wherein all Nations and Ages of the World have so unanimously agreed, as That of a *Fanatick* Strain, or Tincture of *Enthusiasm*; which improved by certain Persons or Societies of Men, and by them practised upon the rest, has been able to produce Revolutions of the greatest Figure in History.
>
> (*Tale*, p. 266)

In *A Tale of a Tub* and the *Fragment* the voices of radical sectarian Whiggism are satirically impersonated and the *Tale* is dedicated by the 'Bookseller' to Somers. In the Williamite polity Swift bitterly observed '*Jack*' was received in '*Court* and *City*' (see *Tale*, p. 204).

Attention to such organs of True Whiggism in the Hanoverian period as the celebrated *Cato's Letters* reveals that the independent Whig publicists John Trenchard and Thomas Gordon are actually closer to the establishment Whigs than they are to men like Swift. *Cato's Letters* makes 'Country' complaints about peculation, bribery, placemen, pensions, standing armies and ministerial mismanagement. But it is the tyranny and dominion of the Anglican prelacy and High Church Tory disaffection which are the publicists' principal targets.[60] In *Cato's Letters* the Tory Peace of Utrecht is regarded as a national shame. The Old Whigs completely endorse the Whig government in prosecuting

---

[60] For a detailed study of the Hanoverian Independent Whig publicists, see Marie P. McMahon, *The Radical Whigs, John Trenchard and Thomas Gordon: Libertarian Loyalists to the New House of Hanover* (Lanham, New York, London, 1990).

Jacobite conspirators and, indeed, call on the government to show no
mercy to Jacobite plotters. Atterbury and High Church Tories are
vilified in six particularly virulent issues (20 April–25 May 1723). They
attack the Tory press and such publicists as Nathaniel Mist. They are
hostile to Charles I and Laud and criticize High Church preaching on
30 January, the anniversary of Charles I's execution. They complain of
Anglican clerical control over education and call for the regulation of
the universities. 'Cato' is spontaneous in affirmation of 'our present
great and glorious sovereign, king George'. Swift, of course, celebrated
and defended the Peace of Utrecht, satirized the Whig prosecution of
Atterbury, and admired and supported Mist, whose paper praised and
publicized him. Swift defended the keeping of the 30 January anniversary and deplored Whig attempts to regulate Anglican pulpits and
educational establishment. Swift publicly said he had no interest in the
ruling royal family. In his writings he depicted the Hanoverians as
tyrants.

   John Toland, in 'A Memorial Presented to a Minister of State, Soon
after his Majesty King George's accession to the Crown', gave this
summary of contemporary Whigs:

The Whigs (I mean those who practise what they profess) are virtuous, wise,
and industrious Church of England men; yet brotherly indulgent towards other
Protestants, and all for a general Naturalization. To these ought to be added
the Sectaries, who heartily join with them on one common bottom, against
Popery and Slavery either in Church or State.

All Whigs, in principle, support civil and religious liberty, trade and
Hanoverian European policy. So far are the Whigs

from being against Kingship (as their enemies foolishly calumniate them) that
they are to a man most zealous for the Act of Succession, particularly faithful to
King GEORGE (whom they admire almost to adoration) absolutely determin'd
to support his progeny, and such, in short, as may be depended upon in all the
particulars aforesaid.[61]

Robert Molesworth complained in his 'Principles of a Real Whig' that
'there has been such chopping and changing both of Names and
Principles, that we scarce know who is who'. But his ideal is a cosmopolitan, tolerant polity, and he notes that a 'Genuine *Whig* is for
promoting a *general Naturalization*'.[62] Swift was not a genuine Whig

---

[61] John Toland, *The Miscellaneous Works . . .*, 2 vols. (London, 1747), pp. 244–5.
[62] See the 'Sentiments of the late Lord *Molesworth*' in *The Memoirs of John Ker, of Kersland in
    North Britain Esq*, 3 pts. (London, 1726), III, 191–221 (pp. 191, 207).

(*PW*, VII, 94–5). Swift's complete and unqualified opposition to mercenary standing armies in times of peace and war[63] and his opposition to the Septennial Act are 'Tory' and, in polemical context, crypto-Jacobite rather than 'Old Whig'. Molesworth wrote:

A *Whig* is against the raising or keeping up a *Standing Army* in Time of Peace; but with this Distinction, that if at any time an *Army* (though even in Time of Peace) should be necessary to the Support of this very Maxim, a *Whig* is not for being too hasty to destroy That, which is to be the Defender of his Liberty.

There is a clear *rapprochement* between Old and establishment Whigs on the question of standing armies and Septennial bills when a threat to the Protestant Whig establishment in Church and State is perceived from Jacobite High Churchmen and Tories, as was the case in the early Hanoverian period. Molesworth wrote that:

a *Whig* (without the just Imputation of having deserted his Principles) may be for the *keeping* up such a Standing Army even in Time of Peace, till the Nation have recovered its *Wits* again, and chuses Representatives who are against *Tyranny in any Hands whatsoever*; till the Enemies of our Liberties want the Power of raising *another* Army of *quite different Sentiments*; for till that time, a *Whiggish* Army is the *Guardian of our Liberties*.[64]

Molesworth, of course, became a placeman after the accession of George I and supported a standing army.[65] *Cato's Letters* accepted a standing army, the suspension of the Habeas Corpus Act and the repeal of the Triennial Act as necessary after the accession of the House of Hanover to prevent Jacobite counter-revolution and to rectify previous Tory abuses. 'Cato', in fact, publicly qualified his well-known, principled opposition to standing armies acknowledging the necessity of the government policy in dealing with Jacobite conspiracy.[66] Cato bitterly reflected on Jacobite Tory appropriation of Old Whig languages in the issue of 20 April 1723 on '*The spirit of the conspirators, accomplices with Dr. Atterbury*': 'They exclaim against armies and taxes, and are the cause of both, and rail at grievances of their own creating.' Conspirators

---

[63] *PW*, V, 80; IX, 31–2; XI, 131.
[64] 'Sentiments of the late Lord *Molesworth*', *Memoirs of John Ker*, III, 210–12.
[65] *Parl. Hist.*, VII, cols. 536–7; Hayton, 'The "Country" Interest and the Party System', p. 51.
[66] See, for example, *Cato's Letters*, II, 200 (no. 60, 6 January 172[2]); III, 223 (no. 95, 22 September 1722); IV, 143–50 (no. 125, 20 April 1723); [Thomas Gordon], 'A short View of the Conspiracy, with some Reflections on the Present State of Affairs. In a Letter to an Old Whig in the Country. By Cato', in *A Collection of Tracts. By the Late John Trenchard, Esq; and Thomas Gordon, Esq.* 2 vols. (London, 1751), II, 127–59 (pp. 128–9, 148).

against the establishment make armies and taxes necessary.[67] The 'Old Whig' Thomas Gordon, in fact, held a government sinecure in the Walpole ministry.[68] Opposition Whigs (and Walpole when in opposition) tended to argue for only a reduction in the size of the standing army.[69] Walpole is perhaps reflected upon when an acute Gulliver reports that one of the 'Methods by which a Man may rise to be Chief Minister' is 'by a *furious Zeal* in publick Assemblies against the Corruptions of the Court. But a wise Prince would rather chuse to employ those who practise the last of these Methods; because such Zealots prove always the most obsequious and subservient to the Will and Passions of their Master' (*PW*, XI, 255). It was Jacobites and Tories who consistently denounced and voted against standing armies and septennial parliaments.

Swift's description of himself as a Whig in politics but a 'High Churchman' in religion is obviously problematic at a time when ecclesiastical and political issues, and Tory and High Church clerical causes, are interconnected. Religion is central to political formation in Swift's lifetime. It is indicative of this interconnection of religion and politics that Swift instinctively compares Ireland's slavery under the English parliament with the Erastian bondage of Anglican Convocations (*Corr*, II, 342); and that one of his most dramatically libertarian declarations – 'I have lived, and by the grace of God will die, an enemy to servitude and slavery of all kinds' – was actually occasioned by a matter of clerical privileges (Swift is responding to Archbishop King's provocative demand that the Dean of St Patrick's supply a proxy for the Archbishop's visitation) (*Corr*, III, 210). There is a demonstrable distinctiveness in religious ideology between Whigs (radical and establishment) and Tories in public debate in the first Age of Party.[70] Religious toleration was a cynosure for all Whigs. Opposition to popish and prelatic imposition and Anglican dominion over the civil magistracy and private judgement was a creed of the Whig party's 'Old' or radical wing. Hanoverian Whig Erastianism expressed itself in the suppression of the Canterbury Convocation in 1717, in the repeal of the

---

[67] *Cato's Letters*, IV, 146 (no. 125, 20 April 1723). See McMahon, *The Radical Whigs*, pp. 187–88, 192.

[68] Joseph Spence, *Observations, Anecdotes, and Characters of Books and Men*, edited by James M. Osborn, 2 vols. (Oxford, 1966), I, 146–7; *An Historical View of the Principles, Characters, Persons, &c. of the Political Writers in Great Britain* (London, 1740), p. 15.

[69] Observed in Cruickshanks, 'The Political Management of Sir Robert Walpole, 1720–42', p. 33.

[70] On the party-political importance of religious controversy under Walpole, see, among others, Stephen Taylor, 'Sir Robert Walpole, The Church of England, and the Quakers Tithe Bill of 1736', *The Historical Journal*, 28 (1985), 51–77.

Tory Occasional Conformity Act (1711) and Schism Act (1714) in 1719, and in Lord Stanhope's attrition against the Test and Corporation Acts. The Walpolean Whig government attempted to avoid 'Church-in-danger' issues by abandoning further tolerationist programmes in favour of Dissent. This deprived the proscribed Tories of a potent, populist party rallying call. An alliance between religious latitudinarianism and political Whiggism and between Dissent, the Crown and Whig government are features of the early Hanoverian regime.[71] Opposed to the tolerant Erastianism of Whigs, the Tories strove for Anglican uniformity and sought to circumscribe the 'indulgence' given to Dissent in the polity. Tory ideology was informed by an exclusivist and intolerant High Church Anglicanism. Antipathy to Dissent and resistance to the tolerationist policies of Erastian princes and Whig administrations are at the core of Toryism and the ideological continuity of the 'Church party' in the Restoration and post-Revolution state.[72]

Much modern criticism represents Swift as an Old Whig who 'split tickets' – a Whig in state politics but a Tory on Church issues. When Swift and Bolingbroke adopted an 'Old Whig' character they occluded a fundamental distinction between Whig and Tory in this partisan world. Contemporary Old Whig publicists pointed out the perverse appropriation of 'the Name of WHIG' by those who propagate 'Slavish Doctrines of Ecclesiastical and Political Tyranny ... by denying the Right of Private Judgment'.[73] The Old Whig: or, The Consistent Protestant denounced 'the Distinction which some Gentlemen have lately seem'd

---

[71] On religion and Hanoverian Whig politics, see Marie McMahon, *The Radical Whigs, John Trenchard and Thomas Gordon*, esp. pp. 127–32; John Gascoigne, *Cambridge in the Age of the Enlightenment: Science, Religion and Politics from the Restoration to the French Revolution* (Cambridge, 1989); James E. Bradley, *Religion, Revolution, and English Radicalism: Nonconformity in Eighteenth-Century Politics and Society* (Cambridge, 1990).

[72] On Tory ideology and the politics of toleration, see Mark Goldie, 'The Nonjurors, Episcopacy, and the Origins of the Convocation Controversy', in *Ideology and Conspiracy: Aspects of Jacobitism, 1689–1759*, edited by Eveline Cruickshanks, pp. 15–35; Goldie, 'Sir Peter Pett, Sceptical Toryism and the Science of Toleration in the 1680s', in *Persecution and Toleration*, edited by W. J. Sheils, Studies in Church History, vol. XXI (Oxford, 1984), pp. 247–73; Goldie, 'Danby, the Bishops and the Whigs', in *The Politics of Religion in Restoration England*, edited by Tim Harris *et al.* (Oxford, 1990), pp. 75–105; Goldie, 'The Political Thought of the Anglican Revolution'; Goldie, 'The Theory of Religious Intolerance in Restoration England', in *From Persecution to Toleration: The Glorious Revolution and Religion in England*, edited by Ole Peter Grell *et al.* (Oxford, 1991), pp. 330–68; Geoffrey Holmes, *Religion and Party in Late Stuart England* (London, 1975); D. Szechi, 'The Politics of "Persecution": Scots Episcopalian Toleration and the Harley Ministry, 1710–12', in *Persecution and Toleration*, edited by W. J. Sheils, pp. 275–87.

[73] *The Old Whig: or, The Consistent Protestant*, no. 20, 24 July 1735.

very fond of, *viz. of being Tories in the Church*, and *Whigs in the State*'. A '*Tory in the Church* hath such peculiar *discriminating* Marks' that 'a *Tory in Church*, and a *Whig in the State*' is an inherent contradiction and cannot exist. For '*Toryism in the Church*, when free from Restraint, will necessarily be productive of *Oppression* and Slavery *in the State*; for it can maintain its Being, and thrive, only by *Civil Penalties*; and is never content, but when it can promote what it calls *the Ends of Religion*, by *temporal* Severities and *Punishments*.'[74]

The Test Act, which excluded from parliament and civil and military office under the Crown all those who would not take the sacrament according to the rites of the Church of England, was regarded as a 'Party Puncto', although even Old Whigs could agree at times with the Walpolean ministry about the imprudence of repealing it.[75] Nevertheless radical, anticlerical Whig publications, like *The Old Whig: or, The Consistent Protestant*, called for relief from persecution by statute and for the repeal of the Test Act. Dissenting-Whig attempts to repeal the Test and Corporation Acts and Quaker agitation against paying Church rates and tithes met with defeat in the 1730s.[76] For High Churchmen and Tories, defence of the Test was almost an act of faith. Swift's polemic against Whig attempts to repeal the Test, the projected tithe legislation, parliamentary and lay encroachment on the Church's rights and temporalities, legislative concessions to Dissent, and the perceived growth of heresy and irreligion is consonant with 'Tory' political attitudes in the Hanoverian period. There is, in fact, only one piece of evidence that Swift ever wrote in support of Whig ecclesiastical policy and that is in a letter of 3 February 1704 when he told his correspondent, William Tisdall, that he 'wrote against the bill that was against Occasional Conformity' (*Corr*, I, 44).[77] The High Church Tory Bill aimed to outlaw a practice whereby many Protestant Dissenters qualified themselves for office under the Test Act by occasionally taking the sacrament according to the rites of the Church of England. Swift's Whig work was never published and is not extant among Swift's manuscript remains. The reference in the letter may well have been just

---

[74] *The Old Whig: or, The Consistent Protestant*, no. 27, 11 September 1735.
[75] See *Cato's Letters*, III, 108–14 (no. 81, 16 June 1722 '*The established church of* England *in no danger from dissenters*'); McMahon, *The Radical Whigs*, pp. 174–75.
[76] Taylor, 'Sir Robert Walpole, The Church of England, and the Quakers Tithe Bill of 1736'; Bradley, *Religion, Revolution, and English Radicalism*, p. 59.
[77] The letter is accepted as documentary evidence of Swift's 'Whig' religious principles in the period in which *A Tale of a Tub* was published: see Frank T. Boyle, 'Ehrenpreis's *Swift* and the Date of *The Sentiments of a Church-of-England Man*', *Swift Studies*, 6 (1991), 30–7 (pp. 35–7).

an epistolary 'bite' (a 'lie' told 'in a serious manner') bantering the
Tory Tisdall (see *Corr*, I, 40, 41). *A Tale of a Tub*, published in 1704,
satirizes prominent Dissenting Occasional Conformists in London.
Swift's actual hatred of Dissenters was lifelong. 'Pox on the Dissenters
and Independents!' he writes to Tisdall in 1704, 'I would as soon
trouble my head to write against a louse or a flea' (*Corr*, I, 43–4). A
principal pamphleteer in the paper war over a Whig attempt to repeal
the Test in Ireland between 1731 and 1733, Swift declaimed violently
against the Dissenting Protestant 'Lice' in his poem *On the Words –
Brother Protestants, and Fellow Christians, so familiarly used by the Advocates
for the Repeal of the Test Act in Ireland, 1733* (lines 29–48, *Poems*, III,
812–13).

Despite calling himself an Old Whig, Swift traduces men who certainly were Old or radical Whigs, such as John Locke (*PW*, II, 80, 85,
97), Robert Molesworth (*PW*, II, 99), Andrew Fletcher (*PW*, V,
262), the astrologer John Partridge (The Partridge Papers, *PW*, II,
139–70), Anthony Collins (author of Whig party 'Atheology', *PW*, IV,
27), John Toland ('the great Oracle of the *Anti-Christians*', *PW*, II, 37)
and Matthew Tindal (the Whig party's 'Apostle', *Exam*, p. 102). The
following chapters will show that Swift's perception of the events
leading to the Revolution, apologia for it, and criticism of post-
Revolution polity are demonstrably those of a contemporary High
Church Tory cleric, not of a radical, anticlerical Revolution Whig
disenchanted by the Whig party's rapid abandonment of primitive
Whig principle. Swift's attitude to foreign policy certainly renders him
'Tory as much as Country'.[78] His animus against the Dutch has Tory
party-political significance. This antipathy found memorable expression in the satire of *Gulliver's Travels*; for instance, when Gulliver in
Japan petitions to be excused the ceremony 'of *trampling upon the Crucifix*'
performed by the Dutch, a scruple which led the Japanese emperor 'to
doubt whether I were a real *Hollander* or no; but rather suspected I must
be a CHRISTIAN' (*PW*, XI, 216). Swift's satiric stroke has echoes in High
Church Jacobite polemical literature. Charles Leslie observed in his
Cassandra papers of 1704: 'The *Test* in *Japan* for a *Christian*, is the
Trampling upon the *Cross*. This is thought a Sufficient Indication, that
he who do's it is no *Christian*. By this the *Dutch* Secure that *Trade* to
Themselves.'[79] The consonance of Swift's texts with militant Jacobite
and Tory literature is not always heard in modern Swift studies, though
it was by contemporaries.

[78] Hayton, 'The "Country" Interest and the Party System', p. 64.
[79] [Charles Leslie], *Cassandra*, no. II (London, 1704), Appendix, no. V, p. 91.

2

Revolution, reaction and literary representation: Swift's Jacobite Tory contexts

The corpus of Tory literature in print and manuscript in the first Age of Party is massive and heterogeneous. Scholarly studies exist on many well-known Tory writers, including, for example, John Arbuthnot, Mary Astell, Francis Atterbury, Tom Brown, Mary Caesar, Jeremy Collier, the newsletter-writer John Dyer, George Granville, Charles Leslie, Roger L'Estrange, Delarivière Manley, William Oldisworth, William Pittis and Ned Ward. There is a substantial critical literature exploring the Jacobite dimension in the later poetry, translations, prose and dramatic writing of John Dryden, who dominates the literature of the 1690s, and in the work of Alexander Pope and Samuel Johnson in the eighteenth century.[1] This chapter explores aspects of the radical idiom of Jacobite Tory literary reaction to the Revolution of 1688-9 and the Williamite, Queen Anne and Hanoverian establishment. What is witnessed in Swift is a post-Revolution Toryism which combined High Church attitudes with a radical political critique of Whig establishment. Swift's imaginative texts are not without Jacobite implication and velleity.

A 'Tory' text might express certain characteristic commitments and hostilities: engagement for the rights, powers and privileges of the Church of England, support for the proscription of Dissent from public

---

[1] Several important essays by Howard Erskine-Hill explore Dryden, Pope and Johnson in relation to affairs of state and Jacobitism: 'Scholarship as Humanism', *Essays in Criticism*, 29 (1979), 33–52 (pp. 42–5); 'Alexander Pope: The Political Poet in His Time', *Eighteenth-Century Studies*, 15 (1981–2), 123–48; 'Literature and the Jacobite Cause: Was There a Rhetoric of Jacobitism?', in *Ideology and Conspiracy*, pp. 49–69; 'The Political Character of Samuel Johnson', in *Samuel Johnson: New Critical Essays*, edited by Isobel Grundy (London and Totowa, NJ, 1984), pp. 107–36; 'The Political Character of Samuel Johnson: *The Lives of the Poets* and a Further Report on *The Vanity of Human Wishes*', in *The Jacobite Challenge*, edited by Eveline Cruickshanks and Jeremy Black (Edinburgh, 1988), pp. 161–76; 'Life into Letters, Death into Art: Pope's Epitaph on Francis Atterbury', *The Yearbook of English Studies*, 18 (1988), 200–20.

life, repudiation of latitudinarian politics, subscription to the doctrines of passive obedience and non-resistance (however modified), detestation of anti-monarchical principles identified with Whiggism, and animus against the naturalization of foreign Protestants and against the Dutch. A 'Tory' text after 1689 might apotheosize royalty in the absent or hidden hereditary king in exile, in the Stuart Queen Anne, or in Charles XII of Sweden, the enemy of George I and Protestant hero of the Jacobites. A 'Tory' text might reflect a royalist *pietas* in its attitude to 'Charles the Martyr'. Tory texts could offer violent 'Country' critiques of the Williamite court and executive and of the Hanoverian Whig regime.

Whig and Tory writers have different emphases in their accounts of the Revolution. What might be called the Whig Authorized Version of the events leading to the Revolution of 1688–9, enshrined in *Bishop Burnet's History of His Own Time*, essentially describes a general Protestant consensus against a despotic Roman Catholic king using an arbitrary prerogative to impose popery.[2] High Church Tory writers disseminated a different construction of the political crisis of 1687–8. In their interpretation, the Church of England was assaulted by papists and Dissenters colluding in latitudinarian politics. Radical Protestant Whig principles legitimating popular and military resistance to an arbitrary monarch (used to justify the Revolution in the 1689 allegiance controversy and later) were impugned as papist in provenance. The claim of a collusion in political purpose and doctrine between popery and Protestant nonconformity had a long pedigree in Anglican polemical literature and anti-Puritan graphic and literary satire. The imputation of a league between Dissenters and papists to destroy the Church and Crown, as John Miller remarks, 'became a Tory cliché'.[3] With sufficient corroborative evidence of Whig and Dissenting accommodation with James II's prerogative toleration and projected repeal of the Test Acts,[4] Tory writers were able to reanimate the cliché

2 *Bishop Burnet's History of His Own Time*, 2 vols. (London, 1724, 1734), I, 702–3.
3 John Miller, *Religion in the Popular Prints 1600–1832*, The English Satirical Print 1600–1832 (Cambridge, 1986), p. 116. A cloud of High Church and Tory witnesses could be produced.
4 A Jacobite tract by Charlwood Lawton arguing for a restoration of James II 'upon composition' represented King James as an acceptable monarch to Whigs because of his latitudinarian politics – an analysis which a High Churchman like Swift would have felt was only too true: see *The Jacobite Principles Vindicated, In an Answer to a Letter Sent to the Author* (London, 1693), in *Somers Tracts*, X, 523–41 (p. 535). See also *A Modest Apology for the loyal Protestant Subjects of King James, who desire his Restoration, without Prejudice to our Religion, Laws or Liberties: In Answer to the Pretences of the French Invasion Examined. In a Letter to a Friend, Somers Tracts*, X, 401–29 (p. 412). Narcissus Luttrell (*A Brief Historical Relation of State Affairs from September 1678 to April 1714*, 6 vols. (Oxford, 1857), I, 395, 399–443) reports the many addresses of thanks presented to James II by Dissenters for 'his declaration of liberty of

into a *parti pris* version of the events of 1687–9. Dissenters were seen to have collaborated with James II's arbitrary attempt to disestablish Anglicanism through the dispensing power. (James's Declaration of Indulgence of April 1687 republished in 1688 suspended the Test Acts, which required all public office-holders to conform to the Church of England.) After the Church party had borne the heat and burden of the day against arbitrary power and popery, the Dissenters, deserting their royal Roman Catholic benefactor upon the Revolution, benefited in the new dispensation under William III. The Dissenting Whig enemies to Church establishment were seen to be still at large after the Revolution under the auspices of 'An Act for exempting their Majesties Protestant Subjects, dissenting from the Church of *England*, from the Penalties of certain Laws' (the so-called Toleration Act of 1689). Whigs and Dissenters were represented as contriving to ruin Anglican orthodoxy and the constitution in Church and State with political and ecclesiastical principles purloined from popery. This High Church Tory topos is well illustrated in the polemical writings of the Jacobite High Churchman Charles Leslie.[5] This remarkable Jacobite outlaw and pamphleteer conducted a news-sheet campaign against the Whig press (particularly John Tutchin's *Observator* and Daniel Defoe's *Review*) and radical Whiggism in Church and State between 1704 and 1709 in *The Rehearsal*. The first issue of *The Rehearsal* (5 August 1704) points to the Jesuitical provenance of the theory of armed resistance to rulers and arguments against episcopacy and monarchy used by the Dissenters. The emissaries of popery are identified as the founders of the sect of Puritans in the reign of Queen Elizabeth.[6] The *Rehearsal* represents Whigs and Dissenters as the '*tools*' of popery. In a short history of the papist project of raising Whigs and Dissenters against the Church of

conscience' which were printed in the *London Gazette* in 1687–8. On the significant support for James II's Declaration of Indulgence among Dissenters and radical Whigs, see J. R. Jones, 'James II's Whig Collaborators', *The Historical Journal*, 3 (1960), 65–73; J. R. Jones, 'James II's Revolution: Royal Policies, 1686–92', in *The Anglo-Dutch Moment: Essays on the Glorious Revolution and Its World Impact*, edited by Jonathan I. Israel (Cambridge, 1991), pp. 47–71 (pp. 59–61); Mark Goldie, 'John Locke's Circle and James II', *The Historical Journal*, 35 (1992), 557–86.

[5] For Leslie's Jacobite career and High Church Tory and Jacobite writings see particularly Bruce Frank, '"The Excellent Rehearser": Charles Leslie and the Tory Party, 1688–1714', in *Biography in the 18th Century*, edited by J. D. Browning (New York and London, 1980), pp. 43–68.

[6] Charles Leslie, *A View of the Times*, I, 7 (*Rehearsal*, no. 1 (5 August 1704)). The first issue was called *The Observator*, but thereafter *The Rehearsal of Observator* and *Rehearsal* (the title by which Leslie's paper is known). All quotations are from the collected edition of 1750, which also contains *Cassandra*.

England, Leslie links Charles II's Declaration of Indulgence of 1672 with the tolerationist policy of 1687–8. The policy by which Whigs and Dissenters were set up against the Church of England was the 'ruin' of Charles II's 'unfortunate *brother*, king *James* II'.[7] After the death of Charles II, wrote Leslie in *The New Association* (1702), 'his Unfortunate *Brother* K. *James* the Second let the *Faction* loose again, by a New *Toleration*: For which they *Hosanna'd* him, even to *Blasphemy*'. In William III's reign 'the *Toleration* granted by King *James*, (and for which, the most of any one thing, he was *Abdicated*) has Enlarg'd'.[8]

This Tory topos is present in Swift's imaginative and polemical texts. The satiric conjunction of Jack (Dissent) and Peter (popery) in section XI of *A Tale of a Tub* (1704) activates the contemporary High Church Tory charge (see *Tale*, pp. 198–200). In this section of the *Tale* there is an acerbic epitome of events, from James II's Declaration of Indulgence in 1687 to the triumph of occasional conformity in Sir Humphrey Edwin's Lord-Mayoralty in 1697, in the allegorical account of the adventures of the three brothers Peter, Jack and Martin (Anglicanism):

how *Peter* got a *Protection* out of the *King's-Bench*; and of a Reconcilement between *Jack* and Him, upon a Design they had in a certain *rainy Night*, to trepan Brother *Martin* into a *Spunging-house*, and there strip him to the Skin. How *Martin*, with much ado, shew'd them both a fair pair of Heels. How a *new Warrant* came out against *Peter*: upon which, how *Jack* left him in the lurch, *stole his Protection, and made use of it himself. How Jack's Tatters came into Fashion in Court* and *City*; How *he got upon a great Horse, and eat Custard.*

(*Tale*, pp. 204–5)

The Dissenters received an 'Indulgence against Law' under James II and 'an Indulgence by Law' under William III, Swift wrote in the *Examiner* of 12 April 1711 (*Exam*, p. 358). It is often supposed in Swift studies that Swift's opposition to James II derives from a basic Whig ideology. In fact, however, Swift's view of events leading to the Revolution is that represented in High Church Tory polemical literature. It is 'liberty of conscience, under the present acceptation', wrote Swift in one of his 'Thoughts on Religion' which 'produces revolutions, or at least convulsions and disturbances in a state' (*PW*, IX, 263). Swift's position is dramatically opposed to that of John Locke. For Locke it is 'the refusal of toleration to those that are of different opinions ... that has produced all the bustles and wars, that have been in the Christian

---

[7] *The Rehearsals*, I, 247–8 (*Rehearsal*, no. 40, 5 May 1705).
[8] [Charles Leslie], *The New Association* ..., third edition (London, 1702), p. 16. See also [Charles Leslie], *The Wolf Stript of His Shepherd's Cloathing* ... (London, 1704), pp. 24–5.

world, upon account of religion'.[9] Swift perceives the events of 1687–9 in religious terms. He sees a design by Peter and Jack to dispossess Martin. Here is the account of the Revolution in *Examiner*, no. 37 (12 April 1711):

the Revolution being wholly brought about by Church of *England* Hands, they hoped one good Consequence of it would be the relieving us from the Incroach-ments of *Dissenters*, as well as those of *Papists*, since both had equally Confeder-ated towards our Ruin; and therefore, when the Crown was new settled, it was hoped at least that the rest of the Constitution would be restored. But this Affair took a very different Turn; the *Dissenters* had just made a shift to save a Tide, and join with the Prince of *Orange*, when they found all was desperate with their *Protector* King *James*. And observing a Party, then forming against the old Principles in Church and State, under the Name of *Whigs* and *Low-Churchmen*, they listed themselves of it, where they have ever since continu'd.

(Exam, pp. 358–9)

The Dissenters had 'boldly enter'd into a League with *Papists* and a *Popish Prince*, to destroy' the Church of England (*Exam*, p. 360). Swift repeatedly argues that it was the Church of England clergy who principally opposed James II's use of the dispensing power and illegal proceedings before the Revolution and he repeatedly witnesses the compliance of the Dissenters with James II's policy of prerogative toleration or implementation of liberty of conscience by royal edict.[10]

At the Revolution the Whig publisher Richard Baldwin printed Philip Hunton's *A Treatise of Monarchy*, in which it is remarked that

there is an art full of Venom, when a truth cannot be beaten down by just reasoning, then to make it odious by hateful comparisons; so in this case Aspersions are cast, as if the Patrons of Resistance did borrow the Popish and

---

[9] John Locke, *A Letter Concerning Toleration*, edited by John Horton and Susan Mendus, Routledge Philosophers in Focus Series (London and New York, 1991), p. 52.

[10] See, for example, *The Sentiments of a Church-of-England Man, With Respect to Religion and Government* (1711), *PW*, II, 9; *The Examiner*, no. 22 (28 December 1710), no. 40 (3 May 1711), *Exam*, pp. 126, 404–5; Marginalia in *PW*, V, 285, 286, 318; *The Presbyterians Plea of Merit* (1733), *PW*, XII, 268–71. Whigs contested Swift's reading of events leading to the Revolution. 'I protested openly', Daniel Defoe declared, 'against the Addresses of Thanks to [James II] for his Illegal Liberty of Conscience, founded upon the Dispensing Power' (*Review*, 24 November 1711, quoted by F. H. Ellis in *Exam*, p. 40n). *The Medley*, no. 15 (8 January 1711) answered *The Examiner* of 28 December 1710: '*The Clergy*, he says, *are known to have rejected all Advances made them to close with the Measures at that time concerting* (he means before the Revolution) *while the Dissenters, to gratify their Ambition and Revenge, fell into the basest Compliances*, &c. This may be true of *Persons*, but shou'd not be affirm'd of whole *Parties*; for the *Clergy* did not All *reject the Advances*, nor did *All* the Dissenters gratify those Passions of Ambition and Revenge' (*Exam*, p. 158).

Jesuitical Grounds, and their Positions as dangerous to Kings, as the Jesuits Hell-bred and bloudy Principles: whereas it appears by all this Discourse ... that there is no Congruity at all betwixt their Doctrines, no more than betwixt Light and Darkness.[11]

Leslie wrote in 1692 that '*Jesuit* and *Puritan* are convertible Terms, in the Point of *Loyalty*, only that the *Jesuit* is the Elder Brother.' After a comparison of Whig and Dissenting revolutionism with popery in the *Rehearsal*, Leslie commented sardonically: 'But *comparisons* are *odious*. Let us defend our selves against them *both*.'[12] Leslie and Swift were masters of the invective 'art full of Venom' imputing congruity and collaboration between Brother 'Jack' and Brother 'Peter'.

Swift has been situated within a Whig Commonwealth intellectual tradition in a modern political biography.[13] Yet Swift subjected Matthew Tindal's *The Rights of the Christian Church Asserted Against the Romish, and All Other Priests Who Claim an Independent Power Over It. With a Preface Concerning the Government of the Church of England, as by Law Establish'd. Part I*, a sensational text of radical Whig anti-priestcraft politics and ecclesiology first published in 1706, to hostile forensic analysis, disparaging some canonical authors of true Whiggism, such as John Locke and Robert Molesworth, in the process. Swift's 'Remarks upon a Book, intitled *The Rights of the Christian Church*' (*c.* 1707) exposes the anticlerical Whig ideologist as a quondam papist and the book itself as crypto-papist.[14] Discovering 'Jack' doing 'Peter's' work in Tindal's pages, Swift effects a familiar Tory polemical strategy, and one deployed by Leslie in his answer to 'The *Rights of the Christian Church*, the labour'd *work* of the whole *party*, and now so *celebrated* by them' in the pages of the *Rehearsal* in 1706.[15]

Leslie anathematized the radical Whig text as '*popery* at the bottom':

And no *emissary* of *Rome* could set up a *topick* more beneficial to *popery* in *England* at this day than what is advanc'd in this *book* of the *Rights*. And it is the more

---

[11] *A Treatise of Monarchy: Containing Two Parts. I. Concerning Monarchy in General. II. Concerning this Particular Monarchy* ... (London, 1643, rpt. 1689), p. 55.

[12] [Charles Leslie], *An Answer to a Book, Intituled, The State of the Protestants in Ireland ...* (London, 1692), p. 71; *The Rehearsals*, II, 105 (*Rehearsal*, no. 85, 9 February 1706).

[13] J. A. Downie, *Jonathan Swift: Political Writer*, p. 246.

[14] Swift owned a copy of the third edition of Tindal's *Rights of the Christian Church Asserted ...* (London, 1707; *SC*, no. 396). His remarks on the book, begun in 1707, remained unfinished. The *Remarks* is included in his 'List of Subjects for a Volume' (1708): see *Swift*, II, 768. See also *Corr*, I, 126. Swift's *Remarks* consists of a prose argument (*PW*, II, 67–84) and remarks (*PW*, II, 85–107). For Swift's aspersions on Locke and Molesworth in the *Remarks* see *PW*, II, 80, 97, 99.

[15] *The Rehearsals*, II, 298 (*Rehearsal*, no. 127, 3 August 1706).

suspicious, that the reputed *author* (and who I hear does not much deny it) turned *papist* and went to *mass* in K. *James's* time, but returned since with the *fashion* ...

To give you the main of this *book*, in one word, it is this. That the *church* has no *authority* but from the *state*, nor the *state* but from the *people*. This is the whole *scope* and *drift* of this *book*.[16]

Swift writes that *The Rights of the Christian Church* is the production 'of one, who, in Hopes of Preferment was reconciled to the *Popish* Religion'. At 'the latter end of King *James's* Reign he had almost finished a learned Discourse in Defence of the Church of *Rome*, and to justify his Conversion: All which, upon the Revolution, was quite out of Season ... by an easy Turn, the same Arguments he had made Use of to advance Popery, were full as properly levelled by him against Christianity itself ... And, therefore every Reader will observe, that the Arguments for *Popery* are much the strongest of any in his Book' (*PW*, II, 68, 70–1; see also *An Argument Against Abolishing Christianity*, *PW*, II, 37). Like Leslie, Swift identifies the principal Erastian project of the book 'making Religion, Church, Christianity, with all their Concomitants, a perfect Contrivance of the Civil Power' (*PW*, II, 70). 'One would think him an Emissary', Swift writes, observing Tindal's promotion of 'Schism' and 'Arguments for Popery' (*PW*, II, 94). Tindal's 'Design is either to run down Christianity, or set up Popery; and the latter is more charitable to think, and, from his past Life, highly probable' (*PW*, II, 106). Swift, again like Leslie, distinguishes the Church's divine and apostolical authority as a spiritual corporation from its legal establishment. Leslie explains in the *Rehearsal* that Tindal

confounds the *constitution* of the *church*, and her *establishment* by *law*. The *establishment* by *law* may be *altered*, or *taken away*, as of *episcopacy* in *Scotland*, but the *constitution* of the *church* she must receive from her *founder*, and is the *same* in all *churches*.[17]

Swift wrote that the legislature

may do any Thing within the Compass of human Power ... the same Law, which deprived the Church, not only of Lands, misapplied to superstitious Uses, but even the Tythes and Glebes, (the antient and necessary Support of Parish Priests) may take away all the rest.

(*PW*, II, 74–5)

---

[16] *The Rehearsals*, III, 78, 80 (*Rehearsal*, no. 165, 14 December 1706).
[17] *The Rehearsals*, III, 81 (*Rehearsal*, no. 165, 14 December 1706).

A distinction is to be made between the Church's *'Being'* and *'Establishment'* which Tindal confounds. Swift writes:

But the Church of *England* is no Creature of the Civil Power, either as to its Polity or Doctrines. The Fundamentals of both were deduced from Christ and his Apostles, and the Instructions of the purest and earliest Ages, and were received as such by those Princes or States who embraced Christianity, whatever prudential Additions have been made to the former by human Laws, which alone can be justly altered or annulled by them.

(*PW*, II, 78, 79)

At one point in his 'Remarks' Swift comments that 'Mr. *Lesly* may carry Things too far, as it is natural, because the other Extreme is so great. But what he says of the King's Losses, since the Church Lands were given away, is too great a Truth, &c.' (*PW*, II, 87). There is sympathy for the High Church politics of the Jacobite pamphleteer here. In Swift's early poetry and *A Tale of a Tub* written in the 1690s, and in his prose and poetry written after the Hanoverian succession, Swift can be read as saying what some Jacobite militants were saying on affairs of state. Swift is an unsettling, extremist political writer. He may have had, from time to time, conditional Jacobite sympathies, and perhaps would have gone over to the Jacobite side if circumstances had been right. In the remainder of this chapter I wish to remark aspects of this congruence between Swift's writing and Jacobite literature, a congruence hitherto largely neglected in literary criticism on Swift.

Two of Swift's early Pindaric odes, 'Ode to the King. On his Irish Expedition. And The Success of his Arms in general' (1691; *Poems*, I, 4–10) and 'Ode to Dr. William Sancroft, Late Lord Archbishop of Canterbury' (1692; *Poems*, I, 33–42) are interesting political texts and important biographical sources for Swift's political views in the early 1690s. Literary criticism has arrived at a number of judgements about the early pindaric odes as a group. They have been dismissed as failures in, for Swift, the uncongenial form of Cowleyean Pindaric; as uncomfortable performances in a fashionable panegyric form before Swift was able to find his natural poetic voice. The poems have been found to contain anticipations of Swift's later satiric manner and themes. They have been studied as repositories of some of Swift's lifelong sentiments and as the poet's exploration of the human condition. They have been read as examples of a minor seventeenth-century tradition, that of satiric Pindarics.[18] There are extended

---

[18] Important received views about the Pindaric odes are summarized in David Sheehan, 'Swift on High Pindaric Stilts', in *Contemporary Studies of Swift's Poetry*, edited by John Irwin

discussions of the 'Ode to Sancroft' in historical context by Edward W. Rosenheim, Jr and F. P. Lock.[19] Yet a specific controversial context for Swift's early poems – that of Jacobite literary response to the Revolution and Williamite settlement and Jacobite polemic rhetoric of the 1690s – has been neglected. The difficulty and obscurity of the highfly-ing Pindaric style offered Swift a protective carapace for oblique political commentary on the Revolution and Williamite regime. Swift's early odes are alive with the rhetoric of Jacobite literature on affairs of state.

The anti-Williamite verse satire generated by the Revolution is, as modern scholarship has witnessed, overwhelmingly Jacobite. That is, it either explicitly supports a Stuart restoration, or would seem to do so implicitly in the violence of its attack on the king and government.[20] In Jacobite satire the Revolution is imaged as illegal, impious and unnatu-ral. William III is, for Jacobite writers, the inglorious, sodomitical, stranger King: a political rapist, parricide, perjured usurper and tyrant; a physically grotesque Tarquin who defecated during his coro-nation and who sleeps on the throne. The vocabulary and motifs of Jacobite political satire are well illustrated in the vitriolic prose political allegory *An Historical Romance of the Wars Between the Mighty Giant Gallieno, and the Great Knight Nasonius, and His Associates* (1694), which narrates William's career of flagitious ambition, rape, usurpation and robbery with demotic, derisive humour.[21] The persons, principles and

Fischer and Donald C. Mell, Jr, with David M. Vieth (Newark, London and Toronto, 1981), pp. 25–35. Sheehan reads the poems as satiric Pindarics.

[19] Edward W. Rosenheim, Jr, 'Swift's *Ode to Sancroft*: Another Look', *Modern Philology*, 73 (1976), S24–S39; F. P. Lock, *Swift's Tory Politics*, esp. pp. 75–93. Rosenheim finds in the poem a 'failure to dwell upon Sancroft's accomplishments' and a sparing admiration, and that Swift writes of William III 'with anything but Jacobite sentiments' (see esp. S33, S34, S37). Lock argues that the 'Ode' 'is not a non-juring or non-juror's poem, still less a Jacobite one' (p. 85).

[20] See Paul Monod, *Jacobitism and the English People*, esp. pp. 45–69.

[21] [John Sergeant], *An Historical Romance of the Wars, Between the Mighty Giant Gallieno, and the Great Knight Nasonius, and His Associates* (Doublin, 1694). The account of the Revolution begins at ch. VI. On the rhetoric of Jacobitism, see Howard Erskine-Hill, 'Literature and the Jacobite Cause: Was There a Rhetoric of Jacobitism?', pp. 49–69. For some examples of Jacobite literary attack on William see, on his homosexuality: 'Satyr', in *A New Collection of Poems Relating to State Affairs, From Oliver Cromwell To this present Time* ... (London, 1705), pp. 531–2 ('Declining *Venus* has no Force o'er Love, / The tender *Ganymede* now rules above ... / B___s are still the Stamp of Revolution'); John Sheffield, Duke of Buckingham, 'A Feast of the Gods', (p. 17), *Buckingham Restor'd: Being Two Essays Which were Castrated from the Works of the late Duke of Buckingham* ('Some Account of the Revolution' (pp. 1–14) and 'A Feast of the Gods' (pp. 15–19)) (Hague, 1727); [John Sergeant], *An Historical Romance, passim*, on '*Nasonius*' and '*Sodomicus*'; [Robert Ferguson], *Whether the Preserving the Protestant Religion was the Motive unto, or the End that was designed in, the late Revolution?* ...

conditions of Revolution government in Church and State anathematized by Jacobite High Churchmen in the 1690s can be consulted in *A Catalogue of Books of the Newest Fashion, to be Sold by Auction at the Whiggs Coffee-House, at the Sign of the Jackanapes in Prating-Alley, near the Deanry of St. Paul's* (1694), a satiric mock-book auction catalogue, attributed to Charles Leslie. Ideologists of the new settlement in Church and State, such as the Erastian Humphrey Hody and the apostate nonjuror William Sherlock, are pilloried on page one. Leslie's Jacobite vilification of an illegitimate regime incorporates 'Country' complaints about war, taxes and pensioners and excoriates latitudinarianism, religious heterodoxy, naturalization of foreigners and the Dutch.[22]

Jacobite writers observed how Williamite Whig panegyric represented the prince as the providential Protestant saviour of the nation's religion and liberties. William's 'rapines and robberies' were being hallowed. 'The panegyrics upon him, on this account, of your Tillotsons, Tenisons, Patricks, and Burnets, &c. are more frontless and fulsome than what your Shadwells, Settles or any of your Grub-street poets' produce.'[23] Jacobites bitterly mocked William by portraying him as a Romance 'Hero'.[24] In Swift's violent, anti-Hanoverian satire 'Directions for a Birth-day Song', written perhaps in 1729 but unpublished in his lifetime, this advice is offered to Whig poets writing an encomium on their royal Caesar or Alexander:

> One Compliment I had forgot,
> But Songsters must omit it not.
> (I freely grant the Thought is old)
> Why then, your Hero must be told,
> In him such Virtues lye inherent,
> To qualify him God's Vicegerent,
> That with no Title to inherit,

(1695), *Somers Tracts*, IX, 543–69 (on the catamite court see p. 564); *POAS*, 5, 37–8, 41–2, 153, 155, 221. And see Swift, *PW*, V, 285. On William's alleged coronation accident: *POAS*, 5, 44. In *An Historical Romance*, 'Nasonius' is told 'you are much better at *Shiting* than *Fighting*' (p. 73). Principal Jacobite satirical motifs can be read in Arthur Mainwaring, *Tarquin and Tullia* (1689), *POAS*, 5, 46–54 and *Suum Cuique* (1689), *POAS*, 5, 117–22. See generally the excellent selection and annotation of political poetry in the Yale *POAS*.

22 [Charles Leslie], *A Catalogue of Books of the Newest Fashion, to be Sold by Auction at the Whiggs Coffee-House, at the Sign of the Jackanapes in Prating-Alley, near the Deanry of St. Paul's* [London, 1694]. British Library shelf-mark 12316.g.26, attributed to Leslie. See Bruce Frank, '"The Excellent Rehearser": Charles Leslie and the Tory Party', p. 54n.

23 [Robert Ferguson], *Whether the preserving the Protestant Religion ...*, *Somers Tracts*, IX, 563; [John Sergeant], *An Historical Romance*, p. 24.

24 [Robert Ferguson], *Somers Tracts*, IX, 555; [William Anderton], *Remarks upon the Present Confederacy, and Late Revolution in England &c* (1693), *Somers Tracts*, X, 507; [John Sergeant], *An Historical Romance, passim.*

He must have been a King by Merit.
Yet be the Fancy old or new,
'Tis partly false, and partly true,
And take it right, it means no more
Than George and William claim'd before.

(*Poems*, II, 464)

To praise a king for his inherent goodness is presented as a fancy of
Whig poets, the artifice by which kings without hereditary title claim
legitimacy. The titles of William III, George I and George II are
brought into question. In the light of this later satiric judgement about
kings who claim to rule on merit, and of contemporary Jacobite
derision of William as a Romance 'Hero', it is extremely interesting to
re-read Swift's 'Ode to the King'. The ode was composed between 1
July 1690 and August 1691 (that is, between the Battle of the Boyne and
when Swift left Ireland) but was first published in 1735, although two
stanzas were quoted by John Dunton in 1699. The poem is routinely
read in Swift studies as an encomium on William III.[25] Yet there may
be covert disturbance of the ostensible praise of William in the 'Ode to
the King'. The poet insists that '*Doing Good*' is 'the best Gemm in
Royalty, / The Great Distinguisher of Blood' (lines 19, 22–3). A
Williamite panegyrical sentiment[26] that, as Swift later wrote, is 'partly
false, and partly true'. One effect of the lines perhaps is to remind
readers that William lacks a direct hereditary title to the crown.
Through a combination of devices – extravagant hyperbole (although
this is conventional in the highflying Pindaric form), artificial simile,
intrusive, parenthetical qualifying remarks by the poet, and opaque or
ambivalent allusion – Swift establishes implicit distance between the
subject of the 'Ode' and the poet and reader. Through such distancing
Swift creates the enabling conditions of satire and sets up the possibility
of detached critical reflection. The conquering Hero William is said to

---

[25] See the headnote and notes to the poem by Pat Rogers in *Complete Poems*, pp. 601–3, where
important critical discussions are listed. See also David Nokes, *Jonathan Swift, A Hypocrite
Reversed: A Critical Biography* (Oxford, 1985), pp. 21–2. A. C. Elias, Jr, posits a private,
Moor Park readership and context for the 'Ode to the King' and 'Ode to Sancroft': see his
Swift at Moor Park: Problems in Biography and Criticism (Philadelphia, 1982), pp. 244–6,
n. 45. Elias parenthetically remarks 'a somewhat ambivalent effect' in the way Swift
imagines William's heroism in the 'Ode to the King' (p. 83). Alan Robinson describes
'Swift's ambivalent approach' in his royal panegyric, which is explained as a stylistic
problem: 'Swift's hesitant adoption of the mythologizing convention' and diffidence with
it, see his 'Swift and Renaissance Poetry: A Declaration of Independence', *British Journal
for Eighteenth-Century Studies*, 8 (1985), 37–49 (esp. pp. 39–40).

[26] Compare P. Sayve, 'To the King' (b2v), in *Musae Cantabrigienses* (Cantabrigiae, 1689):
'*Kings differ not from Men of baser blood, / But in the Godlike Pow'r of doing Good*'.

be 'like a Bold Romantick Knight' rescuing Fame 'from the Giant's Fort' (lines 37–8) and the poet sees William's triumph at the Battle of the Boyne in this way:

> And what I us'd to laugh at in *Romance*,
> And thought too great ev'n for effects of Chance,
> The Battel almost by *Great William*'s single Valour gain'd.
>
> (lines 62–4)

Ostensibly he is flattering William for having actually achieved what would usually be dismissed as an incredible fiction. Yet, as in the Dedication to Somers in *A Tale of a Tub*, the effect of the praise is not straightforward or the irony stable. The possibility of a trace of contempt in this depiction of a bold romantic knight performing what Swift would laugh at in a romance should not be discounted, especially when read in the context of the sardonic humour of such Jacobite polemic rhetoric as that which presented the 'Romance' of the wars between 'the Mighty GIANT GALLIENO' and 'the Great KNIGHT NASONIUS'. Swift's lines may be a sarcastic mimickry of particular Williamite verse panegyric produced by his contemporaries. One tribute 'To the King', for example, enthuses of its hero:

> But Thou, Illustrious WILLIAM, didst withstand
> The threatning Evil Genius of the Land,
> What of Romantick Knights in Fiction's read,
> By whose bright Swords all charms were useless made:
> Such vertue truly We in Thine descry,
> While Priests and all their Incantations fly.
> His Scepter Jove cou'd not in safety sway,
> Till on the ground expiring Giants lay.[27]

Swift was capable of traducing William's rule and even deriding the King indirectly in his poetry of the 1690s. In an unfinished poem, 'On the Burning of Whitehall in 1698', probably written in 1698 and now accepted as canonical (see *Complete Poems*, pp. 80–1, 618–20), Swift, while officially professing admiration and loyalty for King William, nevertheless registers profound disaffection with the Williamite Revolution regime. The following passage alludes to the period between James's flight in 1688 and the fire that destroyed much of the palace of Whitehall on 4/5 January 1698. It attacks the continuation of James II's toleration of Dissent under William, Dutch financial influence, bribery, placemen, corruption and vice:

---

[27] Sayve, 'To the King', b2-(b2v).

> He gone, the rank infection still remains,
> Which to repel requires eternal pains.
> No force to cleanse it can a river draw,
> Nor Hercules could do it, nor great Nassau.
> Most greedy financiers, and lavish too,
> Swarm in, in spite of all that prince could do,
> Projectors, peculates the palace hold,
> Patriots exchanging liberty for gold,
> Monsters unknown to this blessed land of old.
> Heaven takes the cure in hand, celestial ire
> Applies the oft-tried remedy of fire;
> The purging flames were better far employed,
> Than when old Sodom was, or Troynovant destroyed.
> The nest obscene of every pampered vice,
> Sinks down of this infernal paradise.
>
> (lines 30–44; *Complete Poems*, pp. 80–1)[28]

Under the regime of the modern Hercules, William III, monsters infest the land. The Jacobite calumny that William 'burst forth *backwards*' and '*beshit* his Coronation'[29] is present in Swift's 'The Problem' (1699), a scatological satire on Henry Sidney, Earl of Romney. Romney's master is referred to obliquely in lines 19–20:

> We read of Kings, who in a Fright,
> Tho' on a Throne, wou'd fall to sh–.
>
> (*Poems*, I, 66)

Another ambivalent aspect of Swift's royal panegyric is that it does not just compliment the King on the success of his arms, but appears to represent his claim to the crown as founded not in law or social compact, but in successful conquest. William III denounced the idea that his rule was based on conquest, which would have implied that he was merely a successful usurper like Cromwell. Swift later rejected the idea that successful conquest conferred legitimacy (see *PW*, V, 293). The argument that William was a conqueror and that the nation was experiencing corruption and oppression was commonplace among Jacobite writers. In Swift's poetry of the 1690s the nation is observed to be in a chronic state of corruption. In the 'Ode to the King' William is the 'Victor' who 'carves out his Bays' (lines 11, 32). William 'trampled

---

[28] The violence of the moral condemnation in Swift's poem was perhaps typical of the sub-genre of poems on the 'Burning of Whitehall'. See, for example, *Upon the Burning of White-Hall, Jan. 4. 169⅞. Englished from the Latin*, in *A New Collection of Poems Relating to State Affairs . . .* (London, 1705), p. 535.

[29] [John Sergeant], *An Historical Romance*, pp. 37–8.

on this Haughty *Bajazet* [James II], / Made him his Footstool in the War, / And a Grim Slave to wait on his Triumphal Car' (lines 42–4). William is associated with 'a Destroying Angel' (stanza IV). Like Cromwell in Marvell's 'An Horatian Ode upon Cromwel's Return from Ireland' who conquered Ireland ('And now the *Irish* are asham'd / To see themselves in one Year tam'd') and who will over-power Scotland,[30] Swift's William 'controuls' the Scots and is victorious in Ireland: 'thus has our Prince compleated every Victory, / And glad *Ïerne* now may see / Her Sister Isles are *Conquered* too as well as She' (stanza V). Williamite verse pointed out that the *'Great Heroe'* refused *'a Conquerours Name'*. William received *'an unsought Crown'*. He restores peace and order and is likened to God.[31] Swift depicts William as a conqueror in the 'Ode to the King'. Many years later he represents the Revolution as a *coup* effected by William's supporters (*Poems*, II, 468) and regards the prince as a usurper (*PW*, V, 288).

The 'Ode to the King' is unwhiggish in its animus against the people who are described as the *'Giddy Brittish Populace'* (line 72; compare 'Ode to Sancroft', lines 73–83, 117: 'The giddy turns of pop'lar rage', 162: 'Mistaken Ideots! see how giddily they run'). Charles Leslie and Swift's friend Thomas Southerne (*Corr*, IV, 170) write of 'the Giddy Motions of the *Mob*' and the people's 'giddy Humour' in their Jacobite work.[32] Significantly, in stanza V, Swift looks to William to 'controul' the *'Chronical Disease'* of popular Scots Presbyterian revolutionism. An allusion to William as 'Mercury' lulling the people ('Argus') into ease and sleep in the beginning of the stanza has an ambivalent effect:

> The *Giddy Brittish Populace*,
> That *Tyrant-Guard* on *Peace*,
> Who watch Her like a Prey,
> And keep Her for a Sacrifice,
> And must be sung, like *Argus*, into *ease*
> Before this *Milk-white Heifer* can be stole away,
> Our *Prince* has charm'd its many hundred Eyes;
> Has lull'd the Monster in a Deep
> And (I hope) an Eternal Sleep.
>
> (lines 72–80)

30 'An Horatian Ode upon Cromwel's Return from Ireland', lines 73–4, 105–14, in *The Poems and Letters of Andrew Marvell*, edited by H. M. Margoliouth, revised by Pierre Legouis with E. E. Duncan-Jones, third edition, 2 vols. (Oxford, 1971), I, 91–4.
31 *Musae Cantabrigienses*, d2, d2v (cv) (a3), *passim*.
32 [Charles Leslie], *An Answer to a Book . . .* (1692), p. 21, see pp. 18, 32; Thomas Southerne, *The Spartan Dame*, I.i.133, 445–7, in *The Works of Thomas Southerne*, edited by Robert Jordan and Harold Love, 2 vols. (Oxford, 1988), II, 283, 292.

'*Peace*' in this passage changes from 'a Prey' to 'a Sacrifice' to the
'*Milk-white Heifer*' that 'can be stole away'. In the classical story from
Ovid's *Metamorphoses* (I, 601-721) to which Swift alludes, Mercury
charms Argus to sleep, then kills him. There may be an anti-Williamite
implication in Swift's allusion to William (Mercury) lulling the people
(Argus) into an eternal sleep but stealing away their peace. That is, a
view of King William is implied here that is consonant with a remark
Coleridge attributed to Swift: 'Yet Swift was rare. Can any thing beat
his remark on King William's motto, *Recepit, non rapuit*, "That the
receiver was as bad as the thief"?'.[33] Certainly the Jacobite press
depicted William as a conqueror, charming and lulling the people into
a supine state and stealing away their peace, liberty and property.[34]
Williamite verse in 1689 praises the King for ending the '*Charm*' and
removing the '*Plagues*' which oppressed the land.[35]

The High Church poet of 'Ode to the King' has no sympathy for
James II. He is William's 'fond *Enemy*' who tried 'Upon *a rubbish Heap of
broken* Laws / To climb at Victory' and who is now in mourning and
misery. The poem concludes with a combat between kings. The bastard
tyrant Louis XIV receives a wound from William (who is imagined as
Paris) and Louis falls victim to a '*Fistula in Ano*':

> Our Prince has hit Him, like *Achilles*, in the *Heel*,
> The Poys'nous Darts has made him reel,
> Giddy he grows, and down is hurl'd,
> And as a Mortal to his *Vile Disease*,
> Falls sick in the *Posteriors* of the World.

(lines 142-6)

Williamite Whig panegyric praised William as the hero of a Protestant Providence delivering the nation from arbitrary power and
popery which had been sustained by the now discredited non-resistance
principles of Tory High Churchmen. William is celebrated as the
asserter of religious freedom.[36] Swift in the 'Ode to the King' expresses

---

[33] *The Table Talk and Omniana of Samuel Taylor Coleridge* (Oxford, 1917), p. 116. For a possible
origin of this repartee Coleridge attributed to Swift, see Howard Erskine-Hill, 'Literature
and the Jacobite Cause: Was There a Rhetoric of Jacobitism?', p. 62, n. 12.

[34] [Sir James Montgomery], *Great Britain's Just Complaint* ... (1692), *Somers Tracts*, X, p. 468;
Southerne, *The Spartan Dame*, I.i.423-27 in *Works*, II, 291; John Dryden, *Amphitryon*, in *The
Works of John Dryden: Vol. XV. Plays: Albion and Albanius Don Sebastian Amphitryon*, edited
by Earl Miner and others (Berkeley, Los Angeles and London, 1976), esp. Act V.i, pp. 305-7.

[35] John Herbert, 'To the King', in *Musae Cantabrigienses* (b4v).

[36] See, for example, Thomas Shadwell, *A Congratulatory Poem On His Highness the Prince of
Orange His Coming into England*, in *The Complete Works of Thomas Shadwell*, edited by
Montague Summers, 5 vols. (London, 1927), V, 335-40; *Poems on the Reign of William III*,

hostility toward the people and Dissent and looks to William to assert Anglican hegemony. Unlike Whig poets, he does not satirically reflect on Tory non-resistance principles in his poetic depiction of a combat between kings.

Another early Swift poem, 'Ode to Dr William Sancroft, Late Lord Archbishop of Canterbury', on which Swift was working in 1692 can be interpreted as an affirmation of the passive obedience of a Churchman who refused to acknowledge the authority of the Revolution settlement. Sancroft was the subject of a Jacobite hagiography in 1694 in which he is represented as the 'glorious confessor' for passive obedience, 'making a safe passage through storms and tempests', adhering to truth and virtue. After his deprivation he lived in 'just and honourable retirement' and escaped 'a spreading contagion'. In his last hour Sancroft petitioned God to 'preserve this poor suffering church, which, by this revolution, is almost destroyed' and to restore the Stuarts.[37] Swift's praise of Sancroft in 1692 is an act with political implication. In a letter to Thomas Swift on 3 May 1692 Swift wrote: 'I have had an ode in hand these 5 months inscribed to my late L^d of Canterbury Dr Sancroft, a gentleman I admire at a degree more than I can express, putt into me partly by some experience of him, but more by an unhappy reverend Gentleman my L^d the Bishop of Ely with whom I usd to converse about 2 or 3 years ago, and very often upon that Subject' (Corr, I, 8–9). The letter discloses that Swift was in contact with the Jacobite Tory Bishop of Ely soon after the Revolution. Turner, like Sancroft, was deprived in February 1690. The letter affords one of the few glimpses we have of Swift moving in nonjuring circles (see also, for example, PW, II, 21). By 1692 the deprived bishop was a Jacobite outlaw. Swift imagines himself publishing the ode and entering the lists on the nonjuring side in the political and ecclesiastical battle of the books. Swift tells Thomas of the public gesture he intends with his ode: 'I would send it to my Bookseller and make him print it with my name and all, to show my respect and Gratitude to that excellent person, and to perform half a Promise I made His L^{d}ship of Ely upon it' (Corr, I, 9). The criticism of the times and the polemic rhetoric in the 'Ode to Sancroft' elide with Jacobite languages of disaffection.

In the first stanza of the 'Ode' Swift alludes to the political

Introduction and Selection by Earl Miner, Augustan Reprint Society, no. 166 (Los Angeles, 1974).

[37] [Thomas Wagstaffe], A Letter Out of Suffolk to a Friend in London, Giving Some Account of the Last Sickness and Death of Dr. William Sancroft, Late Lord Archbishop of Canterbury, Somers Tracts, IX, 527–40 (pp. 528, 529, 535, 539).

controversy over allegiance to the Revolution regime. Swift searches for 'TRUTH' and is not convinced by Williamite conquest theory:

> How shall we find Thee then in dark disputes?
> How shall we search Thee in a battle gain'd,
> Or a weak argument by force maintain'd?

The 'dagger-contests, and th' artillery of words' cannot 'satisfy the doubt'. In stanza three the nonjuror Sancroft in 'the divin'ty of retreat' is 'the brightest pattern Earth can shew / Of heav'n-born Truth below'. The poem reflects the widespread Anglican angst of the period, but it seems in places only ambiguously within the pale of the Revolution. The poet asks in stanza V which of all the nation's sins 'Has given thee up a dwelling-place to fiends? / Sin and the plague ever abound / In governments too easy, and too fruitful ground.' William is 'a too gentle king' in a time of flourishing evils. Pointedly, the 'British soil' now 'breeds'

> Among the noblest flow'rs a thousand pois'nous weeds,
>   And ev'ry stinking weed so lofty grows,
>   As if 'twould overshade the Royal Rose,
>   The Royal Rose the glory of our morn,
>   But, ah, too much without a thorn.

The poem professes loyalty to the monarch, yet dwells on the sin, pollution and poison in the nation. Stanza nine refers to 'our mighty Prince' and 'his happy influence', yet describes the Erastian ruin of the Church, implies that Heaven's permission of William has not cancelled the sins of subjects and affirms the wisdom of Sancroft. Stanza ten expresses the hope that the events of 1687–8, the Church-destroying revolutionary 'storms' that Sancroft long has borne will not be repeated:

> Ah, may no unkind earthquake of the State,
>   Nor hurricano from the Crown,
> Disturb the present Mitre, as that fearful storm of late,
>   Which in its dusky march along the plain,
>   Swept up whole churches as it list,
>   Wrapp'd in a whirlwind and a mist;
> Like that prophetic tempest in the virgin reign,
>   And swallow'd them at last, or flung them down.
>   Such were the storms good SANCROFT long has borne.
>
>   (lines 190–8)

Swift's implicit comparison of the Dutch and Spanish invasions of 1688 and 1588 respectively and his allusion to the events of 1688 as a 'storm' were commonplace in contemporary correspondence and discourse.[38] There was an earthquake in London in 1692 which Swift metaphorically applies to the events of 1688.[39] This metaphoric depiction of the events of 1688 became very much a Tory (and Swiftian) idiom on the Revolution. 'Jack' and 'Peter' had a design 'in a certain *rainy Night*, to trepan Brother *Martin*' (*Tale*, p. 204). This idiom (and the identification it implies between the 'Protestant' east wind which conveyed William of Orange and a destructive storm) was well parodied by the Whig wit and sometime friend of Swift, Anthony Henley, in a letter printed in *The Medley* of 7 May 1711:

And I wou'd ask any impartial Man, what else but the Revolution cou'd possibly have been the Cause of the great Wind which happen'd some years ago? Can we impute to any other thing the Loss of so many Trees, Houses and Church-Steeples, which were then blown down?

(*Exam*, p. 410)

In the last stanza (XII) of the 'Ode to Sancroft' as we have it, there is an apotheosis of the nonjuring archbishop and an outspoken satiric attack on the Low Church, comprehension party:

Since, happy Saint, since it has been of late
   Either our blindness or our fate,
   To lose the providence of thy cares,
   Pity a miserable Church's tears,
That begs the pow'rful blessing of thy pray'rs.
Some angel say, what were the nation's crimes,
That sent these wild reformers to our times.

(lines 240–6)

Swift does not say what the national crime was that has led to the ruin of religion, but his rhetoric elides with Jacobite High Church satire. In *Suum Cuique* (1689) attributed to Arthur Mainwaring, William 'labors

---

[38] See, for example, *Correspondence of The Family of Hatton Being Chiefly Letters Addressed to Christopher First Viscount Hatton A.D. 1601–1704*, edited by Edward Maunde Thompson, 2 vols. (London: Camden Society, 1878), II, 96, 107; BL Add. MSS, 45, 511, fol. 181, and see also Add. MSS, 45, 512, fol. 78 (Robert Nelson Collection, volumes I and II); John Sharp, *Fifteen Sermons Preach'd on Several Occasions* (London, 1700), Sermon X, p. 264. Swift owned a copy of the *Fifteen Sermons*, see LeFanu, p. 29; *SC*, no. 415; *Tale*, pp. xxxi–xxxvi.

[39] For the 'frightfull earthquake' of September 1692, see *Correspondence of The Family of Hatton*, II, 184–5; [Robert Fleming], *A Discourse of Earthquakes; As they are Supernatural and Premonitory Signs to a Nation; with a respect to what hath occurred in this Year 1692 . . .* (London, 1693), esp. p. 21. Pat Rogers (*Complete Poems*, p. 611) does not record the London earthquake, but notes, however, the disastrous earthquakes at Port Royal in Jamaica, on 7 June 1692 and in Sicily in September 1693 for Swift's allusion. The earthquake in Jamaica was a public sensation in England, see '*The Earth-quake of Jamaica, describ'd in a Pindarick Poem, 1692. By Mr. Tutchin.*', in *Poems on Affairs of State*, volume IV (London, 1707), pp. 327–33.

to assail' the Church and 'keeps fit tools to break the sacred pale'. Gilbert Burnet, John Tillotson, William Lloyd and Henry Compton 'are the leaders in apostasy, / The wild reformers of the liturgy, / And the blind guides of poor elective majesty.'[40] For Swift, Sancroft is an exemplar of and witness to that doctrine of passive obedience from which the people are apostate, his 'daz'ling glory dimms their prostituted sight, / No deflower'd eye can face the naked light' (lines 221–2). Jacobites used a rhetoric of rape and violation in their polemical representation of William's invasion and usurpation of the throne. It was 'an outrageous rape' and 'an open deflowering of the chastity which [the English] church had hitherto preserved in point of allegiance to lawful and rightful monarchs.'[41] But for the Jacobite William Shippen, Sancroft preserved his purity: 'Sancroft's unblemish'd Life, divinely Pure, / In its own heav'nly Innocence Secure, / The teeth of Time, the blasts of Envy shall endure.'[42] Swift in the 'Ode to Sancroft' represents the nation as deflowered and prostitute. The nonjuror Sancroft represents inviolate truth, an 'arch-prelate' who will be translated to the heavenly Church of England as 'arch-angel' (see lines 230–9). Swift's profound respect for Sancroft and his conduct at the Revolution never altered, and he defends him against the Whig Bishop Gilbert Burnet's detraction (see PW, V, 277, 285, 291).

Swift never published this poem, although in a private letter he imagined himself boldly appearing in print on the nonjuror's side. Writing odes to William III and Archbishop Sancroft may seem politically inconsistent. The inconsistency I believe is only nominal. The ambivalence of the presentation of conquering William in the 'Ode to the King' and his praise for the passive obedience of Sancroft, who refused an active part in the Convention and who refused to acknowledge the Revolution monarchs, reflect a consistent Swiftian attitude, that of a High Churchman in the 1690s, opposed to James II's latitudinarian politics, disturbed by the effects of the Revolution, and ambiguous in his attitude to the new King. Swift's literary texts display a strident, anti-court political stance. This is usually understood in Swift studies as a reflection of his 'Old Whig', 'Country' ideology.

---

[40] POAS, 5, 117–22 (lines 14–15, 67–9). Compare also the Jacobite attack on 'Reformers' in Southerne's The Spartan Dame, Works, II, 292–3.

[41] [Robert Ferguson], Whether the Preserving the Protestant Religion ..., Somers Tracts, IX, 560. Charles Leslie asked: 'Whether Dame Britannia were not less culpable in being forc'd to endure a Thirteen Years Rape from Oliver and the Rump, than by living a Five Years Adulteress now by Consent?', A Catalogue of Books, p. 8.

[42] Faction Display'd (1704) in POAS, 6, 657 (lines 152–4).

However, I believe, we are reading in Swift not loyal Whiggism as modern scholars suppose, but what contemporaries recognized as the polemic rhetoric of Jacobite Tory High Churchmen.

Swift and Granville

The transition of Toryism from Court ideology to a stance independent of the Crown is ascribed by historians to the influence of the Robert Harley–Paul Foley Country Whigs on the Tory party in the 1690s, 'the long clericalist tradition of the Church's corporate rights' informing the High Church response to monarchy, and the influence of Jacobitism.[43]

Traditional Tory legitimist sentiment is married to a radical, anti-Court stance in the poetry of George Granville, later first Baron Lansdowne, written when the poet lived in retirement in the country during the reign of William III. Samuel Johnson gave this account of Granville's 'regulated loyalty' in 1688:

However faithful Granville might have been to the King ... he has left no reason for supposing that he approved either the artifices or the violence with which the King's religion was insinuated or obtruded. He endeavoured to be true at once to the King and to the Church.

Johnson quotes a letter written by Granville before the Dutch invasion in 1688 in which the young royalist writes: 'The King has been misled; let those who have misled him be answerable for it. Nobody can deny but he is sacred in his own person, and it is every honest man's duty to defend it ... By what I can hear every body wishes well to the King; but they would be glad his ministers were hanged.'[44] Granville was a High Church Tory and Jacobite, a politician, poet and patron, mentor of Alexander Pope and dedicatee of *Windsor-Forest*, friend of Jonathan Swift and, like Swift in the last years of Anne's reign, a friend of St John, follower of Harley and member of the Tory Brothers' club.[45] A Jacobite

---

[43] See Mark Goldie, 'The Nonjurors, Episcopacy, and the Origins of the Convocation Controversy', pp. 15–35 (p. 30) and Paul Monod, 'Jacobitism and Country Principles in the Reign of William III', 289–310. On the 'Country interest' becoming synonymous with the Tory party, see David Hayton, 'The "Country" Interest and the Party System, 1689–c. 1720', pp. 37–85. For the long history of Tory autonomy and opposition to the crown, see Mark Goldie, 'Danby, the Bishops and the Whigs', pp. 75–105.

[44] Samuel Johnson, 'Granville', in *Lives of the English Poets*, edited by George Birkbeck Hill, 3 vols. (Oxford, 1905), II, 287, 288. On the political significance of Johnson's 'Life of Granville', see Howard Erskine-Hill, 'The Political Character of Samuel Johnson', in *The Jacobite Challenge*, pp. 163, 165, 166, 168–69, 172.

[45] For Granville's career and works, see Elizabeth Handasyde, *Granville the Polite: The Life of George Granville Lord Lansdowne, 1666–1735* (Oxford, 1933). For a list of members of the Tory

activist in the conspiracies of the early Hanoverian period, Granville's 1722 election tract, *A Letter from a Noble-Man Abroad, to His Friend in England*, is a thinly veiled call for a parliament or an armed rising to restore the Stuarts. It appropriates Cato for the proscribed party, exhorts Englishmen to 'take a *Roman* Resolution to save their Country', and admires the example of the republican patriot and tyrannicide Marcus Brutus.[46] The startling Jacobite appropriation of Catonic and republican languages familiar to historians of Jacobitism can be witnessed in Granville's early poems and in other writing by High Churchmen and Jacobite Tories soon after the Revolution.

Johnson's judgement on the youthful effusion of Granville's highflying, Waller-like muse apostrophizing James the Just and Mary d'Este of Modena as earthly god and goddess is not sympathetic:

At the accession of king James ... he again exerted his poetical powers, and addressed the new monarch in three short pieces, of which the first is profane, and the two others such as a boy might be expected to produce.[47]

But there is interest for historical critics of Swift and of later Tory and Jacobite political writing in the early association of James II and royalism with the iconic heroes of virtuous Roman republicanism in Granville's poems. In 'To The King' we read:

> O! cou'd the Ghosts of mighty Heroes dead
> Return on Earth, and quit th' *Elizian* Shade,
> *Brutus* to *James* wou'd trust the Peoples Cause,
> Thy Justice is a stronger Guard than Laws:
> *Marius* and *Sylla* wou'd resign to thee,
> Nor *Caesar*, and Great *Pompey*, Rivals be,
> Or Rivals only who shou'd best obey,
> And *Cato* gives his Voice for Regal Sway.[48]

Brothers' club, see *Letters and Correspondence, Public and Private, of the Right Honourable Henry St. John, Lord Viscount Bolingbroke*, edited by Gilbert Parke, 2 vols. (London, 1798), I, 150n (vol. VI of *The Works of The Right Hon. Henry St. John, Lord Viscount Bolingbroke*, 7 vols. (London, 1754–98)).

[46] [George Granville, Baron Lansdowne], *A Letter from a Noble-Man Abroad, to His Friend in England* (London, 1722). British Library Shelf-mark: 8132.b.59. This work is reprinted in full in Howard Erskine-Hill, 'Alexander Pope: The Political Poet in His Time', 143–6. On the *Letter*, see Erskine-Hill, 'Literature and the Jacobite Cause: Was There a Rhetoric of Jacobitism?', pp. 55–6 and Eveline Cruickshanks and Howard Erskine-Hill, 'The Waltham Black Act and Jacobitism', *Journal of British Studies*, 24 (1985), 358–65 (p. 360n).

[47] *Lives*, II, 286.

[48] *Poems upon Several Occasions* (London, 1712), p. 10; hereafter cited as Granville, *Poems*. See also 'To the Immortal Memory of Mr. Waller: Upon his Death', Granville, *Poems*, p. 17.

Soon after the Revolution the idealized stoic Roman republicans are back in opposition in Granville's verse. In response to the '*Syren* Song' of verses from his cousin Elizabeth Higgons entreating him to leave his country retirement and return to public life, the young Granville pens in 1690 a Jacobite jeremiad against the corruption of this mad time of usurpation. He remarkably enlists Cato for the 'Honest' cause.[49] The poet examines political power and discovers usurpation and illegitimacy behind 'Greatness':

> Survey the World, and with impartial Eyes
> Consider, and examine, all who rise,
> Weigh well their Actions, and their treacherous Ends,
> How Greatness grows, and by what Steps ascends,
> What Murders, Treasons, Perjuries, Deceit,
> How many fall, to make one Monster great.

The poet becomes slightly more specific:

> Wou'd you command? Have Fortune in your Pow'r?
> Hug whom you stab, and smile when you devour:
> Be bloody, false, flatter, forswear, and lie,
> Turn Pander, Pathick, Parasite, or Spy,
> Such thriving Arts may your wish'd Purpose bring,
> At least a General be, perhaps a King.

The 'honest Man' shuns any base embrace with prostitute 'Fortune'.[50] Cato is the type of the 'honest Man' whose conduct is an *exemplum* Granville considers at length. The polemical use of the ancient Roman republican in his Jacobite propaganda *Letter* of 1722 is clearly presaged in this poem of 1690:

> Had *Cato* bent beneath the conquering Cause,
> He might have liv'd to give new Senates Laws;
> But on vile Terms disdaining to be great,
> He perish'd by his Choice, and not his Fate:
> Honours and Life th' Usurper bids, and all
> That vain mistaken Men good Fortune call,
> Virtue forbids, and sets before his Eyes
> An honest Death, which he accepts, and dies.
> O glorious Resolution! Noble Pride!

---

[49] 'Occasion'd by the foregoing [Verses sent to the Author in his Retirement, Written by Mrs. Elizabeth Higgons]', in Granville, *Poems*, pp. 96–101. Higgons's poem is on pp. 94–6. The poems are in *The Genuine Works in Verse and Prose of the Right Honourable George Granville, Lord Lansdowne* (London, 1732), I, 22–4; 24–9.

[50] All quotations from Granville, *Poems*, p. 97.

> More honour'd than the Tyrant liv'd, he dy'd,
> More prais'd, more lov'd, more envy'd in his Doom,
> Than *Caesar* trampling on the Rights of *Rome*.[51]

The mood and rhetoric of such a passage might be compared with Swift's 'Ode to Sancroft', where 'Heaven and Cato both are pleas'd' with 'Saint' Sancroft, high above 'Caesar's court', and in an apotheosized 'retreat' (*Poems*, I, 33–42).

Granville's poem represents the court of King William III as a grotesque and vicious inversion of a natural order. The world of the God-like King 'Just James' and his 'beauteous Queen', the '*Jove* and *Juno*' of Granville's celebratory loyalist verses,[52] has been desecrated with 'endless Noise', 'Blood and Horror', 'unnatural Joys', and a pygmy parody of sacred monarchy. Let others 'cringe in Courts, depending on the Nods / Of strutting Pygmies, who wou'd pass for Gods.'[53] Deploying the topos of the honest happy man in pastoral retirement, Granville's poem concludes in affirmation of quietist retreat from impiety.[54] Granville's poem (and particularly such lines as those comparing the new monarchs to 'strutting Pygmies') is an early instance of a Tory anti-Court rhetoric that attained fine asperity in Swift's satire – in the sneering diminution of the Augustan pretensions of the Hanoverian Whig court to Lilliputian proportions in Part I of *Gulliver's Travels*, in the satiric anthropology of Part IV of the *Travels* where the degenerate rudiments of corrupt modern polity are discovered in the antics of the noisome anthropoid Yahoos, and in the violent anti-Hanoverian satire of such a passage as this from Swift's *An Epistle to a Lady*:

> All the Vices of a Court,
> Do but serve to make me Sport.
> Shou'd a Monkey wear a Crown,
> Must I tremble at his Frown?
> Could I not, thro' all his Ermin,
> Spy the strutting chatt'ring Vermin?
> Safely write a smart Lampoon,
> To expose the brisk Baboon?[55]

---

[51] Granville, *Poems*, p. 98.   [52] See Granville, *Poems*, pp. 12, 13, 17.

[53] Granville, *Poems*, p. 99.

[54] Granville, *Poems*, pp. 100, 101.

[55] *Poems*, II, 634 (lines 147–54). Compare also Ralph Gray, *The Coronation Ballad* (1689), *POAS*, 5, 39–45, for an example of a Jacobite poem describing William III as 'a monkey', a 'strutting thing called a Punchinello', and an 'ape' (p. 41).

It is interesting in the light of Granville's Jacobite Tory appropriation of Cato to read in his important poem *An Essay Upon Unnatural Flights in Poetry* (1701) the criticism of Lucan's famous and controversial line (from *Pharsalia*, I, 128) *Victrix causa deis placuit, sed victa Catoni*.[56] Granville condemns the 'Roman Wit, who impiously divides / His Heroe and his Gods to different sides' but acknowledges that the 'admiring World still stands in his defence'. And indeed, the critic reflects, 'How o'ft, Alas! the best of men in vain / Contend for blessings that the worst obtain!'[57] Granville's literary criticism contains covert contemporary political implication. Should not Cato, the devout 'honest Man', accept the cause sanctioned by the Will of God? Did not William III rule with providential approval? The argument that the Revolution was a work of Providence had perhaps persuaded many Tories to transfer allegiance to the Revolution government. The apostate nonjuror William Sherlock had argued, in his sensational bestseller *The Case of the Allegiance Due to Soveraign Powers* (1691 [1690]), that God's authority was with the monarch in actual, settled possession of the crown.[58] Granville's particular resolution of the apparent difficulty that the gods are on the side of victorious Caesar's cause (i.e. the Williamite or Revolution) and not virtuous Cato's cause (i.e. the Jacobite), looks forward to the assassination of 'Caesar'. In the text of the *Essay* it is explained that 'The Gods, permitting Traitors to succeed, / Become not Parties in an impious deed.' Ultimately Cato and the gods were found to be on the same side against Caesar: 'And, by the Tyrants Murder, we may find / That *Cato* and the Gods were of a mind.'[59] Granville's note to this part of the *Essay* concerning Lucan's line, in the 'Explanatory Annotations' appended to the poem, implies divine approval of the assassination of usurping tyrants:

Victrix Causa deis placuit, sed Victa Catoni. The consent of so many Ages having establish'd the reputation of this Line, the Author perhaps may be judg'd too presuming in this attack. But he cou'd not suppose that *Cato*, who is describ'd to have been a Man of strict devotion, and more resembling the Gods than men, would choose any party in opposition to the Gods ... Besides, success implies

---

[56] Granville's *Essay* is unoriginal and is heavily derived from Bouhours's *La Manière de Bien Penser dans les Ouvrages de l'Esprit* (1687), see George Granville, Lord Lansdowne, *An Essay Upon Unnatural Flights in Poetry* (1701), in *Critical Essays of the Seventeenth Century*, edited by J. E. Spingarn, 3 vols. (Oxford, 1908–9), III, 292–8 and notes, pp. 337–9; Handasyde, *Granville the Polite*, pp. 64–7, 253n, 254n.

[57] *An Essay Upon Unnatural Flights in Poetry*, lines 7–12, *Critical Essays*, III, 294.

[58] See Mark Goldie, 'The Revolution of 1689 and the Structure of Political Argument', 473–564 (p. 557, no. 150).

[59] *An Essay Upon Unnatural Flights in Poetry*, lines 13–16, *Critical Essays*, III, 294.

permission, and not approbation; to place the Gods always on the thriving side is to make 'em partakers in all successful wickedness. They judge before the conclusion of the Action: The Catastrophe will best determine on which side is Providence: And the Violent death of *Caesar* acquits the Gods from being Companions of his *Usurpation*.[60]

Elizabeth Handasyde, in her excellent biography of Granville, notes that his cousins George, Thomas and Bevil Higgons were involved in the Jacobite plots of William's reign, although she remarks of Granville that the 'imitator of Cato was not likely to scheme for the assassination of even so fiercely hated an enemy as William'.[61] But it may be inferred from the evidence produced here that Granville entertained the idea. And he was not alone. The great Jacobite Tory master, John Dryden, anticipates Granville in political approval of the tyrannicide, Marcus Brutus.[62]

Reflecting a strand of revolutionism in his Grotian intellectual inheritance, Swift vicariously entertains the idea of justified rebellion and the assassination of usurpers and tyrants in his great satires. The account in Part III of *Gulliver's Travels* of the Lindalinian rebellion against the court of the flying island Laputa (an ambiguous allegory of Irish resistance to the recent English Court Whig attempt to impose Wood's halfpence) was not in any edition of *Gulliver's Travels* in Swift's lifetime. The rebellion of the Lindalinians 'had like to have put a Period to the Fate of that Monarchy, at least as it is now instituted'. The final sentence of the passage reads:

I was assured by a great Minister, that if the Island had descended so near the Town, as not to be able to raise it self, the Citizens were determined to fix it for ever, to kill the King and all his Servants, and entirely change the Government.

(*PW*, XI, 309–10)

The omission of this passage from printed editions in Swift's lifetime reflects a cautious castration of the political attack on the established monarchy. These radical political sentiments, conveyed here in the carapace of a fictional, mock travel book, were usually only openly expressed in the anonymous extremist Jacobite press (where it was judged to be not unlawful for the body politic to rise against an illegitimate king or usurper) or by Jacobites condemned to the scaffold.

---

[60] *Explanatory Annotations on the foregoing Poem, Critical Essays*, III, 296–7.

[61] Handasyde, *Granville the Polite*, p. 18.

[62] *A Character of Polybius and His Writings* (1693), in *The Works of John Dryden: Volume XX, Prose 1691–1698*, edited by A. E. Wallace Maurer and George R. Guffey (Berkeley, Los Angeles, London, 1989), p. 18.

For example, Robert Charnock's 'Letter to a Friend, Written Shortly Before His Execution' is an open expression of extreme Jacobite views by a man condemned for his part in the Assassination Plot of 1696. Charnock asks in his 'Letter':

shall this Perkin Warbeck of a King be held sacred in his Person, not to be touched, but suffered with impunety to massacre and destroy all the honest part of mankind? Others may judge of this as they please; for my owne part I am convinced that, as Tertulliam says, *In hostes publicos omnis homo est miles*, and that t'is the duty of every loyall subject that has the courage and the opportunity to do it, to rid the world of a Publick Enemy, who has kindled a War all over Europe, and sacrificed more lives of men to his insatiable ambition and usurpation, then all your Marius and Syllas, Cesars and Pompys putt together.[63]

After considering William III as 'an Enemy', Charnock then considers him 'in his particular character of an Usurper'. William is 'an unjust ravisher' and 'what ever may lawfully be attempted against the worst of Theeves and Robbers, not only may, but ought to, be attempted against him'.[64] Charnock's 'Letter' provides a classic formulation of the militant Jacobite libertarian language that the disaffected Swift would echo, not *in propria persona* of course, but through a putative speaker, in *Gulliver's Travels*. Charnock justifies the Jacobite attempt against the Revolution government of William III:

And what can a common Usurper expect, when Julius Cesar himself for usurping upon the freedom of the Roman Commonwealth could not scape the poniards of Brutus and Cassius, and others the best men of that time, and some them (by him reputed) his intimat freinds?

To this may be added the authority of the learned Grotius an Author equally famous for erudition and moderation, and therfor received by all Partys, who in his book *de Jure Belli* tells us that when any one by an unjust war contrary to the law of nations shall usurp the Supreme Power, he may be lawfully killd: *jure potest occidi*, are his words, *a quolibet privato*, by every private person that owes allegeance to him who has the Right.[65]

---

[63] 'Mr Charnock's Letter to a Friend, Written Shortly Before His Execution', reprinted as Appendix 1 in Jane Garrett, *The Triumphs of Providence: The Assassination Plot, 1696* (Cambridge, 1980), pp. 265–71 (p. 267). For an account of Charnock, see pp. 28–32, 204–5. For Jacobite 'dying speeches' after the '45, see *The Lyon in Mourning*, edited by Henry Paton, 3 vols. (Edinburgh, 1895–6). On the 'free Jacobitism' of such printed last words, see Erskine-Hill, 'Literature and the Jacobite Cause: Was There a Rhetoric of Jacobitism?', pp. 56–9. See also Daniel Szechi, 'The Jacobite Theatre of Death', in *The Jacobite Challenge*, pp. 57–73.
[64] 'Mr Charnock's Letter', pp. 268–9.   [65] 'Mr Charnock's Letter', pp. 269–70.

Swift had appropriated Cato and Brutus for the Tory party cause against that modern Caesar, the Duke of Marlborough, in *Some Reasons to Prove, That no Person is obliged by his Principles, as a Whig, to Oppose Her Majesty or Her Present Ministry. In a Letter to a Whig-Lord* (1712). Those icons of Roman virtue, Cato and Brutus, the Whig lord learns, 'joined heartily on that side which undertook to preserve the Laws and Constitution, against the Usurpations of a victorious General, whose Ambition was bent to overthrow them' (*PW*, VI, 134).[66] But the most famous of Swift's references to Brutus occurs in Part III of *Gulliver's Travels* when Gulliver is in Glubbdubdrib, the island of sorcerers or magicians. When antiquity is summoned into Gulliver's presence by the island's governor, Gulliver is afforded the prospect of an imminent Civil War battle, and there is a remarkable celebration of the uncorrupted Senate of Rome, Brutus and tyrannicide:

I SAW *Caesar* and *Pompey* at the Head of their Troops just ready to engage. I saw the former in his last great Triumph. I desired that the Senate of *Rome* might appear before me in one large Chamber, and a modern Representative, in Counterview, in another. The first seemed to be an Assembly of Heroes and Demy-Gods; the other a Knot of Pedlars, Pick-pockets, Highwaymen and Bullies.

The Governor at my Request gave the Sign for *Caesar* and *Brutus* to advance towards us. I was struck with a profound Veneration at the Sight of *Brutus*; and could easily discover the most consummate Virtue, the greatest Intrepidity, and Firmness of Mind, the truest Love of his Country, and general Benevolence for Mankind in every Lineament of his Countenance. I observed with much Pleasure, that these two Persons were in good Intelligence with each other; and *Caesar* freely confessed to me, that the greatest Actions of his own Life were not equal by many Degrees to the Glory of taking it away.

(PW, XI, 195–6)

Swift's vicarious entertainment of tyrannicide in this passage and in his account of the Lindalinian rebellion have startling analogues in Jacobite polemical literature of the 1720s. For example, in defending the Bishop of Rochester (convicted of Jacobite conspiracy) *The True Briton* found this analogue for Atterbury's public spirit in a time of Whig tyranny:

The Great *Brutus* who stabb'd *Caesar*, is a Noble Mark of Publick Spirit. *Caesar* was his Friend, and had served him in many Instances; yet, when he trampled on the Laws, the general Good was preferr'd to his private Inclination; and

---

[66] Cato and Brutus are Swiftian heroes: see, for example: *PW*, I, 222; *PW*, II, 2; *PW*, V, 84; *Poems*, II, 724. Brutus and Cato are members of the illustrious '*Sextumvirate* to which all the

when he imbrued his Hands in his Blood, it was the *Tyrant*, not the *Friend*, he struck.[67]

Granville in *A Letter from a Noble-Man Abroad, to His Friend in England* exhorts 'good *English-men*' to 'take a *Roman* Resolution to save their Country, or perish with it':

Brutus was a sworn Enemy to *Pompey*, the Murderer of his Father; but when it happened that *Rome* must perish, or *Pompey* be supported, *Brutus* became *Pompey*'s Friend.

Brutus took an Oath to *Caesar*, but *Brutus* never swore to be an Enemy to his Country.

Brutus owed much to *Caesar*, but *Brutus* thought private Benefits as well as private Injuries were to be sacrificed to the Publick Safety. And *Brutus* was an honourable Man.[68]

The Jacobite Tory journalist Nathaniel Mist, whose paper industriously publicized Swift's Irish writings against the Hanoverian Whig government in England,[69] printed this explanation of the significance of Cato and Brutus. It is worth quoting at some length, to illustrate how Swift's sortie into Roman history and his invocation of a patriotic Roman assassin had topical polemical resonance and militant innuendo and application:

Some late Circumstances in the World have put me upon the Subject of looking back into History ... And, I find, that most of these adventurous Heroes, who have launched thus voluntarily into Eternity, did it rather because they were *sick* of the *Times*, than of *themselves*: Rather because they could not survive the *Loss* of *Liberty*, or *Oppression* of their *Country* ...

The two most eminent Instances in *Roman* History, of such as thus desperately made an End of themselves, are those of *Cato Uticensis*, and *Marcus Brutus*: The first died because he could not get the better of Tyranny; and the latter, because, when he had struck to root out one Oppressor, he was pursued by more dangerous Tyrants than him whom his Love to *Rome* only moved him to destroy. *Cato* was zealous for the Laws and Liberty of the Commonwealth: And

Ages of the World cannot add a Seventh' in *Gulliver's Travels*, Part III, Chapter VII, *PW*, XI, 196.

67 *The True Briton*, no. 20 (9 August 1723). Paul Chapman has described the radical whiggish and regicidal elements in Jacobite polemic: see his 'Jacobite Political Argument in England, 1714–1766'.

68 [George Granville, Baron Lansdowne], *A Letter* ..., pp. 6–7. Also compare William Shippen, *Faction Display'd* (1704), lines 486–7: 'Where is the Noble *Roman* Spirit fled, / Which once inspir'd thy antient Patriots dead?', *POAS*, 6, 671.

69 On Swift and Mist, see Paul Sawyer, 'Swift, Mist, and a Lincoln's Inn Fields Benefit', *Notes and Queries*, ns, 24 (1977), 225–8; Jonathan Swift and Thomas Sheridan, *The Intelligencer*, edited by James Woolley (Oxford, 1992), Appendix D, pp. 236–43.

Brutus loved *Caesar*, even when he struck him: But when *Caesar* trampled on the Rights of *Rome*, then *Brutus* could forget his Affection to the *Man*, to put an End to the *Tyrant*.[70]

Bolingbroke, in exile, compares himself with Brutus in a letter to Swift in 1724 (*Corr*, III, 29).[71] Roman republican, regicidal radicalism in Swift's *Gulliver's Travels*, consonant as it is with an understood Jacobite political language,[72] has the effect of suggesting not an anachronistic Old or True Whig political stance as is supposed in Swift studies, but the Jacobite velleities of a disaffected High Churchman whose loyalty to the settlement founded upon the Revolution could be radically ambiguous.

It should be said immediately that as a High Church Anglican priest, Swift excoriated the regicide of lawful kings, anathematized the 'murderous Puritan-parliament' and the 'horrid rebellion', venerated 'the excellent King and blessed Martyr CHARLES I, who rather chose to die on a scaffold than betray the religion and liberties of his people, wherewith GOD and the laws had entrusted him', and proscribed the principles whose ultimate provenance was Geneva, which 'carried the blessed Martyr to the scaffold' ('A Sermon Upon the Martyrdom of K. Charles I', *PW*, IX, 219–31). The exiguity of the Anglican establishment in Ireland would have heightened M. B. (perhaps Marcus Brutus) Drapier's sense of the risks of counter-revolution against the Hanoverian monarchy and a Catholic Stuart accession. (Although, of course, some Irish Anglican Tories such as Henry Dodwell, Charles Leslie and George Kelly were Jacobites.) Yet in the 1720s and 1730s Swift is clearly attracted to notions of tyrannicide. In Glubbdubdrib

---

[70] *A Collection of Miscellany Letters, Selected out of Mist's 'Weekly Journal'*, 4 vols. (London, 1722–7), II, 156–7.

[71] Bolingbroke reveals his interest in 'Cato, and Brutus, and Pompey and others' in a 1730 letter to Swift, *Corr*, III, 388.

[72] Whig partisans identified the '*Jacobite* Party' with regicide, see [John Hervey], *The Conduct of the Opposition, and the Tendency of Modern Patriotism* ... (London, 1734), pp. 44–5; E. W. Rosenheim, Jr, 'Swift and the Martyred Monarch', *Philological Quarterly*, 54 (1975), 178–94 (pp. 184–5, 191, quoting Benjamin Hoadly and Francis Hutchinson). In *The Freeholder*, no. 51 (15 June 1716), Addison warns of the pernicious effects of 'following blindly the Examples of Persons to be met with in *Greek* and *Roman* History'. He reminds readers: 'Our Regicides in the Commission of the most execrable Murder used to justify themselves from the Conduct of *Brutus*', Joseph Addison, *The Freeholder*, edited by James Leheny (Oxford, 1979), p. 257. Matthew Tindal warns that approval of Brutus and tyrannicide encourages the regicidal extremism of High Church theocracy, see *The Judgment of Dr. Prideaux, in Condemning the Murder of Julius Caesar, by the Conspirators, as a most Villanous Act, maintain'd* ... (London, 1721), esp. pp. 38–40. For Court Whig response to the Opposition invocation of Cato, see Reed Browning, *Political and Constitutional Ideas of the Court Whigs* (Baton Rouge, 1982), esp. pp. 210–13.

Gulliver relates: 'I chiefly fed mine Eyes with beholding the Destroyers of Tyrants and Usurpers, and Restorers of Liberty to oppressed and injured Nations' (*PW*, XI, 196). Gulliver's entertainment among the dead may contain a buried allusion to Horace's *Odes* (II, xiii, 31–2). The passage in Horace's *Odes* imagines the shades in the underworld packed shoulder to shoulder, drinking in with their ears the recitals by Sappho and Alcaeus of battles and of tyrants driven out. The Latin verse is quoted by Swift in an annotation to *A Short History of the Kings of England. Shewing What Right Every King Had to the Crown, and the Manner of Their Wearing of It. Especially from William the Conqueror, to James the Second, That Abdicated His Three Kingdoms* (1715) – Swift's signature on the annotated pamphlet is dated 1736. Swift wrote:

> ――――― Et exactos Tyrannos
> Densum humeris bibit aure vulgus.[73]

In a letter of 1735 Swift described James II as 'a weak bigoted Papist, desirous like all Kings of absolute power, but not properly a tyrant'.[74] But the Hanoverians were the real thing. Writing to his Jacobite friend John Barber in September 1735, he says that 'without some unexpected assistance from Heaven, many thousand now alive will see [England] governed by an absolute [Mon]arch' (*Corr*, IV, 381). In a letter to William Pulteney of 12 May 1735 Swift wishes 'princes had capacity to read the history of the *Roman* emperors; how many of them were murdered by their own army, and the same may be said of the *Ottomans* by their janissaries; and many other examples are easy to be found' (*Corr*, IV, 337). Swift though an ideological conservative is an imaginative extremist. There is a flirtation with proscribed, extremist political ideas in his literary work. It is not only in *Gulliver's Travels* that the idea of king-killing is entertained.

A Tale of a Tub (largely written, according to Swift's statements in the text, in 1696 and 1697),[75] participates in the political polyphony surrounding the Jacobite Assassination Plot of 1696. Traces of a political discourse of disaffection can be registered in the satire's violent treatment of heroes, Hercules and Henri IV. The satirized putative

---

[73] Michael Treadwell, 'Swift and *A Short History of the Kings of England*', in *Swift and His Contexts*, edited by John Irwin Fischer et al. (New York, 1989), pp. 175–87 (p. 178); Horace, *The Odes and Epodes*, translated by C. E. Bennett, Loeb Classical Library (Cambridge, Mass. and London, 1978), pp. 140–1.

[74] *Corr*, IV, 321 (Swift to Thomas Beach, 12 April 1735). See also *PW*, V, 311–13, 317–19, where James is described as 'a Cowardly Popish King'. He 'unkinged himself for Popery'.

[75] On the date of composition, see *Tale*, pp. xliii–xlvii; *PW*, I, xv–xviii, xxii. The 'Dedication to Somers' and 'The Bookseller to the Reader' were probably written in 1704.

author of the *Tale* is a celebrant of heresy and dissent in religion, faction in the state and modern critical theory in the commonwealth of letters. In Section III, '*A Digression concerning* Criticks', the enthusiastic chronicler links his true 'Criticks' with 'Antient Heroes', but reports that:

Heroick Virtue it self hath not been exempt from the Obloquy of Evil Tongues. For it hath been objected, that those Antient Heroes, famous for their Combating so many Giants, and Dragons, and Robbers, were in their own Persons a greater Nuisance to Mankind, than any of those Monsters they subdued; and therefore, to render their Obligations more Compleat, when all *other* Vermin were destroy'd, should in Conscience have concluded with the same Justice upon themselves: as *Hercules* most generously did.

(*Tale*, p. 94)

A principal target of Swift's satiric animus and exterminatory impulse here is modern criticism and its prominent practitioners. An operation involving 'Ratsbane, or Hemp' is proposed for 'every *True Critick*' (*Tale*, p. 95). But heroes, and in particular, Hercules, are also slaughtered by the satirist. There is a *frisson* of unspeakable political implication if we attend to the historical semantics of a satire condemning Hercules in 1696. After the Revolution, the Protestant Hero, William III, was frequently depicted as, or associated with, Hercules. The image of William as Hercules was overt and ubiquitous in medals, prints, poetry and encomiastic iconography of the period.[76] As we have seen, Swift traduces the Revolution regime and associates William with Hercules in the violent, unfinished poem 'On the Burning of Whitehall in 1698'. In the anonymous *Tale* written around the time of the Jacobite Assassination Plot against William's life, a radical satiric operation on 'Hercules' is performed for the reader. There are classical sources or pre-texts behind the diminution of Hercules in the *Tale*,[77] but there is topical political resonance in Swift's satiric killing.

'*A Digression concerning the Original, the Use and Improvement of* Madness *in a Commonwealth*' in Section IX of *A Tale of a Tub* contains an account of the assassination of Henri IV of France. The putative author, the

---

[76] *The Age of William III & Mary II: Power, Politics, and Patronage 1688–1702: A Reference Encyclopedia and Exhibition Catalogue*, edited by Robert P. Maccubbin and Martha Hamilton-Phillips (Williamsburg, 1989), pp. 8–10, see plates IV, 7–10, 318, 371, 413, 414 (pp. xviii, 8–10, 261, 289, 323); Stephen B. Baxter, 'William III as Hercules: the Political Implications of Court Culture', in *The Revolution of 1688–1689: Changing Perspectives*, edited by Lois G. Schwoerer (Cambridge, 1992), pp. 95–106.

[77] Compare, for example, Lucretius, *De Rerum Natura*, translated by W. H. D. Rouse, revised by Martin Ferguson Smith, Loeb Classical Library (Cambridge, Mass. and London, 1975), Book 5.22–42, pp. 381–3.

Grub Street modernist, tells us that 'the greatest Actions that have been performed in the World, under the Influence of Single Men; which are, *The Establishment of New Empires by Conquest: The Advance and Progress of New Schemes in Philosophy; and the contriving, as well as the propagating of New Religions*' are the products of mad persons. The two examples of the madness of military conquest, violently satirized by Swift, are 'A certain Great Prince' (a note informs us that 'Harry *the Great of* France' is meant) and '*the Present* French *King*' Louis XIV. The account of 'Henri IV' begins:

A certain Great Prince raised a mighty Army, filled his Coffers with infinite Treasures, provided an invincible Fleet, and all this, without giving the least Part of his Design to his greatest Ministers, or his nearest Favourites. Immediately the whole World was alarmed; the neighbouring Crowns, in trembling Expectation, towards what Point the Storm would burst; the small Politicians, every where forming profound Conjectures. Some believed he had laid a Scheme for Universal Monarchy: Others, after much Insight, determined the Matter to be a Project for pulling down the *Pope*, and setting up the *Reformed* Religion, which had once been his own.

The disease of restless military ambition was cured. For in 'the midst of all these Projects and Preparations; a certain *State-Surgeon*' (a note refers to 'Ravillac, *who stabb'd* Henry *the Great in his Coach*') 'attempted the Cure, at one Blow performed the Operation, broke the Bag, and out flew the *Vapour*; nor did any thing want to render it a compleat Remedy, only, that the Prince unfortunately happened to Die in the Performance.' The putative author goes on to explain for the curious, mystified reader that the prince's military 'Projects and Preparations' had a bathetic, circumstantial concupiscent motive – Henri IV's unsatisfied sexual desire for the princess of Condé – concluding:

The very same Principle that influences a *Bully* to break the Windows of a Whore, who has jilted him, naturally stirs up a Great Prince to raise mighty Armies, and dream of nothing but Sieges, Battles, and Victories.[78]

The ironies in this famous section of *A Tale of a Tub* are unstable, but the passage approves the assassination of Henri IV. The choice of Henri IV as satiric victim may have been prompted by the Restoration paper war over toleration. Erastian loyalists and Dissenters during the reigns of Charles II and James II expressed admiration for Henri IV and his

---

[78] *Tale*, pp. 162–5. Swift's source for the story about Henri IV is in François Eudes de Mézeray, *Abregé Chronologique de l'Histoire de France* (Amsterdam, 1696), VI, 368ff; see *Tale*, p. 163 and W. A. Speck, 'Swift and the Historian', in *Proceedings*, pp. 257–68 (pp. 260–1).

Edict of Nantes. They affirmed this example of Catholic tolerance when supporting Stuart attempts at prerogative toleration and opposing persecution by Anglican prelate and magistrate.[79] For anticlerical Whigs the assassinations of Henri III and Henri IV were principal exhibits of the perfidy of priestcraft and popery.[80] Tindal pointedly associated High Church theocratic persecutory ambition and approval of the regicide of a prince 'who usurps on what they call the Rights of God's Holy Church' with the case of 'a Neighbouring Country' where 'two Successive Princes were assassinated on this Account'.[81] Swift abhorred Henri III and compares King George to the French King in his vituperative marginal annotations to *The Historie of the Civill Warres of France*, the English translation of Davila's *Historia delle Guerre Civili de Francia* (1630) published in London in 1647.[82] Although Swift refers to Henri IV as 'that great Prince' and lists him among the persons who *'made great* FIGURES *in some particular Action or Circumstance of their Lives'* (*PW*, V, 109, 83–4), the satiric passage in the *Tale* ambiguously endorses the destruction of the militaristic, tolerationist prince by a priest. There is a clinical account of Henri IV's assassination as a cure for illness in the French body politic in a Restoration tract supporting the Sacramental Test Act. The sardonic diagnosis can be compared with that offered in *A Tale of a Tub*. France was

in danger of becoming totally *Hugonot* it self, had not the Bloody *Vespers* of St. *Bartholomew* in the Year 1572, by the *Parisian Massacre*, as they thought, let out the most dangerous and Feavourish *Protestant* Blood in the *Body*; and after that,

[79] See Mark Goldie, 'Sir Peter Pett, Sceptical Toryism and the Science of Toleration in the 1680s', pp. 247–73 (esp. p. 258), and Goldie, 'The Huguenot Experience and the Problem of Toleration in Restoration England', in *The Huguenots and Ireland: Anatomy of an Emigration*, edited by C. E. J. Caldicott, H. Gough, J.-P. Pittion (Co. Dublin, 1987), pp. 175–203 (esp. pp. 195–6). For examples of Dissenters approving Henri IV, see John Owen, *A Peace-Offering, in An Apology and Humble Plea for Indulgence and Liberty of Conscience* (London, 1667) in *The Works of John Owen, D. D.*, edited by William H. Goold, 24 vols. (London and Edinburgh, 1850–5), XIII, p. 566; William Penn, *The Great Case of Liberty of Conscience* ... ([London], 1670), p. 41; [John Humfrey], *Considerations Moving to a Toleration, and Liberty of Conscience* ... (London, 1685), p. 10; Henry Care, ed., *The King's Right of Indulgence in Spiritual Matters* ... (London, 1688), pp. 5, 11, 13; John Bellers, *Some Reasons for an European State* ... (London, 1710), pp. 17, 20.
[80] [Henry Care], *A Word in Season* ... (London, 1679), pp. 7–8; [Robert Ferguson], *The Third Part of No Protestant Plot* ... (London, 1682), pp. 133–4; 'Popish Treaties not to be rely'd on ... ' in *A Third Collection of Papers Relating to the Present Juncture of Affairs in England* (London, [1688]), p. 33; *Priest-Craft Expos'd* ... (London, 1691), p. 24; [John Dennis], *The Danger of Priestcraft to Religion and Government* ... (London, 1702), p. 17.
[81] [Matthew Tindal], *The Judgment of Dr. Prideaux* ..., p. 39.
[82] Hermann J. Real and Heinz J. Vienken, '"A Pretty Mixture": Books from Swift's Library at Abbotsford House', *Bulletin of The John Rylands University Library of Manchester*, 67 (1984), 522–43 (esp. pp. 538–9).

had it not been rescued from that danger in the *Head*, by the more than *Roman*, the *Roman Catholique* courages of *Clement* and *Ravilliac*, by whose Assassinating Hands the Two *Henries*, the *Third* and *Fourth* fell.[83]

The political focus here is on the fanatical anti-Protestantism and extremism of the Church of Rome. Swift's diagnosis is that the monarch deserved the treatment administered by the monarchomach.

The fact that Swift could choose to write a cold-blooded satire of a militaristic great prince cured by an assassin when the Assassination Plot of 1696 was the sensational topic of public discourse is interesting. The account may have had a further *frisson* of topical political resonance for some readers. The restless but impotent military ambition of William III and his ruinously expensive projects and preparations were a frequent subject of sardonic Jacobite Tory political satire in poems and prose fiction on affairs of state. Chapter XIII of *An Historical Romance of the Wars, Between the Mighty Giant Gallieno, and the Great Knight Nasonius and His Associates* (1694), for example, is a satiric burlesque of William's 'vast attempt' to overthrow Louis XIV and secure 'Immortal Glory':

Long, very long had this mighty Project amused all *Europe*; huge preparations of Cannons, Mortars, Bombs, and other formidable Military Engines had marched with great Solemnity ... and were Embarqu'd. Many hundreds of Transport Ships, and *Well-boats* were taken up, and made ready ... The *Nasonian* Courtiers were all turn'd *Astrologers*, and prognosticated the miserable Downfall of King *Gallieno* ... the Grounds of it so firmly and wisely laid by the *unerring* Politicks of Nasonius ...

The most searching Wits of *Utopia* were too shallow to sound the dark bottom of it, and were at a deadly plunge how to frame the least Conjecture where this *iresistable Thunderbolt* would light ...

It all comes to nothing, however: 'In a word, this grand design, as it was conceived and born in a Mystery, so it died as Mysteriously too. The reason of its miscarriage being so carefully hush'd up, that to this day few know certainly the occasion of it. Some undertake to clear *Nasonius*'s Credit, and Conduct, by alledging that he never meant or designed *any thing* in his Life but to March to and fro with a great Army at his Heels, to shew his Greatness' and to take English money.[84]

[83] *The Established Test, In order to the Security of His Majesties Sacred Person, and Government, and the Protestant Religion. Against the Malitious Attempts and Treasonable Machinations of Rome* (London, 1679), pp. 5-6.
[84] [John Sergeant], *An Historical Romance*, pp. 60-2. For further examples of Jacobite scorn of William's militarism, see *POAS*, 5, 388-9.

William III was called a 'Great Prince' in contemporary panegyric. The note in the *Tale* informing the reader that by a 'certain Great Prince' 'Harry *the Great of* France' is meant, perhaps indicates an awareness of this other signification (*Tale*, p. 163). Henri IV was not the only 'Great Prince' a contemporary reader of the *Tale* would have thought of in juxtaposition with Louis XIV. In seventeenth-century iconography both Henri IV and William III were identified with Hercules, whose destruction is approved in Swift's satire.[85] According to Paul Monod, the Reverend William Cox of Quinton, Gloucestershire, was perhaps the last case of a cleric prosecuted for Jacobitism in William III's reign. At the time the Assassination Plot was discovered he was alleged to have said: '"I see there is a plott & that he [King William] ... has narrowly escaped the hand of justice but vengeance will overtake him he will die the death of a Tyrant, there will a Raveillac arise."'[86] The Jacobite Charlwood Lawton in 1693 hoped for a restoration of James II without bloodshed. 'They are state-quacks, who only understand phlebotomy', he wrote. 'A good physician [James II] will sweeten and compose the mass of humours, and by proper lenitives quiet all our boiling spirits, and correct the temperament of the state into obedience, without creating faintnesses, or destroying our vitals.'[87] *A Tale of a Tub* imagines more radical surgery for one kind of disease in the body politic.

It might be assumed that Swift who, for instance, loyally dedicated Sir William Temple's *Letters* 'To His Most Sacred Majesty William III' in 1699, naturally would have abhorred the Jacobite Assassination Plot of 1695–6, and that this tentative suggestion of a Jacobite political implication in the satire of Hercules and Henri IV in the anonymous *Tale* is an example of a meaning the author never imagined, and for which critics who discover such unintended meanings are satirized in the 'Apology' Swift affixed to the fifth edition of the *Tale* (1710). Yet there is some slight evidence in Swift's case, as perhaps in his friend

---

[85] For William III as a 'Great Prince', see *Musae Cantabrigienses* (c3v). For Henri IV as Hercules, see Corrado Vivanti, 'Henry IV, The Gallic Hercules', *Journal of the Warburg and Courtauld Institutes*, 30 (1967), 176–97. It might be suggestive of an oblique identification of Henri IV and William that in the previous paragraph to the account of Henri IV's '*Vapour*' it is said that 'Fumes issuing from a Jakes, will furnish as comely and useful a Vapor, as Incence from an Altar' (*Tale*, p. 163). William's defecation and stink at his coronation was a Jacobite satiric motif, see *An Historical Romance*, pp. 37–9.

[86] Paul Monod, *Jacobitism and the English People, 1688–1788*, p. 146.

[87] [Charlwood Lawton], *A French Conquest neither Desiderable nor Practicable. Dedicated to the King of England* (London, 1693), *Somers Tracts*, X, 475.

Alexander Pope's,[88] of an ambiguous attitude to the Assassination Plot. In the *Examiner* of 15 March 1711 Swift tries to find an historical parallel for the assassination attempt on Robert Harley by 'a *French Papist*', Antoine de Guiscard. He refers to the assassinations of Caesar, Henri III and Henri IV. 'In our own Country we have, I think, but one Instance of this sort, which has made any Noise', John Felton's stabbing of the first Duke of Buckingham. Although assassins are deplored as 'desperate Villains', it seems to be Swift's view in the *Examiner* that a patriotic and principled motive admits 'some Extenuation' of an assassin's crime. But Guiscard's attempt 'seems to have outdone them all in every heightning Circumstance, except the difference of Persons between a King and a great Minister' (*Exam*, pp. 297–9). The glaring omission in Swift's short history of assassination is duly observed in the Whig *Medley* of 19 March 1711 (and Mainwaring and Oldmixon may have been closer to Swift's private attitudes than they knew):

'Twas very odd in him, when he was reckoning up all the *Assassination-Plots*, not to mention that against King *William*; but no doubt he can tell why 'twas omitted. The Tories don't love to hear of it, and indeed I can't discommend them: For *Charnock* and *Parkins*, I won't say *Friend*, were as much Assassins as *Clement* and *Ravillac*, tho they did not accomplish their execrable Design. I was surpriz'd to see him so very civil to *Felton*, who butcher'd the Duke of *Buckingham*; *that Act*, says he, *will admit of some Extenuation*: For at that rate *Ravillac* and *Clement* are much more entitled to his good Word. *Felton* said, he did it for the good of the *State*; and the *French* Assassins, for the good of the *Church*. There's no Comparison. The *Extenuation* certainly lies all on the side of the *Fryars*: And let my Friend himself be Judg, I am sure he will be of that mind upon second Thoughts.

(*Exam*, pp. 310–11)

The Latin motto of Swift's *Examiner* of 15 March 1711 is taken from Cicero (*Pro P. Sestio*, 135), who was an important classical authority for monarchomachs. The Latin motto (as translated in the edition of *The Examiner* by Frank H. Ellis) reads:

To apply the Knife to a sound and healthy Part of the Body is Butchery and Cruelty; not real Surgery: These are the true Physicians and Surgeons of a State, who cut off the Pests of Society, like Wens from the human Body.

(*Exam*, p. 296)

---

[88] Incised in stone at the entrance to Pope's grotto is an enigmatic inscription 'JR 1696'. Maynard Mack suspects this stands for James Rex 1696 and that it alludes to the Jacobite Assassination Plot, see Maynard Mack, *The Garden and the City: Retirement and Politics in the Later Poetry of Pope 1731–1743* (Toronto, 1969), pp. 64, 287–8. The 'Jacobite half of his being', however, regarded William III as a usurper (see Mack, p. 5). A satiric epigram on

Ravaillac is such a '*State-Surgeon*' in *A Tale of a Tub* (*Tale*, p. 164). The Whig *Observator* seems to have a point when commenting '*On the Examiner's extraordinary Performance upon Thursday last*': 'The *Examiner* by his *Latin* Sentence seems to think that 'tis as necessary to stab some People with Pen-knives.' Whig polemicists identified the inflammatory author of the '*Examiner*' and '*Publick Spirit of the Whiggs*' with a High Church Tory party design to incite 'a *General Massacre* of all they call'd *Whiggs*'.[89] It may be indicative of Swift's attitude to the Jacobite Assassination Plot that in his satiric ridicule of the Whig prosecution of Francis Atterbury in 'Upon the horrid Plot discovered by Harlequin the B---- of R——'s French Dog', a 'perjur'd *Dog*' denotes Thomas Pendergrass (who revealed the plot to assassinate William III) and George Porter (who turned King's evidence) (*Poems*, I, 298). Elsewhere Swift assassinates the character and family of Pendergrass. The man who revealed the existence of a plot against the King's life, and who was rewarded by William, is vilified by Swift as an 'Informer' (see *Poems*, III, 826; *PW*, V, 264).

That Swift was 'no Jacobite' has long been axiomatic in Swift criticism and biography. If in fact he was a Jacobite, he did not commit explicit incriminating evidence to paper. Claude Rawson describes a 'temperamental defensiveness which built a restless indirection into Swift's most casual utterances and made his writing bristle with aggressive mystifications and the concealments of ironic obliquity'.[90] This observation is especially applicable to Swift the political writer, commenting on the Revolution and the Williamite, Queen Anne and Hanoverian establishment under conditions of censorship. To defame William III or to question the motives of the Revolution could lead to prosecution for sedition. Tories and Jacobites generally practised prudence in print, preferring strategies of obliquity and ambiguity to plain political statement. In his published oppositionist political writing Swift typically claims loyalty to the establishment he contrives to criticize radically. *A Tale of a Tub*, with its violent satire on religious Dissent and pointed reflection on the notorious occasional conformity of Sir Humphrey Edwin, is dedicated (not without ambiguity) to the

---

William is probably Pope's first published poem (see David Nokes, 'Lisping in Political Numbers', *Notes and Queries*, ns, 24 (1977), 228–9; *A New Collection of Poems Relating to State Affairs, From Oliver Cromwell ...*, p. 534).

[89] *The Observator*, X, no. 22 (17 March 1711); [Matthew Tindal], *The Defection Consider'd ...* (London, 1717), pp. 13–14.

[90] Claude Rawson, 'The Character of Swift's Satire: Reflections on Swift, Johnson, and Human Restlessness', in *The Character of Swift's Satire: A Revised Focus*, edited by Claude Rawson (Newark, London and Toronto, 1983), pp. 21–82 (pp. 39–40).

Junto Whig Lord Somers. Swift's Irish pamphleteering against the
English Court Whig government draws arguments from the Whig
enemy's own ideological canon. In Swift's case, however, we are
afforded a measure of insight into his private views on the Revolution
and William III in marginal annotations he made in copies of John
Macky's *Memoirs*, William Howell's *Medulla Historiae Anglicanae*, and
Burnet's *History of His Own Time*.[91] Although well known and often
cited, several of Swift's marginal annotations must, it seems to me,
disturb readings of Swift as a Whig or loyal opposition figure.

In the marginal remarks on Macky, Swift expresses contempt for the
Earl of Romney, who for Macky is 'the great *Wheel* on which the
Revolution rolled'. Swift remarks William's 'very infamous Pleasures'
with his companion the Earl of Albermarle. Of the Earl of Middleton,
the prominent Protestant Jacobite 'Compounder', Swift writes: 'Sr Wm
Temple told me he was a very valuable man, and a good Scholar I once
saw him' (*PW*, V, 258, 259, 262). Swift's marginal comments in
Howell's *Medulla Historiae Anglicanae* are hostile to William and he
queries whether William was a king of the 'Dutch or English' (*PW*, V,
264). As Francis Manley has concluded of the overall effect of Swift's
marginalia in Howell, 'almost all his notes in Howell lament that the
Glorious Revolution and ultimately the Hanoverian accession had not
been averted'. Swift describes the death of Anne's last surviving child,
William, Duke of Gloucester, as the 'Ruin of the English Interest and
Politicks'.[92]

Annotations Swift made in the mid- to late 1730s in the margin of a
copy of Gilbert Burnet's *History of His Own Time* belonging to Dr John
Lyon on the arguments propounded in 1688–9 disclose disaffection with
the Revolution. Against Burnet's account of a 'party ... made up of
those who thought that there was an original contract between the
kings and the people of England', Swift wrote: 'I am of this party, and
yet I would have been for a regency' (*PW*, V, 291). The ultra-Tory
regency proposal at the Convention, if implemented, would have preserved James's legal authority, avoided the transfer of the crown and
alteration of the hereditary succession, and preserved the Anglican

---

[91] References are to Swift's marginalia as reprinted in *PW*, V. Swift's editor, Herbert Davis,
did not print Swift's marginal comments on Burnet from the copy belonging to John Lyon
(see *PW*, V, xxxvi). For a significant substantive correction to the Davis text, see Lock,
Swift's Tory Politics, p. 63n.

[92] Francis Manley, 'Swift Marginalia in Howell's *Medulla Historiae Anglicanae*', *PMLA*, 73
(1958), 335–8 (p. 338); *PW*, V, 264–5; William Shippen (in *Faction Display'd* (1704),
POAS, 6, 673) represents William Duke of Gloucester's death as leaving 'Hopes involv'd in
endless Night'.

doctrine of non-resistance to the supreme magistrate. In Burnet's words the proposers of the regency thought,

> their expedient would take in the greatest, as well as the best, part of the Nation: Whereas all other expedients gratified a Republican party, composed of the Dissenters, and of men of no religion, who hoped now to see the Church ruined, and the government set upon such a bottom, as that we should have only a titular King; who, as he had his power from the people, so should be accountable to them for the exercise of it, and should forfeit it at their pleasure. The much greater part of the House of Lords was for this, and stuck long to it: And so was about a third part of the House of Commons. The greatest part of the Clergy declared themselves for it.

Swift commented: 'And it was certainly much the best expedient.'[93] Considering the views of 'those who were for continuing the government, and only for changing the persons', Swift approves, not the radical Whig assertions described by Burnet, but the *in extremis* argument put by those who 'avoided going into new speculations, or schemes of government'.[94] He also appears to be sympathetic to the Tory position in the debate on the word 'abdicated' and the vacancy of the throne (*PW*, V, 291).

Despite the ultra-Tory implications of Swift's support for a regency at the Revolution, John Lyon would have read that Swift is of the party that thought there was an original contract between the kings and people of England, apparently another instance of the profession he made, for example, in his 'Advertisement to *Poems*, 1735' and in his correspondence, especially to Whigs, that he was a Whig in politics and within the pale of the Revolution. However, it is arguable whether Swift's identification with the original contract party (as described by Burnet) means he was endorsing radical Whig versions of contract theory.[95] And it should be recalled that the Jacobite Tory Bishop of Ely, Francis Turner, a leading advocate of the regency scheme (for him it was an expedient until James II could be restored), accepted that there was an original contract between kings and people and argued that the law settling the hereditary succession was part of the original

---

[93] Gilbert Burnet, *Bishop Burnet's History of His Own Time*, I, 811; *PW*, V, 291. See also *Examiner*, no. 44 (31 May 1711), *Exam*, p. 451; *PW*, IX, 229–30.
[94] Burnet, *History of His Own Time*, I, 814; *PW*, V, 291.
[95] See *Bishop Burnet's History of His Own Time*, I, 811–13; J. R. Western, *Monarchy and Revolution* (London, 1972), p. 310; J. P. Kenyon, 'The Revolution of 1688: Resistance and Contract', in *Historical Perspectives*, edited by Neil McKendrick (London, 1974), pp. 43–69; Erskine-Hill, 'Literature and the Jacobite Cause: Was There a Rhetoric of Jacobitism?', esp. p. 50.

contract and that laws could only be altered by the legislative power of King, Lords and Commons in parliament.[96] In a letter of 1692 Swift wrote that he used 'to converse about 2 or 3 years ago' with Turner (*Corr*, I, 9).

The representation of William III in Swift's marginalia in *Bishop Burnet's History of His Own Time* strongly implies Jacobite sympathies. William is said to have contrived the murder of De Witt. William is observed as an inglorious, perjured invader and covert usurper. The warming-pan myth of Williamite propaganda is rejected. There are hostile aspersions on the characters of those involved in inviting over the Prince of Orange (*PW*, V, 275, 277, 285, 287, 288). Jacobitism was born, Burnet believed, when James II, prevented from escaping by some fishermen of Faversham in Kent, was brought back to London:

Yet all the strugglings which that party have made ever since that time to this day, which from him were called afterwards the Jacobites, did rise out of this: For, if he had got clear away, by all that could be judged, he would not have had a party left: All would have agreed, that here was a desertion, and that therefore the Nation was free, and at liberty to secure it self. But what followed upon this gave them a colour to say, that he was forced away, and driven out.[97]

Swift wrote: 'So he certainly was, both now and afterwards' (*PW*, V, 289). The arrest of the Earl of Feversham was 'Base and villanous'. For Swift it was 'certainly true' that the person and government of King James were struck at and that William had effected a disguised usurpation. King William is blamed for the abolition of episcopacy in Scotland. The Jacobite hero, Viscount Dundee, is described by Swift as

[96] See *The Debate at Large, Between The House of Lords and House of Commons, at the Free Conference, Held in the Painted Chamber, in the Session of the Convention, Anno 1688. Relating to the Word, Abdicated, and the Vacancy of the Throne, in the Common's Vote* (London, 1695; rpt. Shannon, 1972), pp. 49, 51–60. Swift owned this book; see Hermann J. Real and Heinz J. Vienken, 'A Catalogue of an Exhibition of Imprints from Swift's Library', in *Proceedings*, p. 363. On Turner at the Convention, see George L. Cherry, 'The Legal and Philosophical Position of the Jacobites, 1688–1689', *The Journal of Modern History*, 22 (1950), 309–21; Robert Beddard, 'The Loyalist Opposition in the Interregnum: a Letter of Dr Francis Turner, Bishop of Ely, on the Revolution of 1688', *Bulletin of the Institute of Historical Research*, 40 (1967), 101–9, and his 'The Guildhall Declaration of 11 December 1688 and the Counter-Revolution of the Loyalists', *The Historical Journal*, 11 (1968), 403–20; Lois G. Schwoerer, *The Declaration of Rights, 1689* (Baltimore and London, 1981), esp. pp. 216–19. For a summary of our fragmentary knowledge of Swift's acquaintance with Turner, see Edward W. Rosenheim, Jr, 'Swift's *Ode to Sancroft*', S24–S39 (S30–S32).

[97] *Bishop Burnet's History of His Own Time*, I, 797.

'the best man in Scotland' (*PW*, V, 290).[98] Elsewhere in these annotations Swift sides with Sancroft, Hickes, Atterbury and Ormonde.[99]

Swift told Charles Wogan, the Irish Jacobite exile who was in
Jacobite service under the Duke of Ormonde, that he highly esteemed
'those Gentlemen of *Ireland*, who, with all the Disadvantages of being
Exiles and Strangers, have been able to distinguish themselves by their
Valour and Conduct in so many Parts of *Europe*' (*Corr*, IV, 51). Praising
Jacobite soldiers abroad, Swift traces corruptions at home to the Revo-
lution of 1688–9. *An Humble Address to Both Houses of Parliament. By M. B.
Drapier* (first published in 1735) remarks roundly: 'whoever is old
enough to remember, and hath turned his Thoughts to observe the
Course of publick Affairs in this Kingdom, from the Time of the
Revolution; must acknowledge, that the highest Points of Interest and
Liberty, have been often sacrificed to the Avarice and Ambition of
particular Persons' (*PW*, X, 120–1). As historian, Swift evokes a pre-
Revolution Stuart age of peace and prosperity, and describes the
Revolution's new financial order and the institution of a National Debt
as a politic Court Whig–Dutch expedient to further Williamite milita-
rist ambitions at English expense (*PW*, VII, 68–9). In 1722 Swift was
linking 'that scheme of politicks, (now about thirty years old) of setting
up a monied Interest in opposition to the landed' with the financial
mismanagement and corruption – the 'Funds of Credit and South-sea
Projects' – experienced under Hanoverian Whig rule (*PW*, IX, 32).
Significantly, Gulliver begins his account of the state of England to the
Houyhnhnm Master – a shocking catalogue of flagitious institutional
corruption – with 'the *Revolution* under the Prince of *Orange*; the long
War with *France* entered into by the said Prince' (*PW*, XI, 245).
William of Orange's successful landing in England on 5 November 1688
is subjected to bathetic re-enactment with Gulliver's inglorious landing
in corrupt Lilliput on 'the fifth of *November*' (*PW*, XI, 20–1). Though a
juring clergyman, Swift is discontented with the Revolution ecclesiastical settlement (see *Exam*, pp. 125–36; *PW*, XII, 271). The growth of
irreligion is associated with the Revolution (*PW*, IV, 30). In the

---

[98] Jacobite writers traduced William for his detention of Feversham: see John Sheffield,
'Some Account of the Revolution', in *Buckingham Restor'd* (p. 9); *An Historical Romance*,
p. 34. On Dundee, see Archibald Pitcairne's Latin verses, translated by John Dryden, in
The Works of John Dryden: Poems 1685–1692, Volume III, edited by Earl Miner (Berkeley and
Los Angeles, 1969), p. 222. Swift publicized the exploits of one of Dundee's men, the
episcopalian, Jacobite cavalier John Creichton, preparing for the press *Memoirs of Capt.
John Creichton* (1731), *PW*, V, 120–81.
[99] *PW*, V, 270, 272, 277, 278, 282, 285, 289, 291, 294.

Memoirs of Capt. John Creichton (1731), which Swift prepared for the press, there is clearly editorial sympathy with the views and conduct of the Jacobite soldier in resisting the Revolution (see particularly *PW*, V, 168). The Revolution is also associated with cultural decline in Swift's writing. For example, modern corrupt refinement in polite language is dated from 'the Time of the Revolution' (*PW*, IV, 106), as is the neglect of philology (*PW*, IV, 231). Swift's idiom on the Revolution Settlement discloses disturbing disaffection rather than the axiomatic approval often alleged in modern Swift studies.

While no positive evidence of Jacobitism exists in Swift's extant writings, there is evidence of self-censorship – omission or suppression of information, secrecy and studied indeterminacy – in his extant correspondence with Tories and suspected Jacobites. Reading through Swift's correspondence of 1714 and after the Hanoverian accession, for instance, it is apparent that the full extent of Swift's political knowledge and opinion and that of his friends is not explicitly disclosed in the written sources.[100] Also, covert modes of communication and signals used among Jacobite Tories, such as the commonplace use of the word 'honest' as an understood synonym for 'Jacobite', and expressions of support for Charles XII of Sweden as an understood register of anti-Hanoverianism and Jacobite sympathy, seem present in the 'Honest' Dean's Tory correspondence.[101] During the last four years of Anne's reign the Whigs sought to expose and exploit the fissile Tory party's

---

[100] *Corr*, II, 156 (Erasmus Lewis to Swift (January 1715)); *Corr*, II, 158–9 (Swift to Matthew Prior, 1 March 1715); *Corr*, II, 166–7 (The Duke of Ormonde to Swift (3 May 1715)); *Corr*, II, 167–9 (John Barber to Swift, 3 May 1715). Barber is writing before the Jacobite Rising in 1715: 'Our Friends here and all the Kingdom over are in great Spirit. we shan't always groan under the Burden. I wish I might speak out' (p. 169); *Corr*, II, 195 (Swift to Bishop Atterbury, 24 March 1716); *Corr*, II, 197 (Bishop Atterbury to Swift, 6 April 1716); *Corr*, II, 218–19 (Viscount Bolingbroke to Swift, 23 October 1716); *Corr*, II, 435 (Swift to Robert Cope, 9 October 1722).

[101] Mrs Caesar, wife of the Jacobite Tory Charles Caesar, concludes her letter to Swift of 6 August 1732: 'so with Mʳ Casars and my best wishes thou Worthy Witty Honest Dean Adieu' (*Corr*, IV, 55). For examples of the Jacobite nuance and association of the label 'honest', see Hearne, *Remarks and Collections of Thomas Hearne, passim*; *The Jacobite Attempt of 1719. Letters of James Butler, Second Duke of Ormonde ...*, edited by William Kirk Dickson, Scottish Historical Society (Edinburgh, 1895), *passim*. The association of 'honest' with Jacobitism is observed by historians of Jacobitism. On Jacobite enthusiasm for and involvement with Charles XII of Sweden and lament at his death in 1718, see *Charles XII of Sweden. A Character and Two Poems*, with an Introduction by Eveline Cruickshanks (Locks' Press, Brisbane, 1983), pp. ii–v. In the pamphlet literature at the time of the Swedish–Jacobite conspiracy of 1716–17, Jacobites are seen to admire and approve Charles XII of Sweden.

division on the succession in the House of Hanover.[102] Swift excoriated
Hanoverian Tories such as the apostate Daniel Finch, second Earl of
Nottingham, and 'such who left us upon the subject of the peace, and
affected jealousies about the succession' (*Corr*, II, 111; see *PW*, XVI,
430–50; *Corr*, I, 339–40; *Exam*, p. 145; *PW*, VI, 129, 139–41; VII,
11–20; VIII, 82–3). In *An Excellent New Song, Being the Intended Speech of a
Famous Orator against Peace* (6 December 1711) Swift satirizes Nottingham for his complicity in the conspiracy that led to the invitation to
William of Orange in 1688 and dispossession of King James:

> When I and some others subscribed our Names
> To a Plot for expelling my Master King *James*;
> I withdrew my Subscription by help of a *Blot*,
> And so might discover, or gain by the Plot.
>
> (lines 27–30, *POAS*, 7, 528–9)

In attacking those Tories who, through concern about the safety of the
Protestant Hanoverian succession, deserted the government to vote
with the Whigs, Swift, of course, denied that there was a hidden Tory
agenda to alter the succession as established by the transfer of the crown
in 1689 and by the Act of Settlement (1701). However, there is a degree
of ambivalence about the possibility of a Jacobite revolution in Swift's
correspondence, ministerial propagandist writings and political commentary which needs to receive more witness.

On 18 May 1714 Swift lamented to the Earl of Peterborough that
despite Queen Anne's failing health it was not possible 'to persuade
people to make any preparations against an evil day' (*Corr*, II, 21 and
see II, 36, 110–11). Swift resolved to withdraw from the political
turmoil of Court and London politics. On 22 May Chiverton Charleton
wrote to Swift encouraging him to remain at his post: 'Hearing from
honest John [Barber] that you still persist in your resolution of retiring
into the country I cannot but give you my thoughts of it.' Swift should
stay and show 'that you are neither afraid nor unwilling to face a storm
in a good cause'. In the postscript, Charleton wrote: 'Honest Townshend & I have the satisfaction to drink your health as often as we do
drink together … at present we have disposed you in the first list of
Rank Tories' (*Corr*, II, 23–5). Swift, however, told Archdeacon Walls
on 11 June 'that I care not to live in *Storms, when I can no longer* do Service
in the ship, and am able to *get out of it*. I have gone thro my Share of

---

[102] Tory division on the succession issue split the party in the last years of Anne's reign, see
Geoffrey Holmes, *British Politics in the Age of Anne*, pp. 82–94, and B. W. Hill, *The Growth of
Parliamentary Parties, 1689–1742* (London, 1976), pp. 139–46.

Malice and Danger, and will be as quiet the rest of my *days, as I can'*
(*Corr*, II, 30). Swift foresaw, as he says in a later letter to Walls, 'the
Storm that would happen' (*Corr*, II, 89). Swift refers to Bolingbroke's
eventual triumph in the ministerial contest with the Earl of Oxford for
the government leadership and Oxford's removal. However, it also
might just possibly have been a more revolutionary political change he
anticipated in June 1714: 'To tell you a Secret, I think as times are like
to be, I should be glad to have my money in another Place' (*Corr*, II,
31). In June 1714 Dr William Stratford, Canon of Christ Church,
Oxford, commented to Edward Harley, afterwards second Earl of
Oxford: 'The transferring of stock looks very like a confession of guilt. I
have not heard of the Dean of St. Patrick's since he went hence, he does
not I believe like these shifting winds, and will scarce appear till the
wind comes to be settled in one point or other.'[103] In a later letter to
Knightley Chetwode of 17 December 1715 Swift appears to use the
word 'storms' to mean the landing of the Pretender and related unrest
(*Corr*, II, 190). Archbishop King later interpreted Swift's retirement at
this time as implying that Swift suspected the Tory ministers were for
the Pretender (*Corr*, II, 248; see II, 238–9).

In the first letter Swift wrote from his retirement in Berkshire he
emphasizes his remoteness from London politics and, perhaps, gives a
glimpse of a reason for his withdrawal from the centre of politics
additional to the well-documented reason of his despair at the interne-
cine contestation between his friends Oxford and Bolingbroke within
the ministry (see *PW*, VIII, 132; *Corr*, II, 63, 70–1, 76, 110). Swift tells
Esther Vanhomrigh: 'The Pretender or Duke of Cambridge may both
be landed and I never the wiser.' Perhaps Swift hoped at this point that
in passivity and ignorance lay innocence. He had received not 'one Line
from any body since I left London; of which I am very glad' (*Corr*, II,
26). Lodging with 'an honest Clergyman of my old Acquaintance' (the
Revd John Geree), Swift, however, was to be regularly informed by
John Arbuthnot and Erasmus Lewis, the remaining two of 'the Triumvirate of honest Councellors', and by other close friends, of the state of
ministerial affairs (*Corr*, II, 35, 46). While the idea of restoring the
Pretender is treated sardonically in Swift's 1714 correspondence (see
Corr, II, 38, 47), Swift interestingly echoes the title of Charles Leslie's
notorious and triumphal Jacobite polemical work *The Finishing Stroke*
(1711) when he describes the last moves in Oxford's demise and the

---

103 Historical Manuscripts Commission. *Report on the Manuscripts of His Grace The Duke of
Portland*, vol. VII (London, 1901), p. 190.

takeover of the administration by Bolingbroke and the Tory extremists as 'a finishing Stroak' (*Corr*, II, 75).

The death of Queen Anne prevented a Tory *coup de grâce* on the Whig party and Dissent. Swift was informed by Barber, Lewis, Ford and Arbuthnot that the Elector of Hanover would succeed without opposition. Lewis commented: 'we are ill prognisticators. every thing goes on with a tranquillity we durst not hope for', and Arbuthnot remarked: 'so far is plain from what has happen'd in publick affairs that what one party affirm'd of the settlement has prov'd true, & that it was firm ... I can assure you the peacable scene that now appears is a disappointment to more than one sett of people' (*Corr*, II, 98, 122, and see 92–5, 102, 117). No public move had been made by suspected Jacobite Tories to proclaim the Pretender. Bolingbroke and Barber hoped Swift would return to London 'and help to save the constitution, which with a little good managemᵗ might be kept in Tory Hands' (*Corr*, II, 101). Swift recommended a united 'Church-interest' to confront the new, pro-Whig dynasty (*Corr*, II, 111–12). But with the increasing evidence of Tory proscription after the Hanoverian accession, Swift's references to the new order become noticeably more ambivalent. He declares to Knightley Chetwode on 6 October 1714: 'Everything is as bad as possible; and I think if the Pretender ever comes over, the present men in power have traced him the way' (*Corr*, II, 135–6). Lord Harley is told on 8 March 1715 that 'there is nothing too bad to be apprehended in my opinion, from the present Face of Things'. In his election year 'Letter to Pope' Swift gave his opinion on 'what is called a Revolution-principle':

That, whenever those evils which usually attend and follow a violent change of government, were not in probability so pernicious as the grievances we suffer under a present power, then the publick good will justify such a Revolution; and this I took to have been the Case in the Prince of Orange's expedition, although in the consequences it produced some very bad effects, which are likely to stick long enough by us.

(*PW*, IX, 31)

In 1715 and 1722 Swift, in common with Jacobite Tories, professed to be witnessing the expiration of liberty in the kingdom. Swift's 'Revolution-principle' is not without certain ambivalence and could easily be construed as covert Jacobite politics if readers felt the present grievances were insupportable. For Swift's Revolution principle would endorse the military expedition of another prince in such an exigency. A 'disaffected' rather than 'Whig' reading is encouraged by Swift's reflection on the Revolution as a violent change of government and by the remark that the post-Revolution order has produced 'some very bad effects'.

In *An Enquiry into the Behaviour of the Queen's last Ministry, with Relation to their Quarrells among themselves, and the Design charged upon them of altering the Succession of the Crown* (begun in 1715, completed some time before 1721, but unpublished in Swift's lifetime), a defence of the government of 1710–14 from the Whigs' 'old slander of bringing in the Pretender' (*Corr*, II, 175) and an attack on the post-1714 Whig administration, Swift implicitly argues that the Tories and the nation have been driven into Jacobitism:

> upon the Queen's Death, if we except Papists and Nonjurers, there could not be five hundred Persons in England of all Ranks who had any Thoughts of the Pretender, and among these, not six of any Quality or Consequence; But how it hath come to pass that severall Millions are said to have since changed their Sentiments, it shall not be my Part to inquire.
>
> (*PW*, VIII, 165; see *Corr*, II, 176, 183–4)

In the last four years of Anne's reign, people 'could have no Scruples of Conscience in submitting to the present Powers'. If 'any Guilt were contracted by the Revolution, it was generally understood that our Ancestors were only to answer for it'. With 'an Exception to professed Nonjurers, there was not one Man in ten thousand through England who had other Sentiments'. Now there is 'prodigious Disaffection' (*PW*, VIII, 168). Swift argues that a parliamentary alteration of the Succession in favour of the Pretender had not been designed under the Oxford ministry:

> in order to have brought such an Affair about in a Parliamentary Way, some years must have been employed to turn the Bent of the Nation, to have rendred one Person odious and another amiable; neither of which is to be soon compassed towards absent Princes, unless by comparing them with those of whom we have had Experience, which was not *then* the Case.
>
> (*PW*, VIII, 173)

Swift's argument that the Tory party was not Jacobite at George I's accession, but was driven toward disaffection and Pretenderism by the violence of the Hanoverian Whig regime, was the line of argument deployed in the contemporary Jacobite press.[104] Swift is more explicit in a manuscript of the unpublished 'Enquiry' where there is a

<hr>

[104] For examples: *The Shift Shifted*, no. 16 (18 August 1716), pp. 94–5; *The Shift Shifted*, no. 17 (25 August 1716), p. 100; *The Second and Last English Advice, To The Freehoulders of Englan[d]* (London, 1722), p. 16.

paragraph entertaining a military solution to Hanoverian tyranny. Swift's tacit support for the Jacobite projects of military invasion and insurrection in 1715, 1717 and 1719 may be legitimately inferred. The paragraph, in Swift's hand but crossed out, reads:

> If the King of a free People will chuse to govern by a Faction inferior in Number and Property to the rest and suspected of Principles destructive to the Religious or Civil part of the Constitution, I do not see how a civil War can be avoyded Because the Bulk of the People and of the Landed Interest, who profess the Established Principles will never endure to see themselves entirely cut out and rendred incapable of all Employm^{ts} of Trust or Profit, and the whole Power most unnaturally vested in the Hands of a Minority, whose Interest it must of necessity be to alter the Constitution, & oppress their Fellow Subjects.
>
> (*PW*, VIII, 218)

Swift's *unqualified* opposition to standing armies expounded, for example, in 1722 in the 'Letter to Pope' means he endorsed the removal of one of the fundamental securities of the Hanoverian establishment in England and Ireland against Jacobite revolutionism (*PW*, IX, 31–2). Swift's position aligns him with the consistent oppositional political stance of William Shippen, 'the head of the veteran staunch Jacobites'.[105]

In a poem written *c*. 1730 Swift takes a vicarious part in a carnivalesque version of a Jacobite rebellion. 'The Revolution at Market Hill' (*Poems*, III, 882–6) is a playful burlesque, but there is insistent allusion to the political reality of a tyrannical reign, Tory proscription from the centre of power, Jacobite plotting and insurrection and cynical Whig ministerial politics. As Pat Rogers has noted of the poem: 'The title suggests to us a *coup d'état* involving the populace; Swift perhaps has in mind a palace revolution, or the kind of power struggle enacted in 1688. Towards the end there are hints of a "plot" such as the Jacobites were accused of, and of a political *coup* of the type by which a minister like Walpole ousted awkward or uncooperative colleagues.'[106] Swift and his Tory friends Sir Arthur Acheson and Henry Leslie, a son of Charles Leslie who had served in the Spanish army, are 'Three Suff'rers in a ruin'd Cause' banished by faction (lines 6–7). Swift and Leslie reproach Acheson (created a baronet of Nova Scotia in 1728) for a lack of commitment and suffering in a dangerous cause:

---

[105] *Lord Hervey's Memoirs*, edited by Romney Sedgwick, revised edition (London, 1963), p. 7; *Parl. Hist.*, VII, cols. 506–11; Lock, *Swift's Tory Politics*, pp. 131–2.
[106] Headnote to 'The Revolution at Market Hill', *The Complete Poems*, p. 804.

PROUD Baronet of *Nova Scotia*,
The D—n and *Spaniard* must reproach ye;
Of *their* two Fames the World enough rings;
Where are *thy* Services and Suff'rings?
What, if for nothing once you kiss't,
Against the Grain, a M—s Fist?
What, if among the courtly Tribe,
You lost a Place, and sav'd a Bribe?
And, then in surly Mode come here
To Fifteen Hundred Pounds a Year,
And fierce against the Whigs harangu'd?
You never ventur'd to be hang'd.
How dare you treat your Betters thus?
Are you to be compar'd to Us?

(lines 29–42)

The disaffected Dean and Spaniard plot to dispossess the knight who 'triumphant reigns' and enslaves them. There is a popular rising:

COME *Spaniard*, let us from our Farms
Call forth our Cottagers to Arms;
Our Forces let us both unite,
Attack the Foe at Left and Right;
From *Market-Hill's* exalted Head,
Full Northward, let your troops be led:
While I from *Drapier's-Mount* descend,
And to the *South* my Squadrons bend:

(lines 43–50)

When 'we execute our Plot' (line 107) and are in possession of 'the Realm' (line 92), Swift and Leslie will act as, it is implied, Whig 'Conqu'rors' (line 91) and 'Politicians' (line 109) do: they will proscribe, subjugate and hang (lines 90–110).[107]

Whatever the extent of Swift's knowledge of Jacobite activity and the degree of political sympathy he had for the Jacobite case, he seems to have resolved to be passive and private in the 'storms' around him. He wrote to Knightley Chetwode on 17 December 1715:

Honest people get into corners, and are as merry as they can. We are as loyal as our enemies, but they will not allow us to be so. If what they said were true, they would be quickly undone. Pray keep yourself out of harm's way. It is the

107 The subversiveness of the poem is observed in Carole Fabricant, *Swift's Landscape* (Baltimore and London, 1982), pp. 160–3. In her reading Swift is subverting the Country House ideal, enacting a class warfare and demystifying differences in economic and social power.

best part a private man can take unless his fortune be desperate, or unless he
has at least a fair hazard for mending the public.

(*Corr*, II, 191)

Unlike his hero the Duke of Ormonde, or Knightley Chetwode or that
'Honest Gentleman' his close friend Charles Ford, 'an honest sensible
firm friendly man' (*Corr*, II, 143, Arbuthnot to Swift, November 1714),
Swift did not become an active Jacobite. However, he seems to have
identified himself to his Tory correspondents as a Jacobite sympathizer.
In the wake of the government arrests of prominent suspected Jacobites
in 1722 Swift wrote to Robert Cope: 'Pray God keep all honest men out
of the hands of lions and bears, and uncircumcised Philistines' (*Corr*, II,
435). There are surely Jacobite political implications in Swift's intention to dedicate his projected 'History of England' to George I's great
enemy Charles XII of Sweden, and in the anti-Hanoverian dedicatory
letter (dated 'Nov. 2, 1719') to Swift's acquaintance, Count Gyllenborg, the Swedish envoy arrested in 1717 for complicity in concerting a
Swedish–Jacobite plot (*PW*, V, 11–12).[108] Although Swift had long
admired Charles XII of Sweden (see *Corr*, I, 153; *PW*, XVI, 650–1), the
following passage in a letter to Ford on 6 January 1719 may contain, as
well as its obvious literal statement, a covert registering of Swift's
goodwill towards those Tories who looked to Charles XII and Sweden
for assistance in 1716–18:

I am personally concerned for the Death of the K of Sweden, because I
intended to have beggd my Bread at His Court, whenever our good Friends in
Power thought fit to put me and my Brethren under the necessity of begging.
Besides I intended him an honor and a Compliment, which I never yet thought
a Crownd head worth, I mean, dedicating a Book to him.

(*Corr*, II, 311)

Swift was fully aware that admiration for Charles XII after 1717
signified Jacobite Tory politics (see *Corr*, II, 312; 'The Part of a
Summer', lines 95–104, *Complete Poems*, p. 237; 'Dick's Variety', lines
23–4, *Poems*, III, 788; *Complete Poems*, p. 347).

In a subsequent letter to Ford on 16 February 1719 Swift allusively
registers his sympathy for the cause of the disaffected, but confesses his
disposition is to be out of danger:

---

[108] On Swift's admiration for Charles XII and the political contexts of his expressed
admiration, see Irvin Ehrenpreis, 'Swift's History of England', *Journal of English and
Germanic Philology*, 51 (1952), 177–85 (esp. pp. 182–5); F. P. Lock, *The Politics of 'Gulliver's
Travels'* (Oxford, 1980), pp. 56–65; Lock, *Swift's Tory Politics*, pp. 125–6.

It would be an admirable Scituation to be neither Whig nor Tory. For a Man without Passions might find very strong Amusements. But I find the turn of Blood at 50 disposes me strongly to Fears, and therefore I think as little of Publick Affairs as I can, because they concern me as one of the Multitude; and for the same Reason I dare not venture to play at threepeny Basset, because it is a Game where Conduct is of no use, and I dare not trust to Fortune as the younger Folks do, and therefore I divert my self with looking upon others at Play *mea sine parte pericli* [Lucretius, ii.6.], which if a Man could do in what concerns the Publick, it would be no ill Entertainment. But when the Diversion grows to throw Fire-balls at Random, how can I be certain that Ucalegon may not live at the Deanry-house [*Aeneid*, ii.311–12.]. — There is a Proverb that shews what is the Time when honest People come by their own. I wonder whether that Proverb hath a Reverse.

(*Corr*, II, 312)[109]

Any interpretation of this epistolary obliquity must be conjectural, but Swift seems to be saying that like Lucretius' philosopher he would observe the warfare in the state without taking part in the peril. The stakes were too high and chances of success too uncertain. Swift was too well aware of the exiguity of the Anglican establishment in Ireland to risk committing himself to a revolution on behalf of a Roman Catholic claimant. In the battle for Troy, neighbouring Ireland and the Dean of St Patrick's would not escape the flames. In early 1719 Swift agonizes over activism for the 'honest' party and their King who sought to enjoy his own again. In 1723 Swift shares his experience of Whig prosecution for alleged Pretenderism with the Jacobite Chetwode and counsels him to forswear politics: 'Do you find that your trees thrive and your drained bog gets a new coat? I know nothing so well worth the enquiry of an honest man, as times run' (*Corr*, II, 449).

Swift's view of the times recorded in one of the notes appended to *Verses on the Death of Dr. Swift, D.S.P.D.* (1731) is profoundly disaffected:

Upon Queen ANNE's *Death the Whig Faction was restored to Power, which they exercised with the utmost Rage and Revenge; impeached and banished the Chief Leaders of the Church Party, and stripped all their Adherents of what Employments they had, after which* England *was never known to make so mean a Figure in Europe. The greatest Preferments in the Church in both Kingdoms were given to the most ignorant Men, Fanaticks were publickly caressed,* Ireland *utterly ruined and enslaved, only great Ministers heaping up Millions, and so Affairs continue until this present third Day of May, 1732, and are likely to go on in the same Manner.*

(*Poems*, II, 568, note 2)

---

109 On card games as a conventional way of alluding to affairs of state, see Howard Erskine-Hill, 'The Satirical Game at Cards in Pope and Wordsworth', *Yearbook of English Studies*, 14 (1984), 183–95.

This note recalls Swift's account in his 'Family of Swift' (dated between 1738 and 1739) of the sufferings of his royalist grandfather during the Interregnum: 'He was deprived of both his Church livings ... and his estate sequestred. His Preferments ... were given to a fanatical Saint' (*PW*, V, 190). In another note to the *Verses on the Death of Dr. Swift, D.S.P.D.*, Swift records his persecution as a suspected Jacobite on his return to Dublin in 1714:

Upon the Queen's Death, the Dean returned to live in Dublin, *at his Deanry-House: Numberless Libels were writ against him in* England, *as a Jacobite: he was insulted in the Street, and at Nights was forced to be attended by his Servants armed*

(*Poems*, II, 568, note 3)

Swift repeatedly assured the Whig Archbishop King that he was not for the Pretender: 'I had no ill designs, nor ever knew any in [Queen Anne's last ministry]'. He was 'always a Whig in Politicks' (*Corr*, II, 206, 236). A letter to King of 13 November 1716 is a significant document in Swift's political biography, for it expresses the dismay and disgust of the Irish clergy at news of the perpetuation of the nonjuring separation and an opinion that the Tory clergy might be regained by the Court (see *Corr*, II, 221–2). The letter was industriously shown in public by the Archbishop. Erasmus Lewis thought Swift must have written 'in an ironical Stile' and that King 'wou'd have it otherwise understood'. Lewis reminds Swift of the dangers of irony: 'this will bring to your mind what I have formerly said to you on that figure' (*Corr*, II, 246)! Atterbury defended Swift from the imputation of political apostasy and Swift wrote to assure the Tory bishop in 1717 of his continued fidelity to 'my party' and that he is 'an honest man' grieved that anyone could think he 'was wholly gone over to other principles more in fashion' (*Corr*, II, 278–80).[110] Swift may have been inconsistent, his allegiances shifting, 'my thoughts change every week', he confessed (*Corr*, II, 279). Interestingly, Charles Leslie was as exasperated as Swift. He advised the nonjuror George Harbin in a letter of 10 October 1716 that the news of a continuing nonjuring schism from the Church of England would destroy the Jacobite cause by alienating the affections of the Church of England and give joy to Whigs and Dissenters.[111] Swift, however, preserved a strong attachment to the

---

[110] Atterbury's final letter to Pope of 23 November 1731 suggests the exiled Jacobite bishop's continued friendship and regard for Swift. He kindly sends a copy of his *Vindication ... relating to the Publication of Lord Clarendon's History* to be conveyed to Swift, see *The Correspondence of Alexander Pope*, edited by George Sherburn, 5 vols. (Oxford, 1956), III, 247, 248.

[111] BL Add. MSS 29,545, fols. 17–18 (G. Harbin Letters).

proscribed Jacobite leaders as he wrote in the letter to Pope of 1723 (*Corr*, II, 464). This attachment extended to seeking to continue a correspondence with the enemies of Hanover. Count Gyllenborg, he tells Reverend James Stopford in 1725, 'if he has not lost his Head, may perhaps be an Ambassad^r somewhere in your way. If he be I would be glad to know where to write to him, upon an Affair wherein he promised to inform me' (*Corr*, III, 63).

Received readings of Swift either as a Whig or as a Hanoverian Tory, a political writer who 'never wavered in accepting the Revolution settlement of 1688, and never doubted the wisdom of maintaining the Protestant succession after the death of Queen Anne', who with 'the Modern Whigs subscribed wholeheartedly to the Act of Settlement', understate the complexity and ambiguity of the case.[112] Such readings necessarily neglect the ambivalence and polemical resonance of aspects of Swift's political language which led contemporaries to identify his political texts as Jacobite Tory. For instance, in his ministerial writing and in the political testament of the 1722 'Letter to Pope' Swift seems ambivalent on the Act of Settlement, reflecting his (and the Tory party's) reservations about the House of Hanover and perhaps a calculated attempt to keep legislative alteration of the succession a theoretically open possibility – an option honest men could consider in a case of necessity. Sir John Percival observed in 1714 that 'there is an unaccountable obscurity in some men's discourse which has giv'n ye Jacobites hopes that more are in their Master's interest than I am persuaded will be found really so'.[113] It is an observation applicable to Swift's writing at certain moments of political high temperature.

While monarchical doctrines of divine right and indefeasible hereditary succession and Filmerian patriarchalism, ably propounded by such publicists as Charles Leslie and George Harbin during Queen Anne's reign, constituted the legitimist mainstream of an essentially variegated Jacobite ideology,[114] Jacobite political aims in Anne's last years were principally 'the repeal of the Act of Succession and the institution of a Tory regime in Church and State'.[115] There was clearly an elision in Country Tory and Jacobite political argument, and although the great

---

[112] See Herbert Davis, 'Introduction', *PW*, II, xvii; Downie, *Jonathan Swift: Political Writer*, p. 82.

[113] Sir John Percival to Philip Percival, 3 April 1714, quoted in D. Szechi, *Jacobitism and Tory Politics 1710–14* (Edinburgh, 1984), p. 197.

[114] Whig polemicists identified such doctrines with the whole Tory party. J. C. D. Clark describes the survival of divine right ideology between 1688 and 1760: see especially his *English Society 1688–1832*, pp. 119–98.

[115] Szechi, *Jacobitism and Tory Politics 1710–14*, pp. 157, 196–9.

majority of Tories before 1714 may have been committed to the
Protestant Hanoverian succession rather than to the exiled Catholic
Stuarts as Swift repeatedly affirmed, a register of ambivalence on the
Act of Settlement could be construed as a crypto-Jacobite speech act.
The treason laws and pragmatic politics effectively meant that prudent
Jacobites would use anonymity and impersonation, and strategies of
indirection, allusion and obliquity in print. Exceptions to this rule were
public, publishing sensations. The 'plain dealing' of the Jacobite
George Lockhart's *Memoirs of the Affairs of Scotland, from Queen Anne's
Accession to the Throne, to the Commencement of the Union of Two Kingdoms of
Scotland and England, in May, 1707*, published anonymously in 1714,
made it 'a very extraordinary piece', and Arbuthnot thought Swift
should come to London just to see it (*Corr*, II, 58). 'I should be glad to
see that Manuscript about the Invasion: & I think I ought to have a
Copy of it', Swift replied (*Corr*, II, 63).[116] At the conclusion of his 'Letter
to Pope', Swift dismissed allegations that he had advanced seditious
principles by pointing to his politic discretion in public political discourse: 'I am too much a politician to expose my own safety' (*PW*, IX,
34). In the absence of explicit evidence of Jacobitism, contemporary
readers of political literature scrutinized a writer's attitude to the Act of
Settlement and to the Dutch to determine political sympathies.

In *The Conduct of the Allies* (1711) the ministerial publicist is indignant
that by the terms of the Barrier Treaty the Dutch should be guarantors
of the Act of Succession, as this prevented legislative defeasibility of the
succession 'how much soever the Necessities of the Kingdom may
require it' (*PW*, VI, 27, 206). Swift added a prudent explanation (but
not, it will be observed, a recantation) in the fourth edition of the
Conduct, as he explained in a 'POSTSCRIPT':

I Have in this Edition explained three or four Lines in the 38th Page [see *PW*,
VI, 206, textual note on page 27, lines 25ff], which mentions the *Succession*, to
take off, if possible, all manner of Cavil; though, at the same time, I cannot but
observe, how ready the Adverse Party is to make use of any Objections, even
such as destroy their own Principles. I put a distant Case of the possibility that
our *Succession*, through extream Necessity, might be changed by the Legislature,
in future Ages; and it is pleasant to hear those People quarrelling at this, who
profess themselves for changing it as often as they please, and that even without
the Consent of the entire Legislature.

(*PW*, VI, 65)

116 Swift possessed a copy of Lockhart's *Memoirs*, see *SC*, no. 416 and Hermann J. Real and
    Heinz J. Vienken, 'A Catalogue of an Exhibition of Imprints from Swift's Library', in
    Proceedings, pp. 351–88 (p. 371).

In the fourth edition Swift writes: 'our Posterity may hereafter, by the Tyranny and Oppression of any succeeding Princes, be reduced to the fatal Necessity of breaking in upon the excellent and happy Settlement now in force' (*PW*, VI, 27). Swift returned to this constitutional point in *Some Remarks on the Barrier Treaty* (1712). He boldly restates the potentially treasonable position of the *Conduct*: 'I make it a Question, whether it were right in point of Policy or Prudence to call in a Foreign Power to be Guarantee to our Succession; because by that means *we put it out of the Power of our own Legislature to alter the Succession, how much soever the Necessity of the Kingdom may require it?* (*PW*, VI, 92). He also obliquely insinuates a nonjuring argument against the Revolution while defending his principle of legislative defeasibility and attacking Whig revolution principles:

> The worst of this Opinion is, that at first sight it appears to be *Whiggish*; but the Distinction is thus, the *Whigs* are for changing the Succession when they think fit, though the entire Legislature do not consent; I think it ought never to be done but upon great Necessity, and that with the Sanction of the whole Legislature. Do these Gentlemen of *Revolution-Principles* think it impossible that we should ever have occasion *again* to change our Succession? And if such an Accident should fall out, must we have no Remedy, 'till the Seven Provinces will give their Consent?
>
> (*PW*, VI, 93)

Swift's statement that the succession should not be changed without the sanction of the whole legislature is a reflection on the Revolution of 1689. 'THE only Difficulty of any Weight against the Proceedings at the Revolution ... offered me some Time ago, with all its Advantages, by a very pious, learned, and worthy Gentleman of the Non-juring Party', Swift wrote in *The Sentiments of a Church-of-England Man* (1711), is:

> that the Laws made by the supreme Power, cannot otherwise than by the supreme Power be annulled: That this consisting in *England* of a King, Lords, and Commons, whereof each have a negative Voice, no Two of them can repeal, or enact a Law without Consent of the Third; much less, may any one of them be entirely excluded from its Part of the Legislature, by a *Vote* of the other Two. That all these Maxims were openly violated at the Revolution ...
>
> (*PW*, II, 21)

Swift declared in his 'Sermon upon the Martyrdom of King Charles I' that James II 'was deservedly rejected, since there could be no other remedy found, or at least agreed on' (*PW*, IX, 229–30). Swift favoured the ultra-Tory 'remedy' of a regency which would have preserved

James II's legal authority and the succession (*PW*, V, 291). It had not been adopted by the Convention in 1689. By raising this 'Difficulty' about the Revolution settlement, by entertaining the possibility of legislative revocation of the Act of Settlement at some future time, and by attacking the Dutch, Swift's ministerial tracts were recognized to signify Tory ambivalence on the succession and a vaguely projected legislative revolution for the Pretender. It is interesting to note in this context that there is some evidence that Swift may indeed have thought that 'the danger of a revolt to a Pretender' might be a useful security against future bad kings (see *PW*, V, 292). In *Remarks upon Remarks* (1712), John Oldmixon italicizes the passage in *Some Remarks on the Barrier Treaty* where Swift declares 'That the Legislature should have Power to change the Succession, whenever the Necessities of the Kingdom require, is so very useful towards preserving our Religion and Liberty, that I know not how to recant' (*PW*, VI, 92–3), and remarks: 'What Occasion was there for such a Thought, if it was not uppermost, and what his Faction most desire?'[117] The alarmed Whig press reacted stridently to legislative defeasibility, reflections on the Revolution, attacks on the Dutch and bantering of the danger of the Pretender in Tory and Swiftian political argument. Swift was regularly convicted of Jacobitism in the press.[118] Swift did not retract his position on the legislative defeasibility of the succession, although he was obliged to modify it. He went on the offensive in *The Public Spirit of the Whigs* (1714). Restating his position, Swift was able to confirm the constitutional propriety of legislative defeasibility of acts of parliament against the privileging of the Union and the Settlement of the Crown as

---

117 [John Oldmixon], *Remarks upon Remarks* ... (London, 1711 [1712]), pp. 26–7, and see pp. 28–30, 38–43. See also *A Letter to the People of England, occasion'd by the Letter to the Dissenters* (signed Cato Brutus) (London, 1714), pp. 23, 62–3. For Swift's response to 'politick Dingley' who found the passage in *The Conduct of the Allies* referring to the Dutch guarantee of the Hanoverian succession 'blameable', see *PW*, XVI, 477–8 and notes.

118 For the pamphlet literature in which Swift figured during the period of the Harley ministry, the peace negotiations culminating in the Treaty of Utrecht and the Jacobite Rising of 1715 and its aftermath, see Pat Rogers, 'The Pamphleteers on Swift, 1710–1716: A Preliminary Checklist', *Analytical and Enumerative Bibliography*, 7 (1983), 16–30. For examples of Whig readings of Jacobitism in Swift's ministerial writing, see John Oldmixon, *The Dutch Barrier Our's* ... (London, 1712), pp. 4, 8, 16–17, 18; [Daniel Defoe], *The Secret History of the October-Club, From Its Original to this Time. By a Member. Part II* (London, 1711), pp. 25–7, 42; [Daniel Defoe], *Hannibal at the Gates: Or, The Progress of Jacobitism. With the Present Danger of the Pretender* (London, 1712), p. 29; [Richard Steele], *Two Letters Concerning the Author of the Examiner* (London, 1713), pp. 9–10; *The Observator*, vol. X, no. 100 (12 December – 15 December 1711); *The Observator*, vol. XI, no. 27 (29 March – 2 April 1712) and *passim*.

unalterable in the work of Whig writers, such as Richard Steele and Daniel Defoe (see *PW*, VIII, 38, 50–3).[119]

As Swift remarked, his advocacy of the principle of legislative defeasibility 'appears to be *Whiggish*'. Later, in marginal comments in copies of Howell's *Medulla Historiae Anglicanae* (1734) and Burnet's *History* (1724–34), Swift in fact approved the Whig Exclusion Bill of 1681 (*PW*, V, 264, 279). When read in polemical context, approval of legislative defeasibility could be understood as an extreme Tory, crypto-Jacobite gambit. High Church and Tory political argument had discovered virtues in legislative defeasibility by 1710.[120] Swift's support in 1714 of a Tory regime in Church and State and Ormonde's purge of Whigs from the army,[121] as well as his provocative entertainment of the possibility

119 For Defoe on the 'Jacobite' argument of legislative defeasibility of the succession and his case for fundamental parts of the constitution (such as the Union, Act of Settlement and Toleration) being legally unalterable: [Daniel Defoe], *The Secret History of the October Club: From its Original to this Time, By a Member* (London, 1711), pp. 54, 55, 73; [Daniel Defoe], *The Present State of the Parties in Great Britain* (London, 1712), esp. pp. 235–43; [Daniel Defoe], *The History of the Jacobite Clubs* (London, 1712), pp. 34–6 (on Swift see esp. pp. 11–14).

120 *The Declaration of an Honest Churchman, Upon Occasion of the Present Times* (London: printed, and sold by J. Morphew, 1710), pp. 14–15, and see pp. 9–11. A pro-Blackall tract that approves the '*Bill of Exclusion*'. William Higden (*A Defence of the View of the English Constitution with Respect to the Sovereign Authority of the Prince, and the Allegiance of the Subject. By way of Reply to the several Answers that have been made to it* (London, 1710)) affirmed that legislative authority is in the King for the time being, with his two Houses of Parliament; that the crown is hereditary but inheritance can, in law, be limited by parliament and the descent of the crown is under the direction of the legislative power. The extreme case of future 'Tyranny and Oppression' (*The Conduct of the Allies*, *PW*, VI, 27) is imagined in *A Discourse on Hereditary Right, Written in the Year 1712. By a Celebrated Clergyman* (London, [1775]). This work has been attributed to Swift: see Daniel Eilon, 'Did Swift Write *A Discourse on Hereditary Right?*', *Modern Philology*, 82 (1985), 374–92 and his *Factions' Fictions*, Appendix, p. 164. A passage on p. 26 seems to be an attack on the Hanoverian monarch, Walpolean bribery and the Whig Septennial Act of 1716: 'However, let us, once for all, state this imaginary question in its utmost height. Suppose, in future ages, an ambitious Prince, designing to enslave the nation, should allow a million a year towards bribing a MAJORITY in both Houses; and, as his first essay, should repeal the act for TRIENNIAL Parliaments, and make THAT which then sat his PERPETUAL PENSIONERS, it is not easy to determine what lengths a *corrupted* people might go with such a King.' Eilon dates this pamphlet as written in late September or October 1710. But this passage, at least, seems to post-date the Hanoverian succession, as does an apparent allusion to *Gulliver's Travels* on page 25. The curious work may be a later 'Swiftian' confection produced for the publisher William Hay. Hay went bankrupt in 1776: see Ian Maxted, *The London Book Trades 1775–1800: A Preliminary Checklist of Members* (Old Woking, Surrey, 1977), p. 106.

121 See *PW*, VIII, 89–90. Whig contemporaries alleged Ormonde was purging the army of pro-Hanoverian Whigs to engage the military for the Jacobites, a view confirmed by the evidence of the Stuart manuscripts available to modern historians; see, for example, *A Letter to the People of England*, p. 133; *Corr*, II, 247–8 (Archbishop King to Swift, 12 January 1717); G. V. Bennett, 'English Jacobitism, 1710–1715; Myth and Reality', *Transactions of the Royal Historical Society*, 32 (1982), 137–51 (p. 145).

of altering the succession, at least complicates the matter of Swift's ultimate political sympathies, although Swift always denied that the Hanoverian succession had been 'attacked by the immortal Tory Ministry' (*PW*, V, 265).

The real difficulties for Swift and the Tory party with the Stuart dynastic option were the Pretender's Roman Catholicism and, after 1714, the oaths of allegiance to the Hanoverian King. It was widely held in Tory circles that only a recantation and conversion would lead to a Stuart restoration. Charles Leslie opined that James would convert to Anglicanism,[122] but the Pretender's absolute refusal in April 1714 to become a Protestant was a blow for Jacobite Toryism. 'As to the Person of this nominall Prince', Swift wrote with disgust in May 1714, 'he lyes under all manner of Disadvantages: The Vulgar imagin him to have been a Child imposed upon the Nation by the fraudulent Zeal of his Parents and their bigotted Councellors; who took special Care, against all the Rules of Common Policy, to educate him in their hatefull Superstition, suckt in with his milk and confirmed in his Manhood, too strong to be now shaken by Mr. Lesley; and, a counterfeit Conversion will be too gross to pass upon the Kingdom after what we have seen and suffered from the like Practice in his Father' (*PW*, VIII, 91).

Swift recorded in 'A Letter From Dr Swift to Mr Pope' 'what my Political principles were in the time of her late glorious Majesty, which I never contradicted by any action, writing or discourse'. The first of these principles was:

I always declared my self against a Popish Successor to the Crown, whatever Title he might have by the proximity of blood: Neither did I ever regard the right line, except upon two accounts; first, as it was established by law; and secondly, as it hath much weight in the opinions of the people. For necessity may abolish any Law, but cannot alter the sentiments of the vulgar; Right of inheritance being perhaps the most popular of all topicks; and therefore in great Changes when that is broke, there will remain much heart-burning and discontent among the meaner people; which (under a weak Prince and corrupt Administration) may have the worst consequences upon the peace of any state.

(*PW*, IX, 31)

Of course, if the Pretender converted to Protestantism then according to Swift's principles a revolution on his behalf and a new settlement could be accepted. Swift argues that 'the right line' (the excluded Stuart dynasty) is only to be regarded when it is established by law and supported by the people. But Swift points out that 'necessity may

---

[122] *A Letter from Mr Lesly to a Member of Parliament in London* ([London], dated 23 April 1714).

abolish any Law' and that hereditary right is 'perhaps the most popular of all topicks'.

Swift in the 'Letter' rehearses, in effect, the Opposition political catechism in the election year of 1722. There is the typically Tory, royalist collocation of Whig principles with Cromwellian parliamentarians and religious fanaticism (*PW*, IX, 30-1) and a recital of dissident Whig and Tory Opposition 'Old Whig' arguments against the Walpolean Whig regime (*PW*, IX, 31–3). Swift disturbingly implies in the 1722 'Letter' that 'a weak Prince and corrupt Administration' might bring the state to just that fatal necessity he presaged in his government writings against the Whigs and the Dutch (*PW*, IX, 31). 'They had a *Revolution* in their Heads, and a King to impose upon us', Arthur Mainwaring alleged of Swift and the Tory ministry he served.[123] A Whig or 'Hanoverian' Tory would have had no interest in being ambiguous about the succession or ambivalent on Jacobitism. There is, however, as I have suggested, a certain degree of ambivalence in Swift's writing in relation to Jacobitism.

In his militant *Letter from a Noble-Man Abroad*, the Jacobite George Granville wrote:

In those Times of Distraction, so like our own, when the Will of a Triumvirate, supported by a Majority of bribed Senators, and an Army at Command was the sole Law; when *Cato* and *Cicero* were in Danger of being torn to Pieces in the Street; when to be honest was to be pr[o]scribed; what Course could good Men take over-power'd by Numbers, and dispairing of the Commonwealth, but to retire to *Athens*, or some remote Corner.[124]

Swift wrote in 1728 of the private satisfaction and pleasure of political satire for persons proscribed from the centre of power:

If I ridicule the Follies and Corruptions of a *Court*, a *Ministry*, or a *Senate*, are they not amply paid by *Pensions*, *Titles*, and *Power*; while I expect, and desire no other Reward, than that of laughing with a few Friends in a Corner?

(*PW*, XII, 34)

In his great satires, *A Tale of a Tub* and *Gulliver's Travels*, Swift can be understood as saying what Tory extremists and Jacobites were saying on affairs of state. The political texture of these works will now be described.

---

[123] John Oldmixon, *The Life and Posthumous Works of Arthur Maynwaring Esq; Containing Several Original Pieces and Translations, in Prose and Verse, never before Printed* (London, 1715), p. 259.
[124] *A Letter*, p. 4.

3

The politics of *A Tale of a Tub*

A Tale of a Tub To which is added The Battle of the Books and the Mechanical Operation of the Spirit is a baroque miscellany book on abuses in religion and learning. Its satiric prosecution of religious enthusiasm draws on Restoration religious polemic and patristic writings against heresy. In particular, the great Restoration satire of the Commonwealth period, Samuel Butler's *Hudibras*, with which Swift was said to be entirely familiar, has been recognized as a significant antecedent text to the *Tale*.[1] Butler, like Swift, satirizes hubris, nonconformity, religious fanaticism (analysed as a psychopathology), pedantry, and dullness. Both satirists impute a nexus between popery and Protestant nonconformity, connect occult learning, astrology and religious enthusiasm as fanatical imposture, and pillory sectarian preaching, predestinarian doctrine, Quakerism and sectarian claims of divine revelation and inspiration such as the Quaker doctrine of the 'Inner Light'.

The religious satire of *A Tale of a Tub* and *A Discourse Concerning the Mechanical Operation of the Spirit*, situated principally in a seventeenth-century tradition of Anglican apologetic and invective, has been regarded by some modern scholars as 'old-fashioned' in content and polemical vision at the time of its composition (*c.* 1696–7) and publication (1704).[2] The work is not regarded as having any immediate political purpose, although, especially in its satire on Dissent, it is seen to be informed by Swift's experience as an Anglican priest at Kilroot near Belfast in 1695–6, a parish comprised largely of Presbyterians. Advocates of the rival Whig and Tory cases for Swift can agree that the

[1] *Memoirs of Mrs Letitia Pilkington 1712–1750 Written by Herself* (1748–1754; rpt. London, 1928), p. 88; Ehrenpreis, *Swift*, I, 197–8.
[2] Phillip Harth, *Swift and Anglican Rationalism: The Religious Background of 'A Tale of a Tub'* (Chicago and London, 1961), p. 153; Kathleen Williams, ed., *Swift: The Critical Heritage* (London, 1970), p. 4; John Traugott, 'A Tale of a Tub', in *The Character of Swift's Satire: A Revised Focus*, edited by Claude Rawson (Newark, Delaware, London and Toronto, 1983), pp. 83–126 (pp. 89–90).

satire is not party-political, although it is claimed to be Whig in its sympathies and political vision.[3] A provenance for the work is located in Swift's experience and work as Sir William Temple's secretary at Moor Park.[4] However, several studies have noted High Church militancy against the Protestant sects in the text and contemporary context of *A Tale of a Tub*.[5] There is now an important corpus of scholarly work which relates *A Tale of a Tub* to late seventeenth-century religious controversy and to the contexts of anti-Puritan satire, anti-Quaker propaganda, anti-atheist and anti-Romanist polemics.[6] Much work on the historical specificity of the satire still needs to be done. The *Tale* is very much the cultural product of the contemporary pamphleteering tradition and writings on affairs of state. There is remarkable intertextuality between *A Tale of a Tub* and the pamphlets of Tory extremists. Swift's satire on Jack and his sect of Aeolists, for example, is a brilliant and complex artistic heightening of the language and ideas of contemporary pamphleteers of religious and political hatred. Swift made out of the quarrel with others not just polemic rhetoric but lasting literary art.

Religious and political issues arising out of the Reformation, the Civil War and the Revolution of 1688–9 were live controversies for Swift and his contemporaries. Swift could ridicule Gilbert Burnet's fear of popery and the High Church party ('He hath been poring so long upon *Fox*'s Book of Martyrs, that he imagines himself living in the Reign of Queen *Mary*' (*PW*, IV, 80)), but for Swift the threat from

---

[3] Richard I. Cook, *Jonathan Swift as a Tory Pamphleteer* (Seattle and London, 1967), p. xii; J. A. Downie, *Jonathan Swift: Political Writer*, p. x.

[4] A. C. Elias, Jr, *Swift at Moor Park*, esp. pp. 164–72, 189–90, 196–7.

[5] John Maybee, 'Anglicans and Nonconformists 1679–1704: A Study in the Background of Swift's *A Tale of a Tub*' (unpublished Ph.D. dissertation, Princeton University, 1942); Ronald Paulson, *Theme and Structure in Swift's 'A Tale of a Tub'* (New Haven, 1960), esp. pp. 158–62; *Swift*, I, 213; II, 328; Robert M. Adams, *Strains of Discord: Studies in Literary Openness* (Ithaca, New York, 1958), pp. 146–79, and 'The Mood of the Church and *A Tale of a Tub*', in *England in the Restoration and Early Eighteenth Century: Essays on Culture and Society*, edited by H. T. Swedenberg, Jr (Berkeley, Los Angeles, London, 1972), pp. 71–99.

[6] See, among others: C. M. Webster, 'Swift's *Tale of a Tub* Compared with Earlier Satires of the Puritans', *PMLA*, 47 (1932), 171–8; Webster, 'Swift and Some Earlier Satirists of Puritan Enthusiasm', *PMLA*, 48 (1933), 1141–53; Webster, 'The Satiric Background of the Attack on the Puritans in Swift's *A Tale of a Tub*', *PMLA*, 50 (1935), 210–23; Webster, 'The Puritans Ears in *A Tale of a Tub*', *Modern Language Notes*, 47 (1932), 96–7; Hugh Ormsby-Lennon, 'Swift and the Quakers (I)', *Swift Studies*, 4 (1989), 34–62, and 'Swift and the Quakers (II)', *Swift Studies*, 5 (1990), 53–89; Roger D. Lund, 'Strange Complicities: Atheism and Conspiracy in *A Tale of a Tub*', *Eighteenth-Century Life*, 13 (1989), 34–58; Marcus Walsh, 'Text, "Text", and Swift's *A Tale of a Tub*', *Modern Language Review*, 85 (1990), 290–303.

Dissent and Whig policies was immediate and radical. In *The Sentiments of a Church-of-England Man* he extenuates the mistake of the clergy in Charles II's and James II's reigns 'who, under the Terms of *Passive Obedience*, and *Non-Resistance*, are said to have preached up the unlimited Power of the Prince':

BESIDES, it is to be considered, that when these Doctrines began to be preached among us, the Kingdom had not quite worn out the Memory of that horrid *Rebellion*, under the Consequences of which it had groaned almost twenty Years.

(*PW*, II, 16, 17)

Swift did not forget or forgive. His 'Sermon upon the Martyrdom of K. Charles I' begins with the classic High Church and Tory defence of the 30 January commemoration:

I KNOW very well, that the church hath been often censured for keeping holy this day of humiliation, in memory of that excellent King and blessed Martyr CHARLES I. who rather chose to die on a scaffold than betray the religion and liberties of his people, wherewith GOD and the laws had entrusted him. But, at the same time, it is manifest that those who make such censures are either people without any religion at all, or who derived their principles, and perhaps their birth, from the abettors of those who contrived the murder of that Prince, and have not yet shewn the world that their opinions are changed.

(*PW*, IX, 219)

Using the favourite Tory metaphor for the events of 1687–8 as a 'Storm' Swift tells his congregation:

as a house thrown down by a storm is seldom rebuilt, without some change in the foundation, so it hath happened, that, since the late Revolution, men have sate much looser in the true fundamentals both of religion and government, and factions have been more violent, treacherous, and malicious than ever, men running naturally from one extreme into another; and, for private ends, taking up those very opinions professed by the leaders in that rebellion, which carried the blessed Martyr to the scaffold.

(*PW*, IX, 224; see also *Exam*, pp. 127–8)

The 'successors of those Puritans' are 'our present dissenters' (*PW*, IX, 226).

The Anglican establishment in the post-Revolution polity was sharply divided on religious issues. A militant High Church movement asserting the episcopal Church's jurisdictional authority in matters of Church government, schism and heresy challenged the moderate, latitudinarian ecclesiology espoused by a majority on the Bishop's bench and endorsed by Whig ministries. The Church's corporate rights became a *cause célèbre* of Tory politics. The nature and extent of the Toleration, for instance, was a topic of violent political partisanship. The Erastian Revolution settlement's apparent political recognition of religious pluralism was challenged by High Church Tories and Jacobites. Between 1702 and 1704 the ecclesiastical and political controversy over occasional conformity seriously disrupted all other public business in parliament and, to Whigs and Dissenters at least, the bill to outlaw the practice seemed to challenge the very basis of the Toleration of 1689. In 1704, the attempted 'Tack' of the third Occasional Conformity Bill to the Land Tax (a money) Bill by the High Church Tories threatened the financing of the English war effort on the continent. The 'Church in Danger' was a *leitmotif* of Tory electoral politics. The representation in *A Tale of a Tub* of the fanatical excesses of Jack and the implication that moderate Martin's appeasement strategy with Jack only encourages Jack's extremist aspiration (see *Tale*, pp. 140–1) is a High Church Tory political parable. The polemical character of the *Tale* suggests one possible reason why Swift, whose *Discourse* of 1701 made him welcome to the Whig political leaders, never received preferment from them.

Contemporary readers reacted to what they saw as the profanity, impiety and scepticism in *A Tale of a Tub*, but also to its polemical implications and meaning. Swift certainly attempted to counter criticism of the *Tale* as irreligious in his 'Apology' prefixed to the work in 1710 and by modifying the more profane strokes of the 1704 text in the fifth edition of 1710.[7] He carefully preserved the official anonymity of the *Tale* and ensured that no formal evidence of his authorship could be produced. Swift could presume that the disorientation within the text itself – mystifications about authorial responsibility for the volume as printed and the formal use of impersonation, parody, irony and putative speakers – would provide further protection from inquisitorial readers. But Swift became known as the author of the notorious volume. It is fairly clear that Swift thought his dangerous and controversial satiric book had advanced his prospects with the Tories. On 7 October 1710, almost certainly alluding to *A Tale of a Tub*, he writes to his intimate friend Esther Johnson that 'They may talk of the *you know what*; but, gad, if it had not been for that, I should never have been able to get the access I have had; and if that helps me to succeed, then that *same thing* will be serviceable to the church' (*PW*, XV, 47 and note).

---

[7] For the significant substantive textual alterations, see *Tale*, p. xxii, note 1; *PW*, I, 296–8.

The context of the passage suggests 'access' to Robert Harley and the Tories. Swift was nicknamed 'Dr. Martin' by Harley 'because *Martin* is a sort of swallow, and so is a *Swift*' (*PW*, XVI, 381), but also most probably in allusion to the Anglican brother in *A Tale of a Tub* (see also *Exam*, p. xxvi, n.). In 1704, Francis Atterbury, the leader of the High Church party among the lower clergy, had recommended *A Tale of a Tub* in a letter to Harley: "'Tis very well written and will do good service.'[8] In *Memoirs, Relating to that Change which happened in the Queen's Ministry in the Year 1710* (written 1714), Swift gives an account of his recruitment as Tory ministerial publicist and apologist in 1710:

> Mr. Harley told me, he and his friends knew very well what useful things I had written against the principles of the late discarded faction; and, that my personal esteem for several among them, would not make me a favourer of their cause: That there was now an entirely new scene: That the Queen was resolved to employ none but those who were friends to the constitution of church and state: That their great difficulty lay in the want of some good pen, to keep up the spirit raised in the people, to assert the principles, and justify the proceedings of the new ministers.
>
> (*PW*, VIII, 123)

Swift's only published works of plain anti-Whig bias before 1710 were *A Letter from a Member of the House of Commons in Ireland to a Member of the House of Commons in England, Concerning the Sacramental Test* (published December 1708) and *A Project for the Advancement of Religion, and the Reformation of Manners* (published April 1709), both of which appeared anonymously. There was also *A Tale of a Tub*, never acknowledged in print by Swift although he was widely reputed to be the author. The fifth edition with the 'Apology' and notes was published in 1710, presumably just before Swift's arrival in London in September (*Corr*, I, 166–7; *Exam*, p. xli, n. 4). The *Tale* may very well have been one of the 'useful things' written against Whig principles, and one of Swift's writings in which Harley and the Tories perceived the presence of an able 'Church party' polemicist.

Despite the *Tale*'s notoriety Swift was not being unreasonable in feeling that the work would ingratiate him with the Tories and serve 'the church'. Eighteenth-century readers seem to have recognized High Church partisanship in the work, which in the divisive period between 1696 and 1710 was implicitly Tory. There is evidence that in Tory circles the *Tale* was regarded as revealing a 'useful' talent. In the

---

[8] Historical Manuscripts Commission. *Fifteenth Report, Appendix, Part IV. The Manuscripts of His Grace The Duke of Portland*, vol. IV (London, 1897), pp. xi, 155.

summer of 1704 Atterbury was also recommending *A Tale of a Tub* to the Tory Bishop of Exeter, Jonathan Trelawny. Atterbury and Trelawny clearly recognized an original polemical talent 'able to do service'.[9] Atterbury undoubtedly appreciated *The Battel of the Books*, which champions the 'Ancient' position of Sir William Temple and Atterbury's former pupil Charles Boyle against Richard Bentley and William Wotton and awards the victory in the Phalaris controversy to the cause of Atterbury and the High Church Tory Christ Church wits. Atterbury may have appreciated what I will suggest is Swift's witty allusion in the *Tale* to a 1687–8 controversy at Oxford over the spirit of Martin Luther, in which Atterbury had written a celebrated treatise. He would have been deeply sympathetic in principle to the *Tale*'s extreme attack on popery and Dissent.

The Tory satirist and Christ Church man William King was alarmed when the profane *Tale* was attributed to him, and he publicly dissociated himself from the book by writing against it. Swift was friendly with King and secured him the post of Gazetteer in 1711.[10] In the 'Apology' Swift remarked that King '*writ against the Conviction of his Talent*' when he composed *Some Remarks on The Tale of a Tub* (1704) (*Tale*, p. 11). King makes some interesting points about the political character of the *Tale*, which have been neglected in Swift scholarship. King interprets the Bookseller's Dedication to Somers as disrespectful. He also assumes that the *Tale* is recognized as the work of a 'violent Tory'.[11] Dr Johnson's famous anecdote in his *Life of Swift* that the High Church extremist Henry Sacheverell tried to flatter the Tory George Smalridge by seeming to think the wild work was his reflects a contemporary view that *A Tale of a Tub* was High Church Tory in provenance. Whigs and Low Churchmen were hostile to the work. William Wotton placed the book explicitly within a contemporary polemical context. Grieved by the alleged irreligion of the *Tale*, Wotton writes: 'This 'tis which makes the difference between the sharp and virulent Books written in this Age against any Sect of Christians, and those which were written about the beginning of the Reformation between the several contending Parties then in *Europe*.' The miscellany volume 'is one of the Prophanest Banters upon the Religion of *Jesus Christ*, as such, that ever yet appeared. In the *Tale*, in the *Digressions*, in

9 *Epist. Corr.*, III, 203, 214, 218.
10 *PW*, XVI, 452; *The Original Works of William King L. L. D.*, 3 vols. (London, 1776), I, xxiii–xxiv.
11 William King, *Some Remarks on The Tale of a Tub*, in *The Original Works*, I, 209–18 (pp. 215, 217).

the *Fragment*, the same Spirit runs through, but rather most in the *Fragment*, in which all extraordinary Inspirations are the Subjects of his Scorn and Mockery, whilst the Protestant Dissenters are, to outward appearance, the most directly levelled at.'[12] Whigs read the book as irreligious and as an attack on principles of 'Moderation'.[13] Swift's eighteenth-century biographer Thomas Sheridan regarded the publication of the *Tale* as a Tory political act.[14]

Swift, of course, still moved in Whig circles until 1710. The anonymous *Tale* with its violent satire of Dissent and pillorying of Sir Humphrey Edwin's occasional conformity appeared in May during the parliamentary recess and as the Tory extremists agitated for the 'Tack' of the Occasional Conformity Bill to the Land Tax Bill. The text draws attention to its 'moment' of publication – the 'Production' of 'a long Prorogation of Parliament'; it 'will serve for an *Interim*'; 'No Man hath more nicely observed our Climate, than the Bookseller who bought the Copy of this Work' (*Tale*, pp. 30, 41, 206). Writing in the *Examiner* of 16 November 1710 Swift provocatively affirmed his support for the Tory 'Church in danger' campaign of 1705, which was mounted after the defeat of the highflyers' third Occasional Conformity Bill in December 1704 (*Exam*, pp. 38–9). This chapter registers the incendiary party-political resonance of Swift's great satire of 1704.

Heretics and High Church politics

A Tale of a Tub is a 'Modernist' raree-show put on by a censorious satiric showman. But the immediate polemical character of Swift's satiric exhibits perceived by Swift's contemporaries has been neglected in modern editorial and critical commentary on the volume. J. R. Crider's excellent and important study of the 'History of *Fanaticism*' in the *Mechanical Operation of the Spirit* (see *Tale*, pp. 283–9) concludes, for instance, that

12 William Wotton, *A Defense of the Reflections upon Ancient and Modern Learning, ... With Observations upon The Tale of a Tub, Observations* rpt. in *Tale*, pp. 313–28 (pp. 324–5).
13 See, for example, *A Morning's Discourse of a Bottomless Tubb, Introducing the Historical Fable of the Oak and her Three Provinces ... Written by a Lover of the Loyal, Honest, and Moderate Party* (London, 1712), see pp. 6, 21–6; *Swift: The Critical Heritage*, edited by Kathleen Williams, pp. 48–9, 52, 70; [Thomas Burnet], *A Letter to the People, To be left for them at the Booksellers; With a Word or Two of the Bandbox Plot* (London, 1712); [Richard Steele], *The Public Spirit of the Tories, Manifested in the Case of the Irish Dean, and his Man Timothy* (London, 1714); [Thomas Burnet], *A Second Tale of a Tub: Or, The History of Robert Powel the Puppet-Show-Man* (London, 1715).
14 Thomas Sheridan, *The Life of the Rev. Dr. Jonathan Swift* (London, 1784; rpt. in *Swiftiana* XV, New York, 1974), pp. 48–9.

As for the sixteenth- and seventeenth-century sectarians cited in the 'History', since all of them stood near the farthest extreme of individualism and, by reputation at least, antinomianism, the view that the *Mechanical Operation* is a satire on Presbyterians, Independents, Baptists, and Quakers is imprecise. All these groups, in fact, repudiated the antinomianism of Swift's fanatics. It is true that Swift names the Quakers, but even here the reference is to the Quakers when they 'first appeared'.[15]

But the project of contemporary High Church and Tory polemic was to collocate modern Dissent with antinomian fanaticism. Swift certainly effects such a satiric collocation in the *Tale* and the *Mechanical Operation of the Spirit*. He does not scruple in the *Tale* to conflate the different sects of Protestant Dissent – English and Scottish Presbyterianism, continental Calvinism, Quakerism, Anabaptism and 'Enthusiasm'. Separating from Martin, Jack is recognized by several denominations:

AND now the little Boys in the Streets began to salute him with several Names. Sometimes they would call Him, *Jack the Bald*; sometimes, *Jack with a Lanthorn*; sometimes, *Dutch Jack*; sometimes, *French Hugh*; sometimes, *Tom the Beggar*; and sometimes, *Knocking Jack of the North*. And it was under one, or some, or all of these Appellations (which I leave the Learned Reader to determine) that he hath given Rise to the most Illustrious and Epidemick Sect of *Aeolists*, who with honourable Commemoration, do still acknowledge the Renowned *JACK* for their Author and Founder.

(Tale, pp. 141–2)

Provocatively, the religious and intellectual aberrations from the satire's implied norms of Established Anglicanism in religion and the 'Ancients' in learning are exposed in the *Tale* as atavistic. Just as flagitious modern criticism is of disreputable antiquity (see Sect. III. '*A Digression concerning* Criticks', *Tale*, pp. 92–104), so modern Dissent is connected with ancient heresy, especially the early Gnostic sects anathematized by the early Church Fathers. Irenaeus' *Adversus Haereses* is recognized as 'one of the major models of Swift's own attack on religious individualism in the *Tale*'.[16] The satirized putative author of the *Tale* is made analogous to a Gnostic heretic (see the quotation from Irenaeus on the title-page and *Tale*, pp. 30, 54, 187). What we formally hear in

[15] J.R. Crider, 'Dissenting Sex: Swift's "History of Fanaticism"', *SEL: Studies in English Literature, 1500–1900*, 18 (1978), 491–508 (p. 508).

[16] C. J. Rawson, 'Cannibalism and Fiction: Reflections on Narrative Form and "Extreme" Situations, Part I', *Genre*, 10 (1977), 667–711 (p. 690), see also pp. 700, 705. See Irenaeus, *Against Heresies*, in *The Ante-Nicene Fathers*, edited by Alexander Roberts and James Donaldson, revised by A. Cleveland Coxe (New York, 1896, rpt. Michigan, 1981), I, 309–567.

the *Tale* is the voice of heretical, Enthusiastical Whig Dissent. Irenaeus' *Adversus Haereses*, and heresiologies such as Thomas Edwards's *Gangraena*, with which Swift was familiar,[17] were much mined and cited by Anglican controversialists in the paper wars of the late seventeenth and early eighteenth centuries. Andrew Marvell, in *The Rehearsal Transpros'd: The Second Part* (1673), observed that his Anglican antagonist Samuel Parker, in attacking religious toleration for Dissenters, adduced a provocative parallel between the ancient Gnostic heretics and the nonconformists: 'There is one thing more in your discussion of Christian Liberty concerning the *Gnosticks*, whom you very frequently parallel to the Non-conformists; which, would I seek for new matter of mirth or stir up fresh controversies, does administer me abundant occasion. But I shall defer that till your Diagnosticks be better.'[18] But the Anglican 'Diagnosticks' of Dissent remained an offensive polemical manoeuvre in the paper wars over passive obedience, religious toleration, liberty of conscience and schism. The Anglican ideologist of absolute non-resistance William Falkner, for instance, explicitly linked the heretical doctrines and '*unclean practises*' of Simon Magus and the Gnostics with Romanist and Presbyterian revolutionism. The papal doctrine of popular resistance, deposition and regicide asserted now by men of 'a *Fanatick strain*' is damnable heresy.[19] Irenaeus' arraignment of Simon Magus and the Gnostics and 'histories' of heretics were High Church polemical idioms in the contemporary offensive against Socinianism, Deism, Quakerism, Enthusiasm and, covertly, the legitimacy of Dissent conferred in effect by the Toleration Act of 1689. The immediate polemical character of Swift's satire is illuminated if the literary text is juxtaposed with non-literary texts of the 1696–1704 period.

Swift's sardonic 'History of *Fanaticism*' proceeds from the 'early Traces we meet with, of *Fanaticks*, in antient Story' (*Tale*, pp. 283–5) to 'the numerous Sects of *Hereticks* appearing in the five first Centuries of

---

[17] Swift studied Saint Irenaeus, *Adversus Valentini & Similium Gnosticorum Haereses Libri Quinque* (Paris, 1675), in 1697. For Swift's reading in 1697 and the *Tale*, see *Tale*, pp. liii–lx; Jonathan Swift, *The Battle of the Books: Eine historisch-kritische Ausgabe mit literarhistorischer Einleitung und Kommentar* von Hermann Josef Real (Berlin and New York, 1978), Appendix B, pp. 128–32. Swift possessed a copy of Edwards's *Gangraena* (1646), see LeFanu, p. 17; *SC*, no. 515.

[18] Andrew Marvell, *The Rehearsal Transpros'd and The Rehearsal Transpros'd The Second Part*, edited by D. I. B. Smith (Oxford, 1971), pp. 257–8. Moderate nonconformist writers repudiated the High Church polemical parallel of nonconformists with '*the old Gnostick Separatists*', see *Moderation a Vertue* (London, 1683), p. 10.

[19] William Falkner, *Christian Loyalty* ... (London, 1679), esp. pp. 326, 334–5, 342–3, 405–7.

the *Christian Aera*, from *Simon Magus* and his Followers, to those of *Eutyches*. The 'Historian' has 'collected their Systems from infinite Reading, and comparing them with those of their Successors in the several Ages since' finds they all agree in 'one fundamental Point', that of a *'Community of Women'*. The 'brief Survey of some Principal Sects, among the *Fanaticks*, in all Ages' concludes with the addition of 'several among our selves, such as the *Family of Love, Sweet Singers of Israel*, and the like' mentioning 'the *Quakers*' by name and satirizing as libidinous the 'Spiritual exercise' of 'the *Saints*'. Religious Enthusiasm and Quaker practices are satirically travestied in the 'History', as elsewhere in the *Mechanical Operation*, as a manifestation of carnal lust (*Tale*, pp. 285–9, 271–3).

Germane to a reading of Swift's religious satire is the pamphleteering of Charles Leslie. As an apologist for the Quakers commented in 1732: '*Leslie* has been long esteem'd by the high-church party, as their greatest champion. The works he has left behind him, are the magazines, from whence they furnish themselves with squibs and crackers, to throw at the *friendly people*.'[20] Swift was aware of Leslie's pamphleteering (*Corr*, I, 43; *PW*, II, 13). At the time of the *Tale*'s composition and publication Leslie was tracing the heretical antiquity of that Socinianism and Quakerism he felt were indulged in the latitudinarian Williamite polity to '*Simon Magus*'. Leslie contends that '*Ancient* and *Pestilent Heresies* are still kept alive amongst us, they are *Gather'd together*, and *Improv'd* by the *Quakers*.'[21] Swift's satire of hubris and self-sufficiency in learning and religion, connection of modern Dissent with Gnosticism, and specific animus against Quakers and the doctrine of the Inner Light have analogues in Leslie's polemic against the Quakers.[22] The account in the *Tale* of how Jack 'rent the *main* Body of his *Coat* from Top to Bottom' (*Tale*, p. 138); the satiric emphasis on Jack's contempt for '*Unity*' (*Tale*, p. 139); and the repudiation of *'Enthusiasm'* and claims of '*Inward Light*' in the *Mechanical Operation of the Spirit* are literary renditions of the contemporary polemical offensive being conducted by High Churchmen such as Leslie against heresy and radical Whig principles in Church and State. Leslie was writing that the Quakers '*Rend asunder the Seamless Coat of Christ Jesus*', '*Promote Factions and Divisions*', and are subject only '*to their* Enthusiastical

---

20 *The Advocate. A Defence of the B. of Lichfield and Coventry ... Including Some Remarks on the Writings of the late Mr. Charles Leslie ...* (London, 1732), pp. 43–4.
21 [Charles Leslie], *The History of Sin and Heresie ...* (London, 1698), pp. 17–18.
22 *The History of Sin and Heresie*, pp. 35–6.

Principle, THE LIGHT WITHIN'. Leslie prescribes an historical parallel of Quakers and earlier heresies as the best method of anathematizing and curing Quakerism.[23] Swift's 'History of Fanaticism' concluding with the Quakers participates in this contemporary polemical project. Swift's reductive satire of the heretics and Quakers as agreeing in the 'fundamental Point' of the *'Community of Women'* reproduces Leslie's insinuation of sectarian and heretical sexual promiscuity. Like Swift, who refers to the libidinous predilection of the Quakers when they 'first appeared' (*Tale*, p. 287), Leslie claims to be only exposing the sexual licentiousness of original Quakerism practised by some Quaker groups and by the Quakers when 'they first appear'd':

I would not be thought, nor is it any Part of my Design, to charge the whole Body of the Quakers with this Heresie [the heresy of the 'Nicolaitans' which is *'that they hold promiscuous use of Women without any respect to marriage, to be lawful'*]; But there is a Party who go under that Name, and who pretend to be more exactly conformable to their Primitive Principles than any of the rest ... who have greedily embraced this Heresie of the *Nicolaitans*.[24]

Leslie's history of heresies juxtaposed with Quakerism draws attention to evidence of sexual promiscuity and to the alleged heretical Quaker principle of women held *'in Common'*. Swift's shorter satiric 'History' in the *Mechanical Operation of the Spirit* concentrates on the heretics in history against whom this charge could be made and adds the Quakers at the end of his catalogue. Leslie forces parallels between George Fox and the Quakers and *'Simon Magus'*, *'Mahomet'*, 'Eutyches', 'John of *Leiden*, a Taylor' and 'David Georgius, *an Impudent Fellow, and a pestilent Heretick'*. Swift also links the Quakers with these heretics in a tradition of dissenting sex.

Jack's radical reformation in the *Tale* left his coat 'either wholly rent to his Shirt; or those Places which had scaped his cruel Clutches, were still in *Peter's* Livery' (*Tale*, p. 140). Jack's 'Rags' resemble Peter's 'Finery', so that 'it fared with *Jack* and his Tatters, that they offered to the first View a ridiculous Flanting, which assisting the Resemblance in Person and Air, thwarted all his Projects of Separation, and left so near a Similitude between them, as frequently deceived the very Disciples

---

23 [Charles Leslie], *A Parallel Between the Faith and Doctrine of the Present Quakers, And that of the Chief Hereticks in all Ages of The Church. And also A Parallel between Quakerism and Popery* (London, 1700). All quotations from the unpaginated 'Preface'.
24 *A Parallel* . . ., pp. 17, 13–14 and see p. 35. In his best sardonic manner Leslie, in his earlier, well-known tract *The Snake in the Grass* (London, 1696) had disclosed the alleged sexual license behind the hypocritical pretence to purity of the Quakers (see esp. pp. 90, 95–6).

and Followers of both' (*Tale*, p. 200). The agreement in principle and practice between popery and the sects is Leslie's favourite theme: 'Quakerism being as Rotten a Fabrick as Popery is, stands in need of the same Crutches, Props and Pillars to support it, that Popery doth.'[25] Swift's 'Jack' is recognizable in Leslie's account of the schism of Quakers and other Dissenters from the Church of England:

And he that will make a *Separation* for every *Error*, will fall into much greater *Error* and *Sin* than that which he would seek to Cure. It is like tearing *Christ's* seamless *Coat*, because we like not the *colour*, or to mend the Fashion of a Sleeve.[26]

In Section I of the *Mechanical Operation of the Spirit* Swift ironically introduces the Anglican 'dangerous Objection' to sectarian claims of inspiration. Charles Leslie, George Hickes and Swift himself would have been among the 'certain Criticks' who positively deny 'that the *Spirit* can by any means be introduced into an Assembly of Modern Saints, the Disparity being so great in many material Circumstances, between the Primitive Way of Inspiration, and that which is practised in the present Age'. These 'Objectors' distinguish between the Pentecost and Conventicles of dissentious illiterates wearing hats (*Tale*, p. 270).[27] The 'Objections' of the Anglican 'Adversaries' to the supernatural inspiration pretended to by the modern saints are accepted, but it is proved that 'our Modern Artificers' practise a mechanical operation of the spirit in their assemblies (*Tale*, p. 271). Swift's violent derision of the doctrine of the Inner Light and the religious practices of his fellow Protestants pained moderate Low Church contemporaries such as William Wotton as well as the contemporary apologists for Quaker principles and liberty of conscience. The satire derives from the invective art of the High Church pamphleteering tradition in which Leslie was a master.

Swift draws attention in the *Mechanical Operation of the Spirit* to the long Anglican offensive against Quakerism: 'It hath continued these

---

25 *A Parallel* ..., p. 49. On the parity of popery and Quakerism, see pp. 49–59.
26 [Charles Leslie], *Primitive Heresie Revived In the Faith and Practice of the People Called Quakers* ... in *Five Discourses By the Author of the Snake in the Grass* (London, 1700), pp. 99–153 (p. 152). Leslie explicitly rejected the Quakers' claim to be 'the *Purest* and most *Perfect* of Christians' (p. 122). Swift lashes 'Pretenders to Purity' (*Tale*, p. 190).
27 See, for example, *The Spirit of Enthusiasm Exorcised: In a Sermon Preach'd Before the University of Oxford, &c. The Fourth Edition, much enlarg'd. By George Hickes D. D. With Two Discourses Occasioned by the New Prophets Pretensions to Inspiration and Miracles* ... (London, 1709), esp. pp. 64–5. Swift possessed this work, see LeFanu, p. 20; *SC*, no. 445. The sermon was first published in 1680. [Leslie], *A Parallel* ..., pp. 2–3, 9.

hundred Years an even Debate, whether the Deportment and the Cant of our *English* Enthusiastick Preachers, were *Possession*, or *Inspiration*, and a World of Argument has been drained on either side, perhaps, to little Purpose' (*Tale*, p. 275). Leslie, for instance, had suggested that George Fox and the Quakers were like Simon Magus because they evidenced demonical possession. In Fox's life 'there are some Instances which make it probable that the Spirit he pretended to, and by which he was acted, was no good Spirit; As Those preternatural Shakings, Foamings, and Swellings, which were usual among them, when he first set up to make Proselytes'.[28] As Swift writes: 'certain Objectors pretend to put it beyond all Doubt, that there must be a sort of preternatural *Spirit*, possessing the Heads of the Modern Saints' (*Tale*, pp. 282–3). Swift describes 'the *Phoenomenon* of *Spiritual Mechanism*' in an assembly of modern saints in what is a scurrilous satire of a Quaker meeting:

It is here to be noted, that in forming and working up the *Spirit*, the Assembly has a considerable Share, as well as the Preacher; The Method of this *Arcanum*, is as follows. They violently strain their Eye balls inward, half closing the Lids; Then, as they sit, they are in a perpetual Motion of *See-saw*, making long Hums at proper Periods, and continuing the Sound at equal Height, chusing their Time in those Intermissions, while the Preacher is at Ebb.

(*Tale*, p. 271, see p. 273)

The satirist is sure that no supernatural inspiration comes to modern Saints and with sardonic seriousness discourses on the mechanical operation of the carnal spirit and the 'Art of Canting' in 'the Commonwealth of *artificial Enthusiasm*' (see *Tale*, pp. 276–83). Like Leslie, Swift attacks the practice of occasional conformity through which the fanatic and heretic mechanical operators he describes have obtained political power under the Williamite regime, instancing Sir Humphrey Edwin's Lanthorn 'Mayoralty, of happy Memory' (*Tale*, p. 279). In *A Dissertation*, Leslie execrated Whig latitudinarian ecclesiastical politics: '*Tender Conscience* and *Moderation* is pleaded on their behalf, who *Tear the Body* of *Christ* in *Pieces* by various *Sects* and *Schisms*.'[29] The High Church Tory polemicist William Baron, in a tract written in 1702 but published in 1703 in support of the Occasional Conformity Bill, reflected:

that a *Common-wealth Ministry* in our *English Monarchy* (asking Pardon for so much boldness with our *Saviour's Simile*) is like *a piece of new Cloth on an old Garment*, it looks *beggarly* at best; and doth constantly break out into such *Rents*,

---

[28] [Leslie], *A Parallel* . . ., p. 2.
[29] [Charles Leslie], *A Dissertation Concerning the Use and Authority of Ecclesiastical History* (London, 1703), p. xvi.

as would have brought any *Nation* but ours, to *beggary*, long since; and if they be suffer'd to *patch* on as hitherto, thither it must come in the *End*.[30]

The author of *A Tale of a Tub* could give a full account of 'How *Jack*'s Tatters came into Fashion in *Court* and *City*' and how Jack became Lord Mayor of London (*Tale*, pp. 204–5). Contemporary Old or True Whigs such as John Toland regarded the attack on the Quakers since the Revolution as an initial stage in the High Tory design against the Toleration and a party-political conspiracy against the Revolution government.[31]

The *Tale*'s satiric association of Jack with Peter, and with the Aeolists and Laplanders would have had political resonance for contemporaries. Ehrenpreis has drawn attention to Swift's technique of associating his enemies with the side they in principle repudiate, observing Swift's association of those apparent opposites, papist and Dissenter. 'This is one of his normal but most cunning devices.'[32] Section XI of the *Tale* contains a famous extended satiric passage where Jack and Peter are brought into conjunction. Their persons and coats have a strong resemblance, their 'Humours and Dispositions were not only the same, but there was a close Analogy in their Shape, their Size and their Mien.' They are confused for each other by arresting authorities and accosting friends. They collude in identical designs (see *Tale*, pp. 198–200, 204). There is some ideological and historical basis for Swift's burlesque. As Wotton conceded in 1705 in a passage Swift introduced into the fifth edition of the *Tale* as a note: '*The Agreement of our Dissenters and the Papists in that which Bishop* Stillingfleet *called,* The Fanaticism of the Church of *Rome, is ludicrously described for several Pages together by* Jack's *Likeness to* Peter, *and their being often mistaken for each other, and their frequent Meeting, when they least intended* it. W. Wotton' (*Tale*, p. 198). The political likeness of popery and Dissent was commonly alleged by contemporary High Churchmen. Theories of popular sovereignty and justified resistance which were associated with radical and dissenting whiggery in Swift's day could be demonstrated to have a Jesuitical and radical Protestant ancestry. Swift's note points out that the '*Papists and Fanaticks, tho' they appear the most Averse to each other, yet bear a near Resemblance in many things, as has been observed by Learned Men*' (*Tale*, p. 198). But the imputation of consonance in political ideology and collaboration in practice between popery and Dissent was the routine

---

[30] William Baron, *Separation and Sedition Inseparable* (London, 1703), p. 3.
[31] John Toland, *The Art of Governing by Parties* ... (London, 1701), pp. 22–3.
[32] *Swift*, III, 763.

signature of a High Church text when Swift published the *Tale*.
William Baron, for instance, would have been an appreciative political
reader of Swift's satiric collocation of Jack and Peter. In *An Historical
Account of Comprehension, and Toleration* (1705) Baron rehearses a received
view of the parallels and borrowing between Roman Catholic and
Calvinist ideologists and their accord in popular revolutionism. Baron's
Romanist Jesuit and Genevan Protestant, like Swift's Peter and Jack,
find 'their *Principles continually meet* and *shake hands*'.[33]

Accounts of plots against the Church of England Establishment in
seventeenth-century Anglican royalist polemical literature routinely
imputed a conspiratorial nexus between Jesuits and nonconformist
sects.[34] Jesuits were witnessed in disguise fermenting rebellion among
the Puritans, Dissenters were 'Papists in Masquerade'. Swift may well
be alluding to the confusion surrounding the 'Meal-Tub Plot' (believed
at first to be a Presbyterian then a Catholic plot) and the 'Popish Plot'
('*Popish Plots*, and *Meal-Tubs*' (*Tale*, p. 70)) when it is reported in the
Tale that 'nothing was more frequent than for a Bayliff to seize *Jack* by
the Shoulders, and cry, *Mr* Peter, *You are the King's Prisoner*' (*Tale*,
p. 199). As indicated in chapter 2, an immediate political context for
Swift's satiric collocation of Jack and Peter is the apparent alliance
between Whig Dissent and James II in 1687 and the post-Revolution
High Church Tory polemic which reminded readers of Whig Dissenting sympathy and collaboration with James II's policy of prerogative
toleration, evidenced in the many addresses of thanks to the King
subscribed by Dissenting groups of all persuasions (see *Tale*, p. 204,
Swift's note).[35]

The Tory Thomas Long in *The Letter For Toleration Decipher'd* (1689),

---

[33] *An Historical Account of Comprehension, and Toleration ... Part I. By the Author of the Dutch Way of Toleration* (London, 1705), pp. 69–70. See also George Smalridge, *A Sermon Preach'd before the Honourable House of Commons, At St. Margarets Westminster, Jan. 30, 1702 ...* (London, 1702), p. 14.

[34] For a masterpiece of lively sardonic invective against Jesuits and Presbyterians in this Anglican royalist polemical genre, see Henry Foulis, *The History of the Wicked Plots and Conspiracies of Our Pretended Saints ...* (London, 1662). See also: [John Nalson], *Foxes and Fire-brands: Or a Specimen of the Danger and Harmony of Popery and Separation. ...* (London, 1680); George Hickes, *The Spirit of Popery Speaking Out of the Mouthes of Fanatical Protestants* (London, 1680). The collusion of 'Jack Presbyter' with Jesuitical popery is a *leitmotiv* in Roger L'Estrange's *The Observator, in Dialogue*, April 13 1681–March 9 1687 (London, 1684–7), see esp. The First Volume (London, 1684), no. 68 (5 November 1681); no. 110 (11 March 168[2]); no. 333 (5 May 1683); no. 341 (19 May 1683).

[35] For a specimen of Presbyterian Jack accepting Peter's protection, see [Vincent Alsop], *The Humble Address of the Presbyterians, Presented to the King ... With His Majesties Gracious Answer* (n.p., 1687).

an attack on John Locke's *Letter on Toleration*, described how the Anglican Establishment in State and Church was assaulted '*the one by an All-Dispensing Power, the other by an Absolute Liberty . . . And there are still a sort of* Lapland *Sorcerers, that would give Vent to the like Winds to encrease our Storms'*. Contending for an '*Absolute and Uncontrolable Liberty in Religious Worship*', for the right of forcible resistance to a magistracy enacting laws against public liberty of conscience in religion, and for a Church that would be a voluntary society, Locke '*like another* Faux, *with his Dark Lanthorn, is ready to blow up the Religion and Loyalty, by God's Blessing, now Established, into meer Air and Atheism*'.[36] While a Tory like Long imagined the ideologists of radical Whig Dissent as Lapland sorcerers turning all into air, in the Jacobite press the Calvinist William of Orange and his Dutch advisers were depicted seeking assistance for their diabolical design in 'the Hellish Country of *Laplandia*' where there are 'certain old Haggs, who have infinite familiarity with the Infernal Spirits, and have often sold Winds' to the Dutchmen.[37] Swift could have read in *Gangraena* the story, repeated in his copy of Roger L'Estrange's *The Dissenters Sayings*, of Samuel Oats, a 'Dipper' in the Interregnum, who was reported to have baptized a woman and then 'bid her gape, and she gaped, and he did blow three times into her mouth, saying words to this purpose, either *receive the holy Ghost*, or now *thou hast received the holy Ghost*'.[38] Late seventeenth-century Tory literature, with its association of Dissenters with Gnostics, imaginative identification of radical whiggery (indeed even William III) with Lapland sorcery and winds, and representation of inspiration among the sects as a literal blowing and inhaling of air, might have provided Swift with 'Hints' which he developed into the full-blown satiric fantasy of Jack's sect of Aeolists, a violent burlesque of sectarian Enthusiasm and the Quakers (*Tale*, Section VIII). The Aeolist priests, 'their *Mouths gaping wide against a Storm*', issue '*Wind* and Vapours' through a distorted mouth and bloated cheeks and 'their *Belches* were received for Sacred, the Sourer the better, and swallowed with infinite Consolation by their meager Devotees'. The tub preacher 'disembogues whole Tempests upon his Auditory'; he delivers 'his oracular *Belches* to his panting Disciples; Of

---

[36] Thomas Long, *The Letter For Toleration Decipher'd* . . . (London, 1689), Dedication, sig. A and pp. 1, 3.

[37] [John Sergeant], *An Historical Romance*, p. 22.

[38] Thomas Edwards, *Gangraena* 3 pts, part II, p. 147; Roger L'Estrange, *The Dissenters Sayings. Two Parts in One* . . . (London, 1685 [1705]), p. 7. Swift owned L'Estrange's *Dissenters Sayings* and other pamphlets, see *SC*, no. 514 (marked in the catalogue as having been annotated by Swift). Swift refers to L'Estrange's writings, see *Tale*, pp. 7, 70, 183.

whom, some are greedily gaping after the sanctified Breath'. Women are prominent among the sects, especially the Quakers, it is explained, because their 'Organs were understood to be better disposed for the Admission of those Oracular Gusts'. Jack's Aeolists, who have literally blown up religion into air in this satiric nightmare, are linked with the '*Laplanders*' who 'appear to be so closely allied in Point of Interest, as well as Inclinations, with their Brother *Aeolists* among Us, as not only to buy their *Winds* by wholesale from the *same* Merchants, but also to retail them after the *same* Rate and Method, and to Customers much alike' (see *Tale*, pp. 153–60).

A Tory tale of the times and Jack in polemical context

The author impersonated by Swift in the *Tale* is a scribbling son of modern faction, his 'Quill worn to the Pith in the Service of the State, in *Pro's* and *Con's* upon *Popish Plots*, and *Meal-Tubs*, and *Exclusion Bills*, and *Passive Obedience*, and *Addresses of Lives and Fortunes*; and *Prerogative*, and *Property*, and *Liberty of Conscience*, and *Letters to a Friend*'. His 'Conscience, thread-bare and ragged with perpetual turning', the party writer confesses: 'Four-score and eleven Pamphlets have I written under three Reigns, and for the Service of six and thirty Factions' (*Tale*, p. 70). A celebrant of schism and heterodoxy, he is the Enthusiastical chronicler of all that High Churchmen regarded as flagitious in modern polity. The author tells us in his 'Preface' that he is retained by 'the Grandees of *Church* and *State*' to divert the Leviathan wits of the present age, who threaten 'to pick Holes in the weak sides of Religion and Government' with 'Pamphlets, and other Offensive Weapons', by producing 'a *Tale of a Tub*' (*Tale*, pp. 39–41). The diversionary book is duly dedicated to one of those grandees – the Junto Whig 'The Right Honourable John Lord Sommers'. Swift's author may be an impersonation of one of those Dissenting Whig pamphleteers complained of by Roger L'Estrange in his address 'To The Reader' in *The Dissenter's Sayings*:

This is precisely the Seven and Thirty'th *Civility of This Kind, that I have Received, within less than Two Months, from the* True Protestant Dissenters: *Which truly I look upon but as so many empty Casks thrown out to divert me from sinking the Rotten Barque they are Engag'd in. These Learned Pieces, I know very well, are Compos'd, and Publish'd at the* Charge, *and for the* Service *of our* Ignatian Society.

The Dissenter's Sayings will expose '*their* Pleas *and* Consciences *still varying with their* Fortunes'.[39] *A Tale of a Tub*, ostensibly the anonymous production of the garrets and printing presses of a modern Grub Street demotic dissenting Whig culture, might be viewed as a literary satiric version of *Dissenter's Sayings*. Speaking in the tongues of Dissent, radical Reformation, and the Good Old Cause and through a putative author who is an apologist for fanaticism and '*the Proceedings of the* Rabble *in all Ages*', Swift attempts to expose the ship of state in the period between 1696 and 1704 as a 'Rotten Barque', a ship of fools. Alluding to Interregnum republicanism, specifically to Harrington's *Oceana* which was republished by John Toland, Swift has his government writer admit that many 'Schemes of Religion and Government' are 'hollow, and dry, and empty, and noisy, and wooden, and given to Rotation' (*Tale*, p. 40). And the '*Commonwealth*' the author defends with his *Tale of a Tub* is 'too apt to *fluctuate*' (*Tale*, pp. 40–1). William Shippen, in his Tory poem *Faction Display'd*, published like the *Tale* in 1704, was exclaiming: 'O *England* how revolving is thy State!' under the influence of the Junto Whig leaders.[40]

Swift's satire of the times in the *Tale*, as in the early odes and 'On the Burning of Whitehall in 1698', is radical. While declaring in 'The Preface' that satire against mankind is ineffectual and pretending to have no talent or inclination for satire, Swift ironically writes a tirade against vice and corruption in the Williamite state in the 1690s. An allusion to sodomy ('Foppery and Fornication, and *something else*') in the moral satirist's list of vices is followed by a declamation against sin and corruption at the very centre of the Williamite court and government: 'Pride, and Dissimulation, and Bribery, at *White Hall*' (*Tale*, p. 52). Swift's satiric allusion to corruption and mismanagement in the navy (*Tale*, pp. 52–3) would have had topical political resonance in

---

[39] Roger L'Estrange, *The Dissenter's Sayings, In Requital for L'Estrange's Sayings. Published in Their Own Words, For the Information of the People* (London, 1681), 'To The Reader', sig. A2b, A3. L'Estrange's style, tone and phrases are specifically parodied by Swift in the *Tale*, see *Tale*, pp. 7, 70 and compare especially *The Observator in Dialogue. The First Volume*, 'To the Reader'. In the preface to *The Observator in Dialogue. The Third Volume* (London, 1687), L'Estrange, for example, appeals "To Posterity' (compare the *Tale*'s Dedication to 'Prince Posterity', *Tale*, pp. 30–8), remarks that 'People are well enough pleas'd to see' abuses stripped and whipped 'provided that they be *Lash'd* upon *Other-Folks Shoulders*' (compare *Tale*, pp. 51–3), compares his papers to a '*Looking-Glass*' (compare *Tale*, p. 215), suffers for his loyalty to the government, debates party questions '*Pro and Con*' (compare *Tale*, p. 70), and says the people are 'not to Trouble their *Heads* about the *Cracking* of *Controversies* that are too *Hard* for their *Teeth*' (compare *Tale*, p. 66). The *Observator* of Saturday, 29 May 1686 (*Observator*, vol. 3, no. 178) considers the subject of whether it is better to be a fool or a knave (compare *Tale*, pp. 171–4).

[40] *POAS*, 6, 648–73 (line 458).

1704. The Country Tory Commission of Public Accounts in the years
1702–4 had targeted the Junto Whig Edward Russell, Earl of Orford,
for financial malpractice as Treasurer of the Navy early in William's
reign.[41] In 'A Digression on Madness' the author recommends to the
volatile Tory MPs Sir Edward Seymour, Sir Christopher Musgrave, Sir
John Bolles, John How, Esq. and other patriots that they 'bring in a
Bill, for appointing Commissioners to Inspect into *Bedlam*'. The 'Commissioners of Inspection' will there find persons naturally suitable for
appointment to 'the several Offices in a State'. A madman could be
given 'a Regiment of Dragoons' and sent 'into *Flanders* among the *Rest*';
others might be assigned to the Inns of Court, the City financial and
commercial centre, the court, and the Royal College of Physicians
(*Tale*, pp. 175–9). The radical derision of the Establishment in the
digression has a political flavour in the general satiric allusion to the
Williamite army and court. The way the derisive contempt is expressed
– appointing madmen to important offices – also has, perhaps, a
political complexion. The mention of 'Sir J——n B——ls' (*Tale*,
p. 175; John Bolles, MP for Lincoln, 1690–1702) would have reminded
contemporary readers of a notorious parliamentary episode in 1701.
The Tory House of Commons placed Bolles, who was reputed to be
mad, in the chair of the committee on the bill for the Act of Settlement.
Putting a madman in the chair of the committee was understood as an
expression of High Tory contempt and aversion for this legislation
personally endorsed by William III.[42] Swift shows his radical aversion
to the present establishment in an analogous fictional strategy. When
he was writing and publishing *A Tale of a Tub* Swift was known as a
Whig. He had supported the Whig leaders in the *Discourse* of 1701. But
his unacknowledged, anonymous *Tale* with its putative Author and
self-protective ironic concealments nevertheless discloses an extremist
political writer disaffected with the Williamite court, and with civil,
military and ecclesiastical affairs.

The *Tale*'s satire on militarism, mercenary armies and war might
seem consistent with loyal Country or Old Whig anti-standing army
rhetoric of the late 1690s and therefore an expression of that Old Whig
politics which modern biography and criticism ascribe to Swift. Yet
attention to this aspect of the book's politics suggests its actual consonance with a disaffected Tory perspective. There is satire of a militaristic 'Great Prince' as a disease that can be cured by assassination (*Tale*,

[41] Geoffrey Holmes, *British Politics in the Age of Anne*, p. 139.
[42] Holmes, *British Politics in the Age of Anne*, p. 89.

pp. 163–4), reflection on William's Dutch regiments (*'Foreign Troops* in a *State'*, *Tale*, p. 144) and violent ridicule of the army in Flanders as blaspheming Bedlamites (*Tale*, p. 176). The ridicule of 'Jack's' cant about the threat of *'the* Pope, *and the* French *King'* has the effect of trivializing the threat (*Tale*, p. 198). There is a possible early instance of Swift's later sneer at 'Nassau, who got the name of glorious / Because he never was victorious' (*Poems*, II, 468) in *The Battel of the Books.* There Swift reflects parenthetically on the expensive military setbacks in William's continental campaigns in the nine-years war with France which concluded in the Peace of Ryswick in 1697: 'the *Grecians,* after an Engagement, when they could not *agree* about the Victory, were wont to set up Trophies on both sides, the beaten Party being content to be at the same Expence, to keep it self in Countenance (A laudable and antient Custom, happily reviv'd of late, in the Art of War)' (*Tale*, p. 221).

But it is the violence of the satire on Dissent – and contemporaries recognized that 'the Protestant Dissenters are … the most directly levelled at' (Wotton, *Observations, Tale*, p. 325) – which reveals that the author of the *Tale* is no Whig. There are unspeakable implications in this satire. The account of the 'Oratorial Machines' in 'The Introduction' contains a particularly frightening *frisson*. A description of the gallows (*'Ladders'*) immediately follows the description of a Dissenting Conventicle (*'Pulpits'* of the Scottish Kirk model). The Tub 'Pulpit' is explained to have a 'near Resemblance to a Pillory'. A plate in the fifth edition visually juxtaposes a tub preacher and an execution (*Tale*, pp. 58–9). The mountebank's stage is 'the great Seminary' of the gallows and Conventicle: 'its Orators are sometimes preferred to the One, and sometimes to the Other, in proportion to their Deservings, there being a strict and perpetual Intercourse between all three' (*Tale*, pp. 59–60). The *'Ladder* is an adequate Symbol of *Faction'* for reasons left unstated, there being an *'Hiatus in MS'* (*Tale*, p. 62). Daniel Defoe would expose just this kind of rhetorical extremism in High Church homiletic and pamphlet literature in *The Shortest Way with the Dissenters* (1702). The unrepentant Leslie wrote of that work in which he had been satirically impersonated:

This *Shortest Way* is a New *Engine* of the *Faction*, being wrote in the *Stile* of a *Church-man*, with an Air of *Wit* and a great deal of *Truth*; which they thought would make the *Severity* to Pass as coming from the *Church-Party*, to have the *Dissenters* Treated according to what he had prov'd to be their *Deserts*, that is, the *Preachers* to be sent to the *Gallows*, and the *Hearers* to the *Galleys*.[43]

43 [Charles Leslie], *The New Association Part II*, p. 6.

A Tale of a Tub disturbingly imagines a short way with the Dissenters in
the gallows humour of 'The Introduction'. Swift's satire suggests what
High Church militants thought the Dissenters deserved.

In a familiar Tory legerdemain, the *Tale* and *Mechanical Operation*
also imply that the modern Dissenters are the heirs of the Puritan
regicides (see *Tale*, pp. 195, 268). Swift's satire of the doctrine of
predestination (see *Tale*, pp. 192–4) is an ecclesiastical–political intervention in a contemporary paper war in which old wounds within the
Church of England were being re-opened. High Churchmen such as
Leslie, who were Arminian on this point in dispute, attacked predestinarian doctrine, identifying it with Calvinist Dissenters and some Low
Church divines. The political implication of Leslie's attack was that
predestinarians posed the threat of schism and that 'moderation' or
latitudinarian politics advocating *rapprochement* with Dissent could not
be countenanced by responsible clergy or the government.[44] The latitudinarian and predestinarian author of *Liberty of Conscience* objected to
the High Church clergy's ridicule of the doctrine of Predestination.[45]
Whereas Leslie was careful to establish his objections to the doctrine by
argument, the High Church satirist's use of sardonic ridicule in the *Tale*
exposed him to the charge of blasphemy. Wotton observed that:
'Things compared, always shew the Esteem or Scorn of the Comparer.
To ridicule Praedestination, *Jack* walks blindfold through the Streets;
the Body of our Dissenters having till of late been *Calvinists* in the
Questions concerning the *Five* Points.' The learned Low-Church Whig
quotes a passage of Swift's burlesque ridicule of predestination and then
anathematizes the author with a stark judgement that surely must have
unnerved Swift: 'This is a direct Prophanation of the Majesty of God'
(*Observations*, in *Tale*, p. 324). In the fifth edition of his book Swift
altered 'Providence' to 'nature' in the passage exposed by Wotton (see
Tale, pp. 193, 324), and in a 'Postscript' to the 1710 'Apology' Swift
anonymously denies an attribution of authorship to Thomas Swift and
himself (*Tale*, p. 20 and Appendix C, pp. 329–48).

A central religious and political concern of the satirist in *A Tale of a*

---

[44] [Charles Leslie], *The History of Sin and Heresie*, p. 49; [Leslie], *The New Association Part II*,
p. 19; [Leslie], *The Rehearsal*, I, p. vii. See esp. *Rehearsal* nos. 231–7 (2–23 August 1707).
The doctrine of predestination was still very much an active issue when the fifth edition of
the *Tale* appeared, see *The Criterion: Or, Touchstone, By which to judge of the Principles of High
and Low-Church, In a Letter to a Friend* (London, 1710), p. 4, and John Edwards, *The Divine
Perfections Vindicated . . .* (London, 1710).

[45] *Liberty of Conscience, or Religion A La Mode, Fitted for the Use of the Occasional Conformist, And
Dedicated to the most Learned Author of the Tale of a Tub* (London, 1704), pp. 20–1.

Tub is the Protestant Dissenters' alleged schism from the episcopal Church of England. The Romanist claim of precedence and the charge that the Church of England as well as the other Reformed Protestant churches were in fact schismatic are summarily dismissed by Swift in a sentence at the beginning of Section II: 'ONCE upon a Time, there was a Man who had Three Sons by one Wife, and all at a Birth, neither could the Mid-Wife tell certainly which was the Eldest' (*Tale*, p. 73). The commonplace standard Protestant charges against Romanist corruptions of primitive Catholic faith are rehearsed in Sections II and IV of the *Tale* (*Tale*, pp. 73–91, 105–22 and notes). But it is the career of Jack for which the satirist has the most intense animus, or, as Swift's putative author puts it in section VI: Brother Jack's 'Adventures will be so extraordinary, as to furnish a great Part in the Remainder of this Discourse' (*Tale*, p. 137). The contemporary political threat is perceived to come principally from Dissent not popery. In the *Tale* Jack's '*Zeal* is never so highly obliged, as when you set it a *Tearing*'. He says to his moderate Brother Martin: '*do as I do, for the Love of God: Strip, Tear, Pull, rent, Flay off all, that we may appear as unlike the Rogue* Peter, *as it is possible*' (*Tale*, pp. 138, 139). In 'a Meddley of *Rags*, and *Lace*, and *Rents*, and *Fringes*, unfortunate *Jack* did now appear: He would have been extremely glad to see his Coat in the Condition of *Martin*'s, but infinitely gladder to find that of *Martin*'s in the same Predicament with his'. Swift describes how Jack 'after as many of the *Fox*'s Arguments, as he could muster up, for bringing *Martin* to *Reason*, as he called it; or, as he meant it, into his own ragged, bobtail'd Condition' separates from Martin. There 'began a mortal Breach' between the two reforming brothers. '*Jack* went immediately to *New Lodgings*' and was reported to be mad (see *Tale*, p. 141).

This satiric account of Protestant Jack tearing his coat, which signifies in the parable the dismantling of pristine Christian faith and doctrine, has profound resonance, activating the Scriptural exhortation to Catholic uniformity and reminding readers of Christ's seamless coat which was not to be rent, parted or patched, and that there should be no schism in the body of Christ.[46] The language of Swift's satire of Jack has specific echoes in contemporary High Church Tory polemical

---

[46] For some key Scriptural texts behind Swift's use of the coat metaphor in his satiric parable of Romanist corruption of Catholic Christian faith and doctrine and the iconoclasm and anti-episcopal character of radical Protestant reformation, see I Corinthians 12.25; John 19.23–4; Psalms 22.18; Joel 2.13; Matthew 9.16; 23.5; Mark 2.21; Luke 5.36; Revelation 3.4; 16.15. Swift's clothing metaphor for Christian faith and doctrine in his satiric parable is conventional in Anglican literature.

literature against 'schismatic' Dissent. Leslie reproves the Dissenters for schism, describing it as the 'Rending' and '*Tearing*' of Christ's body or the Church.[47] Leslie's parable of the 'Countryman's House' (the Church) and some of his servants (the Dissenters) in the *Rehearsal* of 16 December 1704 – an attack on the allegedly causeless separation of Dissenters from the Church of England and argument for their complete exclusion from all public offices in the state – recalls Swift's satiric parable of the three brothers and their coats. In Leslie's ecclesiastical–political parable 'Countryman' tells how the servants in his house

> liv'd at the *beginning* very *peaceably* and *well*, and submitted to the *rules* and *customs* of the *family*, without any *grudging*. And tho' I keep a great *farm*, and employ many *servants*, yet I can say it, no *family* in the *county* was in better *order*, with more *love* and *kindness* among our selves, than mine.
> But at last, some of my *servants* grew *peevish*. They said, that the *colour* of the *cloaths* I was to give them, not being *expressed* in the *articles*, they would no longer *wear* that *colour* they had *worn* before. Nay, they found fault with the *colour* and *shape* of my own *cloaths*; and said, that neither I, my *wife* or *children* shou'd wear *such*, as we always had done *before*. they said it was an *offence* to them to *see* it, tho' upon OUR *backs*! and not being *express'd* in the *articles* with *them*, they were not *oblig'd* to *bear* with it. And that our *wearing* such *sort* of *cloaths*, was an *imposition* upon *them*.[48]

Jack's 'Tearing' and Swift's linkage of the Puritans and modern Enthusiasts with 'the *Scythians*' (see *Tale*, pp. 268, 269, 272) is a language with High Church Tory analogues. Leslie in the *Rehearsal* of 6 January 1705 writes of the modern avatars of '*Knocking Jack of the North*' (*Tale*, p. 142):

> You must know that at the beginning of this *revolution*, in *Decem*. 1688, our *Cameronian* ZEALOTS had the *wink* tipp'd to them, and took *arms*, and shew'd their *moderation* to the *clergy*, like the *Scythians*, O, most CURIOUSLY! *plundering*, *tearing*, and *murdering* at *discretion*. And this was made use of as an argument to shew the *inclinations* of the *people* against *episcopacy*.[49]

Joseph Trapp's Tory tract *Most Faults on One Side* (1710) describes '*Whiggish or Fanatical Moderation*' as consisting 'in *tearing* and *rending*' and denounces the Dissenters' 'Schism': 'Why do They causelessly rend the Church, and tear us in pieces with Quarrels and Factions? For the Distinctions of Parties into *Whig* and *Tory*, *High-Church* and *Low-Church*, are owing to *Their* unreasonable Separation; and Men are said

---

[47] *The New Association Part II*, p. 14; *The Wolf Stript of His Shepherd's Cloathing*, p. 2.
[48] *The Rehearsals*, I, 121–2 (*Rehearsal*, no. 20, 16 December 1704).
[49] *The Rehearsals*, I, 139 (*Rehearsal*, no. 23, 6 January 1705).

to be of This or That Party, according as They are more or less Favourers of the *Dissenters*.'[50] Swift's sermon 'On Brotherly Love', which can be read as a homiletic gloss on the parable of the brothers in *A Tale of a Tub*,[51] declares the Dissenters' schism to be the first cause of the 'great Want of Brotherly Love among us' and original source of party-political division (*PW*, IX, 172–3). The extreme satire of schismatic Jack in the *Tale* is an enduring literary product of the High Church reaction to the Toleration of 1689.

The attack against schism in *A Tale of a Tub* and more generally in *Gulliver's Travels*, where public conformity in a confessional state is represented as a positive (see *PW*, XI, 49–50, 60, 106, 131),[52] is an element identifying these satires as 'Tory' rather than 'Old Whig' in political inspiration. Indeed, it is the danger of schism that Swift invokes when he explicitly insists that heterodox Whig Commonwealth-men should be excluded from positions of public trust. Swift wrote in his 'Remarks upon a Book, intitled *The Rights of the Christian Church*':

> Employments in a State are a Reward for those who intirely agree with it … For Example, a Man who upon all Occasions declared his Opinion, of a Commonwealth before a Monarchy, would not be a fit Man to have Employments; let him enjoy his Opinion, but not be in a Capacity of reducing it to Practice.
>
> (*PW*, II, 102)

Tindal's advocacy of liberty of conscience fails to consider that 'there are some Opinions in several Religions, which, although they do not directly make Men rebel, yet lead to it' (*PW*, II, 89). Papists and

---

50 [J. Trapp], *Most Faults on One Side* (London, 1710), pp. 24, 41–2. Trapp had read Swift's *Tale* and seems to have recognized the parody of the voice of Whig Dissent, see the reference to the *Tale* on p. 39.

51 For a trenchant juxtaposition of *Tale* and sermon, see Martin Price, 'Pope, Swift and the Past', in *Studies in the Eighteenth Century 5: Papers Presented at the Fifth David Nichol Smith Memorial Seminar Canberra 1980*, edited by J. P. Hardy and J. C. Eade (Oxford, 1983), pp. 19–31 (pp. 21–2).

52 The King of Brobdingnag comments that 'he knew no Reason, why those who entertain Opinions prejudicial to the Publick, should be obliged to change, or should not be obliged to conceal them. And, as it was Tyranny in any Government to require the first, so it was Weakness not to enforce the second: For, a Man may be allowed to keep Poisons in his Closet, but not to vend them about as Cordials' (*PW*, XI, 131). The king voices Swift's opinion (compare *PW*, IX, 261). Swift's analogy of liberty of conscience with vending poison may recall Roger L'Estrange's *Dissenter's Sayings*. Compare *The Dissenters Sayings. Two Parts in One*, p. 3: '"A *Toleration* would be the putting a Sword into a mad Man's Hand; a Cup of Poyson into the Hands of a Child …"'; p. 4: '"Will Merciful Rulers set up a Trade for Butchering of Souls, and allow Men to set up a Shop of Poyson, for all Men to Buy, and Take, that will: Yea to Proclaim this Poyson for Souls in Streets and *Church-Assemblies*"'.

Dissenters 'have Opinions that may affect the Peace of the State' (*PW*, II, 107). Swift wholeheartedly supports the Sacramental Test for public employment and 'that it might be no Bribe, the Bill against Occasional Conformity would prevent entirely' (*PW*, II, 103). Tindal's project is schism, for which Swift pillories him: 'The Scripture is full against Schism. *Tindall* promoteth it, and placeth in it all the present and future Happiness of Man' (*PW*, II, 94; see also II, 91).

Swift wrote starkly in the unpublished 'Remarks' that: 'Men must be governed in Speculations, at least not suffered to vent them, because Opinions tend to Actions, which are most governed by Opinion' (*PW*, II, 99; see also II, 88).[53] *A Tale of a Tub* is a hostile distorted mimesis of speculative free-thinking. The putative author declares himself to be

a Person, whose Imaginations are hard-mouth'd, and exceedingly disposed to run away with his *Reason*, which I have observed from long Experience, to be a very light Rider, and easily shook off; upon which Account, my Friends will never trust me alone, without a solemn Promise, to vent my Speculations in this, or the like manner, for the universal Benefit of Human kind.

(*Tale*, p. 180; see also pp. 57, 71, 185)

In the 'Apology' affixed to the fifth edition of 1710 the anonymous real author describes himself as a person who '*had endeavour'd to Strip himself of as many real Prejudices as he could: I say real ones, because under the Notion of Prejudices, he knew to what dangerous Heights some Men have proceeded*' (*Tale*, p. 4). The satirized putative author of the *Tale* is one who has proceeded to dangerous heights. Venting his speculations without restraint, this admiring chronicler of schismatic Jack and the Acolists believes 'it one of the greatest, and best of humane Actions, to remove Prejudices' (*Tale*, p. 161). The satirized putative author speaks an anticlerical, Old Whig language.

---

[53] But speaking 'for the Honour of Liberty' against '*Tyranny*' in *The Sentiments of a Church-of-England Man*, Swift says that '*Slavery* is of all Things the greatest Clog and Obstacle to *Speculation*' (*PW*, II, 18). However, shackling the speculative mind may not be a bad thing in Swift's view when one considers what he writes about the danger of 'Speculations' in this tract and in the 'Remarks' on Tindal's *Rights* (*PW*, II, 13–14, 88). Swift's great satires endorse clogs on speculation. In the *Tale*, the putative Author uses a political metaphor in complaining of Time's 'Methods of Tyranny and Destruction' practised upon modern writings (*Tale*, p. 33). Swift's satire of the ephemerality and worthlessness of modern writings endorses the 'Tyranny' rather than the putative Author's (whiggish) indignation at the tyrant. In *Gulliver's Travels*, the Houyhnhnms are depicted as uniformitarian in sentiments. Swift's fabulous rational animals conspicuously lack that 'wonderful Agility' in 'Speculation' which is a damning characteristic of 'the *Modern* Party' in *The Battel of the Books* (*Tale*, p. 225; see especially *PW*, XI, 264, 267–8, 277). In his polemic Swift certainly supported placing restraints on the anticlerical Whig press (see *PW*, II, 10–11, 106–7).

The project of the classic Old Whig *Cato's Letters*, Trenchard and Gordon wrote in their last paper, had been to show 'the advantage and the beauty of civil and ecclesiastical liberty, and the odious deformity of priestcraft and tyranny' and to vindicate 'our present establishment'. The Old Whig publicist hopes: 'I have removed many of the prejudices imbibed by education and custom.' For 'it is certain, that the capacities of men would carry them much farther than they are suffered to go, if they were not cramped by custom and narrow education'. Cato laments to see 'men dupes and machines to the ambition, pride, and avarice, of selfish and haughty ecclesiastics, or of corrupt statesmen. Nor can I see how this great evil can ever be cured, till we change the education of our youth.'[54] Tindal was a notorious exponent of what Swift in the 'Apology' calls '*the Notion of Prejudices*' and Swift acidly remarked on Tindal's arguments against an imputed pernicious High Church clerical hegemony in education: 'Religion, Morality, Honour, and Honesty ... are, it seems, but Prejudices of Education, and too many get clear of them' (*PW*, II, 103). As Examiner, Swift parodied the Whig-speak of 'the Slavery of believing by *Education* and *Prejudice*' (*Exam*, p. 150) and condemned 'that *Whiggish* Practice of reviling the *Universities*, under the Pretence of their instilling *Pedantry, narrow Principles*, and *High-Church Doctrines*' (*Exam*, p. 419). In the sardonic irony of *An Argument Against Abolishing Christianity* (written in 1708 but first published in 1711) this Old Whig language has become an anti-Christian one: 'It is further objected against the Gospel System, that it obliges Men to the Belief of Things too difficult for Free-Thinkers, and such who have shaken off the Prejudices that usually cling to a confined Education.' The anti-Christians project that the abolition of the gospel and religion will remove 'those grievous Prejudices of Education; which, under the Names of Virtue, Conscience, Honour, Justice, and the like, are so apt to disturb the Peace of human Minds'. From 'Prejudice of Education' are said to derive 'all our foolish Notions of Justice, Piety, Love of our Country; all our Opinions of God, or a future State, Heaven, Hell, and the like'. The concern about 'Prejudices' is needless in 1708, the speaker informs us: 'effectual Care hath been since taken, to remove those Prejudices by an entire Change in the Methods of Education' (*PW*, II, 29, 33). In the non-ironic *Sentiments of a Church-of-England Man*, also written in 1708 during the Junto Whig administration, Swift writes of the affectation of '*removing the Prejudices of Education*; under which Head,

---

[54] John Trenchard and Thomas Gordon, *Cato's Letters*, IV, 244, 245, 247, 248 (no. 138, 27 July 1723).

they have, for some Time, begun to list *Morality* and *Religion*' (*PW*, II, 11). Later in *Gulliver's Travels* the wise King of Brobdingnag's contemptuous reaction to Gulliver's account 'of my own beloved Country; of our Trade, and Wars by Sea and Land, of our Schisms in Religion, and Parties in the State' is attributed by Gulliver to 'the Prejudices of his Education' (*PW*, XI, 106–7). The indignant King of Brobdingnag's lofty denunciation of the social and political 'Corruptions' which Gulliver reports is dismissed by Whig England's obtuse panegyrist as ignorance in affairs of state and polite society. Gulliver's endeavour in his 'many Discourses' had been to 'hide the Frailties and Deformities of my Political Mother, and place her Virtues and Beauties in the most advantageous Light'. The King's condemnation reflects his 'many *Prejudices*, and a certain *Narrowness of Thinking*' (*PW*, XI, 132, 133). Swift's sardonic parody of Old Whig discourse may contain a specific hit at the last of the famous *Cato's Letters* (no. 138, 27 July 1723) where, as we have seen, Trenchard and Gordon proclaimed that their patriotic papers had shown 'the advantage and the beauty of civil and ecclesiastical liberty, and the odious deformity of priestcraft', vindicated the Hanoverian Whig political and ecclesiastical establishment, and opposed the 'prejudices', 'narrow education, and narrow principles' produced by High Church clerical tyranny. Swift, a suspected Jacobite High Churchman, described himself in 1723 as 'sunk under the prejudices of another Education' (*Corr*, II, 465). The ferocious mockery of the Whig project against 'Prejudices of Education', in the *Tale* of 1704, as in his later polemic and satire, discloses the presence of a High Church Tory partisan.

The bookseller's dedication to Somers

Praising Laurence Hyde, Earl of Rochester, the new Tory Lord President of the Council, in the *Examiner* of 1 February 1711 Swift alludes to the ousted Junto Whig Lord Somers with detestation. Commonplace charges against Somers in Tory literature are marshalled by Swift in a bitter sarcastic broadside against the Junto Whig leader. The Tory President of the Council is not descended '*from the Dregs of the People*'. Rochester is 'neither *Deist* nor *Socinian*: He has never convers'd with *T-l-nd*, to open and enlarge his Thoughts, and dispel the Prejudices of Education; nor was he ever able to arrive at that Perfection of Gallantry, *to ruin and imprison the Husband, in order to keep the Wife without disturbance*' (*Exam*, p. 215). It is possible to read the earlier bookseller's dedication to Somers in the *Tale* as Swift's (anonymous and oblique) satiric reflection on a great Whig patron and a Whig publisher, as well as part of the book's satire of the commercialized print culture, debased dedications and decadent panegyric techniques (see also *Tale*, pp. 49–50, 72). A book which is a satiric mimicry of heterodox whiggery, which violently satirizes Dissent as schism and which ridicules the Royal Society (see *Tale*, pp. 64, 242) is with delicious and audacious irony offered as a tribute to Somers. The President of the Royal Society from 1698 to 1704 when Swift was writing the *Tale*, Somers was the epitome of a person who had dispelled 'the Prejudices of Education'. Swift called him, sarcastically, the 'great Genius, who is the Life and Soul, the Head and Heart of [the Whig] Party' (*PW*, VI, 152). The glorious political career of the Williamite Whig statesman and such biographical facts as his latitudinarianism, patronage of anticlerical writers, support for a Williamite standing army and connection with city financiers and the new machinery of public credit are not itemized 'Materials of Panegyrick' (*Tale*, p. 49) in the *Tale*'s dedication to Somers.[55] 'ALL Panegyricks are mingled with an Infusion of Poppy', Swift wrote (*PW*, IV, 252), but the failure to mark specifically and to eulogize the milestones in Somers's Whig career would be extraordinary if Swift really was a wholehearted Whig at this time. Many years later, in 1733, when he writes a 'Prefatory Letter to Poems on Several Occasions by Mrs. Mary Barber', dedicated 'To the Right Honourable *John*, Earl of *Orrery*', a Jacobite Tory, Swift rehearses the common topics of dedicators that he assumes Mrs Barber would insist on, but mentions virtues signally absent from his earlier dedication to Somers:

Perhaps she may be so weak to add the Regularity of your Life, that you believe a God and Providence, that you are a firm Christian, according to the Doctrine of the Church establish'd in both Kingdoms.

(*PW*, XIII, 74)

In the *Tale*'s dedication, Somers is the illiterate bookseller's candidate as 'the sublimest Genius of the Age, for Wit, Learning, Judgment, Eloquence and Wisdom' (*Tale*, p. 23). Somers can be the only possible dedicatee for the stolen encomiums furnished by the mercenary modern

---

[55] For Somers's biography, see Richard Cooksey, *Essay on the Life and Character of John Lord Somers, Baron of Evesham* (Worcester, 1791). This biography, the author states, is intended to vindicate Somers from the hostile charges laid by 'Swift, that monster of ingratitude, perfidy, and prostitution' (pp. 1–2); William L. Sachse, *Lord Somers: A Political Portrait* (Manchester, 1975); Joseph Addison, *The Freeholder*, p. 208, n. 2; Robert M. Adams, 'In Search of Baron Somers', in *Culture and Politics From Puritanism to the Enlightenment*, edited by Perez Zagorin (Berkeley, Los Angeles and London, 1980), pp. 165–202.

bookseller's hackney authors in their garrets in the alleys near his shop (*Tale*, pp. 24–5). The bookseller knows that a dedication to Somers will 'get off' an edition, and recognizes that Somers must be flattered for profit (*Tale*, p. 23). The bookseller in effect does 'ply the World with an old beaten Story of your Wit, and Eloquence, and Learning, and Wisdom, and Justice, and Politeness, and Candor, and Evenness of Temper in all Scenes of Life; Of that great Discernment in Discovering, and Readiness in Favouring deserving Men; with forty other common Topicks' (*Tale*, pp. 25–6). Swift had not received patronage or preferment from Somers when he wrote this, nor would he in the future. He would write in 'Thought on Various Subjects' that 'I HAVE known great Ministers distinguished for Wit and Learning, who preferred none but Dunces' (*PW*, IV, 245).

While contemporaries like William King, responding to the indecorum of the dedication, said that it was disrespectful, modern academic criticism on *A Tale of a Tub* usually, indeed routinely, reads the dedication as a genuine compliment to Somers. What the bookseller (and behind him Swift) is seen to be getting at is that Somers is second to none, the *beau idéal* of the patron. There have been dissenting voices, however. In particular, Robert M. Adams discovers covert hostility to Somers behind the raillery in the bookseller's dedication. In a passage in which Swift is ostensibly ridiculing panegyrics which absurdly praise patrons for qualities they don't possess, Adams has noted the satiric glances at Somers's humble birth, sexual incontinence and libertinism and debilitated physique.[56] The bookseller says:

> I expected, indeed, to have heard of your Lordships' Bravery, at the Head of an Army; Of your undaunted Courage, in mounting a Breach, or scaling a Wall; Or, to have had your Pedigree trac'd in a Lineal Descent from the House of *Austria*; Or, of your wonderful Talent at Dress and Dancing.
>
> (*Tale*, p. 25)

One of Somers's panegyrists, Joseph Addison, celebrated in 1695 'Britain *Advanc'd, and* Europe'*s Peace Restor'd, / By* SOMERS' *Counsels, and by* NASSAU'*s Sword*' and British youth 'Ambitious all / Who first shall storm the Breach, or mount the Wall'.[57] Swift assimilated such lines into a hostile allusion to Somers's sexual rather than military gallantry:

---

[56] Adams, 'In Search of Baron Somers', esp. pp. 185–8 and notes 72–83.

[57] Joseph Addison, *To the King*, dedicated 'To the Right Honourable John Lord Somers, Baron of Evesham', in *Miscellaneous Works*, edited by A. C. Guthkelch (London, 1914), I, 39, 43.

'your undaunted Courage, in mounting a Breach, or scaling a Wall'[58] and indirectly reminds readers of Somers's birth and physical constitution when contemporary Tory poems on affairs of state were sneering at the 'Audacious Upstart' with a syphilitic body.[59] Through a studied, sardonic obliquity Swift contrived to insult a powerful potential patron while ostensibly praising him through raillery.

A parody of a Whig dedication to Somers, the bookseller's dedication is also a satiric demystification of the conditions of literary production and an exposure of the disreputable practices of booksellers. The bookseller is primarily a satiric type, of course, yet he may be distantly modelled on, and intended to satirize, the Whig Kit-Cat publisher Jacob Tonson, a friend and associate of Somers. Tonson's political and literary connection with Somers would make him a topical candidate for a bookseller praising Somers.[60] Tonson's famous association with John Dryden, who is a target of Swift's satiric animus and parody throughout the book, would also have qualified Tonson for satiric attention. Indeed, Swift may obliquely satirize the Tonson–Dryden publishing enterprise in classical translation.[61] The bookseller in his dedication to Somers reveals that neither he nor the authors he employs in translating understand Latin:

> upon the Covers of these Papers, I casually observed written in large Letters, the two following Words, DETUR DIGNISSIMO; which, for ought I knew, might contain some important Meaning. But, it unluckily fell out, that none of the Authors I employ, understood *Latin* (tho' I have them often in pay, to translate out of that Language) I was therefore compelled to have recourse to the Curate of our Parish, who Englished it thus, *Let it be given to the Worthiest.*
>
> (*Tale*, p. 23)

This passage may recall a contemporary literary controversy. Provoked by such Tonson publications, edited by Dryden, as *Ovid's Epistles* (1680 and subsequent editions), *Miscellany Poems* (1684) and *Sylvae* (1685), all

---

58 For the sexual innuendo of such military metaphors, see William Shakespeare, *Henry V*, edited by Gary Taylor, The Oxford Shakespeare (Oxford, 1984), 5.2.136–40, 305–15 and notes pp. 271–2, 279, and for contemporary examples, see Adams, 'In Search of Baron Somers', p. 202, note 82.

59 For some public attacks, see *POAS*, 5, 247; 6, 16, 198, 222, 520, 629, 660–1 and Adams, 'In Search of Baron Somers', pp. 184–5.

60 On the Tonson–Somers connection, see Adams, 'In Search of Baron Somers', p. 187 and note 80; Sachse, *Lord Somers*, pp. 19, 68, 138, 189–92, 197–8.

61 For the Tonson–Dryden connection consult Harry M. Geduld, *Prince of Publishers* (Bloomington and London, 1969); Kathleen M. Lynch, *Jacob Tonson, Kit-Cat Publisher* (Knoxville, 1971); James Anderson Winn, *John Dryden and His World* (New Haven and London, 1987); Stuart Gillespie, 'The Early Years of the Dryden Tonson Partnership: The Background to their Composite Translations and Miscellanies of the 1680s', *Restoration*, 12 (1988), 10–19.

of which consisted largely of translations (many by Dryden), and referring to Dryden's charge in the *Defence of the Epilogue* (1672) that the clergy were corrupters of eloquence, Matthew Prior wrote in a letter of 1685 to Dr Humphrey Gower, Master of St John's:

let our translators know that Rome and Athens are our territories; that our Laureate might in good manners have left the version of Latin authors to those who had the happiness to understand them; that we accuse not others, but defend ourselves, and would only shew that these corruptions of our tongue proceed from him and his tribe, which he unjustly casts upon the clergy.[62]

Prior's *A Satyr on the modern Translators* was published in 1697. It pilloried 'the hireling Drudges of the Age' who have left writing 'bad Plays' to compose 'worse Translations'. The *'dull Translator'* Dryden does not 'know what *Roman* Authors mean'.[63] It may be a particular satiric sneer at Tonson and Dryden that Swift's bookseller, who employs translators who don't understand Latin, should seek enlightenment from a clergyman.

Elsewhere in the *Tale* Swift satirizes a Whig bookseller – the eccentric Dissenting Whig John Dunton, the publicist behind the Athenian Society with whom Swift had unwitting dealing when his *Ode to the Athenian Society* was published in 1692 (*Tale*, p. 59). In connection with the publication of Sir William Temple's manuscripts Swift had some dealings with Tonson. But his own regular publisher was Benjamin Tooke Jr, and during the last four years of Queen Anne's reign John Barber, both of whom were Tory.[64] As Michael Treadwell points out, the anonymity of the publisher of *A Tale of a Tub* was carefully preserved, but the publisher was almost certainly Benjamin Tooke. *A Tale of a Tub* carried the imprint of the trade publisher used to distribute the book: that is, John Nutt, who was succeeded by John Morphew in 1706. The Nutt–Morphew house 'was always very closely associated with the Tory interest'.[65]

Swift's treatment of the bookseller in the dedication to Somers may

---

See the commentary on *A Satyr on the modern Translators* in Matthew Prior, *Literary Works*, edited by H. Bunker Wright and Monroe K. Spears, second edition, 2 vols. (Oxford, 1971), II, 822–3.

A Satyr on the modern Translators, lines 2, 12, 52, 77, *Literary Works*, I, 19–24.

Michael Treadwell, 'London Trade Publishers 1675–1750', *The Library*, 6th series, 4 (1982), 99–134 (pp. 117–18); Treadwell, 'Swift's Relations with the London Book Trade to 1714', in *Author/Publisher Relations during the Eighteenth and Nineteenth Centuries*, edited by Robin Myers and Michael Harris (Oxford, 1983), pp. 1–36 (pp. 8–12, 22, 25). See Samuel Negus's 1724 list of 'High Flyer' printers, in John Nichols, *Literary Anecdotes of the Eighteenth Century*, 9 vols. (London, 1812–15), I, 288–312.

Treadwell, 'London Trade Publishers', pp. 108, 118; Treadwell, 'Swift's Relations with the London Book Trade to 1714', pp. 12, 14, 19.

be compared with the caricatured Tonson in William Shippen's satiric portrait of the leading Whig conspirators against Church and State, meeting on the night of William III's death in *Faction Display'd* (1704). Tonson as '*Bibliopolo*' and Somers as '*Sigillo*' (lines 232–97) are given prominent place in the cabal. The passage in which the Whig bookseller appears reads:

> Now the Assembly to adjourn prepar'd,
> When *Bibliopolo* from behind appear'd,
> As well describ'd by th' old Satyrick Bard,
> *With leering Looks, Bullfac'd, and Freckled fair,*
> *With two left Legs, and Judas-colour'd Hair,*
> *And Frowsy Pores, that taint the ambient Air.*
> Sweating and Puffing for a-while he stood,
> And then broke forth in this Insulting Mood:
> I am the Touchstone of all Modern Wit,
> Without my Stamp in vain your Poets write.
> Those only purchase everliving Fame,
> That in my Miscellany plant their Name.
> Nor therefore think that I can bring no Aid,
> Because I follow a Mechanick Trade,
> I'll print your Pamphlets, and your Rumours spread.
> I am the Founder of your lov'd *Kit-Kat*,
> A Club that gave Direction to the State.
> 'Twas there we first instructed all our Youth,
> To talk Prophane and Laugh at Sacred Truth.
> We taught them how to Toast, and Rhime, and Bite,
> To Sleep away the Day, and drink away the Night.
> Some this Fantastick Speech approv'd, some Sneer'd;
> The Wight grew Cholerick, and disappear'd.
>
> (lines 374–96)[66]

We see in Shippen's caricature of Tonson some of the broad outlines of Swift's satire on the bookseller in the dedication to Somers. Shippen sneers at the profession, 'a Mechanick Trade'. This accent is heard when Swift's bookseller speaks of his 'Shop' and his employees in garrets and 'an Alley hard by' (*Tale*, p. 24). There is contemptuous irony in Shippen's personation of Tonson holding forth that his *Miscellany Poems* will be the only means for modern writers to 'purchase everliving Fame'. Swift's bookseller says "'TIS true, I should be very loth, the Bright Example of your Lordship's Virtues should be lost to After-Ages', but admits that the modern dedication is not the vehicle for transport to

[66] *POAS*, 6, 667–8.

posterity (*Tale*, p. 26). His motives for publishing the dedication are mercenary (p. 23) and Swift accords amusing emphasis to the bookseller's absorption in pecuniary and unscrupulous considerations (*Tale*, pp. 24–5). Like Shippen's Tonson, Swift's bookseller brusquely asserts that he is master of his authors (*Tale*, p. 22).

But it is the bookseller's connection with Somers which suggests that Tonson is a butt of Swift's satire. Later, of course, Swift was to malign the Kit-Cat Club with which Somers and Tonson were famously associated, making similar charges to those made in *Faction Display'd* (lines 388–94).[67] In 1704 his hostility is expressed covertly. The bookseller, after declaring that he does not fear for the sale of the book, since, irrespective of the book's faults or merits, Somers's 'Name on the Front, in Capital Letters, will at any time get off one Edition',[68] adds:

Neither would I desire any other Help, to grow an Alderman, than a Patent for the sole Priviledge of Dedicating to your Lordship.

(*Tale*, p. 23)

In order to help Somers support the dignity of the office of Lord Chancellor which he bestowed upon him in 1697, William III had granted Somers the manors of Reigate and Howleigh in Surrey. Reigate was a burgage borough and Somers's manorial estates enabled him to exercise political influence in the borough. With the parliamentary vote attached to burgages, Somers sought to ensure that the franchise of Reigate burgages was held by dependable Whigs. Before the election of 1698, through Somers's influence, Tonson (along with other Kit-Cats) became one of the new burgesses in Reigate, installed so that Somers could advance his Whig parliamentary interest there.[69] Swift may well be reflecting on Tonson's political recruitment and 'advancement'. In the dedication to Somers Swift satirically imagines that perhaps the grateful bookseller, through his connection with Somers, could hope 'to grow an Alderman'.

Martin in polemical context

The foregoing interpretations present a case for the *Tale* as a satire of heretics, schismatics and Whig authors, patrons and booksellers,

---

[67] See *PW*, IV, 28; *PW*, VI, 149 55.

[68] Ironically, Tonson actually makes a similar declaration to that which Swift imputes to the Bookseller here in the dedication of the 1711 pocket edition of *Paradise Lost* to Somers. Tonson's dedication is quoted in Lynch, *Jacob Tonson, Kit-Cat Publisher*, p. 129.

[69] Sachse, *Lord Somers*, p. 138; Adams, 'In Search of Baron Somers', p. 174.

which had party-political dimension and implication. To conclude this account of the book's politics, the ecclesiastical–political positives explicitly present in the text and intended to control reader response to the *Tale*'s irony and satiric mimesis will be considered.

At the beginning of Section II, the father provides his sons with coats and exhorts them to '*wear them clean, and brush them often*'. A '*Will*' provides '*full Instructions in every particular concerning the Wearing and Management of your Coats*'. The father commands in the will that the sons '*should live together in one House like Brethren and Friends*'. The father's will was observed for seven years and the coats kept 'in very good Order' (*Tale*, pp. 73–4). The High Church satirist's parable inscribes the peremptory authority of Scripture, confirmed and defined by the practice of the primitive Church in the first seven centuries, and places considerable emphasis on the injunction to Catholic uniformity. The father is gone, but his patriarchal authority remains. Swift's satire explores how the human spirit eludes such final authority through intellectual, religious and political corruption and a hermeneutic midwifery that makes the meaning of word and text indeterminate (see particularly *Tale*, pp. 12, 186). Swift emphasizes the proscriptive rather than prescriptive aspect of the Church's authority. What Swift means by the euphemistic instruction in the parable to wear the coats '*clean, and brush them often*' and the practice of keeping them 'in very good Order' might be glossed from the unpublished 'Remarks upon a Book, intitled *The Rights of the Christian Church*'. The fundamentals of the Church of England polity and doctrines 'were deduced from Christ and his Apostles, and the Instructions of the purest and earliest Ages' (*PW*, II, 79). 'And if Heresies had not been used with some Violence in the primitive Age, we should have had, instead of true Religion, the most corrupt one in the World' (*PW*, II, 103–4). In the *Tale* the approval of the early Church's violence against heretics is politely displaced into the idiom of burlesque fairy-tale and allegorical romance. In their early 'Adventures' the sons 'encountred a reasonable Quantity of Gyants, and slew certain Dragons' (*Tale*, p. 74). A year after the first publication of the *Tale*, during the Tory Church-in-danger campaign, John Mather preached a sensational, violent sermon at Oxford on the anniversary of Charles II's restoration, calling for 'the prudent execution of good and wholesome Laws' to eradicate the 'sin of *Schism*, which not only rends in pieces the Sacred Body of Christ' and undermines Protestantism, but raises rebellion and faction in the body politic. The contagion of schism was said to spread from 'Schismatical illegal

Seminaries'.[70] Tindal pillories Mather as a disloyal High Church incendiary. For Swift Mather was merely an 'indiscreet Man' who 'drops an
indiscreet Word' (*PW*, II, 101).

In the *Tale*'s parable of the three brothers it is Martin who embodies
the satire's positive or normative attitude. He expresses the Will's
injunction to unity in his speech to schismatic Jack (*Tale*, p. 139). But
in modern literary criticism of the *Tale* Martin has seemed the most
problematic of positives. The rest of this chapter will be concerned with
the debate about him and Swift's Anglican politics in his creation. For
Martin is a polemical character with a particular provenance and
meaning. Martin's representation is conditioned by Anglican pamphleteering tradition and, importantly, by a polemical controversy
hitherto neglected in Swift studies.

Declaring 'I shall by no means forget my Character of an Historian,
to follow the Truth', the author in section VI of *A Tale of a Tub* picks up
the thread of his narrative of Roman Catholic corruption, papal usurpation, and the beginnings of the Protestant Reformation: 'We left *Lord
Peter* in open Rupture with his two Brethren' (*Tale*, p. 133). The author
records the 'Complexions' and career of the two brothers exiled by
Peter, now distinguished as '*MARTIN*' and '*JACK*' and glossed as '*Martin
Luther*' and '*John Calvin*' (*Tale*, p. 134). The massive, Elizabethan
historical defence of Protestantism, John Foxe's *Acts and Monuments*, had
represented Luther as restoring true religion from papal corruption and
malpractice by 'reducing things to the foundation and touchstone of
the Scripture'.[71] In the *Tale* the two brothers decide to 'reduce all their
future Measures to the strictest Obedience' to the '*Will*' (Scripture).
Comparing 'Doctrine' and past 'Practice' and finding 'horrible down-
right Transgressions of every Point', the reforming brothers resolve
'without further Delay, to fall immediately upon reducing the Whole,
exactly after their Father's Model'. The brothers set out 'to reform their
Vestures into the Primitive State, prescribed by their Father's *Will*' and
'*Martin* laid the first Hand' (*Tale*, pp. 134–5). The two brothers'
'Complexions appear'd extreamly different' (*Tale*, p. 134). The
account of '*Martin*'s Proceedings upon this great Revolution' is a

---

[70] *A Sermon Preached before the University of Oxford, at St. Mary's, on Tuesday May 29th. 1705 ... By
John Mather ...* (Oxford, 1705), see esp. pp. 19–23.
[71] John Foxe, *Acts and Monuments*, edited by S. R. Cattley and George Townsend, 8 vols.
(London, 1837–41), IV, 348–9; Ronald H. Fritze, 'Root or Link? Luther's Position in the
Historical Debate over the Legitimacy of the Church of England, 1558–1625', *Journal of
Ecclesiastical History*, 37 (1986), 288–302 (pp. 290–1). Swift owned a copy of Foxe's *Acts and
Monuments*, 2 vols. (London, 1610), see *SC*, no. 241.

description of a cool, moderate, cautious and conservative attitude to the work of Reformation (*Tale*, pp. 135–7). But Jack 'entred upon the Matter with other Thoughts, and a quite different Spirit' (*Tale*, p. 137). Jack's violent 'Hatred and Spight' is spuriously mystified and privileged as '*Zeal*', and 'brimful of this miraculous Compound, reflecting with Indignation upon PETER's Tyranny, and farther provoked by the Despondency of *Martin*', Jack sets about his career of violent iconoclasm and schism (*Tale*, pp. 137–8). The work of reformation, however, requires the 'sedatest Constitution' (*Tale*, p. 138). Martin's 'Complexion' and his speech in response to Jack's furious, fanatical call to extremism embody what the text declares as the appropriate attitude and temper for Reformation. Martin's speech clearly invokes Scriptural authority against schism. The important passage representing Martin in response to Jack's zealotry reads in part:

But *Martin*, who at this Time happened to be extremely flegmatick and sedate, *begged his Brother of all Love, not to damage his Coat by any Means* ... Desired him *to consider, that it was not their Business to form their Actions by any Reflection upon* Peter's, *but by observing the Rules prescribed in their Father's* Will ... That *it was true, the Testament of their good Father was very exact in what related to the wearing of their* Coats; *yet was it no less penal and strict in prescribing Agreement, and Friendship, and Affection between them. And therefore, if straining a Point were at all dispensable, it would certainly be so, rather to the Advance of Unity, than Increase of Contradiction.*

(*Tale*, p. 139)

The satiric animus in this passage is directed primarily against Calvinism and the radical Reformation on the left of Luther. Yet Martin, the ostensible positive of the satire, is represented as a colour-less, choler-less figure. Focusing on Martin in the text without considering possible polemical contexts that might have conditioned the way he is depicted, readers find Martin to be, at best, satisfactory. Some readers suspect ironic subversion of this moderate in the way he is described as sedate to the point of being soporific. The representation of Martin demands interpretation and Martin's place in the satire has, of course, received detailed attention in literary criticism on *A Tale of a Tub*.

Phillip Harth has provided a lucid summary and analysis of the sections of the *Tale* concerned with the abuses in religion and the altering signification of the three brothers themselves in the course of the tale. Martin's signification shifts from the historical reformer Martin Luther to the English Reformation and Anglicanism. Martin, Phillip Harth points out, in spirit and method exemplifies reason, moderation and charity.[72] Patrick Reilly refers to Martin as 'the unidealistic hero of the *Tale*' who exemplifies an approved 'cautious reformism', conservatism and 'moderationist temper'. 'That Swift endorsed the Martin attitude is incontestable.'[73] Martin Price writes that 'Martin embodies the middle way celebrated by Richard Hooker and the Anglican church of the seventeenth century'.[74] Yet Martin's lack-lustre appearance has suggested to readers that Swift's attitude to the normative brother is not without ambiguity. Pat Rogers argues that

Swift is sceptical regarding golden means, or at any rate about 'moderation' as currently practised – witness the sermon *On Brotherly Love*.

Some have claimed that Swift always does convey some implied norm. But (leaving aside the recognized thinness and insufficiency of Martin, who hasn't even the grace to disappear entirely, and makes periodic shifty entrances, like the untroubled absentee norm he is) I do not see how this view can be sustained.[75]

Gardner D. Stout, Jr, sees in the representation of Martin evidence of ironic tension between Swift's official ideological commitment and his actual imaginative extremism:

Martin embodies Swift's genuine, self-defensive commitment to rational moderation and restraint. But Martin's pallor reflects the emotional weakness of that commitment: though he has all the orthodoxy, Peter and Jack have all the imaginative vitality.[76]

Claude Rawson explores the somewhat ambiguous, slightly subverted projection of Martin's Anglican middle way and ecumenical moderation. Rawson observes 'the similarity in the language, and in the configuration of attitudes, between Martin's correct position, and its Whiggish "Abuse"' described in other works where Swift repudiates Whig moderation. He concludes:

The "admirable Lecture of Morality" and its predicted soporific effect on the reader tend to deflate Martin. The damage should not be exaggerated. Mild ironic underminings of serious statements are common in Augustan writers, as not very damaging (indeed sometimes affectionate) jokes at the speaker's

---

[72] Phillip Harth, *Swift and Anglican Rationalism*, esp. ch. 2, pp. 13–18.

[73] Patrick Reilly, *Jonathan Swift: The Brave Desponder*, pp. 86, 120.

[74] Martin Price, 'Pope, Swift and the Past', p. 27.

[75] Pat Rogers, 'Swift and the Idea of Authority', in *The World of Jonathan Swift*, pp. 25–37 (p. 34).

[76] Gardner D. Stout, Jr, 'Satire and Self-Expression in Swift's *Tale of a Tub*', in *Studies in the Eighteenth Century II. Papers presented at the Second David Nichol Smith Memorial Seminar Canberra 1970*, edited by R. F. Brissenden (Canberra, 1973), pp. 323–39 (p. 327).

expense, which at the same time release the (real) *author* from too solemn a posture of endorsement.[77]

Despite the large corpus of critical commentary and editorial annotation on *A Tale of a Tub*, some of the paper wars which constitute part of the book's context and from which Swift purloined materials have not been fully noted. Martin is often considered divorced from contemporary polemical context. Martin's 'Complexion', however, has a possible provenance in an Oxford battle of books. The phlegmatic Martin can be recognized as Swift's droll literary contribution to a late seventeenth-century skirmish in a longer controversy between apologists for the English Reformation and Roman Catholic polemicists over the character of Martin Luther and his place in debate over the legitimacy of the Church of England.[78] Relocating Martin in contemporary polemical context allows us to understand why Swift specifically represents Martin as rather a pallid, placatory figure. But before describing a polemical genesis for the Martin who appears in the *Tale*, some brief general observations need to be made about Swift's attitude to Martin Luther and about previous constructions of an Anglican *via media* in Anglican polemical literature.

As an Anglican clergyman Swift would have admitted that there were doctrinal differences between Lutheranism and Anglicanism. Also, he would have recognized that a defence of Martin Luther was not central to the contemporary defence of the Church of England (see *Exam*, pp. 260–1 for instance). The legitimacy of the Anglican Church rested principally on its claim of Apostolic succession and as a true Catholic Church reformed from papal corruption, established as national and in agreement with Scripture and the practice of the primitive Church. The High Churchman in Swift deplored the Erastian and anti-episcopal character of the Reformation Luther fathered and its radical Protestant progeny. Such was Swift's hostility that he can sometimes seem barely within the pale of the Reformation. The reductive representation of the Reformation as the adventures and antics of three fops in *A Tale of a Tub* perhaps on some level discloses a disgust with the Reformation that is also expressed in his remarkable unfinished paper, dated 24 May 1736, entitled *Concerning That Universal*

---

[77] Claude Rawson, 'The Character of Swift's Satire', pp. 21–82 (p. 60).
[78] On Luther and the Reformation in England, see particularly, Fritze, 'Root or Link?' See also Michael Mullett, 'Luther: Conservative or Revolutionary? Was Martin Luther the Author of a "Moderate Reformation"? Or Was His Progeny to Prove a "Radical Reformation"?', *History Today*, 33 (December 1983), 39–44.

Hatred, Which Prevails Against The Clergy. The paper has a probable
general occasion in the Whig Quakers Tithe Bill of 1736 and other
controversies concerning the corporate right and temporalities of the
established Church in the mid-1730s. In the reign of Henry VIII, Swift
writes,

> the Church and Court of Rome had arrived to such a height of corruption, in
> doctrine and discipline, as gave great offence to many wise, learned, and pious
> men through most parts of Europe; and several countries agreed to make some
> reformation in religion. But, although a proper and just reformation were
> allowed to be necessary, even to preserve Christianity itself, yet the passions
> and vices of men had mingled themselves so far, as to pervert and confound all
> the good endeavours of those who intended well: And thus the reformation, in
> every country where it was attempted, was carried on in the most impious and
> scandalous manner that can possibly be conceived. To which unhappy pro-
> ceedings we owe all the just reproaches that Roman Catholics have cast upon
> us ever since.

The Erastian Reformation in northern Europe removed the wealth and
authority of the bishops.

> And, in the Protestant monarchies abroad, little more than the shadow of
> Episcopacy is left; but, in the republics, is wholly extinct.
>   In England the Reformation was brought in after a somewhat different
> manner, but upon the same principle of robbing the church.

> > (*PW*, XIII, 125–6)

Sir Thomas More, who stood out against the Erastian Henrician
Reformation in England, is a Swiftian hero and exemplar of passive
obedience under a tyrant (see *PW*, V, 84; XI, 196; XIII, 123).

However, Swift accepted Martin Luther, the biblical and patristic
scholar, as a father of the ideas that produced the English Reformation
and saw him as embodying the ideal of a centrist, moderate Reformation. In *The Mechanical Operation of the Spirit* 'the *Reformation* of *Luther*' is
imaged as a 'Harvest', with the 'Radical Reformers' as the '*Mushrooms*'
that spring up afterwards (*Tale*, p. 286). In *A Preface To the Right
Reverend Dr. Burnet, Bishop of Sarum's Introduction to the Third Volume of the
History of the Reformation, of the Church of England*, Swift writes:

> The Reformation owed nothing to the good Intentions of King *Henry*: He was
> only an Instrument of it, (as the Logicians speak) by Accident; nor doth he
> appear throughout his whole Reign, to have had any other Views, than those of
> gratifying his insatiable Love of Power, Cruelty, Oppression, and other irregu-
> lar Appetites. But this Kingdom, as well as many other Parts of *Europe*, was at
> that Time generally weary of the Corruptions and Impositions of the *Roman*

Court and Church; and disposed to receive those Doctrines, which *Luther* and his Followers had universally spread.

(PW, IV, 73)

'I think, Luther and Calvin seem to have differed as much as any two among the Reformers', Swift wrote *(PW, VIII, 96)*. Clearly, the Anglican clergyman could consider Luther with historical detachment, and Martin is treated with a certain detachment in the *Tale*.

As Martin also comes to signify the Anglican *via media* between the papacy and the 'Radical Reformation', Swift's depiction of him was to some extent pre-scripted or at least influenced by representations of the ideal moderate Anglican middle way in the royalist, anti-puritan pamphleteering tradition. An example of such a royalist anti-Puritan text endorsing Anglican moderation is John Taylor's *A Dialogue Betwixt Three Travellers, as accidentally they did meet on the High-way: Crucy Cringe, a Papist, Accepted Weighall, a Professour of the Church of England and Factious Wrestwrit, a Brownist* (1641). Taylor's three men of the world can be recognized as the polemical ancestors of Peter, Martin and Jack. The ideal of Anglican moderation is positively expounded in the *Dialogue* and embodied in Weighall. It is perhaps indicative of Swift's deep disillusionment with ecclesiastical projects of toleration and moderation, and of the impact on the conservative Anglican mentality of the Civil War and Interregnum, that whereas Taylor represents Weighall's moderate position as triumphant in his text, Martin's correct moderation in Swift's *Tale* merely inflames Jack's fanaticism (*Tale*, p. 140). 'Moderation', considered as a strategy of ecclesiastical politics, is clearly represented by Swift as futile for dealing with Dissent. As already suggested, the polemical dimension of Swift's narrative of Peter, Martin and Jack at the time of publication was not lost on contemporaries. There may be an allusion to Swift's depiction of the Anglican *via media* in the celebrated tracts of the 'Church in Danger' controversy of 1705. For example, the deist and true Whig John Toland's *Memorial of the State of England*, an answer to the High Churchman James Drake's incendiary *Memorial of the Church of England* (1705), may be alluding to the sartorial parable and endorsement of Martin in *A Tale of a Tub*. Toland may have regarded the *Tale* as High Church Tory in provenance, associating it with Drake's book and the Tory 'Church in Danger' campaign of 1705. Defending Whig policies of toleration and moderation, Toland attacks High Churchmen as secret Jacobites. He says the extremist High Churchmen assert:

that *they are the best Reform'd Church in the World*, which may be true, tho' not fit for them to say; *that they steer between the gaudy Dresses of affected* Rome, *and the slovenly Attire of nasty* Geneva; and the *Memorialist* says, That *no Sect or sort of Christians whatsoever can boast of so extensive a Charity, or so good natur'd a Discipline*, when in the same *Libel*, he who pretends to be their Mouth, arraigns the *Government* for not passing the *Bill against Occasional Conformity*, falls foul on the *Bishops* for the Mildness of their Discipline, in relation to their *Protestant* Brethren.[79]

A Tale of a Tub describes Martin's 'Coat so well reduced into the State of Innocence', while Peter's coat is a baroque medley of lace, ribbons, fringe, embroidery and points, and Jack's is rent to a ragged condition (section VI). Swift's book also contains satiric reflections on occasional conformity and the contemporary episcopate (see *Tale*, pp. 79, 204–5, 279).

The particular, forced emphasis in *A Tale of a Tub* on the mildness and moderation of Martin's temper and proceedings as a reformer suggest Swift's allusion to a particular pamphlet controversy in 1687–8 between the Roman Catholic and Anglican interests in Oxford, a controversy within the larger paper war between Romanist and Anglican polemicists and scholars, in which Swift's future friend, the High Church Tory champion Francis Atterbury, first established his reputation as a brilliant controversialist.[80] In the summer of 1687 a work entitled *Two Discourses* by the Roman Catholic polemicist Abraham Woodhead issued from Obadiah Walker's press at Oxford. Obadiah Walker, the Master of University College and a convert to Roman Catholicism, was engaged in a propaganda campaign in support of James II's Catholicizing policies. The 104-page first discourse *Considerations Concerning the Spirit of M. Luther* declaimed against Luther as immoral and possessed by Satan. Luther's relation to other Reformers is represented as wildly immoderate and choleric. Luther 'was noted to suffer impatiently any opposition made to himself, and could not well brook any Reformation different from his own'. He displayed 'presumptive certainty, and plerophory' against the papists and against other Reformers. Luther is represented violently 'censuring and condemning such other [r]eformed doctrines as were contrary to his own'. A section of the *Considerations* describes 'His fierce, contentious, and railing spirit discovered in all his Controversy-writings.' Passages are cited as an 'extract of his raging choler'.[81] Sardonically, Calvin appears at one

[79] [John Toland], *The Memorial of the State of England* ... (London, 1705), p. 14.
[80] For this episode in Atterbury's career, see G. V. Bennett, *The Tory Crisis in Church and State*, pp. 28–30.
[81] [Abraham Woodhead], *Two Discourses. The First, Concerning the Spirit of Martin Luther, and the Original of the Reformation. The Second, Concerning the Celibacy of the Clergy* (Oxford, 1687),

point in the *Considerations* as an appeasing moderate in relation to Luther. '*Calvin* (who liked well, and himself to some degree imitated *Luther*'s reviling spirit, when he wrot [*sic*] against the Church, yet censures, and condemns it, when turned upon his own party)' is quoted as saying of Luther: 'That over-boyling heat and passion in all his writings I wish he had studied more to asswage, and moderate.' But both Calvin and Luther are finally judged to be violent and spiritually proud. The spirit of the Reformation's two 'fore-fathers' does not agree 'with the character of the Holy Spirit'.[82]

Francis Atterbury's *An Answer to Some Considerations* immediately and contemptuously demolishes the central assumption of the Romanist polemic: '*But it look's like a* Jest, *when the Irregularities committed by* Luther *in* Germany, *are turn'd upon* Us *here in* England: *as if any thing that* He *said, or did, could affect a* Church *establish'd upon it's own bottom, and as independent on any forreign authorities.*' But, importantly, Atterbury defended Luther as essentially moderate and reasonable in spirit and in his attitude to Reformation, describing how 'he treated his Adversaries with all mildness' and proposed his views on the gross abuse of pardons 'in a mild Scholastic way'. Denunciation and anathemas 'did not heat him, he went on calmly'. But when no redress came from Rome and Luther's books were burned there, himself condemned and his adversaries supported:

he then, and not 'till then, first chang'd his note, and put on a greater freedom of Expression. Before this time he strove with no man, but in the spirit of meekness ... Thus are the earliest actions of *Luther* in no wise chargeable with contumacy.[83]

Atterbury's tract insists on the distinctiveness of the Church of England from the Lutheran Reformation in Germany but is an apology for the spirit of Martin Luther. Atterbury's answer was itself attacked by the Roman Catholic press, with Thomas Deane's *The Religion of Mar. Luther* again representing Luther as 'destitute of the Virtues of the Holy Spirit, *temperance, meekness, &c*'.[84]

   Considerations Concerning the Spirit of M. Luther, and the Original of the Reformation, see pp. 40, 46, 48, 53, 55.

[82] *Considerations*, pp 56–7, 61.

[83] [Francis Atterbury], *An Answer to Some Considerations on the Spirit of Martin Luther and The Original of the Reformation; Lately Printed at Oxford* (Oxford, 1687), 'The Preface', and pp. 6–7, 7–8.

[84] Thomas Deane, *The Religion of Mar. Luther Neither Catholick Nor Protestant, Prov'd from his own Works. With some Reflections In Answer to the Vindication of Mar. Luther's Spirit, Printed at the Theater in Oxon. His Vindication being another Argument of the Schism of the Church of England*

Martin's phlegm, gravity, patience and moderation in section VI of the *Tale* clearly agree with Atterbury's polemical projection of Martin Luther's spirit during Anglican Oxford's resistance to the Roman Catholic campaign in the last years of James II's reign. Atterbury in the course of his argument had tried to explain away the historical evidence of Luther's intemperate disputation. He conceded that Luther 'had fire in his temper, and a German bluntness' and that in the heat of dispute Luther's opponents provoked perhaps a 'hot word or two, that ought to have been softned'. But Luther can be excused.[85] Woodhead, of course, represented Luther's 'quarrelsom, reviling stile, fierce and impatient' as a fault growing with age 'and his last writings to have bin most violent, and passionate ... tho against those, whom his friends thought of all dissenters from him the most innocent, that is *Zuinglius*, *Bucer's* and *Calvin's* party'.[86] Swift's Martin, after the commencement of the Reformation, 'knew very well, there yet remained a great deal more to be done; however, the first Heat being over, his Violence began to cool, and he resolved to proceed more moderately in the rest of the Work' (*Tale*, p. 136). Martin Luther in the *Tale* is neither choleric nor immoral, indeed Swift drolly presents him as the other extreme. The *Tale's* Historian comments: '*MARTIN* had still proceeded as gravely as he began; and doubtless, would have delivered an admirable Lecture of Morality, which might have exceedingly contributed to my Reader's *Repose*' (*Tale*, pp. 139–40). Woodhead's Luther is scurrilous and flagitious in disputation, freely damning his Romanist and Protestant adversaries as devilish.[87] In the *Tale* it is Peter who 'was very lewdly given in his common Conversation, extream wilful and positive' and who has the faculty of 'swearing' and 'cursing the whole Company to Hell' (*Tale*, pp. 119–20). As Swift points out in the 'Apology', 'Peter *is frequently made to repeat Oaths and Curses.*' Readers are to '*laugh at the Popish Folly of cursing People to Hell*' (*Tale*, p. 18). It is Peter and Jack who vent 'Millions of Scurrilities and Curses' (*Tale*, pp. 122, 141). Answering the Romanist charge of '*Contention and Disobedience*' against Luther, Atterbury described Luther's 'mild Scholastic way' in disputation and scored against Woodhead by noting Luther's passive obedience.[88] The *Tale's* Martin certainly disputes in a 'mild Scholastic way':

(Oxford, Printed by Henry Cruttenden, One of His Majesty's Printers [for Obadiah Walker], 1688), p. 22.
[85] *An Answer to Some Considerations . . .*, pp. 29, 38, and see pp. 39–42.
[86] *Considerations*, pp. 53, 54.
[87] *Considerations*, p. 48.   [88] *An Answer to Some Considerations*, pp. 6, 57.

And as in Scholastick Disputes, nothing serves to rouze the Spleen of him that *Opposes*, so much as a kind of Pedantick affected Calmness in the *Respondent*; Disputants being for the most part like unequal Scales, where the *Gravity* of one Side advances the *Lightness* of the Other, and causes it to fly up and kick the Beam; So it happened here, that the *Weight* of *Martin*'s Arguments exalted *Jack*'s *Levity*, and made him fly out and spurn against his Brother's Moderation. In short, *Martin*'s *Patience* put *Jack* in a *Rage*.

(*Tale*, p. 140)

Martin attempts to dissuade Jack from disobedience and revolt (*Tale*, p. 139).

It would appear that Swift appropriates the polemical language of this Oxford battle of books in a literary representation of the debate about Martin Luther in *A Tale of a Tub*. Echoes of the controversialists can be heard in the *Tale*. Early in his *Considerations Concerning the Spirit of M. Luther*, Woodhead issues an hermeneutic injunction to his readers:

it seems reasonable and of much concernment, that all *Christians* ... do put themselves in the same posture now, as they should have bin in, had they lived at the first appearance of *Luther*, when all remain'd in the bosom, communion, and faith of that Church which he opposed.[89]

Atterbury readily did so: 'let us take the prescrib'd method, and *put our selves in the same posture now, as we should have been in, had we liv'd at the first appearance of Luther*'. Atterbury finds that 'should I put my self into that *posture*, the Considerer desires' he can convict Woodhead of erroneous interpretation:

He advis'd me to *put my self in the same posture I should have been in had I liv'd at Luther's* FIRST APPEARANCE; I have done so, and find that this *first appearance* of his has nothing hideous or frightful in it: the Posture, he put me in, has prov'd flatly against his design: for it represent's *Luther* under the Image of an *holy* and *humble* person, with nothing of *Fleshly Lust*, or *disobedience* about him.[90]

The author of *A Tale of a Tub* writes in his Preface:

I hold fit to lay down this general maxim. Whatever Reader desires to have a thorow Comprehension of an Author's Thoughts, cannot take a better Method, than by putting himself into the Circumstances and Postures ['Posture' edd. 1–4] of Life, that the Writer was in, upon every important Passage as it flow'd from his Pen.

(*Tale*, p. 44)

---

[89] *Considerations*, p. 2.   [90] *An Answer to Some Considerations*, pp. 5, 8.

Swift burlesques the hermeneutic method by literalizing the metaphoric 'Posture' and introducing the Reader to the sick and starving Author in bed in his garret (*Tale*, p. 44). In section VI Swift recalls the method adopted by the antagonists in the controversy over the spirit of Martin Luther. The true nature of Martin and Jack is revealed by attention to the contingent circumstances at their first appearance:

> But when they came forward into the World, and began to display themselves to each other, and to the Light, their Complexions appear'd extreamly different; which the present Posture of their Affairs gave them sudden Opportunity to discover.
>
> (*Tale*, p. 134)

The 'Posture' of affairs presented in the satire implicitly vindicates Atterbury's reading of Martin Luther.

Other parallels and echoes might suggest this specific polemical provenance for section VI of the *Tale*. For example, the circumstantial detail of the parable that Martin and Jack 'took a Lodging together' and fell into argument, after which mad '*Jack* went immediately to *New Lodgings*' (*Tale*, pp. 133, 141), might recall Woodhead's depiction of Luther in hot dispute with another Reformer 'as they were together in an Inn'. However, in Woodhead's version it is Luther who refused to have the doctrinal controversy between them 'privately composed', which divided the Protestant Reformers 'into *two* bands even untill this day'.[91] Atterbury's treatise ends with a eulogy of holy Luther and declares that

> If among this *Crowd of Virtues* a *failing* crept in, we must Remember that an Apostle himself has not been *irreprovable*: If in the *Body* of his Doctrine *one Flaw* is to be seen; yet the greatest Lights of the Church, and in the purest times of it, were, we know, not exact in all their Opinions.[92]

Swift imaginatively transposed Atterbury's apology for a 'Flaw' remaining in the 'Body' of Luther's doctrine in the account of Martin's imperfect reformation of the 'Coat':

> where he observed the Embroidery to be workt so close, as not to be got away without damaging the Cloth, or where it served to hide or strengthen any Flaw in the Body of the Coat, contracted by the perpetual tampering of Workmen upon it; he concluded the wisest Course was to let it remain, resolving in no Case whatsoever, that the Substance of the Stuff should suffer Injury; which he

---

[91] *Considerations*, p. 47.   [92] *An Answer to Some Considerations*, p. 68.

thought the best Method for serving the true Intent and Meaning of his
Father's *Will*.

(Tale, pp. 136–7)

Swift's satiric reflection on Dryden's Roman Catholic poem *The Hind
and the Panther* (1687) in the *Tale* (*Tale*, p. 69) has a polemical analogue
in Atterbury's acid allusion to the baiting of the Anglican Church
under the name of the 'Panther' by the Roman Catholic party.[93]

It was routine in Tory literature to satirize the alleged contumely of
nonconformists.[94] Nevertheless, the 1687–8 Oxford controversy may
have provided Swift with some hints for the *Tale*'s demotic, and
especially the image of Jack uttering 'a Million of Scurrilities' and 'run
mad with Spleen, and Spight, and Contradiction' (*Tale*, p. 141).
Woodhead, for example, gives purported specimens of Calvin's flagitious contumely. Calvin is reported abusing the reverend fathers of the
Council of Trent as 'Impudent, fools, knaves, beasts, horned-beasts,
asses, swine, apes, and such like'. Calvin is quoted as saying 'prating
Monks' lead 'the Council by the nose' one 'tells a tale of a tub; to which
the Fathers, with their ears a foot and half long, give their assent'.[95]

Swift obtained his MA from Oxford in 1692. Atterbury, who had
largely written and supervised *Dr Bentley's Dissertations on the Epistles of
Phalaris, and the Fables of Aesop Examin'd* (1698), recognized that Swift's
satiric volume defended the enterprise of the Christ Church Oxford wits
and the 'Ancient' position in its satire on abuses in learning. Aligned
with Atterbury's side in the battle of the books, *A Tale of a Tub* also
defends a specific 'Oxford' position in its reference to the 1687–8
religious controversy fought out at Oxford in which Atterbury was the
celebrated Anglican champion.[96] Religious controversies before and

[93] *An Answer to Some Considerations*, pp. 42–3.
[94] For example, *The Works of John Dryden, Volume II: Poems 1681–1684*, edited by H. T.
Swedenberg, Jr, *et al.* (Berkeley, Los Angeles, London, 1972), p. 42 and p. 293n; [Charles
Leslie], *A Parallel*, p. 47; John Arbuthnot, *The History of John Bull*, edited by Alan W. Bower
and Robert A. Erikson (Oxford, 1976), p. 51.
[95] *Considerations*, pp. 58–9. On the ill language of Calvin and Atterbury's failure to defend
Calvin as he did Luther, see Thomas Deane, *The Religion of Mar. Luther*, pp. 16–17.
[96] Bishop Burnet thought Atterbury's work one of the best vindications of the Church of
England issued at the time from Oxford, the best short piece on Luther by an Anglican, see
Dictionary of National Biography; G. V. Bennett, *The Tory Crisis in Church and State*, p. 29. On
trial for Jacobite conspiracy against his Lutheran King in 1723, Atterbury in defence of
himself said: 'You will pardon me, my Lords, if I mention, what one of my Counsel also did,
that thirty-seven years ago I wrote in the Defence of *Martin Luther*, the great champion of
the Reformation; and am perhaps the only *Divine*, or *Member* of this Church, that has
defended him in a *Treatise*, expressly writ for that purpose, from the infancy of the
Reformation to this day', *The Speech of Francis Lord Bishop of Rochester, At the Bar of the House*

after the Revolution would still have been 'contemporary' for the author of *A Tale of a Tub*, who declared that the *'greatest Part'* of the book *'was finished above thirteen Years since*, 1696, *which is eight Years before it was published'* (*Tale*, p. 4). An allusion to Luther in a letter Swift wrote to Atterbury on 18 July 1717 might suggest that the reputation and spirit of Martin Luther's Reformation may have been a topic of conversation between these two High Churchmen, Chelsea neighbours and companions in 1711, who had both defended Martin Luther in print (*Corr*, II, 280; see also *PW*, X, 132 for a different application of the same allusion to Luther). While Swift does not specifically refer to Atterbury's treatise or the controversy over the spirit of Martin Luther by name in his extant writings, he did of course allude generally to the religious controversies of the late 1680s and praised Anglican Tory polemic against Roman Catholicism in the dangerous days at the end of James II's reign. In Swift's eyes, High Churchmen in their conduct and writings had confronted the concerted attack of Crown, popery and Dissent with heroic steadiness and learning. In *A Preface to the Right Reverend Dr. Burnet, Bishop of Sarum's Introduction* Swift affirms 'That those whom we usually understand by the Appellation of *Tory* or High-church Clergy, were the greatest Sticklers against the exorbitant Proceedings of King *James* the Second, the best Writers against Popery, and the most exemplary Sufferers for the Established Religion' (*PW*, IV, 63; Atterbury is defended by name on p. 60; see also, for example, *PW*, II, 9; *Exam*, pp. 126–7). In the 'Apology' he prefixed to the fifth edition of *A Tale of a Tub*, Swift claims that his book *'Celebrates the Church of England as the most perfect of all others in Discipline and Doctrine, it advances no Opinion they reject, nor condemns any they receive'* (*Tale*, p. 5). Martin is presented as the most perfect of the brothers in discipline and doctrine. Martin's genesis is in the ideal of a moderate Anglican *via media* in seventeenth-century anti-Puritan satire. His 'Complexion' in the *Tale* has a particular topical provenance in a polemical controversy between the Oxford Anglican interest and Romanist propagandists just before the Revolution over the reputation of Martin Luther, the Reformation and the legitimacy of the Church of England. Swift's imaginative literary depiction of Martin Luther is consonant with Atterbury's celebrated polemical vindication of Luther and may borrow from it.

of Lords, on Saturday, May 11, 1723, In His Defence Against the Bill Then Depending, For Inflicting Pains and Penalties on Him, in *Epist. Corr*, V, Appendix, No. III, pp. 365–96 (p. 388). Atterbury's *An Answer to Some Considerations* was reprinted in 1723. There was much reference to it in the political papers on the Atterbury Plot.

In terms of contemporary polemic, Swift's parable imaginatively affirms the Church of England position. The satire of Peter's usurpation over his brothers in the *Tale*'s religious allegory is a literary rendition of the polemical argument of seventeenth-century Anglican champions such as John Bramhall, who wrote that to make the Pope 'universal or onely Bishop of the world' is 'to dissolve the primitive bonds of brotherly Unity'.[97] The satire of Jack and representation of Martin have specific provenance in High Church Tory polemical languages on affairs of Church and State in the post-Revolution period and in Anglican clericalist pamphleteering against popery before the Revolution. To relocate *A Tale of a Tub* in historical context is a 'Method' which discloses the activist, political 'Postures . . . that the Writer was in'.

---

[97] John Bramhall, *The Works of the Most Reverend Father in God, John Bramhall D. D. Late Lord Archbishop of Ardmagh, Primate and Metropolitane of all Ireland* (Dublin, 1676), Discourse II, p. 125; John Spurr, 'Schism and the Restoration Church', *Journal of Ecclesiastical History*, 41 (1990), 408–24 (p. 414).

4

The politics of *Gulliver's Travels*

Some circumstances of composition

Travels into Several Remote Nations of the World. In Four Parts. By Lemuel Gulliver, First a Surgeon, and then a Captain of several Ships was substantially written between 1721 and 1725 and first published in 1726. The history of the actual composition of the book is evidenced in Swift's correspondence and that of his friends.[1] Empiricist historical criticism of *Gulliver's Travels* attempts to recover the meanings the text had for Swift and his readers in the early Hanoverian period. Reactivating the political meanings of Swift's satiric text and its contexts means exhuming some neglected polemicists and ephemeral literary production. Reading *Gulliver's Travels* alongside political works and writers privileged in modern conceptual analyses of eighteenth-century political literature and thought (such as Bolingbroke's *Craftsman*, Trenchard and Gordon's *Cato's Letters*, Locke, the canonical authors of civic humanism) modern Swift criticism has occluded the presence in Swift's book of some fugitive militant voices from the contemporary paper wars. Swift's political circumstances and whereabouts during the period of *Gulliver's* composition are also of significant contextual interest for an intentionalist and historicist interpretation of the book's politics. Swift's partisan 'Posture', Tory milieu and connections in the period of *Gulliver's* composition will be remarked briefly here before the historical character of the book's political discourse is discussed.

Swift's first reference to *Gulliver's Travels* in his correspondence is in a letter to Charles Ford of 15 April 1721 (*Corr*, II, 379–81). Swift discloses that 'I am now writing a History of my Travells, which will be a large Volume, and gives Account of Countryes hitherto unknown; but they go on slowly for want of Health and Humor' (*Corr*, II, 381). This letter to his Tory friend also shows something of Swift's political

[1] See *PW*, XI, xvi–xxi; Case, *Four Essays on 'Gulliver's Travels'*, pp. 97–102.

144

character and engagement at the time he began writing *Gulliver*. Swift tells Ford of his efforts to help Edward Waters, the High Tory printer who had been prosecuted for publishing Swift's *A Proposal for the Universal Use of Irish Manufacture* (1720; *PW*, IX, 13–22). This pamphlet, written in response to the passing of the Declaratory Act in 1720, had been regarded as seditious, a militant tract inciting insurrection against the English Whig government (see *PW*, IX, 26; *Corr*, II, 358). At the trial of the printer, Swift recorded, Chief Justice Whitshed 'laid his hand on his breast, and protested solemnly that the Author's design was to bring in the Pretender' (*PW*, IX, 27; see also *PW*, XII, 121). As Swift tells Ford, his solicitors on the printer's behalf included Lord Arran (the Jacobite Tory brother of the exiled Duke of Ormonde), 'my Sollicitor Mr Charleton' (the Jacobite Chaplain to the Duchess of Ormonde), and Sir Thomas Hanmer (the leading Hanoverian Tory) (*Corr*, II, 380). Swift also sought the help of his friend the Tory extremist Sir Constantine Phipps and the discontented Irish Whig Lord Molesworth.[2] The 'Whig Jacobite' Duke of Wharton had approved Swift's pamphlet (*Corr*, II, 359).

When Swift began writing *Gulliver's Travels*, then, he had immediate personal experience of a prosecution for sedition. The letter to Ford also reveals Swift's interest at this time in what anti-government writers could get away with in print. After commenting on an outspoken opposition Whig paper, he observes ironically to Ford: 'Your Ministry seems to me to want Credit in suffering so many Libells published against them' (*Corr*, II, 380). Swift also provides Ford with a reading of the political atmosphere in Ireland. He reports: 'The sanguine Stile begins to revive, the D. of Ormonde and his naturall Son were last week in Ireland, and went over to the West, with the like Trumpery' (*Corr*, II, 381). But something was in the wind, as Swift may have heard.

Jacobite hopes for a Stuart restoration had been growing since the South Sea Bubble catastrophe of 1720. In fact in April 1721 when Swift announced that he had begun *Gulliver*, the Atterbury Plot was under way. Swift's Tory 'Brother' Lord Arran was one of the four lords (the others were Lord Orrery, Lord North and Grey and Lord Strafford) planning the plot directed by Bishop Atterbury for 'James III'. Lord Arran was to be commander-in-chief of the projected 1722 Rising until

---

[2] On the pamphlet and its prosecution, see *Corr*, II, 357–9 (Swift to Sir Thomas Hanmer, 1 October 1720); *Corr*, II, 361–2 (Sir Thomas Hanmer to Swift, 22 October 1720); *Corr*, II, 375 (Sir Constantine Phipps to Swift, 14 January 1721); *Poems*, I, 236–8, *Complete Poems*, pp. 217–18, 701–2 ('An Excellent New Song on a Seditious Pamphlet'); *Swift*, III, 122–30.

the arrival of the Duke of Ormonde. A key figure in the Atterbury Plot of 1720–3 was Christopher Layer, Lord North and Grey's agent and legal adviser. In 1721 Swift's 'Sister' and correspondent, the Duchess of Ormonde, acted as proxy for Maria Clementina Sobieska, 'James III's' Queen, at the christening of Layer's child. The Duchess's chaplain, Arthur Charleton, was also Swift's friend and correspondent.[3] The Duchess of Ormonde was in direct correspondence with the Pretender and involved in Jacobite communication and activity.[4] The Duchess of Ormonde's letters to Swift in the early 1720s indicate his continuing credit and friendships in Jacobite Tory circles, and serve to remind modern literary critics of the dangerous conditions under which Swift and his Jacobite friends wrote at this time. In a letter of 18 April 1720 the Duchess of Ormonde tells her 'Brother': 'you'd have great reason to be angry with me, if my long silence had bin occasioned by any thing, but my care of you, for having no safe hand to send by, till now, I wou'd not write, for fear it might be construed a sort of Treason, (Misprision at least) for you to receive a letter from one half of a proscribed man'. She supposes that being in Ireland and 'honest as you are', Swift does not abound in wealth and happiness at the present time (*Corr*, II, 344). Writing on 9 December 1723, the duchess assumes that Swift's letters to her, which she had not received, must have been intercepted and deciphered during the perlustration of letters by the Post Office at the time of the Jacobite plot and government prosecutions in 1722–3 (*Corr*, II, 471). Swift wrote to Pope in 1723 of his 'Infelicity in being so Strongly attached to Traytors (as they call them) and Exiles, and State Criminalls' (*Corr*, II, 464). 'Friendships', as Pat Rogers has observed, 'do not guarantee shared patterns of interest, still less common affections, but they are in themselves a species of elective affinity.'[5] Swift's elective affinity with known or suspected Jacobites might at least suggest that the man did not share Whig fears of a Jacobite restoration under the military direction of his exiled 'Brother' and hero, the Duke of Ormonde. He was certainly loyal to his proscribed Tory friends.

---

[3] See the important revisionist study of the Atterbury Plot by Eveline Cruickshanks, 'Lord North, Christopher Layer and the Atterbury Plot: 1720–23', in *The Jacobite Challenge*, edited by Eveline Cruickshanks and Jeremy Black (Edinburgh, 1988), pp. 92–106. Swift's correspondence with Arthur Charleton has not survived. But for references to their friendship and correspondence, see *Corr*, II, 166n, 173, 250, 253, 254, 271, 274, 331, 348; III, 85, 87, 89; V, 230.

[4] See Ormonde, *The Jacobite Attempt of 1719*, pp. 193–4, 199; Ruth Perry, *The Celebrated Mary Astell: An Early English Feminist* (Chicago and London, 1986), pp. 172–5.

[5] Pat Rogers, 'Gay and the World of Opera', in *John Gay and the Scriblerians*, edited by Peter Lewis and Nigel Wood (London and New York, 1989), pp. 147–62 (p. 160).

There is an interesting reassurance in the poetic testament of fidelity Swift wrote for Harley, some time between July 1715 and July 1717, entitled 'To The Earl of Oxford, Late Lord Treasurer. Sent to him when he was in the Tower, before his Tryal':

> NEXT, faithful Silence hath a sure Reward:
> Within our Breast be ev'ry Secret barr'd:
> He who betrays his Friend, shall never be
> Under one Roof, or in one Ship with me.
>
> (lines 15–18, *Poems*, I, 210)

Though Swift's extant remains betray no complicities in Jacobite activity, we do have Swift's verse image of his political posture in the early Hanoverian period before the publication of *Gulliver*:

> I spend my Time in making Sermons,
> Or writing Libels on the *G——s*,
> Or murmuring at Whigs Preferments.
>
> (*Poems*, III, 993)

In the years when he was at work on *Gulliver's Travels* Swift was spending his summers in Tory country houses. Swift's poem 'The Journal' (or 'The Part of a Summer') gives an amusing account of how he spent his time between June and October 1721 in the Tory household of George Rochfort, whose father, Robert, had been the Chief Baron of the Irish Exchequer until he lost office after the Hanoverian accession. The poem is of political interest. The visiting dean reports the Tory baron's conversation:

> A word or two of Lord Chief *Baron*;
> And tell how little weight he sets,
> On all Whig Papers, and Gazets:
> But for the Politicks of Pue,
> Thinks ev'ry Syllable is true;
> And since he owns the King of *Sweden*
> Is dead at last without evading.
> Now all his hopes are in the *Czar*,
> Why *Muscovy* is not so far,
> Down the black Sea, and up the Streights,
> And in a Month he's at your Gates:
> Perhaps from what the Packet brings,
> By *Christmas* we shall see strange things.
>
> (lines 98–110, *Poems*, I, 282)

The Jacobites, in fact, had been negotiating with both Charles XII of Sweden and Peter the Great of Russia, hoping for a Russo-Swedish

joint action against George I as Elector and King.[6] The Charles
XII–Jacobite connection was a widely suspected fact of foreign affairs
and part of the contemporary domestic political idiom. In Swift's verse
invective against the Whig politician Richard Tighe, entitled 'Dick's
Variety', the victim of Swift's satiric pillory swears that boys who pelt
him 'were with the *Swedes* at *Bender*, / And listing Troops for the
Pretender' (lines 23–4, *Poems*, III, 788). Jacobites had entered the
service of Peter the Great. Jacobites recruited officers from the Royal
Navy for the Russian Navy and Jacobites became admirals in the Tsar's
service.[7] After the death of Charles XII in late 1718, the Tory Baron's
hopes from the North would naturally lie with the Tsar. Appropriately,
the Tory Baron is represented by Swift as imagining a *naval* expedition
which will bring, the poem implies, a modern Hannibal to the
Hanoverian regime's 'Gates'. Swift archly outfaces here the contemporary Whig scaremongering epitomized in such sensationalist tracts
against Tory Pretenderism as (probably Defoe's) *Hannibal at the Gates:
or, the Progress of Jacobitism. With the Present Danger of the Pretender* (1712).
The Duke of Ormonde is described as Hannibal in contemporary
Jacobite verse.[8] Swift has the Baron darkly predict the arrival of
Hanover's foreign enemies by Christmas. Recognizing a Jacobite idiom
in this 'word or two of Lord Chief Baron', the reader starts to wonder if
there might not be some ambiguity about the 'King' signified in the
household's after-dinner loyal toast to 'Church and King' reported at
line 36 of 'The Journal'.

Swift's verse account of his visit to the Rochfort country house in
1721 was printed in Dublin (*c.* 1721–2), and published in London
newspapers in January 1723. Oblique Jacobite sentiment is expressed
in the poem through the character of the Lord Chief Baron speculating
on the foreign news. But in a remarkable unpublished poem written in
this period, and addressed to a close and trusted friend who had been
arrested in 1715 as a suspected Jacobite, Swift speaks more freely. 'To
Charles Ford Esq[r]. on his Birth-day Jan[ry]. 31.st for the Year 1722–3'

---

[6] Ragnhild Hatton, *George I: Elector and King* (London, 1978), p. 221; Edward Gregg, 'The
Jacobite Career of John, Earl of Mar', in *Ideology and Conspiracy*, pp. 179–200 (p. 184).

[7] Eveline Cruickshanks, 'Introduction' to *Ideology and Conspiracy*, pp. 1–14 (p. 11). On
rumours of a Tsarist Jacobite armada, see BL Add. MSS, 6116, fol. 123 (Bishop Nicolson to
Archbishop Wake, 4 April 1723).

[8] For comments on the pamphlet skirmish surrounding *Hannibal at the Gates* and on the
association of Hannibal and Charles XII with Jacobitism, see Howard Erskine-Hill, 'The
Political Character of Samuel Johnson', pp. 131–2. For Ormonde as Hannibal in Jacobite
verse, see Richard Savage, 'Britannia's Miseries', lines 77–88, in *The Poetical Works of Richard
Savage*, edited by Clarence Tracy (Cambridge, 1962), pp. 19–25 (p. 22).

(*Poems*, I, 309–15) is, as Pat Rogers has remarked, 'one of Swift's most openly anti-Hanoverian poems' (*Complete Poems*, p. 726). It was not published in Swift's lifetime, and even when it did appear in 1762 its anti-Hanoverianism had to be toned down: 'Hanoverians' in line 50, for instance, was replaced with 'Presbyterians' (see *Poems*, I, 313; *Complete Poems*, pp. 726, 728). The poem discloses Swift's sympathy for suspected Jacobites and betrays no fear of the cause to which Charles Ford was attached. In a passage referring to the Tory exiles Bolingbroke and Ormonde, the incarceration of Oxford and Prior and the recent arrest and confinement in the Tower of Atterbury for alleged Jacobite conspiracy, Swift tells Ford:

> Your great Protectors, once in Power,
> Are now in Exil, or the Tower,
> Your Foes, triumphant o'er the Laws,
> Who hate Your Person, and Your Cause,
> If once they get you on the Spot
> You must be guilty of the Plot,
> For, true or false, they'll ne'r enquire,
> But use You ten times worse than Pri'r.
>
> (lines 27–34)

Swift ridiculed the Whig prosecution of Atterbury in 'Upon the horrid Plot discovered by Harlequin the B---- of R——'s French Dog. In a Dialogue between a Whig and a Tory' (written 1722, first published 1735, *Poems*, I, 297–301). It is the satire on Walpole's decipherers and the Whig government prosecution of Atterbury in Part III, Chapter VI of *Gulliver's Travels* (*PW*, XI, 190–2) that unmistakably identifies the text as 'Tory'. The bold, but safely generalized, satiric couplets of 'On Dreams. An Imitation of Petronius' (written *c.* 1724, first published in 1727, *Poems*, II, 363–4) also almost certainly allude to the Atterbury Plot and find the monarch as culpable as his murderous ministers:

> The drowsy Tyrant, by his Minion led,
> To regal Rage devotes some Patriot's Head.
> With equal Terrors, not with equal Guilt,
> The Murd'rer dreams of all the Blood he spilt.
>
> (lines 11–14)

The true motive of the Whig ministers is imputed: 'The Statesman rakes the Town to find a Plot, / And dreams of Forfeitures by Treason got' (lines 19–20; compare *PW*, XI, 191). The Petronian satirist (like the disgusted Gulliver in Glubbdubdrib) execrates the 'hireling Senator of

modern Days' who 'Bedaubs the guilty Great with nauseous Praise' and
the poem ends slinging mud in Walpole's face (lines 35–8).

In 'To Charles Ford Esq.' the Whig regime is anathematized and its
flagitious maladministration identified with the ruling German
dynasty:

> In London! what would You do there?
> Can You, my Friend, with Patience bear,
> Nay would it not Your Passion raise
> Worse than a Pun, or Irish Phrase,
> To see a Scoundrel Strut and hector,
> A Foot-boy to some Rogue Director?
> To look on Vice triumphant round,
> And Virtue trampled on the Ground:
> Observe where bloody Townshend stands
> With Informations in his Hands,
> Hear him Blaspheme; and Swear, and Rayl,
> Threatning the Pillory and Jayl.
> If this you think a pleasing Scene
> To London strait return again,
> Where you have told us from Experience,
> Are swarms of Bugs and Hanoverians.
>
> (lines 35–50)

The collocation of 'Bugs and Hanoverians' anticipates a similar satiric
diminution in the linkage of 'the new-devouring Vermin' with 'the
Land of *Huns*' in Swift's later nationalist poem on the political state of
Hanoverian Ireland, 'Verses occasioned by the sudden drying up of St.
Patrick's Well near Trinity College, Dublin' (probably written 1729,
Poems, III, 789–94, lines 59–60). Ostensibly discussing the infestation of
vermin in a 'degenerate and base' Ireland, this poem's suggestive
political diction and its references to, for example, 'A nauseous Brood,
that fills your Senate Walls, / And in the Chambers of your Viceroy
crawls' and to 'Th' amphibious Tyrant, with his rav'nous Band' (lines
57–8, 63) invite the disaffected reader to understand the plague of
toads, frogs and rats as political metaphor. The poem, remarkably,
approves the idea of an armed uprising of patriots and frames its
political criticism of Ireland's rulers in dynastic terms:

> O! had I been Apostle to the *Swiss*,
> Or hardy *Scot*, or any Land but this;
> Combin'd in Arms, they had their Foes defy'd,
> And kept their Liberty, or bravely dy'd.
> Thou still with Tyrants in Succession curst,

> The last Invaders trampling on the first:
> Nor fondly hope for some Reverse of Fate,
> Virtue herself would now return too late.
> Not half thy Course of Misery is run,
> Thy greatest Evils yet are scarce begun.
> Soon shall thy Sons, the Time is just at Hand,
> Be all made Captives in their native Land;
> When, for the Use of no *Hibernian* born,
> Shall rise one Blade of Grass, one Ear of Corn.
>
> (lines 79–92)

The restoration of the cursed land through the return of the virtuous and just king was a Jacobite topos.[9] Swift in this poem refers to the land as being 'with Tyrants in Succession curst'. But in 1729 it seems that 'some Reverse of Fate' is not to be expected. The poet laments that 'Virtue herself would now return too late'. For 'the Use of no *Hibernian* born, / Shall rise one Blade of Grass, one Ear of Corn'. Earlier in the decade in the satiric fiction of *Gulliver's Travels*, the 'least corrupted' of the polities Gulliver visits has an hereditary monarch, who thought 'that whoever could make two Ears of Corn, or two Blades of Grass to grow upon a Spot of Ground where only one grew before; would deserve better of Mankind, and do more essential Service to his Country, than the whole Race of Politicians put together' (*PW*, XI, 292, 135–6). The good monarch absent from modern Britain is offered larger than life in the fictional King of Brobdingnag. Swift's paradigm of a just monarch and political wisdom may owe something to Jacobite Tory propaganda and sentiment. But what can be observed here is that the violent humour of Swift's anti-Hanoverian verse written before and after *Gulliver's* composition in the 1720s, and his willingness to identify the ruling dynasty with the evils of the Whig administration, preclude identifying his political allegiance at this time as Whig or loyal Tory.

In the summer of 1722 Swift was at Loughgall, County Armagh, at the country estate of his friend Robert Cope, a Tory MP who had been arrested as a suspected Jacobite in 1715. There Swift, at work on *Gulliver*, was reading extensively in 'Books of History and Travells' (see *Corr*, II, 430, 431). Swift described for Charles Ford the scene around his Tory friend's estate: 'My Comfort is, that the People, the Churches and the Plantations make me think I am in England. I mean onely the Scene of a few miles about me, for I have passed through miserable

---

[9] See the discussion of Jacobite propaganda art in Paul Monod, *Jacobitism and the English People 1688–1788*, Part I, chs. 1–3.

Regions to get to it' (*Corr*, II, 431). Swift may have specifically remembered Cope's country seat when he came to write Part III of *Gulliver's Travels*, the last part of the book to be completed (see *Corr*, III, 5; *PW*, XI, xvii–xviii). In Part III Gulliver journeys through the ruined wasteland of Balnibarbi before reaching the estate of the conservative Lord Munodi. At Munodi's estate

the Scene was wholly altered; we came into a most beautiful Country; Farmers Houses at small Distances, neatly built, the Fields enclosed, containing Vineyards, Corngrounds and Meadows. Neither do I remember to have seen a more delightful Prospect.

(*PW*, XI, 175–6)

Gulliver says of Balnibarbi, 'I never knew a Soil so unhappily cultivated, Houses so ill contrived and so ruinous, or a People whose Countenances and Habit expressed so much Misery and Want' (*PW*, XI, 175): a judgement that might recall Swift's account of Hanoverian Ireland in his earlier, allegedly seditious and incendiary pamphlet, *A Proposal for the Universal Use of Irish Manufacture*. After provocatively describing the miserable subject Irish, oppressed by rack-renting land-lords, as in '*a worse Condition* than the *Peasants* in *France*, or the *Vassals* in *Germany* and *Poland*' Swift remarked:

Whoever travels this Country, and observes the *Face* of Nature, or the *Faces*, and Habits, and Dwellings of the *Natives*, will hardly think himself in a Land where either *Law*, *Religion*, or *common Humanity* is professed.

(*PW*, IX, 21)

Between 1724 and 1725 Swift was writing the *Drapier's Letters* and other works in the Irish nationalist campaign against the English Whig government's attempt to impose on Ireland a copper coinage manufactured by William Wood. He completed and transcribed *Gulliver's Travels* in 1725 at another country house, that of his friend Thomas Sheridan (*Corr*, III, 87, 102; *PW*, XI, xviii). Sheridan, in Swift's words, was 'famous for a high Tory, and suspected as a Jacobite'. He lay 'under the obloquy of a high Tory and Jacobite' (*PW*, V, 223, 226). In 1725 he revealed his 'Disloyalty in the Pulpit' (*Corr*, III, 94). When Swift's Whig friend Thomas Tickell, Addison's protégé and Secretary to the Lord Lieutenant of Ireland, asked to see the manuscript of 'an Account of imaginary Travels' in May 1726 (see *Corr*, III, 135–6) Swift replied significantly:

As to what you mention of an imaginary Treatise, I can only answer that I have a great Quantity Paper some where or other of which none would

please you, partly because they are very uncorrect, but chiefly because they
wholly disagree with your Notions of Persons and Things.

(*7 July 1726, Corr*, III, 138)

Swift relied on Sheridan to help keep the manuscript papers from the
sight of the Whig government official in Dublin Castle (*Corr*, III,
139–40).

Publication, reception and political context

Prepared for the press in the disaffected air of the Irish countryside,
Gulliver's Travels was published pseudonymously in London by Benjamin Motte Jr on 28 October 1726. Pope's story in his letter to Swift of
16 November 1726 of how the copy of the manuscript of *Gulliver's
Travels* was delivered to the printer suggests all the clandestine circumstance of an anonymous Jacobite night-drop to the printer's shop:

Motte receiv'd the copy (he tells me) he knew not from whence, nor from
whom, dropp'd at his house in the dark, from a Hackney-coach.

(*Corr*, III, 181)

The plea of ignorance attributed to Motte here (and see also *Corr*, III,
182) was a standard response of contemporary publishers when called
to account to the authorities for published works the government found
objectionable. The Tory trade publisher John Morphew, for example,
had testified to the secretaries of state in 1714:

that it is a very usual thing for persons to leave books & papers at his house and
at the houses of other publishers, and a long time after to call for the value
thereof, without making themselves known to the said publishers, and if the
Government makes enquiry concerning the authors of any books or papers so
left, in order to bring them to punishment, it often happens that nobody comes
to make any demand for the value of the said books.[10]

Writing to Swift about the book's immediate reception, both Pope and
Gay were assuring him that the real author's anonymity had been
formally preserved (*Corr*, III, 181, 182). The potentially incriminating
'original Manuscript is all destroyed, since the Publication of my Book',
Gulliver has heard (*PW*, XI, 7; 'A Letter from Capt. Gulliver, to his
Cousin Sympson' added to Faulkner's 1735 edition of *Gulliver's Travels*).

---

[10] PRO, SP 35/1/100, 28 August 1714. Quoted in Laurence Hanson, *Government and the Press,
1695–1763* (London, 1936), p. 51; Michael Treadwell, 'London Trade Publishers', p. 125.

Swift was reputed to be the author of the sensational satire, but there was no formal proof of his connection with the work.

Modern scholarship has described the contemporary reception and political significance of *Gulliver's Travels* as an Opposition work attacking the Walpolean regime, linking it with the political stance of Bolingbroke's circle and the Opposition journal *The Craftsman*.[11] From the time of its first publication readers have looked for topical political allusions and allegories in the text. The tenuousness of the consistent political allegories and much of the particular and personal allusion commonly alleged in modern editorial commentary and literary criticism on the book has been demonstrated by several scholars.[12] Nevertheless, Swift's political satire demonstrably combines topical and general satiric meanings. Swift intended *Gulliver's Travels* as a polemical act against the Whig government and a satire on contemporary European civilization and perennial imperfections, follies and vices of humanity (*Corr*, III, 102, 138, 226). *Gulliver* is a general satire on institutional and individual corruption with topical polemical resonance at the time of its publication. The reader of *Gulliver's Travels* is enabled by analogy, allusion and echo to make topical political applications of the general satire. But, unlike some of the bolder Jacobite pamphleteers and journalists of his day, Swift did not risk publishing explicit anti-government political statements *in propria persona* or allegories against the Court and ministry that were too transparent. Swift could write specific, consistent and transparent political allegory, as his *An Account of the Court and Empire of Japan* (written in 1728) witnesses (see *PW*, V, 99–107). But this thinly disguised political allegory on affairs of

11 See particularly Isaac Kramnick, *Bolingbroke and His Circle: The Politics of Nostalgia in the Age of Walpole* (Cambridge, Mass., 1968); Bertrand A. Goldgar, '*Gulliver's Travels* and the Opposition to Walpole', in *The Augustan Milieu: Essays Presented to Louis A. Landa*, edited by Henry Knight Miller *et al.* (Oxford, 1970), pp. 155–73 and his *Walpole and the Wits: The Relation of Politics to Literature, 1722–1742* (Lincoln, Nebraska, 1976), esp. pp. 5, 30, 49–63; J. A. Downie, 'Walpole, "the Poet's Foe"', in *Britain in the Age of Walpole*, edited by Jeremy Black, Problems in Focus (London, 1984), pp. 171–88, and his 'The Political Significance of *Gulliver's Travels*', in *Swift and His Contexts*, edited by John Irwin Fischer, Hermann J. Real and James Woolley (New York, 1989), pp. 1–19 (p. 15); Simon Varey, 'Exemplary History and the Political Satire of *Gulliver's Travels*', in *The Genres of 'Gulliver's Travels*', edited by Frederik N. Smith (Newark, London, Toronto, 1990), pp. 39–55. On the immediate contemporary reception of *Gulliver*, see Kathleen Williams, ed., *Swift: The Critical Heritage*, esp. pp. 8–15, 61–99; Phyllis J. Guskin, '"A very remarkable Book": Abel Boyer's View of *Gulliver's Travels*', *Studies in Philology*, 72 (1975), 439–53; *Swift*, III, 497–508.

12 Phillip Harth, 'The Problem of Political Allegory in *Gulliver's Travels*', *Modern Philology*, 73 (1976), S40–S47; J. A. Downie, 'Political Characterization in *Gulliver's Travels*', *Yearbook of English Studies*, 7 (1977), 108–20; F. P. Lock, *The Politics of 'Gulliver's Travels*', esp. pp. 89–122.

state attacking the Walpolean regime remained unpublished. In his great satire published in 1726 Swift disappears from the text behind fictive putative speakers and the disorientations and concealments of irony. There is ludic ambiguity and obliquity in his use of allusion, analogy and parallel and a studied generality in the satiric political commentary. The particular political attack is sufficiently disguised and indeterminate so as to confound any attempt by the authorities to convict the author of seditious libel and to afford readers the aesthetic pleasure of interpretation and application.

Pope and Gay reported to Swift in November 1726 that *Gulliver* was received as a bold general satire, but they reassured him that the book was unlikely to be convicted of libel (*Corr*, III, 181; III, 182–3). However, a jocular letter to Swift from the Tory Earl of Peterborough of 29 November 1726 attesting to the popularity of the book also perhaps implies that prosecution of the suspected author of the *Travels* was contemplated. It seems that Swift's artful satire exasperated (or could be imagined to have exasperated) the lawyers trying to make out a case for libel. Gulliver also had influential friends (the Princess Caroline and Mrs Howard, see *Corr*, III, 184–6, 187–8). Amusingly describing what 'strange distempers rage in the nation', the Earl of Peterborough wrote:

Itt was concluded not long agoe that such confusion could be only brought about by the black Art, and by the spells of a notorious scribbling Magitian, who was generally suspected, and was to be recommended to the mercy of the Inquisition.

Inditements were upon the anvill, a charge of Sorcery preparing & Merlin's friends were afraid that the Exasperated Pettyfoggers would persuade the jury to bring in Billa vera.

For they pretended to bring in Certain proofs of his appearing in severall shapes, att one time a Drappier, att another a Wapping Surgeon, sometimes a Nardic, sometimes a Reverend Divine ...

This was the scene not many days agoe, and burning was too good for the Wizard. But what mutations amongst the Lillyputians! the greatest Lady in the nation resolves to send a pair of shoes without heels to Capt Gulliver, she takes vi et Armis the plad from the Lady it was sent too, which is soon to appear upon her Royall person, and Now who but Capt Gulliver?

(*Corr*, III, 191–2)

Swift's summation of the text's reception in a letter to Pope of 27 November 1726 reflects both his concern about possible prosecution and an assessment that he had eluded the pettifoggers:

some think it wrong to be so hard upon whole Bodies or Corporations, yet the general opinion is, that reflections on particular persons are most to be blamed: so that in these cases, I think the best method is to let censure and opinion take their course.

(Corr, III, 189)

Pope assumes that the political writer of Gulliver's Travels might 'fancy none but Tories are your friends' (Corr, III, 182). Swift joked that the ministry might be made to keep him in England 'by a court expedient of keeping me in prison for a plotter' (Corr, III, 189).

Epistolary evidence suggests that Swift believed there was a dimension of seditious criticism in the text of Gulliver's Travels, that the work was dangerous to publish. He wrote in the well-known letter to Pope of 29 September 1725:

I have employd my time (besides ditching) in finishing correcting, amending, and Transcribing my Travells, in four parts Compleat newly Augmented, and intended for the press when the world shall deserve them, or rather when a Printer shall be found brave enough to venture his Eares.

(Corr, III, 102)

In the letter from 'Richard Sympson' to Benjamin Motte of 8 August 1726, offering the manuscript of Gulliver's Travels for publication and stating terms, Swift speaks of showing the Travels 'to several persons of great Judgment and Distinction' and seeks to assure the publisher that 'although some parts of this and the following Volumes may be thought in one or two places to be a little Satyrical, yet it is agreed they will give no Offence'. Nevertheless Swift recognizes there might be a possibility of prosecution in the prevailing political climate, so he writes further 'you must Judge for your self, and take the Advice of your Friends, and if they or you be of another opinion, you may let me know it when you return these Papers, which I expect shal be in three Days at furthest'. And Motte receives an exhortation: 'I require that you will never suffer these Papers to be once out of your Sight' (Corr, III, 153).

After the publication of the first edition of 1726, Swift complained that Motte had made alterations to the text, particularly in Parts III and IV, and he wanted readers to understand that his political satire had been castrated (see Corr, III, 189, 190; IV, 197–8, 211). It is not strictly germane to my discussion to go into the complex and controversial questions of the historical bibliography and textual scholarship on the two substantive editions of Gulliver's Travels in Swift's lifetime (the edition published in London by Benjamin Motte in 1726 and the text published in Dublin in the edition of Swift's Works by George Faulkner in 1735) and the intermediate textual history. But it is worth observing here that ridicule and repudiation of the Whig prosecution of Atterbury, attacks on the House of Lords and a degenerate hereditary nobility, attacks on standing armies, and ideas of justified rebellion and tyrannicide were themes in Jacobite polemic in the 1720s. There are substantive textual variants between the Motte and Faulkner editions in places where Swift's political satire is concerned with these topics. The passage in Motte's 1726 text on 'plots' (which alludes to the Atterbury Plot) at Part III, chapter VI and the satire of the nobility at Part IV, chapter VI are less bold and forthright than the variant passages printed in Faulkner's 1735 edition. The heavily conditional 'plots' passage in 1726 is not specific as to country and implies that there *are* 'Plots and Conspiracies' and that these 'could' or 'might' be exploited. But the 'plots' passage in 1735 specifies Britain and England (the reader is entrapped in the part of a decipherer using the satirized 'Anagrammatick Method' to decode '*Tribnia*' and '*Langden*') and exposes 'Plots' as political fabrications, cynically contrived, conducted and funded by 'Ministers' among a corrupted people. The formulation of the passage in the 1726 text seems to allow some credence to the prosecutors of 'Plots' and is euphemistic. For example, the 1726 text states that care is taken to secure the letters and papers of suspected persons and to 'put the Criminal in safe and secure Custody'. The wording in the 1735 text is 'put the Owners in Chains'. The decipherers in 1726 are 'a Sett of Artists of Dexterity sufficient to find out the mysterious Meanings of Words, Syllables, and Letters'. In 1735 they are 'a Set of Artists very dextrous in finding out the mysterious Meanings of Words, Syllables and Letters', which imputes motive and removes the possible 1726 suggestion that the 'Artists' necessarily have competence and actual coded meanings with which to work (for the evidence on which the above is based, see the text and textual notes at *PW*, XI, 191–2, 311–12). The execrable 'true Marks of *noble Blood*' in the 1735 text were 'no uncommon Marks of a *Great Man*' in 1726 and the attack on the House of Lords in the final paragraph of Part IV, chapter VI in the 1735 text is absent in Motte's edition (for these and other variants, see *PW*, XI, 257, 319).

In Part IV, chapter V of the 1735 text there is a striking attack on mercenary standing armies and the European princes who are said to profit by them. The passage reads:

THERE is likewise a Kind of beggarly Princes in *Europe*, not able to make War by themselves, who hire out their Troops to richer Nations for so much a Day to each Man; of which they keep three Fourths to themselves, and it is the best Part of their Maintenance; such are those in many *Northern* Parts of *Europe*.

(*PW*, XI, 247)

The 1726 edition omits the epithet 'beggarly'. An openly anti-Hanover-ian manuscript amendment of 'Germany and other' for 'many *Northern*' in this passage was not published in either the Motte or Faulkner editions (*PW*, XI, 315). A passage ambiguously alluding to Irish resistance to Wood's halfpence in 1722–4 and imagining tyrannicide and revolution, which would have appeared militantly Jacobitical to the English Whig authorities, remained unpublished in Swift's lifetime (see *PW*, XI, 309–10).

One passage in the *textus receptus* of 1726 does seem to have concerned Swift enough for him to offer, in a manner, a public disclaimer and to omit it in the 1735 edition. The passage in Part IV, chapter VI of the Motte text explicitly celebrates Queen Anne's administration as exem-plary and is a transparent attack on George I's government by innuendo (the passage can be read in *PW*, XI, 318). Approval of Anne's government in the 1720s could register as a disaffected Tory speech act and would certainly have been objectionable to a Whig government which had prosecuted the principals in Queen Anne's Tory ministry for treason.[13] Specific eulogy of Anne, indirect reflection on the honour of George I and implied connection of the monarch with the imputed corruption of his 'First or Chief Minister of State' might have been thought sufficient to bring the outspoken author within reach of the law as administered by Walpole's government. The incautious passage was specifically disclaimed as an interpolated paragraph by Charles Ford, writing to Motte as a friend of the author on 3 January 1727 (*Corr*, III, 194–5). In 'A Letter from Capt. Gulliver, to his Cousin Sympson', first published in 1735 but apparently intended for an earlier revised second edition in 1727, Swift has Gulliver 'renounce' all interpolations, 'par-ticularly a Paragraph about her Majesty the late Queen *Anne*', and complain of other unspecified omissions and alterations (*PW*, XI, 5). This brief witness of some substantive textual variants of political significance suggests that it tends to be Swift's anti-Hanoverian (rather than just anti-ministerial or anti-government) writing which in some passages finds Captain Gulliver sailing too close to the wind. Some relatively explicit aspects of the extremist strain in Swift's political writing were not exposed to the light of day in 1726 or 1735.

---

[13] The Jacobite Matthias Earbery remarks that speaking against King William or for the Tory part of Queen Anne's reign is regarded as seditious, see *The Universal Spy*, fols. 90–1.

While on one level Swift no doubt enjoyed all the mystification and secrecy surrounding the book's pseudonymous publication, which does have a comic Scriblerian aspect, he nevertheless had real reason to feel apprehensive about the reception of the political satire. A number of factors might have encouraged caution when Swift was writing and publishing *Gulliver's Travels*: his prejudicial public reputation as a Jacobite High Churchman and libeller, repeatedly proclaimed in the Whig prints; the prosecution of the recent *A Proposal for the Universal Use of Irish Manufacture*; the proclamation against the author (see *PW*, X, 205) and the arrest and death in custody of John Harding, the printer of *A Letter to the Whole People of Ireland*, the fourth *Drapier's Letter*, which was judged to contain seditious paragraphs; the indictment for libel of *Seasonable Advice* (the 1724 broadside addressed to the Grand Jury preparing a bill against the printer of the Drapier's fourth *Letter*); and the sufferings experienced by his Jacobite Tory friends in Ireland and England. In the 'Letter from Capt. Gulliver, to his Cousin Sympson' added to the 1735 edition, Gulliver complains that the first edition of his book had been altered:

When I formerly hinted to you something of this in a Letter, you were pleased to answer, that you were afraid of giving Offence; that People in Power were very watchful over the Press; and apt not only to interpret, but to punish every thing which looked like an *Inuendo* (as I think you called it).

(*PW*, XI, 5–6)

This passage, in fact, well expresses the conditions under which *Gulliver's Travels* was written and published. It also reflects a view Swift expressed in 'The Answer of The Right Honourable William Pulteney, Esq; To The Right Honourable Sir Robert Walpole', written in 1730: 'there were never heard of so many, so unnecessary, and so severe prosecutions as you have promoted during your ministry, in a kingdom where the liberty of the press is so much pretended to be allowed' (*PW*, V, 118). In 1725 Swift was apprehensive about the safety of his person and papers in returning to England (*Corr*, III, 53). The State Papers Domestic for the reigns of George I and George II provide ample witness to the veracity of this claim about government surveillance of the press.

The demise of pre-publication censorship with the lapse of the Licensing Act in 1695 had led to a considerable increase in the volume of pamphlet and newspaper publication. While there were calls in the following years for the reintroduction of some form of pre-publication censorship, and measures taken (such as the 1712 Stamp Act for

political and economic reasons) to regulate the press, it was the libel
laws, and penal laws against Jacobites, which were to remain the
principal legal means by which the established government could
control political expression. A satirist who used the device of innuendo
and fictitious or classical characters in attacking contemporary persons,
institutions or government was legally safe under the contemporary
libel laws as long as the innuendo was not legally certain, that is, that
the satiric victim had not been specifically named or had not been
identified from other unambiguous evidence in the text.[14] A satirist's
meaning might be apparent to readers, but legal certainty had to be
established in order to secure conviction. The secretaries of state could
initiate official prosecutions against authors and printers on information brought by the Messenger of the Press or the network of
informers and press spies. There is frequent witness in the State Papers
of the Under-Secretary of State, Charles Delafaye, and his officious
press men on the hunt for the authors and printers of seditious works.[15]
From 1722 Nicholas Paxton was employed to monitor papers and
pamphlets published in Britain and to report seditious publication to
the secretaries of state.[16] Seditious libel could be made to cover just
about any expression of disaffection towards the Hanoverian state, but
the evidence suggests that Walpole's government preferred to silence
the Jacobite and Tory voice through harassment, arrest and incarceration of printers and publicists rather than through the problematic
and high-risk method of a full-scale public prosecution of a treasonable,
criminal or seditious libel in a court of law, which would mean incur-
ring costs, adverse publicity, and the considerable legal difficulties of
securing a conviction under the existing libel laws.[17] Such prosecutions
were only contemplated if there were legal grounds to hope for success.
Fiction, for instance, might be prosecuted if it had a criminal double-
meaning or construction, but prosecution could be evaded if it could be

[14] See C. R. Kropf, 'Libel and Satire in the Eighteenth Century', Eighteenth-Century Studies, 8
(1974–5), 153–68.
[15] For reports from informers on the press in the early Hanoverian period, see for example
PRO, SP 35/3/78; SP 35/51/34, 35. For a reported account of the discovery of 'Parson
Carts lodgings' and subsequent apprehension of the Jacobite author Thomas Carte, see
PRO, SP 35/40/2, 3.
[16] PRO, SP 35/31/17; Michael Harris, London Newspapers in the Age of Walpole: A Study of the
Origins of the Modern English Press (London and Toronto, 1987), pp. 136–40.
[17] On this point, see particularly Donald Thomas, 'Press Prosecutions of the Eighteenth and
Nineteenth Centuries: The Evidence of King's Bench Indictments', The Library, 5th series,
32 (1977), 315–32 (pp. 316, 318) and P. B. J. Hyland, 'Liberty and Libel: Government
and the Press during the Succession Crisis in Britain, 1712–1716', English Historical Review,
101, no. 401 (1986), 863–88 (pp. 865, 877).

plainly shown that an innocent sense was meant.[18] In the years when Swift was at work on *Gulliver's Travels*, Walpole's government, provoked by the extremist and populist strain in Jacobite Tory argument, conducted a campaign of harassment, arrest and prosecution of seditious publicists.[19] And as Swift experienced and often attested, the Post Office was used for the surveillance and interception of letters and packets of printed material. As J. C. D. Clark has commented, 'The State Papers Domestic for the reigns of the first two Georges are littered with prosecutions of Jacobite publicists.'[20]

The conditions and nature of political writing against the established Hanoverian monarchy and government in the 1720s need to be recalled when interpreting the political satire in *Gulliver's Travels* and understanding its contemporary reception. Jacobite publications, the vehicles of Tory subversion, used strategies of disguise, indirection, innuendo, allusion and analogy in disseminating anti-Establishment views while seeking to evade prosecution. Elliptical strategies, indeterminacy and ambiguity had functional purposes. The Whig government was willing and able to prosecute unambiguous attacks on the Hanoverian dynasty and disaffected reflections on the motives of the Revolution or the foundations of the Revolution Settlement. Punishment of printers and publicists whose innuendoes against the Hanoverian establishment were so obvious as to be legally certain was severe.

A few examples of the 'People in Power' being 'very watchful over the Press' and punishing 'an *Inuendo*' and explicit statement in the late 1710s and 1720s must suffice. Isaac Dalton, printer of the notorious *The Shift Shifted*, written by the Jacobite George Flint in 1716, was put in Newgate, and another principal behind the publication of the paper absconded. Flint escaped from Newgate and hanging in 1717, reached France and joined the Pretender's service.[21] A young Jacobite

---

[18] PRO, SP 36/19, fol. 102.

[19] See the PRO, SP Domestic, for the reign of George I, covering the years 1714–27; Rocco Lawrence Capraro, 'Political Broadside Ballads in Early Hanoverian London', *Eighteenth-Century Life*, 11 (1987), 12–21.

[20] J. C. D. Clark, *English Society 1688–1832*, p. 144. For important studies of the press and politics, Jeremy Black, *The English Press in the Eighteenth Century* (London and Sydney, 1987), esp. ch. 6, 'Controlling the Press: Censorship and Subsidies', pp. 135–96, and Harris, *London Newspapers in the Age of Walpole*, esp. ch. 7 'The Press and Politics' and ch. 8 'Political Control of the Press', pp. 113–54. For richly documented studies of the Jacobite press, see Paul Chapman, 'Jacobite Political Argument in England, 1714–1766', and Paul Monod, *Jacobitism and the English People 1688–1788*.

[21] R. J. Goulden, '*Vox Populi, Vox Dei*: Charles Delafaye's Paperchase', *The Book Collector*, 28 (1979), 368–90 (pp. 385–6); Clark, *English Society 1688–1832*, p. 145; Black, *The English Press in the Eighteenth Century*, p. 163.

apprentice James Shepheard was arrested and executed in 1718 after information was received of his written undertaking to assassinate King George I.[22] In 1718, Delafaye received a letter from Under-Secretary of State George Tilson assuring him that the Secretary of State, James Craggs, wanted vigorous prosecution and punishment of offending authors and printers, and spoke of employing some attorney who 'knew how to tear & rend those wretches'.[23] In 1719 the young printer John Matthews was hanged after being convicted of high treason against the King and government for printing the overtly Jacobite pamphlet *Vox Populi, Vox Dei*. This inflammatory and militant text declared that the Old Pretender possessed hereditary right and princely virtues and that all asserters of limited monarchy must allow that a person with hereditary right and princely qualities ought to be preferred as monarch. *Vox Populi, Vox Dei* claimed that every Whig who adheres to true Whig principles must perforce be a Jacobite, and called for the popular deposition of a government that does not answer the end of its institution. Delafaye thought that the example of Matthews's execution would 'have the greatest influence upon those of his trade in deterring them from printing treason'.[24] The Jacobite Tory ballad printer Francis Clifton was taken up in 1720 for *The Tory's Wholesome Advice*, which recounts the fate of John Matthews. Clifton was subjected to harassment and arrest in the following years.[25]

The issue of the Jacobite Tory publicist Nathaniel Mist's *The Weekly Journal, or Saturday's Post* of 27 May 1721 was prosecuted by the government for a transparent abuse of George I and his heir. This Restoration Day paper was thought to have been written by Philip

---

[22] On the literature concerned with the Shepheard case and government censorship, see Manuel Schonhorn, 'Defoe and James Shepheard's Assassination Plot of 1718: Two New Pamphlets', *SEL: Studies in English Literature, 1500–1900*, 29 (1989), 447–62.

[23] PRO, SP 35/12, fol. 360; quoted in Goulden, '*Vox Populi, Vox Dei*', p. 371.

[24] See PRO, SP 43/63; Goulden, '*Vox Populi, Vox Dei*', *passim*, quotation on p. 377; Black, *The English Press in the Eighteenth Century*, p. 163. There are copies of *Vox Populi, Vox Dei* at PRO, SP 35/19, fol. 135 and SP 43/61, no. 86.

[25] See Capraro, 'Political Broadside Ballads in Early Hanoverian London', pp. 13–15; Goulden, '*Vox Populi, Vox Dei*', p. 368. Thomas Gent's account of a clandestine meeting between his master Francis Clifton and himself, and the Bishop of Rochester, Francis Atterbury, affords a wonderful glimpse of secret Tory press operations and the constant apprehension of 'direful consequences' under which Tory printers worked in the reign of George I: see Thomas Gent, *The Life of Mr. Thomas Gent, Printer, of York: Written by Himself* (London, 1832; reprinted New York and London, 1974), esp. pp. 85–90. For Gent on Matthews and Clifton, see also pp. 91–3, 95. For the arrests of Gent, Clifton and others at the time of the Atterbury Plot and trial, see pp. 121–9.

Neynoe, a Jacobite clergyman of the Church of Ireland.[26] Swift was
certainly aware of Mist's paper, which was, as Harold Williams
described it, 'the recognized organ of High-fliers and Jacobites', and
Swift commented on the notorious Restoration issue in a letter to his
Jacobite friend Knightley Chetwode written on the Pretender's birth-
day, 10 June 1721: 'There is a paper called Mist come out, just before
May 29th, terribly severe. It is not here to be had. The printer was
called before the Commons. It applies Cromwell and his son to the
present Court. White roses we have heard nothing of to-day' (*Corr*, II,
390–1). *Mist's Weekly Journal* of 20 April 1728 reprinted in part Swift's
A Short View of the State of Ireland. Swift believed or claimed Mist's paper
had been prosecuted by the government: 'Mist, the famous journalist,
happened to reprint this paper in London, for which his press-folks
were prosecuted for almost a twelvemonth; and, for ought I know, are
not yet discharged.' For Swift this was another instance proving 'how
dangerous it hath been for the best meaning person to write one syllable
in the defence of his country, or discover the miserable condition it is in'
(*PW*, XII, 122). Swift's claim about the prosecution of this issue is
unsupported, but Nathaniel Mist and his managers, and Thomas
Payne, printer of the Duke of Wharton's *The True Briton*, were principal
sufferers of concentrated government action in the early 1720s against
expression of disaffection in the press.[27] The transparent Jacobite
allegory of the Duke of Wharton's 'Persian Letter', printed in *Mist's
Weekly Journal* no. 175 of 24 August 1728, led to mass arrests of those
connected with the publication of the issue and to severe sentences.
Mist fled to France and exile in 1728.[28] The issue of *Mist's Weekly
Journal* (no. 176, 31 August 1728) immediately following the treasonable libel lamented how no essay could escape censorship and defended

---

[26] The much-prosecuted Mist describes his sufferings as a Newgate prisoner on account of the
'ever-memorable Letter of the 27th of May' in 'The Preface' of *A Collection of Miscellany
Letters, The Second Volume*, pp. ix–xi. For Neynoe's authorship, see Historical Manuscripts
Commission. *Fourteenth Report, Appendix, Part IX* (London, 1895), pp. 234–5. On Neynoe
and his involvement in the Atterbury Plot where he was an evidence, see Cruickshanks,
'Lord North, Christopher Layer and the Atterbury Plot: 1720–23', pp. 100–1. For a
sympathetic account of Neynoe, who drowned while trying to escape from the Messenger's
custody, see *The Life of Mr. Thomas Gent, Printer, of York: Written by Himself*, pp. 125–8. Cf.
'Upon the horrid *Plot* discovered by *Harlequin* the B---- of *R*——'s *French Dog*', *Poems*, I,
297–301, line 22: '...t'other *Puppy* that was drown'd'.
[27] James Woolley, ed., *The Intelligencer*, pp. 236, 327; Harris, *London Newspapers in the Age of
Walpole*, p. 142.
[28] Goulden, '*Vox Populi, Vox Dei*', p. 368; Jeremy Black, 'Trying Mist's Men: Fresh Material
from the Althorp Papers', *Notes and Queries*, ns, 33 (1986), 497–8; Harris, *London Newspapers
in the Age of Walpole*, pp. 145, 146, 148, 149.

Swift ('the finest Genius the Age has produced') from the calumny of his political enemies.

As a final example, the career of the volatile Jacobite pamphleteer and nonjuror Matthias Earbery illustrates the consequences of out-spoken press criticism of the Hanoverian monarchy and government. He was in trouble with the authorities over a number of publications. He fled the country in 1717 to escape prosecution for seditious libel over *The History of the Clemency of Our English Monarchs* and a sentence of outlawry was imposed on him. In his own words:

Mr. Attorney-General ... mov'd the Court of *King's-Bench* for corporal Tor-tures to be inflicted upon myself, being charg'd with writing *The History of Clemency*, and reflecting, as his Words were, upon the Honour of the King: So tender is every Age of their Princes in Possession.[29]

After his return to England, Earbery was recommended to Swift 'as a sufferer by the times, and desirous to help himself by the translation of an Italian book'. Swift received a bizarre letter from Earbery in August 1727. Swift expressed his sympathy for the sufferings of the Jacobite nonjuror, if not for the manners and pretensions of the person and author (*Corr*, III, 227–8). *Mist's Weekly Journal*, no. 137 (2 December 1727) was also sympathetic to this 'sufferer by the times': 'When the Rev. Mr. *Earbury* was brought to that Bench as an Out Law, I was there, not without Compassion for his Case, he stood upon his last Legs, for Liberty or a Prison.' Perhaps the final witness to the Hanoverian government's surveillance of the press and punishment of 'an *Inuendo*' can be left to Earbery. In the third number of *The Occasional Historian* (1731), a vindication of Charles I from the *Craftsman*'s charge of cruelty in relation to the Star-Chamber, Earbery discusses seditious libel and reflects on the relative severity of the Hanoverian government's press prosecution in comparison with the 'merciful' punishment of William Prynne for *Histriomastix* in 1633. Earbery observes:

In this Age, one *Matthews* was hang'd for Printing the *Vox Populi*, the Hints were thought strong enough to amount to a Persuasive to an Insurrection; but *Prynne*'s was a Persuasive to attack the Person of King *Charles*, and to put him to Death; and yet he was punish'd only with Loss of Ears.

[29] Matthias Earbery, *The Occasional Historian*, Numb. III (London, 1731), p. 17. See also his *The History of the Clemency of Our English Monarchs ... The Second Edition. With Additions* (London, 1720) with *A Vindication of the History of Clemency, With Reflections upon the Late Proceedings against the Author. In a Letter from Himself at Paris, to his Friend in London ...* (dated May. 30. 1718) (London, 1720). Government action against Earbery for *The History of the Clemency of Our English Monarchs* is noticed in Clark, *English Society 1688–1832*, p. 144. See BL Add. MSS, 36,196, fol. 167.

Referring to the example of Thomas Payne, convicted for publishing *The True Briton* (1723–4), Earbery writes:

> Mr. *Payne* was convicted for only an Ironical Expression concerning the present Bench of Bishops, and Irony is so soft, so genteel a Way of Libelling, that in Proportion, putting one Crime against the others, *Leighton, Prynne, Bastwick* and *Burton* ought to have been hang'd, drawn, and quarter'd upon the Spot ...
> In God's Name, is *English* Liberty confin'd only to Republicans, Fanaticks and Rebels? Are not the landed Men of a Nation to Sport in this Sea of Liberty, I thought Liberty was a common Water for all the Natives of *England*, and not to be ingrossed by one Part only.

Earbery concludes his polemical essay on libels by stressing that an intention of malice is essential to the definition of a libel, and for good measure adds an innuendo that the Hanoverian monarch is a latter-day Tiberius:

> To conclude, Libels are certainly a War against an Establishment, and are known by their Malice; but God forbid that Ministers should ever call in Books that plead for Righteousness and Justice, as Libels. *Tiberius* was the first who invented this way to punish Anticourtiers ... *Cremutius Cordus* was accus'd ... of a new and unheard of Crime, that in his Annals by him publish'd, he had prais'd *Brutus*, and called *Cassius* the last of the *Romans*.[30]

In *Gulliver's Travels* Swift implicitly conflates George I with Tiberius in the allusive satire of the Emperor of Lilliput's spurious clemency in Part I, Chapter VII,[31] and explicitly praises Brutus in Part III, Chapter VII. In defending his political and satiric practice in the early 1730s, Swift famously claimed that 'Fair LIBERTY was all his Cry' and that 'Malice never was his Aim' (*Verses on the Death of Dr. Swift* (written in 1731), lines 347, 459, *Poems*, II, 566, 571). Earbery was making similar claims. Swift also humorously described himself at one point in *An Epistle to a Lady* as just a jester and name-caller, a modern Democritus laughing at the corrupt Walpolean regime:

> Safe within my little Wherry,
> All their Madness makes me merry:
> Like the Watermen of *Thames*,
> I row by, and call them Names.

---

[30] *The Occasional Historian*, Numb. III, pp. 23–4, 32–3, 37–8. *The Occasional Historian* was silenced by the government after the publication of the fourth number – an historical essay upon and in defence of English Hereditary Right. Earbery makes similar points to those in the third number of *The Occasional Historian* and again implicitly compares George II with Tiberius in the suppressed paper *The Universal Spy*, fols. 90–1.

[31] *Swift*, III, pp. 453–4.

> Like the ever-laughing Sage,
> In a Jest I spend my rage:
> (Tho' it must be understood,
> I would hang them if I cou'd:)
>
> (lines 163–70, *Poems*, II, 635)

Although these lines are part of an aggressive passage transparently attacking Walpole by innuendo, the poet pretends to leave serious politics to the Opposition publicists (see lines 173–6). However, there is a 'hint' here that the 'Names' and 'Jest' the poet utters in safety would be actionable seditious words. The Thames watermen, with whom Swift as satirist compares himself, were notorious not only for ribald language, as Swift's editors remark, but also for Jacobitism. In the projected Jacobite Rising of 1722 in London the Thames watermen, led by the Duke of Wharton, were to seize the Greenwich powder magazines. When Atterbury left the Tower for permanent exile on the continent, the Duke of Wharton's watermen escorted him down the Thames.[32] The printer and publishers of *An Epistle to a Lady* were prosecuted for seditious libel against the King, his administration and Sir Robert Walpole. Lines 155–72 were among those objected to by the government.[33] It is a striking fact that Swift had correspondence or acquaintance with most of the major Jacobite literary talents – authors such as the Duke of Wharton (*Corr*, II, 285), Thomas Carte (*Corr*, III, 361; IV, 508, 523–4), Matthias Earbery (*Corr*, III, 227–8) and William King, Principal of St Mary Hall, Oxford (*Corr*, V, 266). He was familiar with the work of the brilliant Jacobite publicists Charles Leslie and Nathaniel Mist and was, of course, the friend of Lord Bolingbroke, Lord Lansdowne, the Earl of Mar, the Earl of Orrery and Francis Atterbury, Bishop of Rochester, though such evidence from association does not, of course, make Swift a Jacobite and must be set against the evidence that apparently clears him of any Jacobite commitment. A letter of advice which Swift wrote to the Jacobite Chetwode on 28 April 1731, but then suppressed, indicates his own political prudence and his exasperation at Chetwode's indiscretion in 'a desperate cause' (*Corr*, V, 250–1). For Swift, rather, Jacobitism provided a political rhetoric of militant opposition that could be appropriated and deployed in his

---

[32] See Cruickshanks, 'Lord North, Christopher Layer and the Atterbury Plot: 1722–23', pp. 99 and 105, n. 28. It is not inconceivable that Swift may have had direct knowledge of the political sympathies of the Thames watermen from the Duke of Wharton himself, with whom Swift was acquainted.

[33] See John Irwin Fischer, 'The Government's Response to Swift's *An Epistle to a Lady*', *Philological Quarterly*, 65 (1986), 39–59 (p. 50).

political satire. It is significant that on publication in 1726 *Gulliver's Travels* was received as a disaffected Tory and Jacobite work, as will now be discussed.

'A Letter from Capt. Gulliver to his Cousin Sympson' accurately describes the conditions of censorship in which *Gulliver's Travels* was produced. But in the 'Letter' Swift has the disaffected Redriff recluse deny giving any political offence to the authorities:

> But pray, how could that which I spoke so many Years ago, and at above five Thousand Leagues distance, in another Reign, be applyed to any of the *Yahoos*, who now are said to govern the Herd; especially, at a time when I little thought on or feared the Unhappiness of living under them.
>
> (*PW*, XI, 6)

This denial of topical political application is disingenuous. At the same time that it protests political innocence it artfully invites readers to interpret innuendo in the text and reflect on the 'Unhappiness' of living under the governing Yahoos. Rhetorical disavowals of political offence were an ironically charged routine in anti-government political literature. The Duke of Wharton's notorious Jacobite 'Persian Letter' in *Mist's Weekly Journal*, no. 175 (24 August 1728) is prefaced with the author's heavily ironic address to his printer Mr Mist:

> I observe you have been often under Confinement for having disobliged the present Government, and I must say, that I hope for the future, you will avoid all Occasions of giving Offence to the Ministry: A Ministry equally esteem'd for their Abilities in Domestick, and their great Experience in Foreign Affairs, and whose Lenity, of which you have had the strongest Proofs, renders their Administration as amiable at Home, as it is formidable Abroad.

Similarly, in the 'Preface' to the 1729 printing of *Polly*, a play suppressed by the government, John Gay audaciously disavows any political intent:

> *Since this prohibition I have been told that I am accused, in general terms, of having written many disaffected libels and seditious pamphlets. As it hath ever been my utmost ambition ... to lead a quiet and inoffensive life, I thought my innocence in this particular would never have requir'd a justification ... this kind of writing is, what I have ever detested and never practic'd.*[34]

Howard Erskine-Hill has discussed examples in the work of Pope (*The Rape of the Lock* and *The Key to the Lock*) and the Duke of Wharton (*The*

---

[34] John Gay, *Dramatic Works*, edited by John Fuller, 2 vols. (Oxford, 1983), II, 70.

True Briton) where the idea of political innuendo is denied or ridiculed but where political implication is demonstrably present.[35]

Despite the protestation of injured innocence in the 'Letter', an unapologetic Gulliver complains that his book has been interpreted as disaffected, as well as misanthropic and antifeminist: 'I see myself accused of reflecting upon great States-Folk; of degrading human Nature, (for so they have still the Confidence to stile it) and of abusing the Female Sex' (*PW*, XI, 7). The remark on the political reception of *Gulliver's Travels* is accurate. Certainly Whig commentators professed to see transparent Jacobite intention in the published work, and there were calls for proceedings against the author and printer for seditious libel.[36] Edmund Curll's *A Key, Being Observations and Explanatory Notes, Upon the Travels of Lemuel Gulliver* (1726) seeks at several points to expose the anti-ministerial and anti-Hanoverian applications of Swift's satire. So, for example, the passage in Part I, chapter III of the 1726 text of *Gulliver's Travels* on the purple, yellow and white silk threads given by the Emperor of Lilliput as a reward for dexterity in leaping and creeping is explicated in the *Key* as a reflection on George I's court: 'his Intent could be no other than to ridicule our *three* most noble Orders of the *Garter*, the *Thistle* and the *Bath*'. The commentator loyally counters the disaffected satirist: 'but indeed the Meannesses to which the *Lilliputians* are subjected by an Arbitrary Prince can never be the fate of *Britons* thanks to the Happiness of our admirable Constitution!'[37] In 1725 George I had revived the Order of the Bath and Swift possibly wrote a verse version of this satire on George I's honours system (see 'Verses on the Revival of the Order of the Bath', *Poems*, II, 388–9). In the 1735 text of *Gulliver's Travels*, interestingly, the silk threads are blue, red and green, a specific and explicit allusion to the three major British orders of the Garter, the Bath, and the Thistle, whereas the colours in the 1726 edition are non-specific (*PW*, XI, 39, 304). Swift's alterations

[35] Howard Erskine-Hill, 'Literature and the Jacobite Cause: Was There a Rhetoric of Jacobitism?', in *Ideology and Conspiracy*, pp. 49–69 (pp. 53–4 and p. 67 notes 75 and 76).

[36] For example, see *A Letter from a Clergyman to his Friend, With an Account of the Travels of Capt. Lemuel Gulliver and a Character of the Author. To which is added, The True Reasons why a certain Doctor was made a Dean* (London, 1726), reprinted in *Gulliveriana VI: Critiques of Gulliver's Travels and Allusions Thereto*. Book One. Facsimile Reproductions with an Introduction by Jeanne K. Welcher and George E. Bush, Jr (Delmar, New York, 1976), pp. 8–9.

[37] [Edmund Curll], *A Key, Being Observations and Explanatory Notes, Upon the Travels of Lemuel Gulliver ... In a Letter to Dean Swift* ... (London, 1726), reprinted in *Gulliveriana VI* (Delmar, New York, 1976), 'Observations ... upon the Voyage to Lilliput', p. 16.

to the colours constitute a revision of the 1726 text.[38] For the 1735 edition he perhaps saw no need to preserve the transparent disguise of non-specific colours. After all, the passage had been pointed at in 1726 as a reflection on the King and Walpole's administration, but without any harmful consequence for author or printer. In the 1735 edition Swift presents a text with bolder strokes of the pen.

Elsewhere the *Key* explains apparent topical allusions which imply the Jacobite Tory sympathies of the author. The disarming and detention in custody of the captured and submissive Gulliver and inventory 'of the *Effects* found about Mr *Gulliver* by the *State-Officers*' invite application to the treatment of the Jacobite rebels 'in the Time of the *Preston* Rebellion'. 'The Opposition made to *Lemuel's* Enlargement' suggests 'what some *English* Peers struggled with before they could get out of the *Tower*'. The charge of High Treason and articles of impeachment against Gulliver resemble 'the late Earl of O——d's Sufferings'. 'With how much Glee will a *T——d*, or a *W——p-e* read this Pygmaean Account of *Flimnap* and *Reldresal*', the *Key* leadingly asks. On Gulliver's remark in Glubbdubdrib of how 'many innocent and excellent Persons had been condemned to Death or Banishment, by the practising of great Ministers upon the Corruption of Judges, and the Malice of Faction' (*PW*, XI, 199, 312), the *Key* observes the allusion to the Atterbury Plot and the execution of Christopher Layer, banishment of the Bishop of Rochester, and incarceration of George Kelly:

Now here I am sensible, that the present Disaffected in *England*, will immediately apply the Cases of an executed Barrister, banished Bishop, and an imprisoned Priest.[39]

The Court Whig author of *Gulliver Decypher'd* ... with heavy irony pretended to vindicate Swift from the imputation of authorship of *Gulliver's Travels*. The book cannot be Swift's because of 'the many oblique Reflections it is said to cast upon our present happy Administration, to which 'tis well known how *devoutly* he is attach'd and affected'. It is insinuated that the work gratifies 'Party Malice' and obliges 'a Set of People who are never likely to have it in their Power to serve him or any of their Adherents'.[40] In *Gulliver's Travels* Swift was

---

[38] See Lock, *The Politics of 'Gulliver's Travels'*, pp. 79–81 and Treadwell, 'Benjamin Motte, Andrew Tooke and *Gulliver's Travels*', p. 299, n. 51.

[39] [Edmund Curll], *A Key* ..., 'Observations ... upon the Voyage to Lilliput', pp. 9, 17, 25–26, 13, 'Observations ... upon the Voyage to Laputa &c', p. 27.

[40] *Gulliver Decypher'd: or Remarks on a late Book, intitled, Travels Into Several Remote Nations of the World. By Capt. Lemuel Gulliver. Vindicating the Reverend Dean on whom it is maliciously Father'd* ... (London, [1726]), reprinted in *Gulliveriana VI*, pp. 10, 30.

said to have 'here and there scatter'd up and down some laudable Hints of his Zeal for High Church and Toryism' and the book is seen as coming from the same political stable as '*Mist* or the *Craftsman*'.[41]

It seems likely, as Gay, Pope and the Earl of Peterborough opined, that it was the popularity of the satiric fiction, and the artful obliquity and generality of its political commentary and hit-and-run allusion, which persuaded the Whig government against prosecuting the book for seditious libel. As the Whig writer of *A Letter from a Clergyman to his Friend, With an Account of the Travels of Capt. Lemuel Gulliver and a Character of the Author* ... (1726) observes in arguing for action against *Gulliver*, which is described as the Jacobite work of an incendiary:

But whatever the Doctor deserves, 'tis given out that he has been so much upon his Guard, that no Forms of Law can touch him; in this, Sir, I beg Leave to differ from his Abbettors; for as I take it, that Point has been settled for some Time; and seems by the general Consent, the Determination has met with, to be rightly settled. So that his imaginary Cautions would be in vain; 'twas the Opinion of a late Learned Chief Justice of the King's Bench, that the universal Notion of the People in these Cases, notwithstanding the artful Disguises of an Author, ought much to influence the Determinations of a Jury; for as he very judiciously added; how absurd was it to imagine that all the World should understand his Meaning but just that particular Judge and Jury, by whom he was to be try'd.[42]

The political damage to the Whig government which resulted from the prosecution of the High Church clergyman, Henry Sacheverell, in 1709–10 was not forgotten by contemporaries after the Hanoverian accession. As Dudley Ryder, later an Attorney-General and Chief Justice, noted in his diary in December 1715:

This shows very plainly that the advantage he [i.e. Sacheverell] made by his prosecution has encouraged the clergy to do anything though never so vile from this precedent, that nobody would for the future dare to prosecute a clergyman again. It is certain the clergy in the country have been the greatest instrument in raising this spirit of rebellion through the nation.[43]

A full-scale prosecution of a High Church clergyman of Swift's prominence would have only been contemplated by Walpole and his ministers

[41] [Jonathan Smedley], *Gulliveriana: Or, A Fourth Volume of Miscellanies. Being a Sequel of the Three Volumes, published by Pope and Swift* ... (London, 1728), p. 280.
[42] *A Letter from a Clergyman to his Friend* ..., pp. 10–11, see pp. 9–14.
[43] *The Diary of Dudley Ryder 1715–1716*, edited by William Matthews (London, 1939), p. 152.

if the offending text was explicit and flagitious enough to make conviction certain.[44]

In its political project *Gulliver's Travels* is not just another Opposition attack on Walpole and his government, reflecting unexceptional 'Old Whig' or 'Country' political principles. It is a profoundly disaffected and extremist work. What makes it a candidate for prosecution, as Swift no doubt knew, is its satiric reflection not just on the King's ministry, but on the King and court and the Revolutionary Settlement upon which the Hanoverian dynasty's rule was founded. There are certainly militant implications in aspects of the satire. The consonance between Swift's indirect critique of the Hanoverian regime in *Gulliver's Travels* and the criticism of the government conducted in the Jacobite press is striking. A contextualist reading of Swift's satire – placing the literary text in juxtaposition with Jacobite pamphleteering and Jacobite papers such as *The Shift Shifted, Mist's Weekly Journal* and its successor *Fog's Weekly Journal, The Freeholder's Journal* of 1722–3 with which Thomas Carte was involved and the Duke of Wharton's *The True Briton* of 1723–4 – activates for the modern reader the dimension of seditious criticism in Swift's satire. *Gulliver's Travels* can be shown not only to share the disaffected political discourse of Jacobite publications but also to entertain recognized Jacobite alternative options – ideas of resistance and tyrannicide, demands for free elections and parliaments, ideas of composition and reversion to the principles of 'Old England'. Assuming Swift was not a Jacobite and regarding Jacobitism as a lost cause, modern Swift scholars do not seem to have considered seriously the possibility of a Jacobite context for interpreting *Gulliver's Travels*. The concentration in criticism on the civic humanist and 'Country' Opposition languages in the text, illuminating as it has been, nevertheless has led to the neglect of other possible ways of reading the politics of *Gulliver's Travels*. There is, of course, no explicit Swiftian call for a Jacobite restoration in *Gulliver's Travels* or elsewhere in his canon, and Swift renounced Jacobitism several times in print. But I am not arguing that Swift was a committed Jacobite or that the Jacobite publications to which I refer are 'sources' for Swift's political language in *Gulliver's Travels*. Rather, by describing the consonance between Swift's political expression and Jacobite press argument I can suggest how it was

---

[44] Bishop Nicolson told Archbishop Wake in October 1724 that 'if no Mark be set on this insolent Writer, little Safety will be expected'. But in October 1725 Nicolson opines that Swift's popularity in Ireland probably rules out prosecution of him, see BL, Add MSS, 6116, fols. 137, 148.

possible for contemporaries to construe *Gulliver's Travels* as a work of
Jacobite Tory provenance. Despite his disclaimers (and Swift, like some
committed Jacobite publicists, called himself an 'Old Whig' or
renounced party labels),[45] it is not difficult to see why contemporaries
regarded this political writer as a Tory extremist, a *de facto* Jacobite.

Political significance

Jacobite publicists after 1715 adopted constitutionalist and libertarian
stances, criticized the monarch and not just his ministry, and purveyed
the view of the Hanoverian regime as a tyranny. The distinctive
signature of a Jacobite Tory paper was its readiness to impugn the
monarch for the policies of his ministers. The provenance of that
corruption perceived in the polity by Opposition Whigs and Tories is
located in the monarch and court by the Jacobite writer. Jacobite
arguments against corruption emphasize the betrayal of the people's
trust by their representatives and hold the King and court responsible
for the corruption in the body politic. The monarchy is assailed for its
illegitimacy, conduct and intentions. As direct criticism of the King was
treasonable libel, Jacobite publicists were taking great risks. Recognition of the conditions of writing under the treason laws, the strategies of
indirection used by anti-government writers and the typical signature
of a crypto-Jacobite text attunes a reading of Swift's illocutionary acts
in the political satire of *Gulliver's Travels*.

Swift's topical political satire in *Gulliver's Travels* is directed against
the monarch as well as the ministry. A celebrated episode of comic
satire in Part I describes the '*Diversions of the Court of* Lilliput'. Gulliver
is most diverted by the rope dancing, which 'is only practised by those

---

[45] For example the Jacobite Roman Catholic George Flint (*The Shift Shifted*, no. 16, 18
August 1716, pp. 94–5) claims 'I, for Example, am an honest Low-Churchman, love K.
GEORGE very well, and the *Protestant Succession*' but he is shocked by George I's lack of
clemency, perpetuated parliaments and a standing army, and witnesses a universal
discontent and a general voice for the Pretender since the Hanoverian accession. The
Jacobite Duke of Wharton's *The True Briton* (19 August 1723) celebrates '*The old Whigs of
Rome*'. Among Jacobite works rejecting 'Party' in 1722: *The Freeholder's Journal* (31 January
172[2]), p. 3; [George Granville, Baron Lansdowne], *A Letter*, p. 6; *The Second and Last
English Advice, To The Freehoulders of Englan[d]* (London, 1722) rejects 'talk of *Whig* or *Tory*'
but admits in the course of argument a leaning 'to what is called the Tory or Church-party'
(pp. 40, 23); [Matthias Earbery], *An Historical Account of the Advantages that have Accru'd to
England, By the Succession in the Illustrious House of Hanover* (London, 1722), p. 44: 'I am no
Party Writer; I neither prefer the Interests of *Whig* or *Tory* ... the Question now is not
whether *Whig* or *Tory* Church of *Englandman* or *Dissenter* is to prevail, but between *English*
Liberty and Foreign arbitrary Dominion.'

Persons, who are Candidates for great Employments, and high Favour, at Court. They are trained in this Art from their Youth, and are not always of noble Birth, or liberal Education'. Gulliver tells us that '*Flimnap*, the Treasurer, is allowed to cut a Caper on the strait Rope, at least an Inch higher than any other Lord in the whole Empire. I have seen him do the Summerset several times together, upon a Trencher fixed on the Rope, which is no thicker than a common Packthread in *England*.' Gulliver 'was assured, that a Year or two before my Arrival, *Flimnap* would have infallibly broke his Neck, if one of the *King's Cushions*, that accidentally lay on the Ground, had not weakened the Force of his Fall' (*PW*, XI, 38–9). Swift had 'put the case' of rope dancing as a qualification for high office in a derisive polemical remark on Tindal's *Rights of the Christian Church*:

Put the Case, that walking on the slack Rope were the only Talent required by Act of Parliament for making a Man a Bishop; no Doubt, when a Man had done his Feat of Activity in Form, he might sit in the House of Lords, put on his Robes and his Rotchet, go down to his Palace, receive and spend his Rents; but it requireth very little Christianity to believe this Tumbler to be one whit more a Bishop than he was before.

(*PW*, II, 75)

The rope-dancing episode in Part I of *Gulliver's Travels* is a general satire on the politics of intrigue and refinement and the incongruity between qualification or talent and office in the corrupt state. The rope-dancing passage is commonly interpreted as also containing topical political satire. The traditional reading of the passage is succinctly put by Harold Williams in his introduction to the standard Davis edition of the text: 'The Emperor becomes George I ... Flimnap is Walpole; and the cushion which broke his fall is the Duchess of Kendal whose interest he gained (1721)' (*PW*, XI, xix). Pat Rogers connects the moral and topical satire of the rope-dancing episode with the technique of Scriblerian farce and with a running critique of contemporary sights and shows conducted by Swift and his fellow Scriblerians.[46] The reading of a topical political satire of Walpole and George I's mistress, the Duchess of Kendal, in the episode derives from Sir Walter Scott and is now commonplace in Swift criticism. But it has been challenged controversially by F. P. Lock, who urges that more 'than any particular incident, Swift intended Flimnap's near-fall to illustrate

---

[46] Pat Rogers, *Literature and Popular Culture in Eighteenth Century England* (Brighton, 1985), ch. 2 'Shapes and Postures. Swift, Walpole and the Rope-Dancers', pp. 71–86. The essay originally appeared in *Papers on Language and Literature*, 8 (1972), 159–71.

one of Sir William Temple's favourite historical maxims, the idea of
trifling circumstances affecting great historical events'. Lock strongly
emphasizes the paradigmatic rather than tenuous topical allegorical
aspect of the episode: 'Any attempt to pin down this or other incidents
in *Gulliver's Travels* in too topical a manner should be resisted. Walpole
was only an example; it was the idea that he represented that Swift was
satirizing.'[47]

Certainly, it is unlikely that the King's mistress, the Duchess of
Kendal, is signified by 'one of the *King's Cushions*' as she was Walpole's
enemy. As Lord Hervey observed:

For as the Duchess of Kendal never loved Sir Robert Walpole, and was weak
enough to admire and be fond of Lord Townshend, so in any nice points that
were to be insinuated gently and carried by favour ... the canal of application
to the royal ear had always been from Lord Townshend to the Duchess and
from the Duchess to the King.[48]

But the general or paradigmatic significance of Swift's 'Scriblerian'
comic satire in the depiction of Lilliputian high politics in the farcical
terms of an English popular entertainment does not, however, preclude
the possibility that a hit-and-run reflection on the contemporary
Hanoverian court and ministers was also intended. Significantly, in the
episode of the rope dancers in Part I Chapter III, satiric blame is
directed against the court, not just against Flimnap and the ministers.
The ministers perform their grotesque antics to recommend themselves
to the monarch. Gulliver reports that the 'infamous Practice of acquir-
ing great Employments by dancing on the Ropes' (*PW*, XI, 60) is a
corruption encouraged by the monarch (*PW*, XI, 38). While Swift does
not expose himself or printer to danger by writing simple one-to-one
allegory, the reader is enabled to see the Court of Lilliput as a diminu-
tive parallel to England's. The Court is recognizable with a monarch,
'Treasurer' and chief ministers, and the incongruous diversion of rope
dancing represents the Court of this remote nation in the reductively
familiar light of an English popular entertainment. The specific detail
in the rope-dancing passage that 'one of the *King's Cushions*' saved the
dexterous Flimnap's neck may just possibly allude to the *lits de justice*,
the ceremonies by which absolutist French kings by-passed parliament.
The king reclined on cushions during the ceremony, hence the name *lits*

---

[47] Lock, *The Politics of 'Gulliver's Travels'*, pp. 86–7.
[48] *Some Materials Towards Memoirs of the Reign of King George II* By John, Lord Hervey, edited
by Romney Sedgwick, 3 vols. (London, 1931 [1970]), I, 84; *The History of Parliament*, edited
by Romney Sedgwick, 2 vols., II, 514.

de justice.[49] The reader, enabled by the satirist to see the court of Lilliput as a fictional proxy for George I's, now finds its dexterous practices associated with the ceremonies of hated continental despots as well as with the antics and properties of a street show. Swift's polemical project in this passage is to insinuate to readers the Hanoverian King's contempt for parliamentary government and natural justice. Walpole's neck is saved at the court of a continental despot.

King George is particularly attacked throughout *Gulliver's Travels.* The Emperor of Lilliput is a paradigm of a despotic king, but the character also specifically reflects on George I. The Emperor has determined to use 'only low Heels [*innuendo* Low Church or Whig party] in the Administration of the Government, and all Offices in the Gift of the Crown' and has proscribed the 'high Heels [*innuendo* High Church or Tory party]' from power, though the 'high Heels' 'are most agreeable to our ancient Constitution' and exceed the 'low Heels' in number (*PW*, XI, 48). The Emperor, like George I when Swift was at work on *Gulliver's Travels*, had reigned for 'about seven' years. The description of the Emperor's person in Part I, Chapter II (*PW*, XI, 30) is a satiric mock-encomium of George I – the Emperor being praised for physical features George I conspicuously lacked. The italicized '*Austrian Lip*' in the catalogue of the Emperor's features may have invited hostile reflection on the House of Hanover's alleged abandonment of the Protestant cause on the continent. A Jacobite pamphleteer posed these rhetorical questions in a 1722 arraignment of the Hanoverian monarch:

Was it for the *Interest of the Protestant Cause* to Divest the late King of *Sweden* of his Dominions in *Germany*? To enable the *Regent* to suppress the growing Reformation in *France*? To leave the reformed *Palatines* to the fury of a Bigotted Prince? To maintain or permit a *Popish* College in *Hannover*? And to extend the Power of the House of *Austria*, the Ancient and perpetual Enemy to the *Reformation*?[50]

The sardonic satire on the spurious and cynically proclaimed '*Lenity*' of the Emperor of Lilliput and on the 'great Clemency' of the cruel and arbitrary King of Luggnagg (*PW*, XI, 69–73, 204–5) reflects on George I and on Whig and parliamentary encomiums on George I's 'clemency'. Swift alludes to the capital punishment inflicted on Jacobite lords who had surrendered after the 1715 rebellion and to the imprisonment of and proceedings against Tories suspected of

---

49 For a later 'Swiftian' play with the absolutist ceremony, see Laurence Sterne, *The Life and Opinions of Tristram Shandy, Gentleman*, edited by Ian Campbell Ross, The World's Classics (Oxford, 1983), vol. VI, chap. XVI, p. 349 and note on p. 582.
50 *The Second and Last English Advice*, p. 39.

involvement in Jacobite plots in the 1720s. Swift's satire is an intervention on the Jacobite Tory side in the paper war between Whig defend-
ants and Jacobite Tory plaintiffs concerning the honour of the King
and the nature of his rule.[51] Swift implies an arbitrary Hanoverian
reign of terror, the euphemism for which is the King's 'clemency'. The
division in the Lilliputian court, between the cabal of ministers who
want capital punishment inflicted on Gulliver and the Emperor and
Secretary Reldresal who thought 'there was room for Mercy', parallels
a division in George I's Whig Court in 1723. Whether the death penalty
should be inflicted on Atterbury 'divided the Court much and made the
leaders very uneasy, who were for tempering justice with mercy as the
prudenter way'.[52] The Emperor of Lilliput's 'mercy' manifests itself in
his determination to blind and starve Gulliver rather than inflict
immediate death by torture. The Lilliputian Court expedient to blind
Gulliver might have suggested to Swift's readers the exotic customs of
remote countries. Swift may have derived the idea of blinding from an
account of such a court practice in the Dutch voyager Jan Huygen Van
Linschoten's *Discours of Voyages in ye Easte & West Indies*.[53] But Swift
ensures that readers of this satire on the spurious clemency of arbitrary
kings reflect on the severity of monarchs closer to home. Gulliver
confesses that he could not 'discover the *Lenity*' of the Lilliputian
monarch's sentence of blinding and 'thought of standing my Tryal':

But having in my Life perused many State-Tryals, which I ever observed to
terminate as the Judges thought fit to direct; I durst not rely on so dangerous a
Decision, in so critical a Juncture, and against such powerful Enemies.

                                                                 (*PW*, XI, 72–3)

Gulliver wishes that 'Monarchs of *Europe* would imitate' the King of
Luggnagg's 'great Clemency' and 'Care' of his subjects (*PW*, XI, 205)!
    In Part III of *Gulliver's Travels* there is an arresting possibility that the
satirist is suggesting that the settlement of the crown in the House of

---

[51] For close Jacobite analogues to Swift's allusive satire on the clemency of George I, see *The
Shift Shifted*, no. 1 (5 May 1716); no. 3 (19 May 1716); no. 8 (23 June 1716); *To Robert
Walpole Esq.* (n.p., [1717]), p. 2; *The Freeholder's Journal* (31 January 172[2]), p. 5;
Matthias Earbery, *The History of the Clemency of Our English Monarchs . . . The Second Edition;
The Second and Last English Advice*, pp. 17, 20, 23, 30–1; [George Granville, Baron Lans-
downe], *A Letter from a Noble-Man Abroad*, pp. 4–5. Swift, of course, was well aware of the
polemical controversy over George I's 'clemency, mercy, and forgiving temper' (*Corr*, II,
436; *PW*, V, 254).

[52] Quotation is from an entry for March 1723 in the Tory Sir Edward Knatchbull's
Parliamentary Diary, in Sedgwick, ed., *The House of Commons 1715–1754*, I, p. 66.

[53] See my 'Possible "Hints" for *Gulliver's Travels* in the *Voyages* of Jan Huygen Van Linschoten', *Notes and Queries*, ns, 33 (1986), 47–50 (pp. 47–8).

Hanover has been a political, social and economic catastrophe. There are sufficient 'hints' enabling readers to associate Laputa, the '*Flying* or *Floating Island*' (*PW*, XI, 161), with contemporary Britain and George I's Whig Court.[54] For example, the King and Court are preoccupied to distraction with abstract speculations upon the subjects of 'Mathematicks and Musick' (*PW*, XI, 163). George I approved and patronised mathematicians and musicians, and music was the 'reigning Amusement' in London, Gay told Swift in 1723 (*Corr*, II, 447).[55] Like Gulliver's countrymen, the people of Laputa display a 'strong Disposition . . . towards News and Politicks . . . passionately disputing every Inch of a Party Opinion' (*PW*, XI, 164). The King of Laputa 'would be the most absolute Prince' but his ministers, it seems, are landed men with estates to protect and they 'would never consent to the enslaving their Country' (*PW*, XI, 171). This King is 'distinguished above all his Predecessors for his Hospitality to Strangers'. There are a considerable number of 'Strangers' from the continent attending at Court (*PW*, XI, 160–1, 165). Arraignment of George I for absolutism and for being a foreigner, hostility to Hanoverian 'Strangers', and appeals for a free parliament of landed men to defend the '*Liberties of* England' against a Hanoverian court alleged to be for '*Absolute Power*, and *Enslaving* the Nation' are topoi in Jacobite Tory pamphleteering of the 1710s and 1720s.[56] Swift's satire specifically alludes to the Hanoverian government's repeal of the provision in the Act of Settlement (1701) forbidding the King to leave England without parliamentary permission. Gulliver reports: 'ʙʏ a fundamental Law of this Realm, neither the King nor either of his two elder Sons, are permitted to leave the Island; nor the Queen till she is past Child-bearing' (*PW*, XI, 172). The passage is not without libellous innuendo. This line of satiric attack also has Jacobite analogues. Jacobite pamphleteers were saying that George

---

54 The *Weekly Journal* discussed a reported sighting of a floating island near Gibraltar in 1718, see Black, *The English Press in the Eighteenth Century*, p. 213. The italicized '*Floating Island*' might have amusingly reminded contemporaries of earlier satires on imaginary voyages, see Richard Head, *The Floating Island* (London, 1673). Sir William Temple refers to England as a 'floating island' in his *Works*, see Charles Firth, 'The Political Significance of "Gulliver's Travels"', in his *Essays Historical & Literary* (Oxford, 1938), pp. 210–41 (pp. 232–3).

55 The satire on George I is annotated in Paul Turner's World's Classics edition of *Gulliver's Travels* (Oxford, 1986), see esp. pp. 341–2. Pat Rogers remarks Hanover's 'highly musical court' in 'Gay and the World of Opera', p. 151. In Swift's disaffected 'Directions for a Birth-day Song', the Whig poet is instructed to take his panegyrical song on the Hanoverian monarch to 'Minheer Hendel' to be set 'to some Italian Tune' (*Poems*, II, 469).

56 *The Second and Last English Advice*, p. 40 and *passim*; *To Robert Walpole Esq.*, *passim*; [Earbery], *An Historical Account . . . Part II*, esp. pp. 43–4; Granville, *A Letter*, *passim*.

I had violated the legislative contract or settlement upon which his right to rule was founded. In the explicit words of one Jacobite pamphlet circulated at the time of the 1722 election, the Hanoverian court and its client Whig parliament

pass'd another Act, which although it then seemed of no great consequence, was however an ill Precedent and hath proved in the highest manner detrimental to the Nation. It was entitled an Act *to Repeal part of the Act for the Limitation of the Crown, and better securing the Rights and Liberties of the Publick.* This Act of *Limitation* provided *that no Person who should come to the Possession of the Crown should go out of the Dominions of* England, Scotland *or* Ireland *without consent of Parliament.* The reasons of that part of the Act of *Limitation* were obvious, lest the King, *pro tempore,* by visiting or residing long in his Foreign Dominions might continue estranged from the People of *England.* Besides Voyages of that kind might give opportunities for *Leagues and Alliances* prejudicial to the *English* interest, which could not be so privately Negotiated here as at *Hannover.* And again those Voyages would afford his *German* followers the means to Transport to their own Country the Wealth, they might Collect here.[57]

Swift may, in fact, encode in Part III disaffection with the Act of Settlement itself by which the Hanoverian dynasty ruled. During Gulliver's stay with that disaffected conservative Lord Munodi he is desired to observe a distant 'ruined Building upon the Side of a Mountain'. Munodi tells Gulliver

That he had a very convenient Mill within Half a Mile of his House, turned by a Current from a large River, and sufficient for his own Family as well as a great Number of his Tenants. That, about seven Years ago, a Club of those Projectors came to him with Proposals to destroy this Mill, and build another on the Side of that Mountain ... that being then not very well with the Court, and pressed by many of his Friends, he complied with the Proposal.
(*PW*, XI, 177–8)

The Laputan 'Experiment' miscarried and the result was ruin. The Mill episode has been thought to refer to the disastrous South Sea scheme and to the contemporary mania for entrepreneurial projects. Pat Rogers suggests that it 'is likely that Swift has a subsidiary political point: undesirable innovations include the kind of notions imported when the English leaders went across to Holland to invite over William of Orange'. Contesting received allegorical interpretation of the episode, F. P. Lock nevertheless observes appositely that the 'design of the new mill replacing the old is a better type of an attempt to replace

---

[57] *The Second and Last English Advice*, pp. 25–6; *To Robert Walpole Esq., passim*; [Earbery], *An Historical Account ... Part II*, p. 52; Granville, *A Letter from a Noble-Man Abroad*, p. 4.

one dynasty with another than it is of a trading and financial concern'. In line with his thesis, Lock does not propose this as 'a serious interpretation' but as an example of how easily allegorical readings can be generated in criticism.[58] But what if a Jacobitical dynastic critique is obliquely present in the text? The consequence should be a major revision of our understanding of the politics of the text and its author. Munodi, out of favour with the Court, complied with this project 'about seven Years ago' (i.e. *c.* 1701, see *PW*, XI, 154). In 1701, the Tories, out of favour with William III, complied with the alteration of the hereditary succession in the Act of Settlement, the Act being framed with significant limitations restricting the power of future monarchs (see *PW*, VIII, 94 for Swift's witness of Tory framing of the Settlement in 1701). Gulliver tells us that 'I had my self been a Sort of Projector in my younger Days' (*PW*, XI, 178). As the *Discourse of the Contests and Dissentions* indicates, Swift had been (at least nominally) a Whig in 1701. The fact that in contemporary political iconography a windmill was associated with the Pretender[59] might have enabled a Tory dynastic reading of the Mill episode in Swift's text: the destruction of the succession in the hereditary House of Stuart in 1701 and radical deviation to the distant House of Hanover with ruinous consequences.

Gulliver's Travels does offer a paradigm of a wise and good monarch in the King of Brobdingnag. Of all the remote nations Gulliver visits, 'the least corrupted are the *Brobdingnagians*, whose wise Maxims in Morality and Government, it would be our Happiness to observe'. Gulliver does not incriminate himself further. 'But I forbear descanting further, and rather leave the judicious Reader to his own Remarks and Applications' (*PW*, XI, 292). There has been much critical speculation about whom the idealized King of Brobdingnag might suggest, if he suggests anyone. He has been identified with William III, the Hanoverian Prince of Wales, and Sir William Temple, and seen more generally as a type of a pacific, patriotic and Platonic philosopher king offered as a complete contrast to the Emperor of Lilliput.[60] But a reader is enabled by the text to make disaffected 'Applications' also. The hereditary king

---

[58] Case, *Four Essays on 'Gulliver's Travels'*, pp. 88–9; Pat Rogers, 'Gulliver and the Engineers', *Modern Language Review*, 70 (1975), 260–70 (p. 262); Lock, *The Politics of 'Gulliver's Travels'*, pp. 102–3.

[59] See Lois G. Schwoerer, 'Propaganda in the Revolution of 1688–89', *American Historical Review*, 82 (1977), 843–74 (pp. 861, 865 and see the Dutch print 'Qualis vir Talis Oratio', dated 16 October 1688, reproduced as fig. 1 on p. 863).

[60] See Paul Turner, ed., *Gulliver's Travels*, p. 328; Lock, *The Politics of 'Gulliver's Travels'*, pp. 16–17, 121, 131–2, 138–9.

of Brobdingnag's rule is founded not on revolution principles but on 'a general Composition'. Brobdingnag had

been troubled with the same Disease, to which the whole Race of Mankind is Subject; the Nobility often contending for Power, the People for Liberty, and the King for absolute Dominion. All which, however happily tempered by the Laws of that Kingdom, have been sometimes violated by each of the three Parties; and have more than once occasioned Civil Wars, the last whereof was happily put an End to by this Prince's Grandfather in a general Composition; and the Militia then settled with common Consent hath been ever since kept in the strictest Duty.

(*PW*, XI, 138)

Is there nostalgia here for the lost alternative to the Revolution of 1688–9 proposed by the Jacobite compounders – a 'composition' between lawful King and people and replacement of a mercenary standing army with a 'militia'?[61] A Jacobite compounder tract had argued that 'there are in all climates ebbings and flowings of the monarchical, aristocratical, and democratical particles of the composure' of regular government. The writer concluded:

that since the princes have had an inclination to greater power than the people will comply with, and the people a stronger lust after liberty than our kings were willing to satisfy, that the one has mistaken prerogative, and the other as much their privileges, it would be well if a new Magna Charta was made ... We must deal impartially if we would ever compose things.[62]

The King of Brobdingnag has a militia guard of cavaliers (*PW*, XI, 115, 138) and displays impeccable 'Country' Opposition principles in his obvious opposition to the institutional corruption, party and faction, systems of modern credit and standing armies disclosed to him by Gulliver during Gulliver's Court Whig panegyric on Britain (*PW*, XI, 127–38). The King's rhetoric on standing armies closely resembles Jacobite formulations on the issue. The King of Brobdingnag, says Gulliver,

was amazed to hear me talk of a mercenary standing Army in the Midst of Peace, and among a free People. He said, if we were governed by our own Consent in the Persons of our Representatives, he could not imagine of whom we were afraid, or against whom we were to fight; and would hear my Opinion, whether a private Man's House might not better be defended by himself, his Children, and Family; than by half a Dozen Rascals picked up at a Venture in

---

[61] Charlwood Lawton, *The Jacobite Principles Vindicated*, in *Somers Tracts*, X, 536, 527.
[62] *Honesty is the Best Policy*, in *Somers Tracts*, X, 212, 213.

the Streets, for small Wages, who might get an Hundred Times more by cutting their Throats.

(*PW*, XI, 131)

The Jacobite George Flint was similarly amazed and outraged:

So it is, with all humble Submission Queried, Whether it is not possible for a standing Army to know its own Strength? And then, Whether a Conjurer may not unluckily raise a Devil which he does not know how to lay again. I am amaz'd, astonish'd, stupified, how it is possible for a Man that has a Life, Liberty and Property to lose, a Wife, Sister or Daughter to be ravish'd, can be pleased to see a standing Army.[63]

The King of Brobdingnag's indictment of the management of the treasury, public debt and a standing army was recognized by contemporary readers as 'a common *Jacobite* Insinuation, from King *William*'s *Dutch Guards* to the last *Augmentation*'.[64] When Swift has 'the Plague' signify 'a standing Army' during the satire of Walpole's deciphering branch in the 'Plots' passage in Part III (*PW*, XI, 191), he not only expresses his life-long detestation of armies but registers a topical anti-government political reflection alluding to the proclaimed Quarantine Act (1721) and the clauses giving emergency powers to the government. The linkage of the standing army and the plague was sardonically made in contemporary Tory Jacobite writing. A Jacobite tract of 1722 observed: 'because in Times of Tranquility, standing Armies might be thought a Grievance, a new kind of War was contrived, a Plague was denounced, Forces were decreed to be kept on Foot'.[65] The distinctively Tory satire of Walpole's decipherers and the Whig government prosecution of Atterbury in the 'Plots' passage was reproduced in the Jacobite *Fog's Weekly Journal* of 29 August 1730.[66]

---

63 *The Shift Shifted*, no. 7 (16 June 1716), p. 41. Compare John Gay, *To my ingenious and worthy Friend W[illiam] L[owndes]*, lines 55-7: 'Why need we armys when the land's in peace? / Soldiers are perfect devils in their way, / When once they're rais'd, they're cursed hard to lay', John Gay, *Poetry and Prose*, edited by Vinton A. Dearing with Charles E. Beckwith, 2 vols. (Oxford, 1974), I, 246. Total opposition to standing armies is a topos of Jacobite publicists. Old Whigs called for a reduction in the size of the army, see *Cato's Letters*, 4 vols. (n. p., 1754), III, 212-23 (no. 95, 22 September 1722).

64 *Gulliver Decypher'd*, p. 38; [Jonathan Smedley], *Gulliveriana*, p. 282 (identifying the King's words against a standing army as libel).

65 [Lansdowne], *A Letter*, p. 5. And for Tory agitation to repeal clauses in the Act, see *Parl. Hist.*, VII, cols. 929-35. For Swift's refusal to read the Act of Parliament concerning the plague, see his letter to Chetwode of 13 March 1722 (*Corr*, II, 422).

66 *Select Letters Taken from Fog's Weekly Journal*, II, 72-8. For a later Swiftian ridicule of Whig deciphering, see *An Examination of Certain Abuses, Corruptions, and Enormities, in the City of Dublin* (1732), *PW*, XII, 213-32. The True Whig Anthony Collins observed that Swift

The political critique in works of Tory or Jacobite provenance such as Francis Atterbury's *English Advice to the Freeholders of England* (dated 1714, published 1715), *The Second and Last English Advice, To the Freehoulders of Englan[d]* (1722) and Earbery's two-part *An Historical Account of the Advantages That have Accru'd to England, By the Succession in the Illustrious House of Hanover* (1722) can be readily identified in *Gulliver's Travels*. Swift's satire in *Gulliver's Travels* on the 'clemency' of arbitrary monarchs, Hanoverian violation of the Act of Settlement, the corrupt management of the treasury, fraud, foreign military intervention, mercenary standing armies, corrupt elections, informers, party and faction and 'Corruption' have analogues in Jacobite Tory pamphleteering and in the discourse of Jacobite journalism. *The Freeholder's Journal* of 1722–3, for instance, attacks 'Corruption', standing armies and standing parliaments, and struggles for 'the Liberties of old *England*' against repressive Court Whig legislation. *The True Briton* of 1723–4 defends 'the Liberties of *Old England*', discourses on '*Public Spirit*', compares the 'present Race of Statesmen' with 'the Heroes of Old', defends Atterbury and execrates 'those obnoxious Vermin called *Informers*'. And so on. The violent attack on the degeneration of the hereditary nobility in *Gulliver's Travels* (see esp. *PW*, XI, 129, 198–200, 256–7) is a traditional topos of satirists, Juvenal's *Satire VIII* being an important model. To modern readers, Swift's satire on the aristocracy might suggest radical Whig rather than Tory politics. In fact, however, the degeneration of the hereditary nobility was a virulent motif of Jacobite Tory writing against the Williamite and Hanoverian regimes.[67] As historian, Swift traced the corruption of the nobility to the Revolution and Williamite creations (*PW*, VII, 19, 21). Elsewhere, the source of corruption in the nobility is traced to the cataclysm of the Civil War and Interregnum (*PW*, XII, 47).

The parallels between the political expression in *Gulliver's Travels* and that of a Jacobite Tory work of 1722, George Granville, Baron Lansdowne's *A Letter from a Noble-Man Abroad*, are striking. This tract begins: '*AT* this critical Conjuncture when the Rumour of a new Parliament sounds like the last Trumpet, to awaken the Genius of Old *England*, and raise departed Liberty to Life, it would be a Crime to be silent'. It claims 'We have lived to see the first Honours of Peerage bestowed to

performed 'on the Jacobite Stage of *Mist's* and *Fogg's* Journal', quoted in *The Intelligencer*, edited by James Woolley, p. 236.

[67] See, for example, [Francis Atterbury], *English Advice to the Freeholders of England* (n. p., 1714 [1715]), p. 26; [Lansdowne], *A Letter*, p. 4; *The Second and Last English Advice*, pp. 3–5, 38.

dignifie Prostitution, the Freedom of the People, the most inestimable Article of their Freedom, the Freedom of Elections, betrayed by their own Representatives.' It excoriates the 'Tyranny' of those 'raised from the Dirt of Faction, supported by Senates, chosen and directed by Corruption'. The tract is a militant call to 'stand for Liberty and Old *England*'.[68] In Glubbdubdrib Gulliver has raised to life before him 'some *English* Yeomen of the old Stamp ... once so famous for the Simplicity of their Manners, Dyet and Dress; for Justice in their Dealings; for their true Spirit of Liberty; for their Valour and Love of their Country'. Such 'pure native Virtues were prostituted for a Piece of Money by their Grand-children; who in selling their Votes, and managing at Elections have acquired every Vice and Corruption that can possibly be learned in a Court' (*PW*, XI, 201–2). In the 'Advertisement To The Reader' of the *Memoirs of Captain John Creichton* (1731) which Swift prepared for the press, the Jacobite Captain is described as '*a very honest and worthy Man; but of the old Stamp: And it is probable, that some of his Principles will not relish very well, in the present Disposition of the World. His* Memoirs *are therefore to be received like a Posthumous Work*'. The memoirs are offered '*in their native Simplicity*' and the man himself is distinguished by his '*personal Courage and Conduct*' (*PW*, V, 121–2).

Swift's political rhetoric in *Gulliver's Travels* intersects with contemporary Jacobite texts significantly in the satire of the Dutch in the first and last chapters of Part III (*PW*, XI, 154–5, 216–17). After the Revolution, hatred of the Dutch, a ubiquitous strain in Jacobite vitriol, became the recognized signature of High Church Toryism, which was said to be characterized by 'railing at the Dutch'.[69] There is now a substantial bibliography of specialist studies tracing the anti-Dutch animus in Swift's writings to such factors as Swift's association with Harley's predominantly Tory ministry during the government peace negotiations leading to the Treaty of Utrecht, a traditional xenophobia in English attitudes to the Dutch reflected in seventeenth-century literature and his own hostile view of Dutch religious, political, diplomatic, maritime and trading practices. Swift scholars have suggested sources for some particular details of the famous satiric attack on the

---

[68] [Lansdowne], *A Letter*, pp. 3, 4, 5, 8. See my 'Swift's Politics: A Preface to *Gulliver's Travels*', *Monash Swift Papers*. Number One, edited by Clive T. Probyn and Bryan Coleborne (Monash University, 1988), pp. 41–65 (pp. 51–3).

[69] [Matthew Tindal], *New High-Church Turn'd Old Presbyterian* (London, 1709), p. 20. See my 'The Sentiments of a Church-of-England Man: A Study of Swift's Politics' (unpublished Ph.D. thesis, University of Warwick, 1989), ch. 5, 'Swift and the Dutch: The Question of Swift's Jacobitism', p. 234 and *passim*.

Dutch in Part III of *Gulliver's Travels* – such as the '*trampling upon the Crucifix*' episode and Gulliver's passage on a Dutch ship called the '*Amboyna*' – in his reading of contemporary voyage literature and accounts therein of the Dutch East India traders in Japan, and in imaginary, historiographical and geographical literature on Japan.[70] Swift mined material for his satire from anti-Dutch war literature of 1672–3.[71] The contemporary Jacobite dimension of *Gulliver's* anti-Dutch satire has been relatively neglected in Swift scholarship, however.

Jacobite polemicists like Leslie and Robert Ferguson drew upon polemical accounts of the Dutch East India trade. Charges against the Dutch, such as their perfidy and attrition against the English in the East Indies, their massacre of Englishmen at Amboyna (now Ambon in Indonesia) in 1623, their abjuration of Christ in Japan and recorded practice of trampling upon the crucifix in order to secure trading privileges from the anti-Christian Japanese Emperor, are activated in post-Revolution Jacobite and Tory tracts. Leslie's *Delenda Carthago*, a tract written in opposition to a continental land war against France, is a violent indictment of the Dutch. Leslie reminds readers of 'the Murder of the *English* at *Amboyna* ... and other Depredations in the *East Indies.* You may see a whole History of their Breach of Treaties, and most *Barbarous* and *Perfidious* Cruelties upon the English, By Dr. Stubbe, Printed in 1673.'[72] In *A Justification of the Present War. Against The United Netherlands* and *A Further Justification of the Present War Against The United Netherlands*, violently anti-Dutch books written in support of the third Anglo-Dutch war, to which Leslie refers and from which he quotes, Henry Stubbe presents evidence of Dutch apostasy and anti-Christian activity. This representation figures prominently in Jacobite polemic of the 1690s and in the High Tory and Jacobite tracts of Anne's reign, where the ideological and polemical enterprise was to indict Dutch principles in religion and government and to alienate English public

[70] 'The Sentiments of a Church-of-England Man', p. 380, note 51 for a list of Swift studies. On British opinion of the Dutch in Swift's time, with many references to Swift's Tory opinion, see especially Douglas Coombs, *The Conduct of the Dutch: British Opinion and the Dutch Alliance During the War of the Spanish Succession* (The Hague, 1958). See also Michael Duffy, *The Englishman and the Foreigner*, The English Satirical Print 1600–1832 (Cambridge, 1986), esp. pp. 27–31, and plates 8, 9, 11, 14–18, 25, 37.

[71] 'The Sentiments of a Church-of-England Man, ch. 5, pp. 268ff.; Anne Barbeau Gardiner, 'Swift on the Dutch East India Merchants: The Context of 1672–73 War Literature', *Huntington Library Quarterly*, 54 (1991), 235–52.

[72] Charles Leslie, *Delenda Carthago. Or, The True Interest of England, in Relation to France and Holland* (n. p., [1695]), p. 3.

opinion from the Dutch in order to prepare the nation for a peace with France. For High Churchmen, the Dutch were the international face of Dissent. Leslie in *Cassandra* (1704) connects anti-Episcopalian icono-clasm in Scotland after the Revolution with the Dutch 'Trampling upon the *Cross*' in Japan.

Stubbe's books are an authority and source for Jacobite polemic against the Dutch, with parallels in theme and detail to Swift's satire of the Dutch in *Gulliver's Travels*. A few examples of the intertextuality may suffice here. When Gulliver's petition to be excused the ceremony (performed by Dutchmen, one of whom he pretends to be) of '*trampling upon the Crucifix*' in Japan was interpreted to the Emperor, 'he began to doubt whether I were a real *Hollander* or no; but rather suspected I must be a CHRISTIAN' (*PW*, XI, 216). Stubbe wrote that 'I should injure Christendom to reckon the *United Netherlands* a part thereof.' The Dutch in Japan declined 'that Profession of *Christianity*, to which *Christ* and his *Apostles* oblige them'. The Japanese believe the Dutch '*are as perfect Heathens as themselves*'.[73] While a Dutchman is satirized in Part III of *Gulliver's Travels* as worse than 'a Heathen' (*PW*, XI, 154–5), a Portu-guese captain, '*Pedro de Mendez*', is presented sympathetically as humane, moral and charitable in Part IV (*PW*, XI, 286–9). Much has been made of Don Pedro, particularly in 'soft school' readings of the meaning of Part IV of *Gulliver's Travels* where he is said to function as the satire's supposed positive of moderation, but it can be observed that the Portuguese appear positively in the anti-Dutch literature which the Jacobites and Tories culled. The good Portuguese captain has a polemi-cal political provenance. Stubbe makes the following marginal comment in *A Justification*:

The Portugueses *refused to trade there* [in Japan] *upon* those terms. *Which are the* best Christians, *those* Papists, *or these* Protestants? *Is it not manifest that the* Dutch *are hereby* [in the conditions of trade in Japan] obliged *to deny themselves absolutely to be* Christians, *in case any* Japanner *doth put such a* Question *unto them?*[74]

The 'jabbering' Dutchman in Part III of *Gulliver's Travels* presages the Yahoos of the fourth voyage in his restless and mindless violence. The only difference we infer between Gulliver's reprobate 'Brother Chris-tian' (*PW*, XI, 154–5) and his 'Brother Brutes in *Houyhnhnmland*' is that human Yahoos 'use a Sort of *Jabber*, and do not go naked' (*PW*, XI, 8).

---

[73] Henry Stubbe, *A Justification of the Present War. Against The United Netherlands* ... (London, 1673), pp. 2–3. In all quotations gothic print used for emphasis in the original is repro-duced in italics.

[74] Stubbe, *A Justification*, p. 3.

The Dutchman assails Gulliver 'with all the Curses and injurious Terms his Language could afford' (*PW*, XI, 155). Stubbe had described Dutch belligerence similarly and was willing to endorse the solution that Swift's Houyhnhnms would project for the Yahoos:

We do complain that *these Netherlanders*, who ... do so highly pretend to *Piety* and *Protestancy*, should violate all *divine* and *humane* Rules of *Civility*, that they *rail* instead of *fighting*, that they attacque us with *contumelious* language, and aggravate their *unjust enmity* with an *insolence* that is *not to be endured* ... and *common humanity* obligeth every one to endeavour their *extirpation*.[75]

For Stubbe, the Dutch are only problematically part of the human species: 'whilst others behold the *Dutch* as *Protestants* and *Christians*, I cannot but rank them amongst the *worst of mankind*, not to be parallel'd by any known race of *Pagans* and *Savages*'.[76]

The example of the Dutch in Japan provides a rhetorical climax in Leslie's account of Dutch atrocity in the East Indies.[77] In strident anti-Dutch books the Jacobite Robert Ferguson explicitly linked Dutch treachery in the East Indies with their involvement in the Revolution.[78] When in a Jacobite tract, such as Ferguson's *A Brief Account*, there are anticipations of some of the more audacious rhetorical strategies of Swift's Tory Peace pamphleteering it is not difficult to understand how contemporaries could read in works such as *The Conduct of the Allies* and *Some Remarks on the Barrier Treaty* a rhetoric of Jacobitism. Swift, in *Some Remarks on the Barrier Treaty*, connects Dutch atrocities in the East Indies with alleged Dutch military designs against Britain (*PW*, VI, 97): Ferguson's polemical argument in *A Brief Account*. Ferguson's reiterated use of '*Dutch* King' or '*Belgick* King' for William III,[79] anticipates Swift's reflection in *The Conduct of the Allies* that William, 'although King of *England*, was a Native of *Holland*' (*PW*, VI, 11). Jacobite political literature ceaselessly alleged that the House of Orange and the House of Hanover served Dutch and German interests at the expense of Britain's. Swift appropriates Jacobite Tory language in a sardonic attack on William III and on the Hanoverian dynasty in the later, violent poem 'Directions for a Birth-day Song':

---

[75] Stubbe, *A Justification*, p. 5.   [76] Stubbe, *A Justification*, p. 28.
[77] Leslie, *Delenda Carthago*, p. 5, see also p. 8.
[78] *A Brief Account of Some of the Late Incroachments and Depredations of the Dutch upon the English; and of a Few of Those Many Advantages Which by Fraud and Violence they have made of the Brittish Nations since the Revolution, and of the Means enabling them thereunto* (n. p., 1695 [1696]), p. 8, and Robert Ferguson, *An Account of the Obligations The States of Holland Have to Great-Britain ...* (London, 1711), pp. 32–3: on this work, see Coombs, *The Conduct of the Dutch*, pp. 289–90. On Ferguson, see James Ferguson, *Robert Ferguson the Plotter* (Edinburgh, 1887).
[79] See particularly, *A Brief Account*, p. 40.

A skilfull Critick justly blames
Hard, tough, cramp, gutt'rall, harsh, stiff Names.
The Sense can ne're be too jejune,
But smooth your words to fit the tune,
Hanover may do well enough;
But George, and Brunswick are too rough.
Hesse Darmstedt makes too rough a sound,
And Guelph the strongest ear will wound.
In vain are all attempts from Germany
To find out proper words for Harmony:
And yet I must except the Rhine,
Because it clinks to Caroline . . .
 Nassau, who got the name of glorious
Because he never was victorious,
A hanger on has always been,
For old acquaintance bring him in.
(lines 209–20, 251–4, *Poems*, II, 467, 468; see *Complete Poems*,
pp. 393, 394 and notes pp. 802, 803)

Swift's declamation in the *Conduct* that 'we are thus become the *Dupes* and *Bubbles* of *Europe*' recalls the Jacobite's outburst against England's ruinous folly in underwriting Dutch military expansion: 'a bubbling of this Kingdom'.[80] In Ferguson and Swift there are shared charges that England has become a tributary state of the Dutch, that England has been reduced to a dependence on the Dutch, who have assumed a power to depose a King of England, that English expenditure of men and money in continental war has only served to enlarge Dutch dominions.[81]

The Jacobite Tory valence of the particular treatment of the Dutch in *Gulliver* can be noted. For example, the Amboyna massacre to which Swift alludes in *Gulliver* (*PW*, XI, 217) was certainly in polemical currency in the early eighteenth century. Swift could have read about it in a voyage literature primary source such as *Purchas His Pilgrimes*.[82] But in terms of polemical intention and contemporary reception it is important to note that Whigs ignored, understated or extenuated such incidents in the East Indies, while 'Amboyna' remained a centrepiece of the Jacobite and Tory rehearsal of Dutch atrocity and attrition in the

[80] *PW*, VI, 40; *A Brief Account*, p. 40.
[81] Compare, for example, Swift's *Some Remarks on the Barrier Treaty* (*PW*, VI, 87) with Ferguson's *A Brief Account*, pp. 12, 40.
[82] *Purchas His Pilgrimes. In Five Bookes* (London, 1625), Part II, pp. 1853–8. Swift owned this work: see LeFanu, p. 27; *SC*, no. 261.

1690s and in the first half of the eighteenth century.[83] Swift's provocative, casually intruded assumption that the Dutch are anti-Christian –
the ironic disjunction between a Hollander and a Christian (*PW*, XI,
154–5, 216–17) – was the strident aspersion of Jacobite and Tory
writers, and in the 1720s Mist's *Weekly Journal* was rehearsing the
accusations against the Dutch in Japan.[84] Jacobite polemicists like
Leslie and Ferguson referred readers to particular cases of English ships
despoiled by the Dutch East India Company. The case of William
Courten and partners whose ships were seized by the Dutch became the
subject of a long, notorious litigation between George Carew (admini-
strator of the goods and chattels of Courten and partners) and the
Dutch East India Company, who refused reparation for damages
sustained by the Englishmen. Reading the tracts occasioned by the case
and cited by contemporary polemicists, the reader finds reiterated
charges which are clearly present in Swift's paradigm of the perfidious
Dutchman in *Gulliver's Travels*: that the Dutch behave like pirates,
committing depredations upon English shipping in breach of oaths,
peace treaties, the laws of nations and common humanity, and that
they are worse than pagans.[85]

Swift indeed may allude obliquely to this case. In Part III Gulliver
sets out on a voyage to the East Indies. He is made master of a sloop
which, like Courten's ship the *Bona Esperanza*, is chased by two ships – in
the *Travels* they are 'Pyrates', in the case of Courten's ship it was two
Dutch East India boats acting like pirates. Gulliver's sloop is boarded
by both the pirates and 'they pinioned us [Gulliver and the prostrate
crew] with strong Ropes' (*PW*, XI, 154). Swift's satire of the Dutch and
their conduct in the East Indies (*PW*, XI, 154–5) makes the point that
the Dutch have an influence over the Japanese authorities and exercise
this power to the detriment of England. Swift alludes acidly to the
method of murder employed by the Dutch on Englishmen in the East

---

[83] For Whig references, see Daniel Defoe's diminution of Amboyna in *POAS*, 6, 169, 413.
See also: [Daniel Defoe], *A Justification of the Dutch From Several Late Scandalous Reflections . . .*
(London, 1712), pp. 13–14; John Oldmixon, *The Dutch Barrier Our's*, p. 18; John Withers,
The Dutch Better Friends than the French, To the Monarchy, Church, and Trade of England . . ., 2nd
edition (London, 1713), pp. 34–6. For Stubbe on Amboyna, see *A Justification*, pp. 31–2, 80
and his *A Further Justification*, pp. 134–6. For Jacobite reference, see *Select Letters Taken From
Fog's Weekly Journal*, 1, 74. The Jacobite Thomas Carte records the massacre of the English
at Amboyna in *A General History of England*, 4 vols. (London, 1747–55), IV, 120: 'Scarce any
age affords an instance of the like barbarity.'

[84] *A Collection of Miscellany Letters, Selected out of Mist's 'Weekly Journal'*, IV, 276–7.

[85] For 'the Courten case' see: *Severall Remarkable Passages Concerning the Hollanders . . .* (n. p.,
1673); George Carew, *Fraud and Oppression detected and arraigned . . .* (n. p., 1676) and his *Lex
Talionis . . .* (London, 1682); Thomas Browne, *Vox Veritatis . . .* (n. p., 1683).

Indies as made familiar to contemporaries in the anti-Dutch pamphleteering in England:

I OBSERVED among them a *Dutchman*, who seemed to be of some Authority, although he were not Commander of either Ship. He knew us by our Countenances to be *Englishmen*, and jabbering to us in his own Language, swore we should be tyed Back to Back, and thrown into the Sea.

(*PW*, XI, 154)

Leslie, citing as his authority 'The Remonstrance of G. Carew, Esq; Printed 1662', gives an identical account of Dutch treatment of English commanders and crew in *Delenda Carthago*: '*and causing them to be tied back to back, they were cast into the Sea . . . the* Dutch *. . . went aboard the* English *Ships, and served every Man in the same manner*'. Ferguson cites the seizure of Courten's ships and describes the Dutch method of murder: 'the Men tied back to back and thrown over-board, the Cargo seiz'd for the use of the States . . . So much for the return they made us in the *Indies*, and that in time of Peace.' The circumstantial details of Dutch atrocity in the Carew case, often repeated in anti-Dutch polemic, are reproduced by Swift in his satire.[86] Swift develops the familiar disjunction of Tory and Jacobite rhetoric between a Dutchman and a Christian and Protestant, thus undermining the usual Whig argument that Dutch–English friendship and alliance was necessary to safeguard European Protestantism. The Dutchman is shown violating international law and allied treaties. It is suggested that the Dutch procure the slaughter of Christians in Japan and that a heathen is better than a Dutch Protestant ally. The constant utterance of profane oaths by Swift's Dutchman (and the Japanese Captain's fidelity to his word) suggest the central charge of Tory and Jacobite polemic against the Dutch, namely, their flagrant abuse of oaths and alliances, and causeless belligerence against the English.[87]

---

[86] Leslie, *Delenda Carthago*, pp. 4–5; Ferguson, *An Account of the Obligations The States of Holland Have to Great-Britain*, p. 39; see also Stubbe, *A Further Justification*, p. 69; *The History of the Dutch Usurpations. Their Maxims and Politicks in Point of Government, And Their Remarkable Ingratitude to England. Particularly their unheard of Cruelties at Amboyna . . .* (London, 1712), p. 25. See also Michael Duffy, *The Englishman and the Foreigner*, plate no. 14. Duffy parenthetically comments that the supposed atrocity inflicted on the crews 'was still being used by Swift in 1726 in *Gulliver's Travels* Part III, ch. 1' (p. 80). Swift's information may have been derived from a variety of print sources. He certainly appropriates the phraseology of anti-Dutch polemic in the Jacobite press.

[87] The Dutchman's contumelious and imprecatory language has a polemical provenance as remarked above, but Swift's specific insult that the Dutchman (and human Yahoos) 'jabber' (*PW*, XI, 8, 154) has a long literary pedigree. The Dutchman's 'jabbering' identifies him with the simian and barbarian in literature since Homer: see Claude

Gulliver's confrontation with the Dutchman may be seen then as a paradigm of the charges made in seventeenth-century anti-Dutch propaganda tracts and reiterated in the 1690s, during the Tory peace campaign, and later by Tory and Jacobite authors. Swift's satire of the Dutch in 1726 is sometimes seen by modern readers as gratuitous, an incidental satiric eruption reflecting Swift's personal animus. Scholars have laboured to show that even this gratuitous outburst says nothing against the Dutch that cannot be documented as derived from sources in voyage literature, geographical and historiographical writings. But the polemical nature of this anti-Dutch satire as an understood language of Jacobite Toryism would suggest that Swift designed to vex gentle readers of whiggish political persuasion. The correspondence between Swift's treatment of the Dutch and Tory argument can also be witnessed in earlier works such as *The Sentiments of a Church-of-England Man* and the 'Remarks' on Tindal's *Rights of the Christian Church*.

Swift's Irish writings after *Gulliver* are also resonant with echoes of Jacobite polemic. For example, the famous cannibal motif in *A Modest Proposal* (1729; *PW*, XII, 109–18) may have several possible sources, but it does have a specific polemical provenance. Cannibalism was an idiom of Oppositionist political language in the 1720s. One of *Cato's Letters* (no. 35, 1 July 1721) describes the misery of Europeans living under arbitrary power:

It is as astonishing as it is melancholy, to travel through a whole country, as one may through many in *Europe*, gasping under endless imposts, groaning under dragoons and poverty, and all to make a wanton and luxurious court.

There are similarities with the melancholy reflection at the beginning of Swift's sermon on the 'Causes of the Wretched Condition of Ireland' (*PW*, IX, 199) and the opening of *A Modest Proposal* (*PW*, XI, 109). 'Cato' observes of European misery under arbitrary rulers:

Such indeed is their misery, that their case would be greatly mended, if they could change conditions with the beasts of the field; for then, being destined to be eaten, they would be better fed: such a misfortune is it to them that their governors are not *Cannibals*! Oh happy *Britain*, mayest thou continue ever so!

In another paper (no. 99, 20 October 1722) exhorting members of parliament to attend parliament and preserve the liberty of the subject, 'Cato' wrote:

Rawson, 'Narrative and the Proscribed Act: Homer, Euripides and the Literature of Cannibalism', in *Literary Theory and Criticism. Festschrift in Honor of René Wellek*, edited by Joseph P. Strelka, 2 parts (Berne, Frankfurt-on-Main, New York, 1984), Part II, pp. 1159–87 (p. 1169).

Whatever has happened in former reigns, we have reason to hope, that none come now into parliament, with an execrable intention to carry to market a country which has trusted them with its all; and it would be ridiculous to throw away reason upon such banditti, upon public enemies to human society. Such men would be worse than *Cannibals*, who only eat their enemies to satisfy their hunger, and do not sell and betray into servitude their own countrymen, who trust them with the protection of their property and persons.[88]

The Jacobite press was even more outspoken, representing the Hanoverian Whig regime as cannibalistic. Condemning 'a STANDING *Parliament*' and 'a STANDING *Army*', *Mist's Weekly Journal* remarks: 'We read, that the Negroes in *Guiney* sell the Prisoners which they take in the Wars for Slaves; but we seldom hear of any who sell themselves, or their Children.' The betrayed British subjects are likened to slaves being sold, their rights sacrificed 'to the Pleasures of a *devouring* MINISTRY'.[89] Swift, in *A Modest Proposal* of 1729, is writing that Ireland, oppressed by discriminatory laws imposed by England, is ready for wholesale cannibalism. Swift imputes cannibalism to both the oppressors (the English Whig government, their Irish ruling class clients and Irish landlords) and the oppressed (the brutalized Irish poor). Swift's satiric black fantasy shocks readers by literalizing and animating such cannibal metaphors and analogies. It confronts readers with the horror of a nation prepared for devouring by its inhumane rulers and a people so brutalized and savage that they would be prepared to sell and eat their children.

Swift's imaginative texts turn the current polemical metaphors and imputations of the partisan pamphleteers and journalists into an arresting art of attack. In *A Modest Proposal* the Jacobite claim that a cannibalistic Hanoverian Whig regime was devouring its victims is transformed (although not beyond recognition) into the savage irony and black humour of the clinically elaborated cannibal fantasy. In its topical satire, *Gulliver's Travels* is a disaffected Tory political commentary on the times. *A Modest Proposal* is the Tory satirist's jeremiad against his people and their oppressors (see Jeremiah 19.9). Swift's

[88] *Cato's Letters*, II, 12, 13; III, 247.
[89] *A Collection of Miscellany Letters, Selected out of Mist's Weekly Journal*, III, p. 89. Swift was reading both 'Cato' and Mist in 1721–2, see *Corr*, II, 380, 422. For other Jacobite examples, see *The Shift Shifted*, no. 7 (16 June 1716), p. 41; *The Shift Shifted*, no. 8 (23 June 1716), p. 46; *The Shift Shifted*, no. 10 (7 July 1716), pp. 56–7; *The Shift Shifted*, no. 16 (18 August 1716), p. 94 (King George as *Moloch*); *The Freeholder's Journal*, no. 10 (23 March 172[2]), pp. 56–7. Mary Caesar remarks on the Whigs' love of 'Devouring', BL Add. MSS, 62 558, fols. 20–1, 85.

Jacobite Tory correspondents would have been responsive readers of
Swift's satire. Lord Bathurst wrote to Swift in 1737:

those complaints yᵘ make of the deplorable state of Ireland made me reflect
upon the condition of England, and I am inclin'd to think it is not much better,
possibly the only difference is that we shall be last devour'd.

(*Corr*, V, 78)

David Hume, in his Essay 'Of the Parties of Great Britain', remarked
that the 'Tories have been so long obliged to talk in the republican
style, that they seem to have made converts of themselves by their
hypocrisy, and to have embraced the sentiments, as well as language of
their adversaries'.[90] Sir Roger Newdigate in his 'Essays on Party' (*c.*
1760) noted that during George I's and succeeding reigns 'the two
parties generally distinguished as Whigs and Tories continued to
espouse principles directly contradictory to those from whom they
inherited those names. Tories were the friends of liberty, watchful
against every encroachment of prerogative, enemies of oppression and
corruption and every ministerial art or abuse. From the Whigs, the
boasted advocates for liberty, proceeded Septennial Parliaments,
standing armies, revenue officers without number, Riot Act, martial
law.'[91] A modern historian has observed that 'the "country" strand in
the ambiguous Jacobite heritage could lead on paradoxically to
republicanism and even regicide'.[92]

Such witness of the paradox of Tory and Jacobite appropriation of
Country and even republican idioms is germane to interpretation of the
political significance of Swift's enigmatic 'Voyage to the Country of the
Houyhnhnms'. It is, of course, a remarkable political paradox that the
ideal condition or polity offered in the militant Tory satire of *Gulliver's
Travels* should be an 'Ancient' arcadian stoic republic. The mythic
Houyhnhnm state of nature is modelled principally on ancient Sparta[93]
and is a radical, ascetic alternative to the cosmopolitan, pluralistic,

---

[90] David Hume, *Essays: Moral, Political and Literary* (1741–2; London, Oxford University
Press, 1963), p. 74.

[91] Reproduced in Peter D. G. Thomas, 'Sir Roger Newdigate's Essays on Party, c. 1760', *The
English Historical Review*, 102 (1987), 394–400 (p. 398).

[92] Bruce Lenman, 'Physicians and Politics in the Jacobite Era', in *The Jacobite Challenge*,
pp. 74–91 (p. 89).

[93] For the presence of Lycurgan Sparta in Swift's work, see the evidence brought together in
my 'Swift and Sparta: The Nostalgia of *Gulliver's Travels*', *Modern Language Review*, 78
(1983), 513–31.

commercial and 'Athenian' society posited in the writings of contemporary Whig authors such as the Third Earl of Shaftesbury, Molesworth, Addison and Bernard Mandeville. A radical disaffection with monarchy eliding into republican sympathy may be read in Swift. In one of his 'Thoughts on Religion', for instance, there is the remark:

Perhaps, in my own thoughts, I prefer a well-instituted commonwealth before a monarchy; and I know several others of the same opinion. Now, if, upon this pretence, I should insist upon liberty of conscience, form conventicles of republicans, and print books, preferring that government, and condemning what is established, the magistrate would, with great justice, hang me and my disciples.

(PW, IX, 263)

Swift, of course, is putting a case here. His primary argument stated with characteristic animus and intensity is the commonplace Tory one for a strictly limited Toleration and for the proscription from public life of Commonwealth principles and the persons who subscribe to them. When Matthew Tindal put the Old Whig argument for the removal of the civil disabilities imposed on non-Anglicans under the Test Act, Swift remarked: 'Employments in a State are a Reward for those who intirely agree with it ... For Example, a Man who upon all Occasions declared his Opinion, of a Commonwealth before a Monarchy, would not be a fit Man to have Employments; let him enjoy his Opinion, but not be in a Capacity of reducing it to Practice' *(PW, II, 102)*. As Tory *Examiner* Swift exhorted conformity to the established constitution in Church and State:

'Tis possible, that a Man may speculatively prefer the Constitution of another Country, or an *Utopia* of his own, before that of the Nation where he is born and lives; yet from considering the Dangers of Innovation, the Corruptions of Mankind, and the frequent impossibility of reducing Idea's to Practice, he may join heartily in preserving the present Order of Things, and be a true Friend to the Government already settled.

(Exam, p. 256)

Houyhnhnmland is a mythic 'well-instituted commonwealth' and is offered in the satire as the positive rational and virtuous social order and standard of reproach to a corrupt modern civilization. But the virtuous republic of *Gulliver's Travels* is non-human and thus unattainable for the vicious human species. Of the 'remote nations where *Yahoos* preside', it is the balanced, mixed polity of Brobdingnag ruled by an hereditary king which the text approves. For Swift in the fable of Part IV, as for Dryden in the 1690s, the order of ancient Sparta afforded a nostalgic model of civic virtue for a time of corruption.[94]

Matthias Earbery wrote in *The Occasional Historian* of 1731 that it 'was certainly a very wise and just Observation of Mr. *Hobbes*, That many of our *English* Gentry were poison'd by the *Greek* and *Roman* Histories'. He denounces the Commonwealth Interregnum, 'a wretched, hideous Republick, justly hated by all Men of Honour and Sense'.[95] Yet the anti-Hanoverian polemicist could also write elsewhere: 'I must needs own I think the Republican Whigs are more in the Interests of their Country than the others; for no doubt if such a Scheme of Government prevail'd it would be more eligible and better for the Interest of *England* than the Dominion of a Foreigner.'[96] Swift hated the Commonwealth Interregnum, but the experience of Hanoverian monarchy prompted the High Churchman into the radical political margins:

I can recollect, at present, three Civil Establishments, where *Calvinists*, and some other Reformers who rejected *Episcopacy*, possess the supreme Power; and, these are all Republicks; I mean, *Holland*, *Geneva*, and the reformed *Swiss* Cantons. I do not say this in Diminution, or Disgrace to Commonwealths; wherein, I confess, I have much altered many Opinions under which I was educated, having been led by some Observation, long Experience, and a thorough Detestation for the Corruptions of Mankind: Insomuch, that I am now justly liable to the Censure of *Hobbs*, who complains, that the Youth of *England* imbibe ill Opinions, from reading the Histories of ancient *Greece* and *Rome*, those renowned Scenes of Liberty and every Virtue.

                    (*The Presbyterians Plea of Merit* (1733); *PW*, XII, 278)[97]

Tory monarchism reached its apogee in Restoration royalism and nadir after the Hanoverian accession.

Coda

The Tory view that passive obedience and non-resistance were peremptory duties of the subject informed Swift's support of the regency at the

---

[94] 'A Character of Polybius and His Writings', in *The Works of John Dryden: Vol. XX: Prose 1691–1698*, p. 34. Gulliver's voyage to the Houyhnhnms is identified with a Tory time, being dated between the ministerial revolution which replaced Whigs with Tories in September 1710 (*PW*, XI, 221) and February 1715 (*PW*, XI, 283, 288) when Whig ascendancy was restored under the Hanoverian dynasty: see W. A. Speck, 'From Principles to Practice: Swift and Party Politics', in *The World of Jonathan Swift*, p. 85.

[95] *The Occasional Historian*, Numb. II, pp. 4, 6.

[96] *An Historical Account of the Advantages That have Accru'd to England*, p. 21.

[97] Compare also *PW*, II, 17–18, VIII, 37, 120. For contemporary Whig animadversion on the Jacobite '*Republican Scheme*', see *The Freeholder's Alarm to his Brethren: Or, The Fate of Britain Determin'd by the Ensuing Election* (London, 1734), esp. pp. 14, 19–21, 23.

Revolution, his praise of Sancroft and his understanding of the oath he made to subsequent monarchs. As historian of the reign of King Stephen, Swift observed how 'all the miseries of this kingdom' during that period 'were manifestly owing to that continual violation of ... oaths of allegiance' (*PW*, V, 63). The Tory party polemicist and apologist believed 'that no true Member of the Church of England, can easily be shaken in his Principles of Loyalty, or forget the Obligation of an Oath by any Provocation' (*PW*, VIII, 95), a Tory principle given expression in *Gulliver's Travels*. Gulliver in Lilliput (like his creator in the 1720s perhaps) experiences temptation but knows the Church-of-England man's duty:

Once I was strongly bent upon Resistance: For while I had Liberty, the whole Strength of that Empire could hardly subdue me, and I might easily with Stones pelt the Metropolis to Pieces: But I soon rejected that Project with Horror, by remembering the Oath I had made to the Emperor.

(*PW*, XI, 73)

Despite the violence of Swift's satire on Hanoverian Court Whiggism and vicarious entertainment of revolt, it is the Church Tory doctrine of non-resistance and passive obedience that is exemplified and endorsed in *Gulliver's Travels*; for example, in the passive conduct of the oppressed Lord Munodi, whose patience under extreme provocation is intended to be poignant and admirable (*PW*, XI, 176). High Church and Tory ideologists of absolute non-resistance represented submission, prayer, appeals and petitions, or leaving the country, as the private subject's options when lawful governors acted tyrannically.[98] Gulliver in his travels goes through these routines of a loyal subject. For instance, in Part I he petitions to be excused from complying with the Emperor's commands which would have forced the consciences and destroyed the liberties and lives of innocent people (*PW*, XI, 69). In the third voyage Gulliver acts out the principle of passive obedience in a classic exigency – when his religion and the law of the state conflict. Gulliver is expected by the Emperor of Japan to perform the ceremony 'of *trampling upon the Crucifix*'. Gulliver petitions to be excused from active obedience to this law of Japan to which Dutchmen (one of whom he pretends to be) are subject (*PW*, XI, 216). A despairing Gulliver in the fourth voyage is obedient to the (literally inhuman) rational rigour of a Houyhnhnm

---

[98] See, for instance, John Kettlewell, *The Religious Loyalist* ... (London, 1686), esp. pp. 15–16; Luke Milbourne, *The Measures of Resistance* ... (London, 1710), esp. pp. 27–9; William Oldisworth, *A Vindication of The Right Reverend The Lord Bishop of Exeter* ... (London, 1709), pp. 68–9.

Assembly '*Exhortation*' (*PW*, XI, 280). The Houyhnhnms, exemplars of stoic 'sociableness' who live in accord with reason and nature and in total obedience to the determinations of the Representative Council of the whole nation, might be seen as fabulous embodiments of the stoic-influenced state of nature described in the 'Prolegomena' to Grotius's *De Jure Belli ac Pacis*. The Houyhnhnms certainly exemplify that 'rule of the law of nature' to abide by pacts and to conform to what the majority, or those upon whom authority is conferred, have determined.[99] The hypothetical Houyhnhnm state of nature where all obey what is enjoined by natural law without the necessity of divine injunction may be an imaginative version of a Grotian proposition.[100] But Swift's Grotian state of nature is a non-human world. The fable's image of a human state of nature is the brutish, violent anarchy of the anthropoid Yahoos – a mythic version of a Hobbesian state of nature.[101] The idyllic order of those equine Ancients, the Houyhnhnms, is unattainable. Gulliver lives in a world of political opinions and choices, in a history of 'Conspiracies, Rebellions, Murders, Massacres, Revolutions, Banishments'. Gulliver feeds his eyes on 'the Destroyers of Tyrants and Usurpers', but as a private subject he pays obedience to the powers that be. As Swift wrote to Archbishop King in 1727:

My Lord, I have lived, and by the grace of God will die, an enemy to servitude and slavery of all kinds: And I believe, at the same time, that persons of such a disposition will be the most ready to pay obedience wherever it is due.

(*Corr*, III, 210)

---

[99] Hugo Grotius, *De Jure Belli ac Pacis Libri Tres*, trans. by Francis Kelsey (Oxford, 1925), 'Prolegomena', 15, pp. 14–15. Swift's library was well stocked with editions of Grotius' works: see LeFanu, p. 19; *SC*, nos. 151, 322. Swift owned one of the two 1712 Amsterdam editions of *De Jure Belli ac Pacis*. He recommended the great work to Gay in 1714 (*Corr*, II, 33).

[100] Grotius, *De Jure Belli ac Pacis*, 'Prolegomena', 11, 50, pp. 13, 27.

[101] A reader of *Gulliver's Travels* in 1726 saw it as an answer to Whig writers who 'consider men as reasoning creatures – as they should be, not as they are', see Joseph Spence, *Observations, Anecdotes, and Characters of Books and Men*, I, p. 393.

Bibliography

This is a select bibliography principally of cited works. Most contemporary tracts were published anonymously. Authors have been supplied where known.

Swift's works

Swift, Jonathan, *The Account Books of Jonathan Swift*, transcribed and with an Introduction by Paul V. Thompson and Dorothy Jay Thompson (Newark and London, 1984)

The Battle of the Books: Eine historisch-kritische Ausgabe mit literarhistorischer Einleitung und Kommentar, Hermann Josef Real (Berlin and New York, 1978)

The Complete Poems, ed. by Pat Rogers (Harmondsworth, 1983)

The Correspondence of Jonathan Swift, ed. by Harold Williams, 5 vols. (Oxford, 1963–5)

A Discourse of the Contests and Dissentions Between the Nobles and the Commons in Athens and Rome, ed. by Frank H. Ellis (Oxford, 1967)

[?], *A Discourse on Hereditary Right, Written in the Year 1712. By a Celebrated Clergyman* (London, [1775])

An Enquiry into the Behaviour of the Queen's Last Ministry, ed. by Irvin Ehrenpreis (Bloomington, 1956)

Gulliver's Travels, ed. by Peter Dixon and John Chalker with an Introduction by Michael Foot (Harmondsworth, 1967, 1985)

Gulliver's Travels, ed. by Paul Turner, The World's Classics (Oxford, 1986)

The Intelligencer (with Thomas Sheridan), ed. by James Woolley (Oxford, 1992)

The Letters of Jonathan Swift to Charles Ford, ed. by David Nichol Smith (Oxford, 1935)

Memoirs of Martinus Scriblerus (with Pope, *et al.*), ed. by Charles Kerby-Miller (New Haven, 1950)

Miscellanies in Prose and Verse (London, 1711; rpt. Menston, 1972 with an Introductory Note by C. P. Daw)

The Poems of Jonathan Swift, ed. by Harold Williams, 2nd edn, 3 vols. (Oxford, 1958)

Poetical Works, ed. by Herbert Davis (London, 1967)

197

The Prose Writings of Jonathan Swift, ed. by Herbert Davis and others, 16 vols. (Oxford, 1939–74)

Swift vs. Mainwaring: 'The Examiner' and 'The Medley', ed. by Frank H. Ellis (Oxford, 1985)

A Tale of a Tub and Other Works, ed. by Angus Ross and David Woolley (Oxford and New York, 1986)

A Tale of a Tub To which is added The Battle of the Books and the Mechanical Operation of the Spirit, ed. by A. C. Guthkelch and D. Nichol Smith, 2nd edn (Oxford, 1958 [1973])

Manuscript sources

British Library Additional Manuscripts
  6116 (Bishop Nicolson's Letters to Archbishop Wake)
  29,545 (G. Harbin, Letters)
  29,612 (Letter-Book of Silvester Jenks 1703–1707)
  36,196 fol. 167 (State of the Proceedings against Matthias Earbery)
  45,511; 45,512 (Robert Nelson Collection)
  62,558 (Journal of Mary Caesar)
Public Record Office, Chancery Lane, London
  The State Papers Domestic. SP 35 (George I), SP 36 (George II) and SP 43. (The Harvester Press, Microfilm)

Printed primary sources

Addison, Joseph, *The Freeholder*, ed. by James Leheny (Oxford, 1979)
  The Miscellaneous Works, ed. by A. C. Guthkelch, 2 vols. (London, 1914)
The Advocate. A Defence of the B. of Lichfield and Coventry . . . Including Some Remarks on the Writings of the late Mr. Charles Leslie . . . (London, 1732)
[Alsop, Vincent], *The Humble Address of the Presbyterians, Presented to the King . . . With His Majesties Gracious Answer* (n.p., 1687)
[Anderton, William], *Remarks upon the Present Confederacy, and Late Revolution in England &c.* (London, 1693), in *Somers Tracts*, X, 491–523
Arbuthnot, John, *The History of John Bull*, ed. by Alan W. Bower and Robert A. Erickson (Oxford, 1976)
Astell, Mary, *A Fair Way with the Dissenters and their Patrons. Not Writ by Mr. L—y, or any other Furious Jacobite, Whether Clergyman or Lay-Man; but by a very Moderate Person and Dutiful Subject to the Queen* (London, 1704)
[Atterbury, Francis], *An Answer to Some Considerations on the Spirit of Martin Luther and The Original of the Reformation; Lately Printed at Oxford* (Oxford, 1687)
  English Advice to the Freeholders of England (n.p., 1714 [1715])
  The Epistolary Correspondence, Visitation Charges, Speeches and Miscellanies of the Right Reverend Francis Atterbury, D.D., Lord Bishop of Rochester, ed. by J. Nichols, 5 vols. (London, 1783–90)
  The Rights, Powers, and Priviledges of an English Convocation . . . (London, 1700)

Baron, William, *The Dutch Way of Toleration, Most Proper for our English Dissenters* (London, 1698)

An Historical Account of Comprehension, and Toleration ... Part I. By the Author of the Dutch Way of Toleration (London, 1705)

An Historical Account of Comprehension, and Toleration ... Part II (London, 1706)

Separation and Sedition Inseparable ... (London, 1703)

Bellers, John, *Some Reasons for an European State ...* (London, 1710)

Blackall, Offspring, *The Divine Institution of Magistracy ...* (London, 1709)

The Subjects Duty ... (London, 1705)

Bolingbroke, Henry St John, Lord, *Contributions to the Craftsman*, ed. by Simon Varey (Oxford, 1982)

The Works of The Right Hon. Henry St. John, Lord Viscount Bolingbroke, 7 vols. (London, 1754–98)

Boyer, Abel, *The History of the Reign of Queen Anne, Digested into Annals*, volume III (London, 1705)

Reflections upon the Examiner's Scandalous Peace (London, 1711)

Bramhall, John, *The Works of the Most Reverend Father in God, John Bramhall D.D. Late Lord Archbishop of Ardmagh, Primate and Metropolitane of all Ireland* (Dublin, 1676)

Brief Remarks On the late Representation of The Lower House of Convocation; As the same respects the Quakers only (London, 1711)

Browne, Thomas, *Vox Veritatis ...* (n.p., 1683)

Burnet, Gilbert, *Bishop Burnet's History of His Own Time*, 2 vols. (London, 1724, 1734)

[Burnet, Thomas], *A Letter to the People, to be left for them at the Booksellers; With a Word or Two of the Bandbox Plot* (London, 1712)

A Second Tale of a Tub: Or, The History of Robert Powel the Puppet-Show-Man (London, 1715)

Butler, Samuel, *Hudibras*, ed. by John Wilders (Oxford, 1967)

Care, Henry, ed., *The King's Right of Indulgence in Spiritual Matters ...* (London, 1688)

A Word in Season ... (London, 1679)

Carew, George, *Fraud and Oppression detected and arraigned ...* (n.p., 1676)

Lex Talionis ... (London, 1682)

Carte, Thomas, *A General History of England*, 4 vols. (London, 1747–55)

Charles XII of Sweden. A Character and Two Poems, with an Introduction by Eveline Cruickshanks (Locks' Press, Brisbane, 1983)

Clarke, Rev. J. S., *The Life of James The Second King of England, &c.*, 2 vols. (London, 1816)

Cobbett, William, ed., *The Parliamentary History of England*, 36 vols. (London, 1806–20). Vols. IV–VIII cover the period 1660–1733

Coleridge, Samuel Taylor, *The Table Talk and Omniana of Samuel Taylor Coleridge* (Oxford, 1917)

A Collection of Scarce and Valuable Tracts (known as *Somers Tracts*) ed. by Walter Scott, 2nd edn, 13 vols. (London, 1809–15)

A Collection of the Several Statutes, and Parts of Statutes, Now in Force, relating to High Treason, And Misprision of High Treason (London, 1709)

Collier, Jeremy, *An Ecclesiastical History of Great Britain* ..., 2 vols. (London, 1708, 1714)

Collins, Anthony, *A Discourse of Free-Thinking, Occasion'd by the Rise and Growth of a Sect Call'd Free-Thinkers* (London, 1713)

Cooksey, Richard, *Essay on the Life and Character of John Lord Somers, Baron of Evesham* (Worcester, 1791)

Craik, Henry, *The Life of Jonathan Swift*, 2nd edn, 2 vols. (London, 1894)

The Criterion: Or, Touchstone, By which to judge of the Principles of High and Low-Church. In a Letter to a Friend (London, 1710)

Curll, Edmund, *A Complete Key to the Tale of a Tub* (London, 1710; rpt. *Swiftiana I: On the Tale of a Tub 1704–1712*, New York, 1975)

   A Key, Being Observations and Explanatory Notes, Upon the Travels of Lemuel Gulliver. By Signor Corolini ... (London, 1726; rpt. *Gulliveriana VI*, New York, 1976)

Davila, [Enrico Caterino], *The Historie of the Civill Warres of France, Written in Italian by H. C. Davila*, translated by Charles Cottrell and William Aylesbury, 2 vols. in 1 (London, 1647–8)

Deane, Thomas, *The Religion of Mar. Luther* ... (Oxford, 1688)

The Debate at Large, Between the House of Lords and House of Commons, at the Free Conference, Held in the Painted Chamber, in the Session of the Convention, Anno 1688. Relating to the Word, Abdicated, and the Vacancy of the Throne, in the Common's Vote (London, 1695; rpt. Shannon, 1972)

The Declaration of an Honest Churchman, Upon Occasion of the Present Times (London, 1710)

[Defoe, Daniel], *A Defence of the Allies and The Late Ministry: Or, Remarks on the Tories New Idol. Being a Detection of the Manifest Frauds and Falsities, in a late Pamphlet, Entituled, The Conduct of the Allies and of the Late Ministry, in the Beginning and Carrying on the War* (London, 1712)

Defoe, Daniel, *Defoe's Review*, Reproduced from the original editions, with an Introduction and Bibliographical Notes by Arthur W. Secord, in 22 facsimile books (New York, 1937, 1965)

   Hannibal at the Gates: Or, The Progress of Jacobitism. With the Present Danger of the Pretender (London, 1712)

   The History of the Jacobite Clubs (London, 1712)

   A Justification of the Dutch From Several Late Scandalous Reflections ... (London, 1712)

   The Present State of the Parties in Great Britain (London, 1712)

   The Secret History of the October Club: From its Original to this Time. By a Member (London, 1711)

   The Secret History of the October-Club, From Its Original to this Time. By a Member. Part II (London, 1711)

[Dennis, John], *The Danger of Priestcraft to Religion and Government* ... (London, 1702)

Dr. S—'s Real Diary (London, 1715; rpt. *Swiftiana II: Bickerstaffiana and Other Early Materials on Swift 1708–1715*, New York, 1975)

Dryden, John, *The Works of John Dryden: Poems 1685–1692, Volume III*, ed. by Earl Miner (Berkeley and Los Angeles, 1969)

The Works of John Dryden, Vol. II: Poems 1681–1684, ed. by H. T. Swedenberg, Jr, *et al.* (Berkeley, Los Angeles and London, 1972)

The Works of John Dryden: Vol. XV. Plays: Albion and Albanius Don Sebastian Amphitryon, ed. by Earl Miner and others (Berkeley, Los Angeles and London, 1976)

The Works of John Dryden: Vol. XX: Prose 1691–1698, ed. by A. E. Wallace Maurer and George R. Guffey (Berkeley, Los Angeles and London, 1989)

Dunton, John, *The Life and Errors of John Dunton* ... ed. by John Nichols, 2 vols. (1818: rpt. New York, 1969)

[Earbery, Matthias], *An Historical Account of the Advantages that have Accru'd to England, by the Succession in the Illustrious House of Hanover* (London, 1722)

An Historical Account of the Advantages that have Accrued to England by the Succession in the Illustrious House of Hanover. Part II (London, 1722)

The History of the Clemency of Our English Monarchs ... 2nd edn (London, 1720)

The Occasional Historian, 4 parts (London, 1730–2)

The Universal Spy or, the Royal Oak Journal Reviv'd, no. 9 (2 September 1732) in Public Record Office, State Papers Domestic 36/28

Edwards, John, *The Divine Perfections Vindicated* ... (London, 1710)

Edwards, Thomas, *Gangraena*, 3 parts (London, 1646; rpt. The Rota, 1977)

The Established Test, In order to the Security of His Majesties Sacred Person, and Government, and the Protestant Religion. Against the Malitious Attempts and Treasonable Machinations of Rome (London, 1679)

Falkner, William, *Christian Loyalty* ... (London, 1679)

Ferguson, Robert, *An Account of the Obligations The States of Holland Have to Great-Britain, And The Return They Have Made Both in Europe and the Indies. With Reflections upon the Peace* (London, 1711)

A Brief Account of Some of the Late Incroachments and Depredations of the Dutch upon the English ... (n.p., 1695 [1696])

The Third Part of No Protestant Plot ... (London, 1682)

Whether the Preserving the Protestant Religion was the Motive unto, or the End that was designed in the late Revolution? ... (1695) in *Somers Tracts*, IX, 543–69

[Fleming, Robert], *A Discourse of Earthquakes; As they are Supernatural and Premonitory Signs to a Nation; with a respect to what hath occurred in this Year 1692* ... (London, 1693)

Flint, George, *Robin's Last Shift: Or, Weekly Remarks and Political Reflections Upon the most Material News Foreign and Domestick* (London, 1717)

The Shift Shifted: Or, Weekly Remarks and Political Reflections Upon the most Material News Foreign and Domestick (London, 1716)

Forbes, Robert, *The Lyon in Mourning*, ed. by Henry Paton, Scottish Historical
    Society, 3 vols. (Edinburgh, 1895–6)
Foulis, Henry, *The History of the Wicked Plots and Conspiracies of Our Pretended
    Saints . . .* (London, 1662)
Foxe, John, *Acts and Monuments*, ed. by S. R. Cattley and George Townsend, 8
    vols. (London, 1837–41)
*The Freeholder's Alarm to his Brethren: Or, The Fate of Britain Determin'd by the
    Ensuing Election* (London, 1734)
The Freeholder's Journal (London, 1722–3)
Gay, John, *Dramatic Works*, ed. by John Fuller, 2 vols. (Oxford, 1983)
    Poetry and Prose, ed. by Vinton A. Dearing with Charles E. Beckwith, 2 vols.
    (Oxford, 1974)
Gent, Thomas, *The Life of Mr. Thomas Gent, Printer, of York: Written by Himself*
    (London, 1832; rpt. New York and London, 1974)
[Gordon, Thomas], *A Dedication to a Great Man, Concerning Dedications. Discover-
    ing, Amongst other wonderful Secrets, what will be the present Posture of Affairs a
    thousand Years hence* (London, 1718)
The Grand Accuser The Greatest of all Criminals, Part I (London, 1735)
Granville, George, Baron Lansdowne, *The Genuine Works in Verse and Prose*, 2
    vols. (London, 1732)
    A Letter from a Noble-Man Abroad, to His Friend in England (London, 1722)
    Poems upon Several Occasions (London, 1712)
Grotius, Hugo, *The Law of War and Peace. De Jure Belli ac Pacis Libri Tres*, trans.
    by Francis Kelsey (Oxford, 1925)
*Gulliver Decypher'd: or Remarks on a late Book, intitled, Travels Into Several Remote
    Nations of the World. By Capt. Lemuel Gulliver. Vindicating The Reverend Dean on
    whom it is maliciously Father'd . . .* (London, [1726]; rpt. *Gulliveriana VI*, New
    York, 1976)
Gulliveriana VI: Critiques of Gulliver's Travels and Allusions Thereto, book one.
    Facsimile reproductions, Introd. by Jeanne K. Welcher and George
    E. Bush, Jr (New York, 1976)
Head, Richard, *The Floating Island* (London, 1673)
Hearne, Thomas, *Remarks and Collections of Thomas Hearne*, ed. by C. E. Doble,
    Oxford Historical Society, 11 vols. (Oxford, 1885–1921)
Herbert, George, *The English Poems of George Herbert*, ed. by C. A. Patrides
    (London, 1974)
[Hervey, John, Lord], *The Conduct of the Opposition, and the Tendency of Modern
    Patriotism, (More particularly in a late Scheme to Establish a Military Government
    in this Country) Review'd and Examin'd* (London, 1734)
    Lord Hervey's Memoirs, ed. by Romney Sedgwick, revised edition (London,
    1963)
    Some Materials Towards Memoirs of the Reign of King George II, ed. by Romney
    Sedgwick, 3 vols. (London, 1931 [1970])
Hickes, George, *The Spirit of Enthusiasm Exorcised: In a Sermon Preach'd Before the
    University of Oxford, &c.* 4th edn (London, 1709)

The Spirit of Popery Speaking Out of the Mouthes of Fanatical Protestants (London, 1680)

Higden, William, *A Defence of the View of the English Constitution with Respect to the Sovereign Authority of the Prince, and the Allegiance of the Subject. By way of Reply to the several Answers that have been made to it* (London, 1710)

A View of the English Constitution, with Respect to the Sovereign Authority of the Prince, and the Allegiance of the Subject, &c. The Third Edition. With a Defence of the View, by way of Reply to the several Answers that have been made to it (London, 1710)

Historical Manuscripts Commission, *Appendix to Second Report* (London, 1874)

Historical Manuscripts Commission, *Fifteenth Report, Appendix, Part IV. The Manuscripts of His Grace The Duke of Portland*, vol. IV (London, 1897)

Historical Manuscripts Commission, *Fourteenth Report, Appendix, Part IX. The Manuscripts of the Earl of Buckinghamshire, the Earl of Lindsey, the Earl of Onslow, Lord Emly, Theodore J. Hare, Esq., and James Round, Esq., M.P.* (London, 1895)

Historical Manuscripts Commission, *Report on the Manuscripts of His Grace The Duke of Portland*, vol. VII (London, 1901)

An Historical View of the Principles, Characters, Persons, &c. of the Political Writers in Great Britain (London, 1740)

The History of the Dutch Usurpations. Their Maxims and Politicks In Point of Government, And Their Remarkable Ingratitude to England, Particularly their unheard of Cruelties at Amboyna ... (London, 1712)

Honesty is the Best Policy, in *Somers Tracts*, X, 211–18

Horace, *The Odes and Epodes*, trans. by C. E. Bennett, Loeb Classical Library (Cambridge, Mass. and London, 1978)

An Hue and Cry after Dr. S— T (London, 1714; rpt. *Swiftiana II: Bickerstaffiana and Other Early Materials on Swift 1708–1715*, New York, 1975)

Hume, David, *Essays: Moral, Political and Literary* (1741–2; London, Oxford University Press, 1963)

[Humfrey, John], *Considerations Moving to a Toleration, and Liberty of Conscience ...* (London, 1685)

[Hunton, P.], *A Treatise of Monarchy: Containing Two Parts. I. Concerning Monarchy in General. II. Concerning this Particular Monarchy ...* (London, 1643; rpt. 1689)

Irenaeus, Saint, Bishop of Lyons, *Against Heresies*, in *The Ante-Nicene Fathers*, vol. I, ed. by Alexander Roberts and James Donaldson, rev. by A. Cleveland Coxe (New York, 1896; rpt. Michigan, 1981), pp. 309–567

Johnson, Samuel, *Lives of the English Poets*, ed. by George Birkbeck Hill, 3 vols. (Oxford, 1905)

[Johnston, Nathaniel], *The Dear Bargain: or, a True Representation of the State of the English Nation under the Dutch. In a Letter to a Friend* (1690?), in *Somers Tracts*, X, 349–77

Kenyon, J. P., ed., *The Stuart Constitution Documents and Commentary*, 2nd edn (Cambridge, 1986)

Kettlewell, John, *The Religious Loyalist* ... (London, 1686)

King, William, *The Original Works*, 3 vols. (London, 1776)

Knatchbull, Edward, *The Parliamentary Diary of Sir Edward Knatchbull, 1722–30*, ed. by A. N. Newman (London, 1963)

Laud, William, *A Relation of the Conference betweene William Lawd ... and Mr. Fisher the Jesuite* ... (London, 1639)

[Lawton, Charlwood], *A French Conquest neither Desiderable nor Practicable, Dedicated to the King of England* (London, 1693), in *Somers Tracts*, X, 471–91

  The Jacobite Principles Vindicated, In an Answer to a Letter sent to the Author (London, 1693), in *Somers Tracts*, X, 523–41

[Leslie, Charles], *An Answer to a Book, Intituled, The State of the Protestants in Ireland* ... (London, 1692)

  The Best Answer Ever was Made, And to which no Answer Ever will be Made ... (London, 1709)

  Best of All. Being The Student's Thanks to Mr. Hoadly ... (London, 1709)

  Bishop of Salisbury's Proper Defence, From a Speech Cry'd about the Streets in his Name, and Said to have been Spoken by him in the House of Lords, upon the Bill Against Occasional Conformity (London, 1704)

  The Case of the Regale and of the Pontificat Stated ... (n.p., 1700)

  Cassandra (London, 1704)

  A Catalogue of Books of the Newest Fashion, to be Sold by Auction at the Whiggs Coffee-House, at the Sign of the Jackanapes in Prating-Alley, near the Deanry of St. Paul's [London, 1694]

  Considerations of Importance to Ireland, In a Letter to a Member of Parliament there; upon Occasion of Mr. Molyneux's late Book: Intituled, The Case of Ireland's being Bound by Acts of Parliament in England, Stated (n.p., 1698)

  Delenda Carthago [n.p., 1695?]

  A Dissertation Concerning the Use and Authority of Ecclesiastical History (London, 1703)

  The Finishing Stroke, Being a Vindication of the Patriarchal Scheme of Government, In Defence of the Rehearsals, Best Answer, and Best of All ... To which are Added, Remarks on Dr. Higden's late Defence, In a Dialogue between Three H—'s (London, 1711)

  Five Discourses By the Author of the 'Snake in the Grass', viz. 'On Water-Baptism'. 'Episcopacy'. 'Primitive Heresie of the Quakers'. 'Reflections on the Quakers'. 'A Brief Account of the Socinian Trinity' (London, 1700)

  Gallienus Redivivus, or, Murther Will Out, &c. Being a True Account of the De-Witting of Glencoe, Gaffney, &c. (Edinburgh, 1695)

  The History of Sin and Heresie ... (London, 1698)

  A Letter from Mr Lesly to a Member of Parliament in London (dated 23 April 1714 [London, 1714])

  The New Association Of those Called, Moderate-Church-Man, with the Modern-Whigs and Fanaticks, to Under-mine and Blow-up the Present Church and Government. Occasion'd by a Late Pamphlet, Entituled, The Danger of Priest-Craft, &c. With a Supplement, on Occasion of the New Scotch Presbyterian Covenant. By a True-Church-Man, 3rd edn (London, 1702)

The New Association. Part II ... (London, 1703)

A Parallel Between the Faith and Doctrine of the Present Quakers, And that of the Chief Hereticks in all Ages of The Church. And also A Parallel between Quakerism and Popery (London, 1700)

Querela Temporum: or, the Danger of the Church of England ... (London, 1694), in *Somers Tracts*, IX, 509–27

The Right of Monarchy Asserted ... (London, 1713)

The Snake in the Grass ... (London, 1696)

A View of the Times, Their Principles and Practices in The Rehearsals. By Philalethes [The Rehearsal], 2nd edn, 6 vols. (London, 1750)

The Wolf Stript of His Shepherd's Cloathing ... (London, 1704)

L'Estrange, Roger, *The Character of a Papist in Masquerade: Supported by Authority and Experience. In Answer to the Character of a Popish Successor* (London, 1681)

The Dissenter's Sayings, In Requital for L'Estrange's Sayings. Published in Their Own Words, For the Information of the People (London, 1681)

The Dissenters Sayings. Two Parts in One ... (London, 1685 [1705])

The Observator, in Dialogue (London, 1684–7)

A Letter from a Clergyman to his Friend, With an Account of the Travels of Capt. Lemuel Gulliver and a Character of the Author. To which is added, The True Reasons why a certain Doctor was made a Dean (London, 1726; rpt. *Gulliveriana VI*, New York, 1976)

A Letter to the People of England, occasion'd by the Letter to the Dissenters [signed Cato Brutus] (London, 1714)

A Letter to the Reverend Mr. Dean Swift, Occasion'd by a Satire Said to be written by Him, Entitled, A Dedication to a Great Man, concerning Dedications ... (London, 1719)

Liberty of Conscience, or Religion A La Mode, Fitted for the Use of the Occasional Conformist. And Dedicated to the most Learned Author of the Tale of a Tub (London, 1704)

Locke, John, *A Letter Concerning Toleration*, ed. by John Horton and Susan Mendus, Routledge Philosophers in Focus Series (London and New York, 1991)

Two Treatises of Government, ed. by Peter Laslett, 2nd edn (Cambridge, 1970)

Lockhart, George, *Memoirs Concerning the Affairs of Scotland, from Queen Anne's Accession to the Throne, to the Commencement of the Union of Two Kingdoms of Scotland and England, in May, 1707* (London, 1714)

Long, Thomas, *The Letter For Toleration Decipher'd, And The Absurdity and Impiety of an Absolute Toleration Demonstrated* ... (London, 1689)

Lord, G. deF. and others, ed., *Poems on Affairs of State*, 7 vols. (New Haven, 1963–75)

Lucretius, *De Rerum Natura*, trans. by W. H. D. Rouse, revised by Martin Ferguson Smith, Loeb Classical Library (Cambridge, Mass. and London, 1975)

Luttrell, Narcissus, *A Brief Historical Relation of State Affairs from September 1678 to April 1714*, 6 vols. (Oxford, 1857)

Mandeville, Bernard, *The Fable of the Bees*, ed. by Phillip Harth (Harmondsworth, 1970, 1989)

Marvell, Andrew, *The Poems and Letters of Andrew Marvell*, ed. by H. M. Margoliouth, rev. by Pierre Legouis with E. E. Duncan-Jones, 3rd edn, 2 vols. (Oxford, 1971)

  The Rehearsal Transpros'd and The Rehearsal Transpros'd The Second Part, ed. by D. I. B. Smith (Oxford, 1971)

Mather, John, *A Sermon Preached before the University of Oxford, at St. Mary's, on Tuesday May 29th. 1705. Being the Anniversary of K. Charles II. Restoration* (Oxford, 1705)

Milbourne, Luke, *The Measures of Resistance To The Higher Powers, So far as becomes a Christian: In a Sermon Preach'd on January the 30th, $17\frac{19}{10}$* ... (London, 1710)

Mist, Nathaniel, *A Collection of Miscellany Letters, Selected out of Mist's 'Weekly Journal'*, 4 vols. (London, 1722–7)

Mist's Weekly Journal (London, 1725–8)

Moderation a Vertue (London, 1683)

A Modest Apology for the loyal Protestant Subjects of King James, who desire his Restoration ... in *Somers Tracts*, X, 401–29

Molesworth, Robert, Lord, 'Sentiment of the late Lord Molesworth', in *The Memoirs of John Ker, of Kersland in North Britain Esq.*, 3 parts (London, 1726), III, 191–221

Molyneux, William, *The Case of Ireland Stated* (1698), introd. and afterword by J. G. Simms and Denis Donoghue (Dublin, 1977)

[Montgomery, Sir James], *Great Britain's Just Complaint for her late Measures, present Sufferings, and the future Miseries she is exposed to* (1692), in *Somers Tracts*, X, 429–71

A Morning's Discourse of a Bottomless Tubb, Introducing the Historical Fable of the Oak and her Three Provinces ... Written by a Lover of the Loyal, Honest, and Moderate Party (London, 1712; rpt. in *Swiftiana I: On the Tale of a Tub 1704–12*, New York, 1975)

Musae Cantabrigienses (Cantabrigiae, 1689)

[Nalson, John], *Foxes and Fire-brands: Or a Specimen of the Danger and Harmony of Popery and Separation* ... (London, 1680)

A New Collection of Poems Relating to State Affairs, From Oliver Cromwell to this present Time ... (London, 1705)

Nichols, J., *Literary Anecdotes of the Eighteenth Century*, 9 vols. (London, 1812–15)

The Observator (London, 1711–12)

The Old Whig (London, 1719)

The Old Whig: or, The Consistent Protestant (1735–8)

Oldisworth, William, *A Dialogue between Timothy and Philatheus* ..., 3 vols. (London, 1709–11)

  A Vindication of The Right Reverend the Lord Bishop of Exeter ... (London, 1709)

Oldmixon, John, *The Dutch Barrier Our's* ... (London, 1712)

The History of England, 3 vols. (London, 1735)

The Life and Posthumous Works of Arthur Maynwaring, Esq... (London, 1715)

Memoirs of the Press, Historical and Political, For Thirty Years past, From 1710 to 1740 (London, 1742)

Reflections on Dr. Swift's Letter to Harley (London, 1712; rpt. intro. by Louis A. Landa, The Augustan Reprint Society, no. 15 (Los Angeles, 1948)

Remarks upon Remarks: Or The Barrier-Treaty and The Protestant Succession Vindicated. In Answer to the False and Treasonable Reflections of the Author of The Conduct of the Allies, &c. (London, 1711 [1712])

Ormonde, James Butler, Second Duke of, *The Jacobite Attempt of 1719. Letters of James Butler, Second Duke of Ormonde* ..., ed. by William Kirk Dickson, Scottish Historical Society (Edinburgh, 1895)

Owen, John, *The Works of John Owen, D.D.*, ed. by William H. Goold, 24 vols. (London and Edinburgh, 1850–5)

Penn, William, *The Great Case of Liberty of Conscience* ... ([London], 1670)

Pilkington, Letitia, *Memoirs of Mrs Letitia Pilkington 1712–1750 Written by Herself* (1748–54; rpt. London, 1928)

Poems of Affairs of State, volume IV (London, 1707)

Poems on the Reign of William III, introd. and selected by Earl Miner, Augustan Reprint Society, no. 166 (Los Angeles, 1974)

Pope, Alexander, *The Correspondence of Alexander Pope*, ed. by George Sherburn, 5 vols. (Oxford, 1956)

The Twickenham Edition of the Poems of Alexander Pope, ed. by John Butt and others, 11 vols. in 12 (London, 1939–69)

Priest-Craft Expos'd ... (London, 1691)

Prior, Matthew, *Literary Works*, ed. by H. Bunker Wright and Monroe K. Spears, 2nd edn, 2 vols. (Oxford, 1971)

Purchas His Pilgrimes. In Five Bookes (London, 1625)

Ryder, Dudley, *The Diary of Dudley Ryder 1715–1716*, ed. by William Matthews (London, 1939)

Sacheverell, Henry, *The Perils of False Brethren, both in Church, and State: Set forth in a Sermon Preach'd before The Right Honourable, The Lord-Mayor, Aldermen, and Citizens of London, at the Cathedral-Church of St. Paul, On the 5th of November, 1709* (London,1709; rpt. The Rota, 1974)

Savage, Richard, *The Poetical Works of Richard Savage*, ed. by Clarence Tracy (Cambridge, 1962)

The Second and Last English Advice, To The Freehoulders of Englan[d] (London, 1722)

Select Letters Taken from Fog's Weekly Journal, 2 vols. (London, 1732)

[Sergeant, John], *An Historical Romance of the Wars, Between the Mighty Giant Gallieno, and the Great Knight Nasonius, and His Associates* (Doublin, 1694)

Severall Remarkable Passages Concerning the Hollanders Since the Death of Queene Elizabeth, Untill the 25'th of December, 1673 ... With the Continuation of the Case betweene Sr William Courten His Heires and Assignes and The East-India Company of the Netherlands ... (n.p., 1673)

Shadwell, Thomas, *The Complete Works of Thomas Shadwell*, ed. by Montague Summers, 5 vols. (London, 1927)

Shakespeare, William, *Henry V*, ed. by Gary Taylor, The Oxford Shakespeare (Oxford, 1984)

Sharp, John, *Fifteen Sermons Preach'd on Several Occasions* (London, 1700)

Sheffield, John, Duke of Buckingham, *Buckingham Restor'd: Being Two Essays Which were Castrated from the Works of the late Duke of Buckingham* (Hague, 1727)

The Works of John Sheffield, Earl of Mulgrave, Marquis of Normanby, and Duke of Buckingham, 2 vols. (London, 1723)

Sheridan, Thomas, *The Life of the Rev. Dr. Jonathan Swift* (London, 1784; rpt. *Swiftiana XV*, New York, 1974)

Sherlock, William, *The Case of the Allegiance Due to Soveraign Powers* ... (London, 1690; rpt. The Rota, 1979)

Smalridge, George, *A Sermon Preach'd before the Honourable House of Commons, At St. Margarets Westminster, Jan. 30. 1702* ... (London, 1702)

[Smedley, Jonathan], *Gulliveriana: Or, a Fourth Volume of Miscellanies. Being a Sequel of the Three Volumes, published by Pope and Swift* ... (London, 1728)

Southerne, Thomas, *The Works of Thomas Southerne*, ed. by Robert Jordon and Harold Love, 2 vols. (Oxford, 1988)

The Spectator, ed. by Donald F. Bond, 5 vols. (Oxford, 1965)

Spence, Joseph, *Observations, Anecdotes, and Characters of Books and Men*, ed. by James M. Osborn, 2 vols. (Oxford, 1966)

Spingarn, J. E., ed., *Critical Essays of the Seventeenth Century*, 3 vols. (Oxford, 1908–9)

Steele, Richard, *The Public Spirit of the Tories, Manifested in the Case of the Irish Dean, and his Man Timothy* (London, 1714)

Two Letters Concerning the Author of the Examiner (London, 1713)

Sterne, Laurence, *The Life and Opinions of Tristram Shandy, Gentleman*, ed. by Ian Campbell Ross, The World's Classics (Oxford, 1983)

Stubbe, Henry, *A Further Justification of the Present War Against The United Netherlands. Illustrated with several Sculptures* (London, 1673)

A Justification of the Present War, Against The United Netherlands ... (London, 1673)

[Taylor, John], *A Dialogue Betwixt Three Travellers, as accidentally they did meet on the High-way: Crucy Cringe, a Papist, Accepted Weighall, a Professour of the Church of England, and Factious Wrestwrit, a Brownist* (London, 1641)

Temple, Sir William, *The Works of Sir William Temple, Bar'.*, 2 vols. (London, 1731)

A Third Collection of Papers Relating to the Present Juncture of Affairs in England (London, [1688])

Thompson, Edward Maunde, ed., *Correspondence of The Family of Hatton Being Chiefly Letters Addressed to Christopher First Viscount Hatton A.D. 1601–1704*, 2 vols. (London, 1878)

Thompson, Nathaniel, *A Collection of 86 Loyal Poems* (London, 1685)

[Tindal, Matthew], *The Defection Consider'd* ... (London, 1717)

The Judgment of Dr. Prideaux, in Condemning the Murder of Julius Caesar, by the Conspirators, as a most Villanous Act, maintain'd ... (London, 1721)

New High-Church Turn'd Old Presbyterian (London, 1709)

The Rights of the Christian Church Asserted, Against the Romish, and all other Priests who claim an Independent Power over it. With a Preface concerning the Government of the Church of England, as by Law Establish'd. Part I, 3rd edn (London, 1707)

Tint for Taunt. The Manager Managed: Or, The Exemplary Moderation and Modesty, of a Whig Low-Church-Preacher discovered, from his own Mouth ... (London, 1710)

To Robert Walpole Esq (n.p., [1717], subscribed by Wm. Thomas)

[Toland, John], *The Art of Governing by Parties* ... (London, 1701)

The Memorial of the State of England, In Vindication of the Queen, the Church, and the Administration ... (London, 1705)

The Miscellaneous Works ..., 2 vols. (London, 1747)

[Trapp, J.], *Most Faults on One Side* (London, 1710)

Trenchard, John and Thomas Gordon, *Cato's Letters*, 4 vols. (London, 1723–4)

Cato's Letters: Or, Essays on Liberty, Civil and Religious, And other important Subjects, 4 vols. (n.p., 1754)

A Collection of Tracts. By the Late John Trenchard, Esq; and Thomas Gordon, Esq. 2 vols. (London, 1751)

The Independent Whig: or, A Defence of Primitive Christianity, And of our Ecclesiastical Establishment, Against the Exorbitant Claims and Encroachments of Fanatical and Disaffected Clergymen, 6th edn, 3 vols. (London, 1735)

Undone again; or, The Plot discover'd. Being A Detection of the Practices of Papists with Sectaries, For Overthrowing the Government, and the National Church ... (London, 1710)

[Wagstaffe, Thomas], *A Letter Out of Suffolk to a Friend in London, Giving Some Account of the Last Sickness and Death of Dr. William Sancroft, Late Lord Archbishop of Canterbury* (1694), in *Somers Tracts*, IX, 527–40

The Weekly Journal, or Saturday's Post (London, 1715–25)

[Wharton, Philip Duke of], *The True Briton* (London, 1723–4)

Withers, John, *The Dutch Better Friends than the French, To the Monarchy, Church, and Trade of England* ..., 2nd edn (London, 1713)

[Woodhead, Abraham], *Two Discourses. The First, Concerning the Spirit of Martin Luther, and the Original of the Reformation. The Second, Concerning the Celibacy of the Clergy* (Oxford, 1687)

Wotton, William, *A Defense of the Reflections upon Ancient and Modern Learning, In Answer to the Objections of Sir W. Temple, and Others. With Observations upon The Tale of a Tub* (London, 1705; rpt. *Swiftiana I: On the Tale of a Tub 1704–1712*, New York, 1975)

Secondary sources

Adams, Robert M., 'In Search of Baron Somers', in *Culture and Politics from Puritanism to the Enlightenment*, ed. by Perez Zagorin (Berkeley, Los Angeles and London, 1980), pp. 165–202

'The Mood of the Church and *A Tale of a Tub*', in *England in the Restoration and Early Eighteenth Century: Essays on Culture and Society*, ed. by H. T. Swedenberg, Jr (Berkeley, Los Angeles and London, 1972), pp. 71–99

Strains of Discord: Studies in Literary Openness (Ithaca, New York, 1958)

Allen, Robert J., 'William Oldisworth: "the Author of *The Examiner*"', *Philological Quarterly*, 26 (1947), 159–80

Anderson, Perry, *Arguments within English Marxism* (London, 1980)

Babcock, Robert W., 'Swift's Conversion to the Tory Party', *University of Michigan Publications in Language and Literature (Essays and Studies in English and Comparative Literature)*, 8 (1932), 133–49

Baxter, Stephen B., 'William III as Hercules: the Political Implications of Court Culture', in *The Revolution of 1688–1689: Changing Perspectives*, ed. by Lois G. Schwoerer (Cambridge, 1992), pp. 95–106

Beckett, J. C., 'Swift as an Ecclesiastical Statesman', in *Essays in British and Irish History in Honour of James Eadie Todd*, ed. by H. A. Cronne, T. W. Moody and D. B. Quinn (London, 1949), rpt. in *Fair Liberty Was All His Cry: A Tercentenary Tribute to Jonathan Swift 1667–1745*, ed. by A. Norman Jeffares (London, 1967), pp. 146–65

Beckett, J. V., 'Introduction: Stability in Politics and Society, 1680–1750', in *Britain in the First Age of Party 1680–1750: Essays Presented to Geoffrey Holmes*, ed. by Clyve Jones (London and Ronceverte, 1987), pp. 1–18

Beddard, Robert, 'The Guildhall Declaration of 11 December 1688 and the Counter-Revolution of the Loyalists', *The Historical Journal*, 11 (1968), 403–20

'The Loyalist Opposition in the Interregnum: A Letter of Dr Francis Turner, Bishop of Ely, on the Revolution of 1688', *Bulletin of The Institute of Historical Research*, 40 (1967), 101–9

ed., *The Revolutions of 1688* (Oxford, 1991)

Bennett, G. V., 'English Jacobitism, 1710–1715; Myth and Reality', *Transactions of the Royal Historical Society*, 5th series, 32 (1982), 137–51

The Tory Crisis in Church and State 1688–1730: The Career of Francis Atterbury, Bishop of Rochester (Oxford, 1975)

Black, Jeremy, 'Archibald Hutcheson as Author', *Notes and Queries*, ns, 32 (1985), 207–8

The English Press in the Eighteenth Century (London, and Sydney, 1987)

'Trying Mist's Men: Fresh Material from the Althorp Papers', *Notes and Queries*, ns, 33 (1986), 497–8

'An Underrated Journalist: Nathaniel Mist and the Opposition Press during the Whig Ascendency', *British Journal for Eighteenth-Century Studies*, 10 (1987), 27–41

Boyce, Benjamin, *Tom Brown of Facetious Memory: Grub Street in the Age of Dryden* (Cambridge, Mass., 1939)

Boyle, Frank T., 'Ehrenpreis's *Swift* and the Date of *The Sentiments of a Church-of-England Man*', *Swift Studies*, 6 (1991), 30–7

'Profane and Debauched Deist: Swift in the Contemporary Response to *A Tale of a Tub*', *Eighteenth-Century Ireland*, 3 (1988), 25–38

Bradley, James E., *Religion, Revolution and English Radicalism: Nonconformity in Eighteenth-Century Politics and Society* (Cambridge, 1990)

Brown, William J., 'Gulliver's Passage on the Dutch *Amboyna*', *English Language Notes*, 1 (1964), 262–4

Browning, Reed, *Political and Constitutional Ideas of the Court Whigs* (Baton Rouge and London, 1982)

Bywaters, David, '*Gulliver's Travels* and the Mode of Political Parallel during Walpole's Administration', *ELH*, 54 (1987), 717–40

Capraro, Rocco Lawrence, 'Political Broadside Ballads in Early Hanoverian London', *Eighteenth-Century Life*, 11 (1987), 12–21

Carnochan, W. B., 'Swift, Locke, and the *Tale*', *Swift Studies*, 1 (1986), 55–6

Case, Arthur E., *Four Essays on 'Gulliver's Travels'* (Princeton, NJ, 1945; rpt. Gloucester, Mass., 1958)

Chambers, Karl D., 'Swift and the *Trampling* Dutch', *Christian Scholar's Review*, 3 (1973), 51–4

Champion, J. A. I., *The Pillars of Priestcraft Shaken: The Church of England and Its Enemies 1660–1730* (Cambridge, 1992)

Chapman, Paul, 'Jacobite Political Argument in England 1714–1766' (unpublished Ph.D. thesis, University of Cambridge, 1983)

Cherry, G. L., 'The Legal and Philosophical Position of the Jacobites, 1688–1689', *The Journal of Modern History*, 22 (1950), 309–21

Christie, Ian R., 'The Tory Party, Jacobitism and the 'Forty-Five: A Note', *The Historical Journal*, 30 (1987), 921–31

Clark, J. C. D., *English Society 1688–1832: Ideology, Social Structure and Political Practice during the Ancien Regime* (Cambridge, 1985)

'A General Theory of Party, Opposition and Government, 1688–1832', *The Historical Journal*, 23 (1980), 295–325

'The Politics of the Excluded: Tories, Jacobites and Whig Patriots 1715–1760', *Parliamentary History*, 2 (1983), 209–22

Revolution and Rebellion: State and Society in England in the Seventeenth and Eighteenth Centuries (Cambridge, 1986)

Clark, J. Kent, 'Swift and the Dutch', *Huntington Library Quarterly*, 17 (1954), 345–56

Clements, Frances M., 'Lansdowne, Pope and the Unity of *Windsor-Forest*', *Modern Language Quarterly*, 33 (1972), 44–53

Colley, Linda, *In Defiance of Oligarchy: The Tory Party 1714–1760* (Cambridge, 1982)

and Mark Goldie, 'The Principles and Practice of Eighteenth-Century Party', *The Historical Journal*, 22 (1979), 239–46

Cook, Richard I., *Jonathan Swift as a Tory Pamphleteer* (Seattle and London, 1967)

Coombs, Douglas, *The Conduct of the Dutch: British Opinion and the Dutch Alliance During the War of the Spanish Succession* (The Hague, 1958)

Corns, T. N., W. A. Speck and J. A. Downie, 'Archetypal Mystification: Polemic and Reality in English Political Literature, 1640–1750', *Eighteenth-Century Life*, 7 (1982), 1–27

Crider, J. R., 'Dissenting Sex: Swift's "History of Fanaticism"', *SEL: Studies in English Literature, 1500–1900*, 18 (1978), 491–508

Cruickshanks, Eveline, ed., *Ideology and Conspiracy: Aspects of Jacobitism, 1689–1759* (Edinburgh, 1982)

   'Lord Cornbury, Bolingbroke and a Plan to Restore the Stuarts 1731–1735', *Royal Stuart Papers*, 27 (1986), 1–12

   'Lord North, Christopher Layer and the Atterbury Plot: 1720–23', in *The Jacobite Challenge*, ed. by Eveline Cruickshanks and Jeremy Black (Edinburgh, 1988), pp. 92–106

   'The Political Management of Sir Robert Walpole, 1720–42', in *Britain in the Age of Walpole*, ed. by Jeremy Black (London, 1984), pp. 23–43

   Political Untouchables: The Tories and the '45 (London, 1979)

   'Religion and Royal Succession – The Rage of Party', in *Britain in the First Age of Party 1680–1750*, ed. by Clyve Jones (London and Ronceverte, 1987), pp. 19–43

   and Howard Erskine-Hill, 'The Waltham Black Act and Jacobitism', *Journal of British Studies*, 24 (1985), 358–365

   and Jeremy Black, eds., *The Jacobite Challenge* (Edinburgh, 1988)

Daw, C. P., '"A Tast of Wit": Laud, Swift, and *A Tale of a Tub*', in *Swift and His Contexts*, ed. by John Irwin Fischer, *et al.* (New York, 1989), pp. 159–74

Dickinson, H. T., *Liberty and Property: Political Ideology in Eighteenth-Century Britain* (London, 1977)

Downie, J. A., *Jonathan Swift: Political Writer* (London, 1984)

   'Political Characterization in *Gulliver's Travels*', *The Yearbook of English Studies*, 7 (1977), 108–20

   'The Political Significance of *Gulliver's Travels*', in *Swift and His Contexts*, ed. by John Irwin Fischer, *et al.* (New York, 1989), pp. 1–19

   Robert Harley and the Press: Propaganda and Public Opinion in the Age of Swift and Defoe (Cambridge, 1979)

   'Swift's Politics', in *Proceedings of The First Münster Symposium on Jonathan Swift*, ed. by Hermann J. Real and Heinz J. Vienken (Munich, 1985), pp. 47–58

   'Walpole, "the Poet's Foe"', in *Britain in the Age of Walpole*, ed. by Jeremy Black (London, 1984), pp. 171–88

Duffy, Michael, *The Englishman and the Foreigner*, The English Satirical Print 1600–1832 (Cambridge 1986)

Dussinger, John A., '"Christian" vs. "Hollander": Swift's Satire on the Dutch East India Traders', *Notes and Queries*, ns, 13 (1966), 209–12

Ehrenpreis, Irvin, 'Swift on Liberty', *Journal of the History of Ideas*, 13 (1952), 131–46

Swift: The Man, his Works, and the Age, 3 vols. (London, 1962–83)

'Swift's History of England', *Journal of English and Germanic Philology*, 51 (1952), 177–85

Eilon, Daniel, 'Did Swift Write *A Discourse on Hereditary Right*?', *Modern Philology*, 82 (1985), 374–92

Factions' Fictions: Ideological Closure in Swift's Satire (Newark, London, Toronto, 1991)

'Private Spirit: The Prosecution of Self-Interest and Faction in Swift's Satire', *History of Political Thought*, 5 (1984), 79–89

'Swift's Satiric Logic: On Parsimony, Irony, and Antinomian Fiction', *The Yearbook of English Studies*, 18 (1988), 18–40

Elias, A. C. Jr, *Swift at Moor Park: Problems in Biography and Criticism* (Philadelphia, 1982)

Ellis, Frank H., '"A Quill worn to the Pith in the Service of the State": Swift's *Examiner*', in *Proceedings of The First Münster Symposium on Jonathan Swift*, ed. by Hermann J. Real and Heinz J. Vienken (Munich, 1985), pp. 73–82

Erskine-Hill, Howard, 'Alexander Pope: The Political Poet in His Time', *Eighteenth-Century Studies*, 15 (1981–2), 123–48

The Augustan Idea in English Literature (London, 1983)

'Life into Letters, Death into Art: Pope's Epitaph on Francis Atterbury', *The Yearbook of English Studies*, 18 (1988), 200–20

'Literature and the Jacobite Cause', *Modern Language Studies*, 9 (1979), 15–28

'Literature and the Jacobite Cause: Was There a Rhetoric of Jacobitism?', in *Ideology and Conspiracy: Aspects of Jacobitism, 1689–1759*, ed. by Eveline Cruickshanks (Edinburgh, 1982), pp. 49–69

'The Political Character of Samuel Johnson', in *Samuel Johnson: New Critical Essays*, ed. by Isobel Grundy (London and Totowa, NJ, 1984), pp. 107–36

'The Political Character of Samuel Johnson: *The Lives of the Poets* and A Further Report on *The Vanity of Human Wishes*', in *The Jacobite Challenge*, ed. by Eveline Cruickshanks and Jeremy Black (Edinburgh, 1988), pp. 161–76

'The Satirical Game at Cards in Pope and Wordsworth', *The Yearbook of English Studies*, 14 (1984), 183–95

'Scholarship as Humanism', *Essays in Criticism*, 29 (1979), 33–52

The Social Milieu of Alexander Pope (New Haven and London, 1975)

'Under Which Caesar? Pope in the Journal of Mrs Charles Caesar 1724–1741', *Review of English Studies*, 33 (1982), 436–44

Every, George, *The High Church Party, 1688–1718* (London, 1956)

Fabricant, Carole, *Swift's Landscape* (Baltimore and London, 1982)

Feiling, Keith, *A History of the Tory Party 1640–1714* (Oxford, 1924)

Ferguson, James, *Robert Ferguson the Plotter* (Edinburgh, 1887)

Ferguson, Oliver W., *Jonathan Swift and Ireland* (Urbana, 1962)

Fink, Z. S., 'Political Theory in *Gulliver's Travels*', *ELH*, 14 (1947), 151–61

Firth, Charles, *Essays Historical & Literary* (Oxford, 1938)

Fischer, John Irwin, 'The Government's Response to Swift's *An Epistle to a Lady*', *Philological Quarterly*, 65 (1986), 39–59

'Review of *Jonathan Swift: Political Writer*. By J. A. Downie' (London, 1984), *Scriblerian*, 17 (1985), 170–3

et al., eds., *Swift and His Contexts* (New York, 1989)

Fitzgerald, Robert P., 'Science and Politics in Swift's Voyage to Laputa', *Journal of English and Germanic Philology*, 87 (1988), 213–29

Foot, Michael, *The Pen and the Sword* (London, 1957)

Frank, Bruce, '"The Excellent Rehearser": Charles Leslie and the Tory Party, 1688–1714', in *Biography in the 18th Century*, ed. by J. D. Browning (New York and London, 1980), pp. 43–68

French, David P., 'Swift, the Non-Jurors, and Jacobitism', *Modern Language Notes*, 72 (1957), 258–64

Fritz, Paul S., *The English Ministers and Jacobitism between the Rebellions of 1715 and 1745* (Toronto and Buffalo, 1975)

Fritze, Ronald H., 'Root or Link? Luther's Position in the Historical Debate over the Legitimacy of the Church of England, 1558–1625', *Journal of Ecclesiastical History*, 37 (1986), 288–302

Gallagher, F. P., 'The Polemical Writings of Jonathan Swift' (unpublished Ph.D. dissertation, University of Wisconsin, 1968)

Gardiner, Anne Barbeau, 'Swift on the Dutch East India Merchants: The Context of 1672–73 War Literature', *Huntington Library Quarterly*, 54 (1991), 235–52

Garrett, Jane, *The Triumphs of Providence: The Assassination Plot, 1696* (Cambridge, 1980)

Gascoigne, John, *Cambridge in the Age of the Enlightenment: Science, Religion and Politics from the Restoration to the French Revolution* (Cambridge, 1989)

Geduld, Harry M., *Prince of Publishers: A Study of the Work and Career of Jacob Tonson* (Bloomington and London, 1969)

Gillespie, Stuart, 'The Early Years of the Dryden–Tonson Partnership: The Background to their Composite Translations and Miscellanies of the 1680s', *Restoration*, 12 (1988), 10–19

Goldgar, Bertrand A., *The Curse of Party: Swift's Relations with Addison and Steele* (Lincoln, Nebraska, 1961)

'*Gulliver's Travels* and the Opposition to Walpole' in *The Augustan Milieu: Essays Presented to Louis A. Landa*, ed. by Henry Knight Miller *et al.* (Oxford, 1970), pp. 155–73

Walpole and the Wits: The Relation of Politics to Literature, 1722–1742 (Lincoln, Nebraska, 1976)

Goldie, Mark, 'Danby, the Bishops and the Whigs', in *The Politics of Religion in Restoration England*, ed. by Tim Harris *et al.* (Oxford, 1990), pp. 75–105

'Edmund Bohun and *Jus Gentium* in the Revolution Debate, 1689–1693', *The Historical Journal*, 20 (1977), 569–86

'Historiographical Review: Obligations, Utopias, and their Historical Context', *The Historical Journal*, 26 (1983), 727–46

'The Huguenot Experience and the Problem of Toleration in Restoration England', in *The Huguenots and Ireland: Anatomy of an Emigration*, ed. by C. E. J. Caldicott, H. Gough, J.-P. Pittion (Dublin, 1987), pp. 175–203

'John Locke and Anglican Royalism', *Political Studies*, 31 (1983), 61–85

'John Locke's Circle and James II', *The Historical Journal*, 35 (1992), 557–86

'The Nonjurors, Episcopacy, and the Origins of the Convocation Controversy', in *Ideology and Conspiracy: Aspects of Jacobitism, 1689–1959*, ed. by Eveline Cruickshanks (Edinburgh, 1982), pp. 15–35

'The Political Thought of the Anglican Revolution', in *The Revolutions of 1688*, ed. by Robert Beddard (Oxford, 1991), pp. 102–36

'Review of *Subjects and Sovereigns: the Grand Controversy over Legal Sovereignty in Stuart England. By C. C. Weston and J. R. Greenberg*', *The Historical Journal*, 26 (1983), 1029–30

'The Revolution of 1689 and the Structure of Political Argument: An Essay and an Annotated Bibliography of Pamphlets on the Allegiance Controversy', *Bulletin of Research in the Humanities*, 83 (1980), 473–564

'The Roots of True Whiggism 1688–94', *History of Political Thought*, 1 (1980), 195–236

'Sir Peter Pett, Sceptical Toryism and the Science of Toleration in the 1680s', in *Persecution and Toleration*, ed. by W. J. Sheils, Studies in Church History, vol. XXI (Oxford, 1984), pp. 247–73

'The Theory of Religious Intolerance in Restoration England', in *From Persecution to Toleration: The Glorious Revolution and Religion in England*, ed. by Ole Peter Grell *et al.* (Oxford, 1991), pp. 330–68

'Tory Political Thought 1689–1714' (unpublished Ph.D. dissertation, University of Cambridge, 1977)

Goulden, R. J., '*Vox Populi, Vox Dei*: Charles Delafaye's Paperchase', *The Book Collector*, 28 (1979), 368–90

Greene, Donald, 'Review of *The Curse of Party: Swift's Relations with Addison and Steele. By Bertrand A. Goldgar* (Lincoln, Nebraska, 1961)', *Philological Quarterly*, 41 (1962), 629–30

'Swift: Some Caveats', in *Studies in the Eighteenth Century II: Papers Presented at the Second David Nichol Smith Memorial Seminar 1970*, ed. by R. F. Brissenden (Canberra, 1973), pp. 341–58

Greenwood, David, *William King: Tory and Jacobite* (Oxford, 1969)

Gregg, Edward, 'The Jacobite Career of John, Earl of Mar', in *Ideology and Conspiracy: Aspects of Jacobitism, 1689–1759*, ed. by Eveline Cruickshanks (Edinburgh, 1982), pp. 179–200

Guskin, Phyllis, J., '"A very remarkable Book": Abel Boyer's View of *Gulliver's Travels*', *Studies in Philology*, 72 (1975), 439–53

Haakonssen, Knud, 'Hugo Grotius and the History of Political Thought', *Political Theory*, 13 (1985), 239–65

Haley, K. H. D., *The British and the Dutch: Political and Cultural Relations through the Ages* (London, 1988)

Hall, Basil, '"An Inverted Hypocrite": Swift the Churchman', in *The World of Jonathan Swift: Essays for the Tercentenary*, ed. by Brian Vickers (Oxford, 1968), pp. 38–68

Hammond, Brean, *Gulliver's Travels*, Open Guides to Literature (Milton Keynes and Philadelphia, 1988)

Handasyde, Elizabeth, *Granville the Polite: The Life of George Granville Lord Lansdowne, 1666–1735* (Oxford, 1933)

Hanson, Laurence, *Government and the Press, 1695–1763* (London, 1936)

Harris, Michael, *London Newspapers in the Age of Walpole: A Study of the Origins of the Modern English Press* (London, and Toronto, 1987)

Harth, Phillip, 'The Problem of Political Allegory in *Gulliver's Travels*', *Modern Philology*, 73 (1976), S40–S47

Swift and Anglican Rationalism: The Religious Background of 'A Tale of a Tub' (Chicago and London, 1961)

Hatton, Ragnhild, *George I: Elector and King* (London, 1978)

Hayton, David, 'The Beginnings of the "Undertaker System"', in *Penal Era and Golden Age: Essays in Irish History, 1690–1800*, ed. by Thomas Bartlett and D. W. Hayton (Belfast, 1979), pp. 32–54

'The "Country" Interest and the Party System, 1689–c. 1720', in *Party and Management in Parliament, 1660–1784*, ed. by Clyve Jones (Leicester, 1984), pp. 37–85

'Walpole and Ireland' in *Britain in the Age of Walpole*, ed. by Jeremy Black (London, 1984), pp. 95–119

'The Williamite Revolution in Ireland, 1688–91' in *The Anglo-Dutch Moment: Essays on the Glorious Revolution and Its World Impact*, ed. by Jonathan I. Israel (Cambridge, 1991), pp. 185–213

Higgins, Ian, 'Possible "Hints" for *Gulliver's Travels* in the *Voyages* of Jan Huygen Van Linschoten', *Notes and Queries*, ns, 33 (1986), 47–50

'The Sentiments of a Church-of-England Man: A Study of Swift's Politics' (unpublished Ph.D. thesis, University of Warwick, 1989)

'Swift and Sparta: The Nostalgia of *Gulliver's Travels*', *Modern Language Review*, 78 (1983), 513–31

'Swift's Politics: A Preface to *Gulliver's Travels*', *Monash Swift Papers* Number One, ed. by Clive T. Probyn and Bryan Coleborne (Monash University, 1988), pp. 41–65

Hill, Brian, *The Growth of Parliamentary Parties, 1689–1742* (London, 1976)

Hill, Christopher, *Collected Essays. Volume One: Writing and Revolution in 17th Century England* (Brighton, 1985)

Holden, William P., *Anti-Puritan Satire 1572–1642* (New Haven, 1954; rpt. Archon Books, 1968)

Holmes, Geoffrey, *British Politics in the Age of Anne*, rev. edn (London and Ronceverte, 1987)

Religion and Party in Late Stuart England (London, 1975)

Holzknecht, G. K., 'Swift and the Text of *A Tale of a Tub*', *English Studies*, 54 (1973), 470–8

Horsley, Lee Sonsteng, 'Paper Wars in the Reign of Queen Anne: A Study of Political Journalism' (unpublished Ph.D. dissertation, University of Birmingham, 1970)

Horwitz, Henry, *Parliament, Policy and Politics in the Reign of William III* (Manchester, 1977)

Hyland, P. B. J., 'Liberty and Libel: Government and the Press during the Succession Crisis in Britain, 1712–1716', *English Historical Review*, 101 (1986), 863–88

Israel, Jonathan I., ed., *The Anglo-Dutch Moment: Essays on the Glorious Revolution and Its World Impact* (Cambridge, 1991)

Jacob, James R., *Henry Stubbe, Radical Protestantism and the Early Enlightenment* (Cambridge, 1983)

Jones, George Hilton, *The Main Stream of Jacobitism* (Cambridge, Mass., 1954)

Jones, J. R., *The First Whigs: The Politics of the Exclusion Crisis 1678–1683*, rev. edn (London, 1970)

'James II's Revolution: Royal Policies, 1686–92', in *The Anglo-Dutch Moment: Essays on the Glorious Revolution and Its World Impact*, ed. by Jonathan I. Israel (Cambridge, 1991), pp. 47–71

'James II's Whig Collaborators', *The Historical Journal*, 3 (1960), 65–73

The Revolution of 1688 in England (London, 1972)

Jones, Myrddin, '*Further Thoughts on Religion*: Swift's Relationship to Filmer and Locke', *Review of English Studies*, 9 (1958), 284–6

Kelly, Patrick, 'Ireland and the Glorious Revolution: From Kingdom to Colony', in *The Revolutions of 1688*, ed. by Robert Beddard (Oxford, 1991), pp. 163–90

'William Molyneux and the Spirit of Liberty in Eighteenth-Century Ireland', *Eighteenth-Century Ireland*, 3 (1988), 133–48

Kennedy, R. F., 'Swift and Suetonius', *Notes and Queries*, ns 16 (1969), 340–1

Kenyon, J. P., 'The Revolution of 1688: Resistance and Contract', in *Historical Perspectives*, ed. by Neil McKendrick (London, 1974), pp. 43–69

Revolution Principles: The Politics of Party 1689–1720 (Cambridge, 1977)

Kitchin, George, *Sir Roger L'Estrange* (London, 1913)

Klein, Lawrence, 'The Third Earl of Shaftesbury and the Progress of Politeness', *Eighteenth-Century Studies*, 18 (1984–5), 186–214

Korshin, Paul J., 'Deciphering Swift's Codes', in *Proceedings of The First Münster Symposium on Jonathan Swift*, ed. by Hermann J. Real and Heinz J. Vienken (Munich, 1985), pp. 123–34

Kramnick, Isaac, *Bolingbroke and His Circle: The Politics of Nostalgia in the Age of Walpole* (Cambridge, Mass., 1968)

Kropf, C. R., 'Libel and Satire in the Eighteenth Century', *Eighteenth-Century Studies*, 8 (1974–5), 153–68

Lacey, Douglas R., *Dissent and Parliamentary Politics in England, 1661–1689* (New Brunswick, NJ, 1969)

Landa, Louis A., *Swift and the Church of Ireland* (Oxford, 1954 (1965))

Langford, Paul, *The Excise Crisis: Society and Politics in the Age of Walpole* (Oxford, 1975)

LeFanu, William, *A Catalogue of Books belonging to Dr Jonathan Swift Dean of St Patrick's, Dublin Aug. 19. 1715: A Facsimile of Swift's Autograph with an Introduction and Alphabetic Catalogue*, Cambridge Bibliographical Society Monograph no. 10 (Cambridge, 1988)

Lenman, Bruce, 'The Jacobite Diaspora 1688–1746: From Despair to Integration', *History Today*, 30 (1980), 7–10

   The Jacobite Risings in Britain 1689–1746 (London, 1980)

   'Physicians and Politics in the Jacobite Era', in *The Jacobite Challenge*, ed. by Eveline Cruickshanks and Jeremy Black (Edinburgh, 1988), pp. 74–91

   'The Scottish Episcopal Clergy and the Ideology of Jacobitism', in *Ideology and Conspiracy: Aspects of Jacobitism, 1689–1759*, ed. by Eveline Cruickshanks (Edinburgh, 1982), pp. 36–48

Leslie, Rev. R. J., *Life and Writings of Charles Leslie, M.A. Nonjuring Divine* (London, 1884)

Lewis, Peter and Nigel Wood, eds., *John Gay and the Scriblerians*, Critical Studies Series (London and New York, 1988)

Leyburn, Ellen Douglass, 'Swift's View of the Dutch', *PMLA*, 66 (1951), 734–45

Lock, F. P., 'Gulliver's Politics Revisited', Paper read at Queen's University, Canada, 3 February 1987

   The Politics of 'Gulliver's Travels' (Oxford, 1980)

   'Swift and English Politics, 1701–14', in *The Character of Swift's Satire: A Revised Focus*, ed. by Claude Rawson (Newark, Delaware, London and Toronto, 1983), pp. 127–50

   Swift's Tory Politics (London, 1983)

   'The Text of "Gulliver's Travels"', *Modern Language Review*, 76 (1981), 513–33

Lund, Roger D., 'Strange Complicities: Atheism and Conspiracy in *A Tale of a Tub*', *Eighteenth-Century Life*, 13 (1989), 34–58

Lynch, Kathleen M., *Jacob Tonson, Kit-Cat Publisher* (Knoxville, 1971)

McCarthy, Muriel, 'Swift and the Foundation of the First Public Library in Ireland', *Swift Studies*, 4 (1989), 29–33

Maccubbin, Robert P. and Martha Hamilton-Phillips, eds., *The Age of William III & Mary II: Power, Politics, and Patronage 1688–1702: A Reference Encyclopedia and Exhibition Catalogue* (Williamsburg, 1989)

Mack, Maynard, *Alexander Pope, A Life* (New Haven and London, 1985)

   The Garden and the City: Retirement and Politics in the Later Poetry of Pope 1731–1743 (Toronto, 1969)

McLynn, F. J., 'The Ideology of Jacobitism on the Eve of the Rising of 1745 – Part I', *History of European Ideas*, 6, no. 1 (1985), 1–18

   'The Ideology of Jacobitism – Part II', *History of European Ideas*, 6, no. 2 (1985), 173–88

The Jacobites (London, 1985)

McMahon, Marie P., *The Radical Whigs, John Trenchard and Thomas Gordon: Libertarian Loyalists to the New House of Hanover* (Lanham, New York, London, 1990)

McMinn, Joseph, 'A Weary Patriot: Swift and the Formation of an Anglo-Irish Identity', *Eighteenth-Century Ireland*, 2 (1987), 103–13

Manley, Francis, 'Swift Marginalia in Howell's *Medulla Historiae Anglicanae*', *PMLA*, 73 (1958), 335–8

Maxted, Ian, *The London Book Trades 1775–1800: A Preliminary Checklist of Members* (Old Woking, Surrey, 1977)

Maxwell, J. C., 'The Text of "A Tale of a Tub"', *English Studies*, 36 (1955), 64–6

Maybee, John Ryerson, 'Anglicans and Nonconformists 1679–1704: A Study in the Background of Swift's *A Tale of a Tub*' (unpublished Ph. D. dissertation, Princeton University, 1942)

Mayhew, George P., 'Swift's Political "Conversion" and his "Lost" Ballad on the Westminster Election of 1710', *Bulletin of The John Rylands Library*, 53 (1971), 397–427

Metscher, Thomas, 'The Radicalism of Swift: *Gulliver's Travels* and the Irish Point of View', in *Studies in Anglo-Irish Literature*, ed. by Heinz Kosok (Bonn, 1982), pp. 13–22

Mezciems, Jenny, 'Swift and Orwell: Utopia as Nightmare', *Dutch Quarterly Review of Anglo-American Letters*, 15 (1985), 189–210

'The Unity of Swift's "Voyage to Laputa": Structure as Meaning in Utopian Fiction', *Modern Language Review*, 72 (1977), 1–21

'Utopia and "the Thing which is not": More, Swift, and Other Lying Idealists', *University of Toronto Quarterly*, 52 (1982), 40–62

Miller, John, *James II: A Study in Kingship* (Hove, 1978)

Popery and Politics in England, 1660–88 (Cambridge, 1973)

'Proto-Jacobitism? The Tories and the Revolution of 1688–89' in *The Jacobite Challenge*, ed. by Eveline Cruickshanks and Jeremy Black (Edinburgh, 1988), pp. 7–23

Religion in the Popular Prints 1600–1832, The English Satirical Print 1600–1832 (Cambridge, 1986)

Monod, Paul Kléber, 'For The King To Enjoy His Own Again: Jacobite Political Culture in England, 1688–1788', 2 vols. (unpublished Ph. D. dissertation, Yale University, 1985; reproduced University Microfilms International, 1986)

'Jacobitism and Country Principles in the Reign of William III', *The Historical Journal*, 30 (1987), 289–310

Jacobitism and the English People, 1688–1788 (Cambridge, 1989)

Moody, T. W. and W. E. Vaughan, eds., *A New History of Ireland, IV: Eighteenth-Century Ireland 1691–1800* (Oxford, 1986)

Moore, John Robert, 'Was Jonathan Swift a Moderate?', *South Atlantic Quarterly*, 53 (1954), 260–7

Morton, A. L., *The English Utopia* (London, 1952)

Mullett, Michael, 'Luther: Conservative or Revolutionary? Was Martin Luther the Author of a "Moderate Reformation"? Or Was His Progeny to Prove a "Radical Reformation"?', *History Today*, 33 (December, 1983), 39–44

Napier, Elizabeth R., 'Swift, Kaempfer, and Psalmanaazaar: Further Remarks on "Trampling Upon The Crucifix"', *Notes and Queries*, ns, 28 (1981), 226

'Swift's "Trampling Upon The Crucifix": A Parallel', *Notes and Queries*, ns, 26 (1979), 544–8

Needham, Gwendolyn B., 'Mary de la Rivière Manley, Tory Defender', *Huntington Library Quarterly*, 12 (1949), 253–88

Newton, Theodore F. M., 'William Pittis and Queen Anne Journalism', *Modern Philology*, 21 (1935–6), 169–86; 279–302

Nokes, David, *Jonathan Swift, A Hypocrite Reversed: A Critical Biography* (Oxford, 1985)

'Lisping in Political Numbers', *Notes and Queries*, ns, 24 (1977), 228–9

'The Radical Conservatism of Swift's Irish Pamphlets', *British Journal for Eighteenth-Century Studies*, 7 (1984), 169–76

Novak, Maximillian E., 'Swift and Defoe: Or, How Contempt Breeds Familiarity and a Degree of Influence', in *Proceedings of The First Münster Symposium on Jonathan Swift*, ed. by Hermann J. Real and Heinz J. Vienken (Munich, 1985), pp. 157–73

Ormsby-Lennon, Hugh, 'Swift and the Quakers (I)', *Swift Studies*, 4 (1989), 34–62

'Swift and the Quakers (II)', *Swift Studies*, 5 (1990), 53–89

Orwell, George, 'Politics *vs.* Literature: An Examination of *Gulliver's Travels*', in *The Collected Essays, Journalism and Letters*, volume IV, ed. by Sonia Orwell and Ian Angus (London, 1968), pp. 205–23

Parlato, Paul C., 'Vesture in Anglican Tradition: A Frame of Reference for Swift's *Tale of a Tub*' (unpublished Ph. D. dissertation, University of Notre Dame, 1971)

Passmann, Dirk Friedrich, *'Full of Improbable Lies': 'Gulliver's Travels' und die Reiseliteratur vor 1726* (Frankfurt on Main, Berne, New York and Paris, 1987)

Paulson, Ronald, *Theme and Structure in Swift's 'Tale of a Tub'* (New Haven, 1960)

Perry, Ruth, *The Celebrated Mary Astell: An Early English Feminist* (Chicago and London, 1986)

Philmus, Robert M., 'Swift's "Lost" Answer to Tindal', *Texas Studies in Literature and Language*, 22 (1980), 369–93

Pocock, J. G. A., *The Machiavellian Moment: Florentine Political Thought and the Atlantic Republican Tradition* (Princeton, NJ, 1975)

'*The Machiavellian Moment* Revisited: A Study in History and Ideology', *Journal of Modern History*, 53 (1981), 49–72

'Radical Criticisms of the Whig Order in the Age between Revolutions', in

The Origins of Anglo-American Radicalism, ed. by Margaret Jacob and James Jacob (London, 1984), pp. 33–57

Preu, James A., *The Dean and the Anarchist* (Tallahassee, 1959)

Price, Martin, 'Pope, Swift and the Past', in *Studies in the Eighteenth Century 5: Papers Presented at the Fifth David Nichol Smith Memorial Seminar Canberra 1980*, ed. by J. P. Hardy and J. C. Eade (Oxford, 1983), pp. 19–31

Swift's Rhetorical Art: A Study in Structure and Meaning (New Haven, 1953)

Probyn, Clive T., ' "Haranguing upon Texts": Swift and the Idea of the Book', in *Proceedings of The First Münster Symposium on Jonathan Swift*, ed. by Hermann J. Real and Heinz J. Vienken (Munich, 1985), pp. 187–97

Quintana, Ricardo, *Swift: An Introduction* (London, 1955; rpt. Oxford Paperbacks 1962)

Two Augustans: John Locke, Jonathan Swift (Madison, 1978)

Rawson, C. J., 'Cannibalism and Fiction: Reflections on Narrative Form and "Extreme" Situations, Part I', *Genre*, 10 (1977), 667–711

'Cannibalism and Fiction Part II: Love and Eating in Fielding, Mailer, Genet and Wittig', *Genre*, 11 (1978), 227–313

ed., *The Character of Swift's Satire: A Revised Focus* (Newark, London and Toronto, 1983)

'The Character of Swift's Satire: Reflections on Swift, Johnson, and Human Restlessness', in *The Character of Swift's Satire: A Revised Focus*, ed. by Claude Rawson (Newark, London and Toronto, 1983), pp. 21–82

ed., *Focus: Swift* (London, 1971)

Gulliver and the Gentle Reader: Studies in Swift and Our Time (London and Boston, 1973)

Henry Fielding and the Augustan Ideal under Stress: 'Nature's Dance of Death' and Other Studies (London and Boston, 1972)

' "I the Lofty Stile Decline": Self-Apology and the "Heroick Strain" in Some of Swift's Poems', in *The English Hero, 1660–1800*, ed. by Robert Folkenflik (Newark, Delaware, London and Toronto, 1982), pp. 79–115

'The Injured Lady and the Drapier: A Reading of Swift's Irish Tracts', *Prose Studies*, 3 (1980), 15–43

'Narrative and the Proscribed Act: Homer, Euripides and the Literature of Cannibalism', in *Literary Theory and Criticism. Festschrift in Honor of René Wellek*, ed. by Joseph P. Strelka, 2 parts (Berne, Frankfurt-on-Main and New York, 1984), Part II, pp. 1159–87

Order from Confusion Sprung: Studies in Eighteenth-Century Literature from Swift to Cowper (London, 1985)

Real, Hermann J. and Heinz J. Vienken, 'A Catalogue of an Exhibition of Imprints from Swift's Library', in *Proceedings of The First Münster Symposium on Jonathan Swift*, ed. by Hermann J. Real and Heinz J. Vienken (Munich, 1985), pp. 351–88

' "A Pretty Mixture": Books from Swift's Library at Abbotsford House', *Bulletin of The John Rylands University Library*, 67 (1984), 522–43

eds., *Proceedings of The First Münster Symposium on Jonathan Swift* (Munich, 1985)

'Swift's "Trampling upon the Crucifix" Once More', *Notes and Queries*, ns, 30 (1983), 513–14

Reilly, Patrick, *Jonathan Swift: The Brave Desponder* (Manchester, 1982)

Rivington, Charles A., *'TYRANT': The Story of John Barber 1675 to 1741 Jacobite Lord Mayor of London and Printer and Friend to Dr. Swift* (York, 1989)

Robbins, Caroline, *The Eighteenth-Century Commonwealthman* (Cambridge, Mass., 1961)

Robinson, Alan, 'Swift and Renaissance Poetry: A Declaration of Independence', *British Journal for Eighteenth-Century Studies*, 8 (1985), 37–49

Rogers, Pat, 'The Dunce Answers Back: John Oldmixon on Swift and Defoe', *Texas Studies in Literature and Language*, 14 (1972), 33–43

'Gay and the World of Opera', in *John Gay and the Scriblerians*, ed. by Peter Lewis and Nigel Wood (London and New York, 1989), pp. 147–62

Grub Street: Studies in a Subculture (London, 1972)

'Gulliver and the Engineers', *Modern Language Review*, 70 (1975), 260–70

Literature and Popular Culture in Eighteenth Century England (Brighton, 1985)

'The Pamphleteers on Swift, 1710–1716: A Preliminary Checklist', *Analytical and Enumerative Bibliography*, 7 (1983), 16–30

'Plunging in the Southern Waves: Swift's Poem on the Bubble', *The Yearbook of English Studies*, 18 (1988), 41–50

'Swift and the Idea of Authority', in *The World of Jonathan Swift: Essays for the Tercentenary*, ed. by Brian Vickers (Oxford, 1968), pp. 25–37

Roscelli, William John, '*A Tale of a Tub* and the "Cavils of the Sour"', *Journal of English and Germanic Philology*, 64 (1965), 41–56

Rosenheim, Edward, Jr, 'Swift and the Atterbury Case', in *The Augustan Milieu: Essays Presented to Louis A. Landa*, ed. by Henry Knight Miller *et al.* (Oxford, 1970), pp. 174–204

'Swift and the Martyred Monarch', *Philological Quarterly*, 54 (1975), 178–94

'Swift's *Ode to Sancroft*: Another Look', *Modern Philology*, 73 (1976), S24–S39

Rumbold, Valerie, 'The Jacobite Vision of Mary Caesar', in *Women, Writing, History 1640–1740*, ed. by Isobel Grundy and Susan Wiseman (London, 1992), pp. 178–98

Sachse, William L., *Lord Somers: A Political Portrait* (Manchester, 1975)

Said, Edward W., 'Swift's Tory Anarchy', *Eighteenth-Century Studies*, 3 (1969), 48–66

The World, the Text, and the Critic (Cambridge, Mass., 1983)

Sawyer, Paul, 'Swift, Mist, and a Lincoln's Inn Fields Benefit', *Notes and Queries*, ns, 24 (1977), 225–8

Schmidt, Johann N., '*The Drapier's Letters*', *Englisch Amerikanische Studien*, 1 (1988), 29–49

Schonhorn, Manuel, 'Defoe and James Shepheard's Assassination Plot of 1718: Two New Pamphlets', *SEL: Studies in English Literature, 1500–1900*, 29 (1989), 447–62

Schwoerer, Lois G., *The Declaration of Rights, 1689* (Baltimore and London, 1981)

'Propaganda in the Revolution of 1688–89', *American Historical Review*, 82 (1977), 843–74

Sedgwick, Romney, ed., *The History of Parliament, The House of Commons 1715–54*, 2 vols. (London, 1970)

Sheehan, David, 'Swift on High Pindaric Stilts', in *Contemporary Studies of Swift's Poetry*, ed. by John Irwin Fischer and Donald C. Mell, Jr, with David M. Vieth (Newark, London and Toronto, 1981), pp. 25–35

Simms, J. G., *War and Politics in Ireland 1649–1730*, ed. by D. W. Hayton and Gerard O'Brien (London and Ronceverte, 1986)

William Molyneux of Dublin, ed. by P. H. Kelly (Blackrock, County Dublin, 1982)

Skinner, Quentin, *The Foundations of Modern Political Thought: Volume Two: The Age of Reformation* (Cambridge, 1978)

'The Principles and Practice of Opposition: The Case of Bolingbroke versus Walpole', in *Historical Perspectives*, ed. by Neil McKendrick (London, 1974), pp. 93–128

Sledd, James and Gwin Kolb, 'Johnson's Definitions of Whig and Tory', *PMLA*, 67 (1952), 882–5

Slusser, M., 'Abraham Woodhead (1608–78): Some Research Notes, Chiefly About His Writings', *Recusant History*, 15 (1979–81), 406–22

Smith, Lawrence Bartlam, *Spain and Britain 1715–19: The Jacobite Issue* (New York and London, 1987)

Snyder, Henry L., 'The Contributions of Abel Boyer as Whig Journalist and Writer of the *Protestant Post-Boy*, 1711–1712', in *The Dress of Words: Essays on Restoration and Eighteenth Century Literature in Honor of Richmond P. Bond*, ed. by Robert B. White, Jr (Lawrence, Kansas, 1978), pp. 139–49

'Newsletters in England, 1689–1715, With Special References to John Dyer – A Byway in the History of England', in *Newsletters to Newspapers: Eighteenth-Century Journalism*, ed. by Donovan H. Bond and W. Reynolds McLeod (West Virginia University, 1977), pp. 3–19

Speck, W. A., '*The Examiner* Examined: Swift's Tory Pamphleteering', in *Focus: Swift*, ed. by C. J. Rawson (London, 1971), pp. 138–54

'From Principles to Practice: Swift and Party Politics', in *The World of Jonathan Swift: Essays for the Tercentenary*, ed. by Brian Vickers (Oxford, 1968), pp. 69–86

'Polemical Purposes', *The Times Higher Education Supplement*, 7 November 1986, 16

Reluctant Revolutionaries: Englishmen and the Revolution of 1688 (Oxford, 1988)

Society and Literature in England 1700–60 (Dublin and Atlantic Highlands, NJ, 1983)

'Swift and the Historian', in *Proceedings of The First Münster Symposium on Jonathan Swift*, ed. by Hermann J. Real and Heinz J. Vienken (Munich, 1985), pp. 257–68

Spurr, John, 'Schism and the Restoration Church', *Journal of Ecclesiastical History*, 41 (1990), 408–24

Steele, Margaret, 'Anti-Jacobite Pamphleteering, 1701–1720', *The Scottish Historical Review*, 60 (1981), 140–55

Stephens, F. G. and M. D. George, eds., *Catalogue of Political and Personal Satires Preserved in the Department of Prints and Drawings in the British Museum*, 11 vols. (London, 1870–1954)

Stout, Gardner D., Jr, 'Satire and Self-Expression in Swift's *Tale of a Tub*', in *Studies in the Eighteenth Century II. Papers Presented at the Second David Nichol Smith Memorial Seminar Canberra 1970*, ed. by R. F. Brissenden (Canberra, 1973), pp. 323–39

Szechi D., *Jacobitism and Tory Politics 1710–14* (Edinburgh, 1984)

'The Jacobite Theatre of Death' in *The Jacobite Challenge*, ed. by Eveline Cruickshanks and Jeremy Black (Edinburgh, 1988), pp. 57–73

'The Politics of "Persecution": Scots Episcopalian Toleration and the Harley Ministry, 1710–12', in *Persecution and Toleration*, ed. by W. J. Sheils, Studies in Church History, vol. XXI (Oxford, 1984), pp. 275–87

and David Hayton, 'John Bull's Other Kingdoms: The English Government of Scotland and Ireland', in *Britain in the First Age of Party 1680–1750*, ed. by Clyve Jones (London and Ronceverte, 1987), pp. 241–80

Taylor, Stephen, 'Sir Robert Walpole, The Church of England and The Quakers Tithe Bill of 1736', *The Historical Journal*, 28 (1985), 51–77

Teerink, H. and Arthur H. Scouten, *A Bibliography of the Writings of Jonathan Swift*, 2nd edn (Philadelphia, 1963)

Thomas, Donald, 'Press Prosecutions of the Eighteenth and Nineteenth Centuries: The Evidence of King's Bench Indictments', *The Library*, 5th series, 32 (1977), 315–32

Thomas, Peter D. G., 'Party Politics in Eighteenth-Century Britain: Some Myths and a Touch of Reality', *British Journal for Eighteenth-Century Studies*, 10 (1987), 201–10

'Sir Roger Newdigate's Essays on Party, c. 1760', *The English Historical Review*, 102 (1987), 394–400

Thompson, E. P., *The Poverty of Theory and Other Essays* (London, 1978)

Whigs and Hunters. The Origin of the Black Act (London, 1975)

Townend, G. M., 'Religious Radicalism and Conservatism in the Whig Party under George I: The Repeal of the Occasional Conformity and Schism Acts', *Parliamentary History*, 7 (1988), 24–44

Traugott, John, 'A Tale of a Tub', in *The Character of Swift's Satire: A Revised Focus*, ed. by Claude Rawson (Newark, Delaware, London and Toronto, 1983), pp. 83–126

Treadwell, Michael, 'Benjamin Motte, Andrew Tooke, and *Gulliver's Travels*', in *Proceedings of The First Münster Symposium on Jonathan Swift*, ed. by Hermann J. Real and Heinz J. Vienken (Munich, 1985), pp. 287–304

'London Trade Publishers 1675–1750', *The Library*, 6th series, 4 (1982), 99–134

'Swift and *A Short History of the Kings of England*', in *Swift and His Contexts*, ed. by John Irwin Fischer *et al.* (New York, 1989), pp. 175–87

'Swift's Relations with the London Book Trade to 1714', in *Author/Publisher Relations during the Eighteenth and Nineteenth Centuries*, ed. by Robin Myers and Michael Harris (Oxford, 1983), pp. 1–36

Troyer, Howard William, *Ned Ward of Grub Street: A Study of Sub-Literary London in the Eighteenth Century* (1946; London, 1968)

Tuck, Richard, *Natural Rights Theories. Their Origin and Development* (Cambridge, 1979)

Varey, Simon, 'Exemplary History and the Political Satire of *Gulliver's Travels*' in *The Genres of 'Gulliver's Travels'*, ed. by Frederik N. Smith (Newark, London and Toronto, 1990), pp. 39–55

Vienken, Heinz J. and Hermann J. Real, '"Ex Libris" J. S.: Annotating Swift', in *Proceedings of The First Münster Symposium on Jonathan Swift*, ed. by Hermann J. Real and Heinz J. Vienken (Munich, 1985), pp. 305–19

Vivanti, Corrado, 'Henry IV, The Gallic Hercules', *Journal of the Warburg and Courtauld Institutes*, 30 (1967), 176–97

Wallis, Norman Richard, 'The Political Context of Jonathan Swift's Tracts on Church and State: 1707–1709' (unpublished Ph. D. dissertation, University of Chicago, 1974)

Walsh, Marcus, 'Text, "Text", and Swift's *A Tale of a Tub*', *Modern Language Review*, 85 (1990), 290–303

Ward, Addison, 'The Tory View of Roman History', *SEL: Studies in English Literature, 1500–1900*, 4 (1964), 413–56

Webster, C. M., 'The Puritans Ears in *A Tale of a Tub*', *Modern Language Notes*, 47 (1932), 96–7

'The Satiric Background of the Attack on the Puritans in Swift's *A Tale of a Tub*', *PMLA*, 50 (1935), 210–23

'Swift and Some Earlier Satirists of Puritan Enthusiasm', *PMLA*, 48 (1933), 1141–53

'Swift's *Tale of a Tub* Compared with Earlier Satires of the Puritans', *PMLA*, 47 (1932), 171–8

Weinbrot, Howard D., *Augustus Caesar in 'Augustan' England: The Decline of a Classical Norm* (Princeton, NJ, 1978)

Western, J. R., *Monarchy and Revolution* (London, 1972)

Wilding, Michael, 'The Politics of *Gulliver's Travels*', in *Studies in the Eighteenth Century II: Papers Presented at the Second David Nichol Smith Memorial Seminar Canberra 1970*, ed. by R. F. Brissenden (Canberra, 1973), pp. 303–22

Williams, G. H., *The Radical Reformation* (London, 1962)

Williams, Harold, *Dean Swift's Library. With a Facsimile of the Original Sale Catalogue and Some Account of Two Manuscript Lists of his Books* (Cambridge, 1932)

The Text of 'Gulliver's Travels' (Cambridge, 1952)

Williams, Kathleen, *Jonathan Swift and the Age of Compromise* (Lawrence, Kansas, 1958)

ed. *Swift: The Critical Heritage* (London, 1970)

Willman, Robert, 'The Origins of "Whig" and "Tory" in English Political Language', *The Historical Journal*, 17 (1974), 247–64

Wing, Donald L., 'Swift and Holland' (unpublished Ph. D. dissertation, Wayne State University, 1980)

Winn, James Anderson, *John Dryden and His World* (New Haven and London, 1987)

Woolley, David, 'The Canon of Swift's Prose Pamphleteering, 1710–1714, and *The New Way of Selling Places at Court*', *Swift Studies*, 3 (1988), 96–117

'Swift's Copy of *Gulliver's Travels*: The Armagh *Gulliver*, Hyde's Edition, and Swift's Earliest Corrections', in *The Art of Jonathan Swift*, ed. by Clive T. Probyn (London, 1978), pp. 131–78

Woolley, James, 'The *Intelligencer*: Its Dating and Contemporaneity', in *Proceedings of The First Münster Symposium on Jonathan Swift*, ed. by Hermann J. Real and Heinz J. Vienken (Munich, 1985), pp. 337–49

Index

CAMBRIDGE STUDIES IN EIGHTEENTH-CENTURY ENGLISH LITERATURE AND THOUGHT

Lightning Source UK Ltd.
Milton Keynes UK
UKOW031357211212

203995UK00001B/

Ollscoil na hÉireann, Gaillimh

3 1111 40268 3898

9 780521 025683